John R. Nicholson
Rebecca D. Halbasch
Sean R. Nicholson

SAMS
Teach Yourself
Outlook™ 98
in 24 Hours

SAMS

A Division of Macmillan Computer Publishing
201 West 103rd St., Indianapolis, Indiana, 46290 USA

EXECUTIVE EDITOR
Jim Minatel

ACQUISITIONS EDITOR
Jill Byus

DEVELOPMENT EDITOR
Brian Kent-Proffitt

TECHNICAL EDITOR
Ben Schorr

MANAGING EDITOR
Thomas F. Hayes

PROJECT EDITOR
Gina Brown

COPY EDITOR
Tom Cirtin

INDEXER
Cheryl Jackson

PRODUCTION
Betsy Deeter
Brad Lenser

BOOK DESIGNER
Gary Adair

BOOK COVER
Aren Howell

Overview

Contents

Dedication

This book is dedicated to our loving families, who had to put up with the stress caused by a high pressure deadline, but who, as always, stood at our respective sides saying, "Aren't you done with that yet?"

Acknowledgments

Although this book appears to be the work of three authors, it is actually the result of many behind-the-scenes people. **Jill Byus**, the Acquisitions Editor at Sams, kept us on track throughout the project. The Development Editor, **Brian Proffitt** (who co-authored *Sams' Teach Yourself Microsoft Outlook 97 in 24 Hours* with **Kim Spilker**), gave us unconditional support, as well as terrific advice on how to improve this book. His sense of humor at 4 a.m. was unflagging. **Ben Schorr**, the Technical Editor for this book, obviously did his superb technical editing on the beaches of Hawaii. (I could tell by the sand in my email.) His sense of humor also helped create a book that is fun to read, and not just a "regular computer book." **Gina Brown** and **Tom Cirtin** were very instrumental in taking our battered prose and turning it into a grammatical wonder.

The people at Timex were very helpful in providing a DataLink watch and associated material. Shameless Plug: If you haven't got one of these yet, look at Hour 20 to see what it is, head for the store and buy one, and then read Hour 20 to learn how it works. Thanks to **Woody Leonhard** for providing me with a copy of his book. Be sure to check out Woody's Office Watch Web site at http://www.wopr.com. This will tell you what you need to use Microsoft Office 97 and Outlook 98 in the "real world" (if such a thing really exists).

Thanks also to **David Fugate** and his cohorts at Waterside Literary Agency for thinking of me when this book became available. And as always, thanks to **Glenna Stites**, the friend who got me into the writing business. Glenna, don't worry, I don't hold it against you. You're still my friend.

About the Authors

John R. Nicholson is a Professor at Johnson County Community College in Overland Park, Kansas. He is a Certified Office Automation Professional, and is Microsoft Office User Specialist (MOUS) certified for Microsoft Outlook. He wrote two Excel books, one with his son, Sean. He has authored five textbooks on computer applications, and has been the Microsoft Certification (MOUS) editor for five other books. He was named one of the top ten percent of beta testing sites for Microsoft Office 97 Professional. John has been married to his editor and best friend, Pam, for over 30 years. John is the very proud father of Matt, an aircraft electrician in the Air Force, and Molly, a Phi Theta Kappa Honor Student who is preparing to enter Kansas State University (Go Wildcats!), much to the surprise of her University of Kansas parents (Go Jayhawks!), Rebecca, and Sean. John can be reached at jnichols@johnco.cc.ks.us or wryterjccc@aol.com.

Rebecca D. Halbasch is the Help Desk Administrator for Concorde Career Colleges, Inc. in Kansas City, and has owned her own consulting and training company, User Friendly Consultants, for two years. Rebecca has been working with Outlook since it was released. She is excited to be writing a book showing off the new Outlook 98 program. She has been working with computers for over 12 years. Rebecca is married to Robert Halbasch and has three children, Jessica, Kristopher, and Ashley.

Sean R. Nicholson is completing his final year at the University of Missouri—Kansas City School of Law, with the loving (and financial) help offered by his wife, Deborah. He is studying to become an Intellectual Property Attorney. Sean is on the editorial staff of the UMKC Law Review, which published his article *Mutiny as to the Bounty: Preservation Law's Failing Efforts Regarding Shipwrecks and their Artifacts Located in International Waters*. Sean is also an editorial staff member of the Urban Lawyer legal digest, which published his case digest of the United States Supreme Court case *Chandler v. Miller*. Sean has received Dean's List Academic Honors, is the President of the UMKC Intellectual Property Law Society, and has recently been involved in advanced Intellectual Property training at the number one ranked Intellectual Property Law School in the nation—the Franklin Pierce Law Center. He also co-authored a book during his second year of law school. Sean owns his own computer consulting business and has provided hardware system and asset management recommendations to businesses ranging from small, one-man firms to multi-million dollar technology corporations.

About the Technical Editor

Ben M. Schorr is the Director of Information Services at Damon Key Leong Kupchak Hastert in Honolulu, Hawaii. Prior to making the sacrifice of moving to Hawaii he was the Director of Operations for Watson/Schorr Consulting in Los Angeles for six and half years, and Ben has been an Information Services professional for over a decade. In addition to being a Microsoft Outlook MVP and a beta tester for Outlook 98, Ben teaches technology classes at Kapi'olani Community College and is an occasional columnist for *WindoWatch* magazine. Ben lives in Kaimuki, Hawaii and is taller, better looking, and more successful than his high school classmates remember.

Introduction

If you believe your life needs a little more organization (like I do), then you are in luck. The book you are holding shows you how to get a free upgrade from Microsoft Outlook 97 to Outlook 98, a product that will help you organize those precious hours in your day. I have been told there are 24 hours in every day, but most days seem to have many less.

If you haven't previously used Outlook, you may be unaware of its powerful features. It can help you keep track of how your time is spent, remind you when it's time to do something, and tickle your memory about people who you contact on either a regular or occasional basis. It can act as your email editor, and allow you to access the thousands of newsgroups offered by your Internet service provider.

By the time you finish this book (in about 24 hours, if you don't stop for mundane activities, such as sleeping, eating, and going to work), you'll have a good idea of the basic features of Outlook 98. Using it correctly will improve your organization skills, make you appear as though you know what you're doing, and make you handsome (or beautiful), wise, and rich. (Oh, sorry, those last three require the talents of a genie.)

This book is divided into 24 easy-to-digest topics that can each be absorbed in about an hour. It is designed for the beginning to intermediate user of Outlook. It contains tips, notes, and warnings. It tells you how to get the help you need to become an expert user of the program. And, it does all this for one low price. So, head for the checkout line, take it home, and get busy organizing your life, so you have time for family, entertainment, travel, and the many other vital components of the good life.

Conventions Used in this Book

Features used in this book include the following:

Notes give you comments and asides about the topic at hand, as well as full explanations.

Tips give you great shortcuts and hints on how to get more productivity from Outlook.

Cautions tell you how to make your life miserable if you do something wrong. Heed these, or suffer.

New terms are introduced using the New Term icon. The new term appears in italic.

At the end of each hour, frequently asked questions about Outlook are asked and answered in the Q&A sections.

PART I

Introducing Outlook 98

Hour

HOUR 1

The View from the Outlook

Did you know that, "A weekday edition of *The New York Times* contains more information than the average person was likely to come across in a lifetime in seventeenth-century England". According to Saul Wurman, author of the best-selling *Information Anxiety: What to Do When Information Doesn't Tell You What You Need to Know* (Bantam Doubleday Dell Publishing, 1990), this overwhelming glut of information is something we must learn to deal with on a daily basis. As toolmakers, humans design tools to help complete tasks. To manage the vast amount of information that you encounter every day, Microsoft developed Outlook 98.

When you want to buy a car, the first thing you do is take it out for a test drive. You aren't concerned with how the engine works or the g-force that's required to release the air bags. Instead, you want to know how it rides, how the instrument panel is arranged, if there are enough cup holders, and if the sound system includes a CD player. Then, if the car pleases you, you will want additional information. In this first hour, we are going to take Outlook 98 for a spin around the block. You'll see how it looks, check out its various parts (accessories), and learn a few tasks it can help you do.

> If you haven't installed Outlook 98 yet, see Appendix A, "Getting, Installing, and Upgrading Outlook 98," for instructions on getting a copy and installing it.

First, you'll examine the basics of Outlook 98. You'll be introduced to various Outlook 98 components without studying them in depth. Just think of this as similar to a party where you are greeting the guests. You don't have a lot of time to stop and chat; you need to save that for later.

Indeed, after this whirlwind tour, you may feel a little dizzy, and wonder if you can ever learn it all. Don't worry, that's the purpose of the other 23 hours in this book. You'll get to know each component on a more personal level in subsequent hours. For now, sit down at your computer with a cup of coffee, herbal tea, or soft drink (keep it away from the keyboard), and relax.

Starting and Exiting Outlook 98

As with all tasks in Windows 95, there are several ways of completing any task, and starting Outlook is no exception. Here are two different ways to start Outlook.

To Do: Starting Outlook 98

▼ To Do

1. Turn on the computer and wait for Windows to open (unless Windows is already open, in which case just skip this step).

2. Click Start, Programs, Microsoft Outlook. The Outlook opening screen, as shown in Figure 1.1, is displayed. Unless you or someone else has already used Outlook, there will probably only be one message in your mailbox. Your screen may look slightly different from the one shown in Figure 1.1.

▼

FIGURE 1.1.

The Outlook screen shows only one message in the Inbox the first time you use Outlook.

Inbox icon —

Maximize/Minimize button

Close button

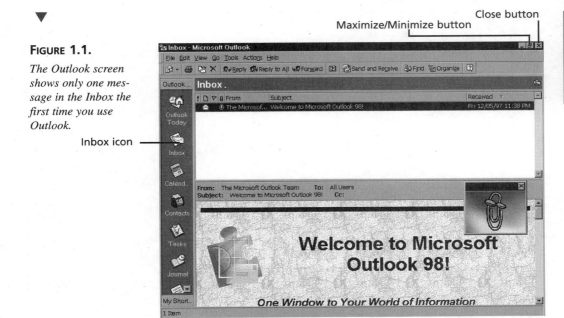

The Office Assistant starting panel may be open. If so, click the option box next to Show These Choices at Startup, and click OK. Unless you have changed it, your Office Assistant will be an animated paper clip.

3. If the Outlook window doesn't take up the entire screen, click the Maximize/Restore button. The Inbox should be displayed. If any other component (such as the Calendar) is displayed, click the Inbox icon in the vertical panel at the left edge of the window.

4. Click the Close button in the top-right corner of the screen to close Outlook. You can also choose File, Exit.

5. Although your desktop may look different from the one shown in Figure 1.2, you should still be able to see the Outlook icon on the desktop. Double-click it to open Outlook again. This is just another way to open Outlook.

▲

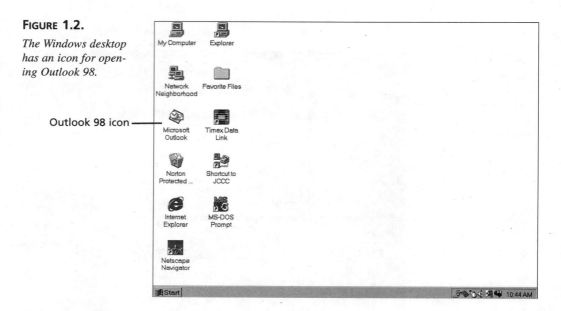

Figure 1.2.

The Windows desktop has an icon for opening Outlook 98.

Outlook 98 icon ——

Office Assistant

If you have worked with other Office 97 modules, you are probably already familiar with Office Assistant. Its purpose is to offer advice and help you access a "plain English" help system. Let's take a brief look at it.

To Do: Working with Office Assistant

1. Outlook should still be open. Office Assistant is in a separate window and probably looks like a paper clip (which is named Clippit).

2. Click inside the Office Assistant box to display the dialog box for typing your question. Often, questions are suggested based on the task you are currently performing. The Office Assistant panel should be similar to the one shown in Figure 1.3. To see more questions, you can click the See More button. When the text above the Search button is highlighted, just type your question if it isn't among the suggestions. Now type, How can I create a new mail message? Click the Search button.

> There are several variations of Office Assistant. If it isn't displayed, click the Office Assistant button (it looks like a question mark) near the right end of the toolbar.

FIGURE 1.3.

Office Assistant is used to answer questions typed as sentences.

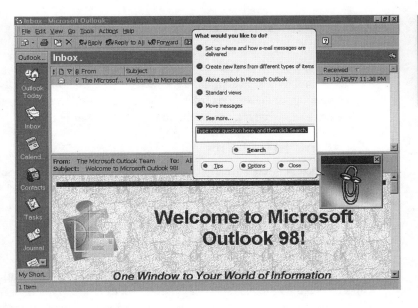

3. Click the button to the left of the subject (Create a Message). Keep your eyes (and ears) open while Office Assistant looks for the answer to your question. The Create a Message help window, as shown in Figure 1.4, is displayed. If the window is too small to display all the text, use the scroll arrows to see the rest of the help screen.

FIGURE 1.4.

Office Assistant displays Create a Message help.

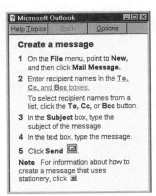

4. Click the Close button in the Help window. Close Office Assistant by clicking its Close button.

Using the Shortcuts Bar

The Outlook Bar is located along the left edge of the Outlook window. It contains short-cuts to frequently used folders. Information for each Outlook component (mail, contacts, calendar, and others) is kept in a separate folder. The shortcuts in the Outlook Bar are icons pointing to the various folders. The Outlook Bar contains three different sets of shortcuts, each of which can be modified to meet your needs.

Outlook Shortcuts

The Outlook shortcuts usually consist of eight icons. You may not be able to see all of them at once. If you see a down-pointing arrow near the bottom of the Outlook Bar or an up-pointing arrow near the top of the Outlook Bar, you can click it to view the other icons.

My Shortcuts

To see the second set of shortcuts, click near the bottom of the Outlook Bar on the My Shortcuts bar. Outlook displays a different set of icons. By default, you may see other icons that can be used to store drafts, outgoing items, and previously sent items.

Other Shortcuts

The last set of shortcuts (Other Shortcuts) contains icons used to open My Computer, My Documents, and the Favorites folder. All three of the shortcut areas can be customized. Later, you learn to add and delete folders.

To Do: Navigating with Shortcuts

1. Make sure that only the Outlook Shortcuts bar is at the top of the Outlook Bar. Click Outlook Today. The screen changes, as shown in Figure 1.5. You may want to make this your starting screen, rather than the Inbox. Later, you'll learn to make the changes.

2. Since you've already looked at the Inbox screen (where email is stored), click the Calendar shortcut (either double-click the Calendar icon in the Outlook Today window or click the Calendar icon on the Outlook Bar). Your screen should be similar to Figure 1.6.

3. At some time during your work with Outlook, you may not be able to see the shortcut icon you need. Remember, use the up- or down-pointing arrow on the Outlook Bar to see additional icons. Now, click the Contacts icon. Currently, your list is probably empty. You'll remedy that a little later. Your screen should be similar to that in Figure 1.7.

▼ To Do

FIGURE 1.5.

The Outlook Today screen can be used as a table of contents, leading to other functions logically used in conjunction with Outlook.

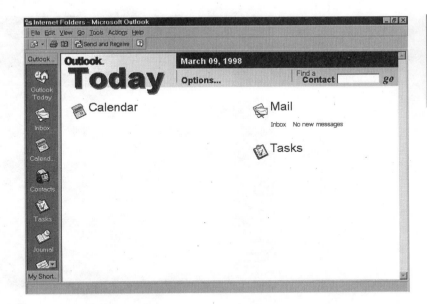

FIGURE 1.6.

The Calendar enables you to make appointments and add tasks to the Task List using the TaskPad.

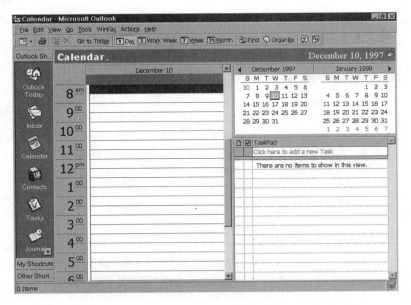

▼ FIGURE 1.7.

The Contact Manager acts as an extremely powerful phone book and contact log.

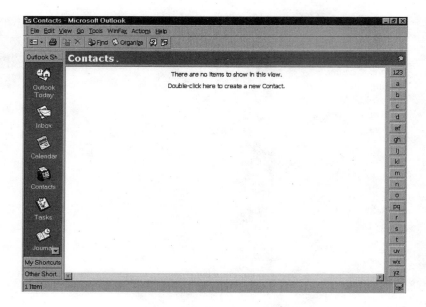

4. Now that you have an idea of how to move among Outlook components, check out
▲ each one and then return to the Outlook Today screen.

Outlook Today

The Outlook Today page provides a preview of the current day (as well as several days in the future). You can see a summary of your appointments for the day, a list of scheduled tasks, and even a listing of your new email messages. You can also quickly find a contact by using the Lookup Person text box, which searches through your list of contacts. As mentioned above, the Outlook Today page makes a good table of contents for each day's appointments, tasks, and contacts. The Outlook Today page can be set as the first page to open when you start Outlook. You may find this more helpful than having the Inbox open first.

To change the default opening page to Outlook Today, click the Options button in the lower-left corner of the Outlook Today window. The Outlook Today Options window, shown in Figure 1.8, is displayed. Click the Startup option box and then click Back to Outlook Today. From now on, Outlook Today will be the opening page when you open Outlook 98.

FIGURE 1.8.

The Outlook Today Options window enables you to set Outlook Today as your beginning screen in Outlook.

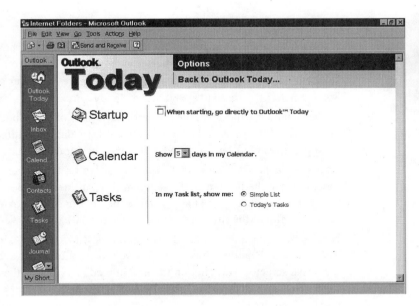

Using the Inbox for Email

The Inbox is a storage folder for incoming email. It is divided into two windows. The top window contains a listing of multiple messages in table view (where each message is displayed as a single line of text). Beneath that is the Preview Pane, where you can see the first several lines of the message. The lower set of scroll arrows on the right side of the window are used to scroll through the selected message.

If you have more messages than can be displayed in the upper window, you can use the upper set of scroll arrows to scroll through the list of messages. The height of the upper and lower windows can be modified by pointing at the dividing bar between the two windows. When the icon turns into a horizontal bar with a double-headed vertical arrow through the middle, you can drag the boundary up or down to adjust the size of the windows.

Keeping a Calendar

Although you have had a brief look at the Calendar, now you have a chance to enter some data and see how it interacts with other Outlook modules. Data in the Calendar and other modules is integrated: Making a change in one module affects the display in other modules.

To Do: Making a Calendar Entry

1. Click the Calendar shortcut on the Outlook Bar. Notice, as shown earlier in Figure 1.6, that the day is divided into half-hour segments. Later, you learn to control the segment length. Click in the 12 p.m. bar. The entire half-hour segment turns blue. Type Lunch at Big Ben's BBQ with Sandy. Press Enter.

2. In the Calendar window in the upper-right portion of the window, click the day on either side of the current day. Notice that today's date is boldfaced. That means that an appointment has been entered. Click the current date again.

3. Because this is a business lunch, a half-hour isn't really enough time. To extend the time, point to the bottom of the segment (it's outlined in blue). The cursor changes to a double-headed vertical arrow. Drag the bottom of the box down until two segments are filled (the time between 12:00 and 1:00).

4. Next, you will use the TaskPad to enter a task. In Hour 11, "Time Is on My Side: The Calendar Feature," you learn to have more control over adding tasks by using the Tasks screen. Now, click in the box immediately below the TaskPad title bar. Type Call Jim about the board meeting schedule. Press Enter. The task is moved down into the Task area. Again, you'll learn to have more control over this a little later.

5. Click the Outlook Today icon. Your screen should be similar to that shown in Figure 1.9. If you have already been using Outlook, you may have additional entries displayed.

FIGURE 1.9.

The Outlook Today screen now shows an appointment and a task.

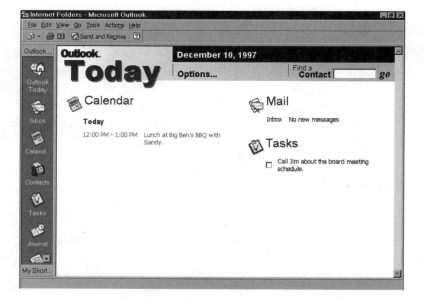

Working with Contacts

The Contacts module of Outlook acts as a high performance telephone book. Not only can you enter basic information about each person, but you can add information about his family or business, and document each contact that you have with him.

To Do: Entering Personal Information in the Contact Manager

1. Click the Contact icon in the Outlook Bar. Because you haven't input any data yet, there is no information displayed.

2. Click the New Contact button (the left-most button on the toolbar). Your screen is now similar to that shown in Figure 1.10. In Hour 4, "Establishing First Contact," and Hour 5, "Manipulating Contacts," you learn to use the advanced features. For now, you'll just enter some basic data.

FIGURE 1.10.

This screen is used to input contact data.

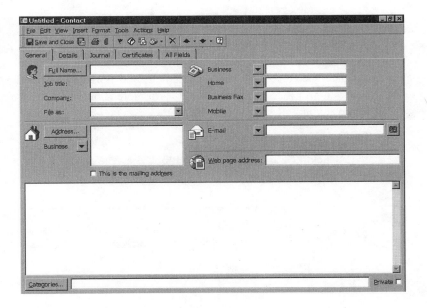

3. Click in the Full Name text box. Type James Nelson. You can move to the next field by pressing the Tab key (or Shift+Tab to move to the previous field), or you can click in a field to drop the insertion point. Press Tab to move to the Job Title field.

4. Look in the File As text box. You see that Outlook automatically files the name by last name followed by first name. The drop-down arrow also enables you to file the information by first name rather than last.

▼　　　　In the Job Title box, type Owner. Press Tab. Type Sandy's Hideaway. Press Tab
three times to move to the Business phone field. Type 555-9988. Press Tab until
the insertion point is in the Address box. Type 1234 South Oak. Press Enter. Type
Overland Park, KS 66210 and press Tab several times to move to the E-mail text
box. Type Sandy@sandyshideaway.com.

5. So far, you have entered information only on the General tab. Click each of the
other four tabs (Details, Journal, Certificates, and All Fields) to get a feel for the
other information that can be stored. Click the Save and Close button on the toolbar. The screen now contains the basic contact information you entered. Notice that
not all fields (such as Job Title and Company) are visible from this screen. To open
▲　　　　the contact information, double-click anywhere on it. Click the Save and Close button again.

Assigning and Managing Tasks

You have already entered a simple task from the Calendar screen. If you want to add
more information, you can use the Task Manager. Here you can change the status, the
due date, the current percentage complete, and assign the task to a specific category. You
can even prioritize each task. You'll learn more about the Task Manager in Hour 11, but
for now, you will enter another task.

To Do: Entering a Task

To Do

1. Click the Tasks icon in the Outlook Bar. The task you entered earlier is displayed,
as shown in Figure 1.11.

> You may not be able to see all the columns. (Categories should be in the
> right-most column.) You can drag the column edges to resize them to fit
> your screen.

2. Click the Subject box to enter a new task. Type Research buying a new
printer. Click in the Status box. Click the drop-down arrow. Click the In Progress
option. Click the Due Date text box. You can either type in a date, or click the
drop-down arrow to see a calendar. Type 12/12/98. Click in the % Complete box.
Type 25. At this point, you could add a category, but for now, just press Enter.

3. To see the full list of possibilities for the task, double-click anywhere on the task.
The Task dialog box for the specific task is displayed. You may have to resize the
window to be able to see all of it, as shown in Figure 1.12. Look at the Details tab.
▼　　　　Click the Save and Close button on the toolbar.

FIGURE **1.11.**

A single task has been entered into the Task Manager.

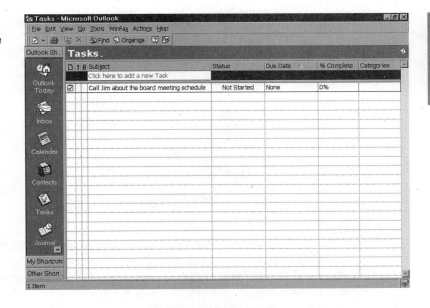

FIGURE **1.12.**

The task information has been expanded, and additional information can now be added.

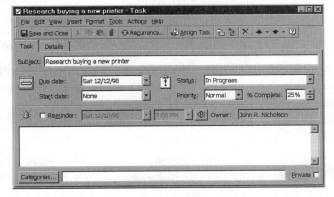

 Notice that there is no place to enter a category. If you want to enter a category, you need to enter all other information and close the box. Then you can right-click the text box in the Categories column and choose Categories. Do not place the insertion point in the Categories text box, or right-clicking will result in the Cut/Copy/Paste options being displayed.

4. Right-click in the Categories field for the "printer" task. Choose Categories. The Categories dialog box, as shown in Figure 1.13, is displayed.

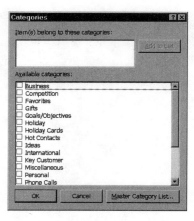

▼ **FIGURE 1.13.**

The Categories dialog box is used to add an existing category or categories to the task.

5. Click the Business category. To add a category to the Master List, click the Master Category List button. In the New text box, type `Research`. Click the Add button. Click OK. Scroll down, and place a check mark in the Research category. Click

▲   OK to close the category list. Business, Research is now displayed in the Categories column for the printer entry.

Keeping a Journal

Have you ever thought about keeping a record of everything important that you do each day? Have you ever wanted to know what you discussed the last time you spoke with a specific customer? Has your boss ever asked how you spend your time? Have you ever wondered where the week went and what you really accomplished? The Outlook Journal can help you answer some (though not all) of these questions.

Journal is a semi-automatic diary. It can be used to track phone calls you make, track the time you spend working on a specific project, and even automatically log the time you spend working in each Office application. Like most Outlook tools, Journal can be customized to fit your needs and the way you work.

To Do: Looking at the Journal Entries

1. Click the Journal button on the Outlook Bar. Your screen should be similar to that shown in Figure 1.14. If you have just begun using Outlook, you will not have many entries in the text area.

FIGURE 1.14.

The Journal helps keep track of how you spend your day.

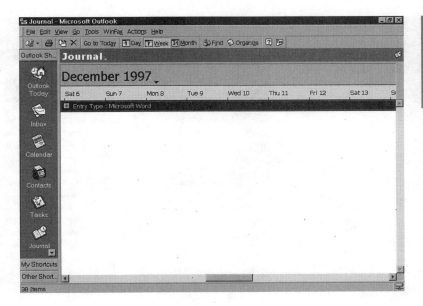

If you don't see the Journal icon on the Outlook Bar, click the down-pointing arrow to see additional icons.

2. Journal has three views: daily, weekly, and monthly. Each can be selected by clicking the appropriate button on the toolbar. In Figure 1.14, the Journal has only one entry category: Microsoft Word. You can easily create other categories, such as meetings, email you have sent and received, and phone calls or other contacts you have made during the day.

   Click the plus sign at the left side of Entry Type to expand your view of your activities, as shown in Figure 1.15. (If you don't yet have any activities listed, don't worry about it.)

3. The screen shown in Figure 1.15 acts as a table of contents of your activities. To see more detail for any portion of a task, you can double-click the icon to the left of the filename to expand it. Your expanded entry should resemble that shown in Figure 1.16. The files used in the activity are displayed on the title bar of the Journal Entry dialog box.

FIGURE 1.15.

When the Journal window is expanded, you get a more complete list of your activities.

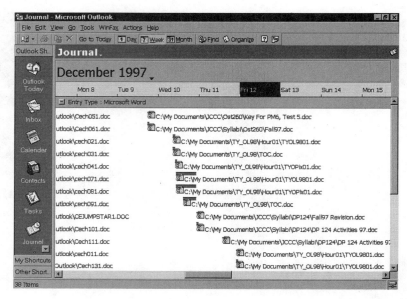

If you have an entry, try expanding it now. You may need to adjust the size of the window. Notice all the different information that can be kept about this particular document. Click the Save and Close button.

FIGURE 1.16.

An expanded Journal entry shows more specific information about the task you have been working on.

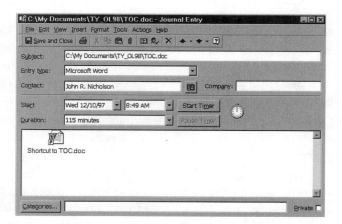

4. Next, click the Day and Month buttons on the toolbar to see different Journal views. When you are finished, click the Week button on the toolbar.

Using Outlook Notes

Do you have pieces of scratch paper or sticky notes all over your office (your car, your home)? You know that you wrote down the information that you need somewhere. The question is *where?* The Notes feature of Outlook can help clean up your sticky note problems.

The Notes window shown in Figure 1.17 is blank. In the next few minutes, you will create three notes and then search to find the information you need.

FIGURE 1.17.

The Notes window can contain hundreds or even thousands of notes, which can be easily searched and organized.

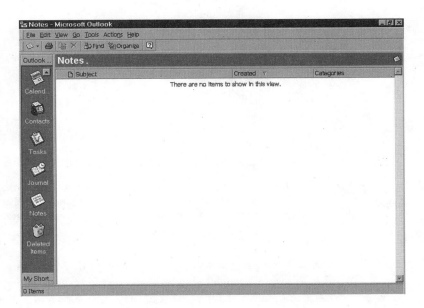

To Do: Putting Notes on Your Desktop

1. Click the Notes icon on the Outlook Bar. The screen should be similar to the one shown in Figure 1.17.

2. To create your first note, click the New Note button on the left edge of the toolbar. A yellow note appears on the screen with the insertion point already positioned. Type `Samantha Candleton, Day: 555-2387. Home 555-0093`. Close the note by clicking the Close button.

3. Create two more notes. Click the New Note button and type `UST Support, 888-555-7142`. Close the note. Click the New Note button again and type `Questions for Jill: How soon? From scratch? No disk. Updated beta?` Close the note. As shown in Figure 1.18, if the notes are short, all the text is used as the note title. Otherwise, only the first few lines are displayed.

▼

FIGURE 1.18.

*A short note uses all
its text as its title,
whereas a long note
displays only a portion
of its text.*

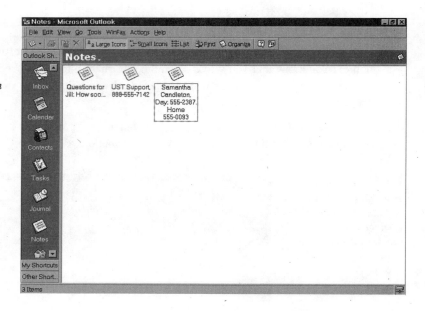

> If you're going to be organized, why not put the information directly into
> the contact list or task list? Contacts, tasks, and journal entries are normally
> used for semipermanent information, whereas notes are usually temporary.

4. With only three notes, it's easy to see what each one contains. What if you had 300
   notes to search through? Simple: Click the Find button on the toolbar. Type `beta`,
   and click Find Now! Jill's note is displayed, as shown in Figure 1.19. You'll learn
   to use the more advanced search features in Hour 14, "The Journal: My So-Called
   Diary," and Hour 16, "Not-So-Sticky Notes."

5. Close the Find box by clicking the Close button in the upper-right corner (just to
   the right of the Advanced Find command).

FIGURE 1.19.

The Find option is used to find specific text from a multitude of notes.

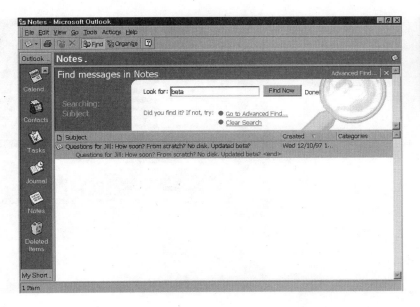

Managing Deleted Items

Luckily, deleting items in Outlook is not necessarily permanent. In this section, you'll delete a note, and then learn to recover it.

To Do: Deleting Unwanted Items

1. If necessary, click the down arrow in the Outlook Bar until you can see the Deleted Items bin. Make sure Jill's note is highlighted, and press Delete. (There are several other ways to delete notes, including dragging and dropping, but we won't cover them here.)

2. Double-click the Deleted Items bin to see its contents. Previously deleted items (if there are any) are shown in the upper-half of the window. The item highlighted in the upper half of the window (usually the most recently deleted item) is displayed in the lower portion of the window, as shown in Figure 1.20.

▼ **FIGURE 1.20.**

The highlighted text item in the upper half of the window is displayed in the lower half.

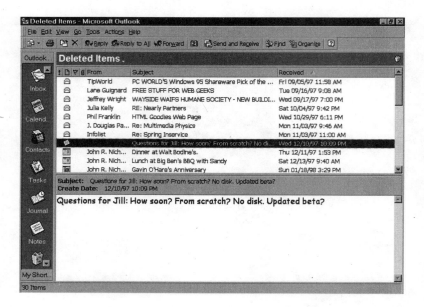

3. To *undelete* the item, drag the note icon on the left side of the selected item in the upper-half of the window to the appropriate folder on the Outlook Bar (in this case, the Notes folder). Click the Notes folder again. Jill's note has been restored.

▲

Closing Outlook 98

Like other Windows programs, you want to be sure to shut Outlook down properly when you are finished with it. You can click the Close button in the top-right corner of the screen, or you can choose File, Exit from the menu bar. If you are in the middle of a task, you may be asked if you want to save your work before quitting Outlook.

Summary

When comparing the features learned this hour to the actual capabilities of Outlook 98, you can't even say they're just the tip of the iceberg. Rather, they're closer to an ice cube sitting on the tip of an iceberg. Outlook 98 offers many tools to help organize your life. However, to get the most from Outlook, you must use it regularly, keeping the information updated. In the next few hours, you'll learn the real power behind Outlook, and find many tips for easily integrating it into your normal workday.

Q&A

Q I find Office Assistant annoying. Can I get rid of it?

A Just click the Close button. When you need it again, click the Office Assistant button on the toolbar (it is a question mark).

Q Why should I upgrade to Outlook 98?

A Several reasons, not the least of which is because it is free (if you already own Outlook 97). However, the main advantage is the additional speed you will notice in the upgrade. There are also new features that you may want to use, and we'll discuss them in later hours. For a list of new features, see Appendix B, "What's New in Outlook 98."

Q Do I have to keep all the icons on the Outlook Bar?

A No. You can drag any of them to the Deleted Items icon on the Outlook Bar. Later, you will learn to add other icons to the Outlook Bar.

Q The Outlook Bar takes up a lot of room on the screen, and I can navigate using the Go menu. Can I hide the Outlook Bar?

A Yes. Just choose View, Outlook Bar. Repeat the process to display it again.

HOUR 2

Customizing Outlook 98 to Fit Your Needs

When you purchase an expensive suit or dress, it often needs minor alterations to make it fit you just right. Similarly, the standard setup for most software may not exactly fit the way you work: It may need to be *customized*.

During this hour, you learn about the *standard* configuration of Outlook 98, and how to modify it to fit your needs. You'll learn about folders, and how to make them work *for* you rather than against you. Finally, you'll learn how to make a few additional configuration modifications. You might choose to change some configurations, while you might leave others at their default settings.

Although the terms *folder* and *subfolder* are not really synonymous, to keep things simple, we'll use the terms interchangeably, unless it is important to differentiate between the two.

Working with Folders

In Hour 1, "The View from the Outlook," you learned to add information to the various components of Outlook, including Calendar, Tasks, and Contacts. You may find it useful to create other folders to better organize your information. For example, you may want to keep all the data for a single project in a separate folder.

The data you enter into Outlook may be stored on your local hard drive or the network server. If you aren't sure where it's stored, ask your system administrator if you are on a network. If you aren't, then your data is on your hard drive.

You can create folders, change their names, arrange them in a different order on the Outlook Bar, copy them, and even delete them. By learning to manipulate the Outlook files on your hard drive, you will find it easier to organize your information.

Figure 2.1 shows a sample view of a folder structure. Several ways to display the folder structure are the following:

- Choose <u>V</u>iew, Fold<u>e</u>r List. (This changes the size of the viewing pane.)
- Click the folder name in the viewing pane. (This temporarily displays the Folder List, but doesn't resize the viewing pane.) Click the folder name again to remove the Folder List.
- Click the folder name in the viewing pane, then click the push pin as indicated. The push pin is located where you would normally find the Close box. As soon as you click the push pin, it changes to the Close icon.

In this hour, you will explore many different dialog boxes that enable you to control how Outlook works. It is not feasible to fully discuss all the possibilities involved in configuring Outlook. Whenever there is an option you would like to know more about, point the mouse cursor at it and right-click. You will be shown a brief explanation of what the feature controls.

FIGURE 2.1.

The Folder List view is displayed.

Folder List ———

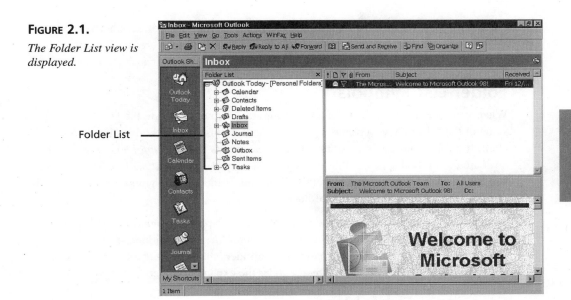

In Figure 2.1, notice that several folders are beneath the main folder. These are called *subfolders*. The term subfolder is relational. For example, in your family the same woman might be a mother, daughter, wife, cousin, and aunt. In the case of subfolders, one subfolder may be acting as a folder for other subfolders. So, a folder can be both a folder and a subfolder, depending on its relationship to other folders. You can change folders in many ways, as you will learn shortly.

The way that folders are handled in Outlook is quite different from the way folders are handled in Windows. If you use Windows Explorer to view the directory structure, you will find that only the first-level folders (such as Mailbox.pst or Outlook.pst) are displayed as files. All subfolders (such as Inbox and Contacts) are kept within the folder file, and are not visible using Windows Explorer.

Depending on which programs you have used in the past (such as Schedule+, Lotus CC:Mail, or even Outlook 97), your folder structure might be very different from the one shown in the figures.

The Folder List is contained within your profile. If you change profiles, the Folder List and contents change accordingly.

Profile: A set of instructions that defines a specific Outlook session. You can use separate profiles for different users, or the same user can create different profiles (for example, one for working at home and one for working on the network).

Folder List Symbols

When you look at your screen (or back at Figure 2.1), notice that to the left of the name, some of the folders have a minus sign, some have a plus sign, and others have no symbol at all. If a folder has a minus sign next to it, that means that *all subfolders on the next level* are currently displayed. If a plus sign is displayed, additional subfolders are located beneath the folder, but are not currently displayed. If there is no symbol next to the folder name, the folder contains no subfolders.

You can use the icons to control the level of folders displayed at any time. Clicking a minus sign collapses the folder; that causes all subfolders to be hidden. The symbol changes to a plus sign to indicate there are subfolders that are not displayed. Clicking a plus sign displays all subfolders *directly* under the expanded folder.

Creating a Subfolder

The purpose of the Folder List is to enable you to organize how your information is stored so that you can access it quickly and efficiently. You can direct Outlook to store various types of information in specific folders.

Creating a subfolder can be done in several ways. The method you choose is simply the one you prefer, or the one that is easiest at the time. If the Folder List is displayed, do the following:

- Right-click the folder icon and click New Folder. (Don't click the folder name, or you will display a different menu.)
- Click the drop-down arrow to the right of the New Contact button on the toolbar and click Folder.
- Choose File, New Folder from the menu bar.

In the next exercise, you'll get a chance to practice changing the view, expanding and collapsing folders, and creating a subfolder to store additional information. The skills you learn in the next few minutes are the ones that you will continue to use as your proficiency at using Outlook 98 increases.

To Do: Basic Skills for Managing Folders

1. Open Outlook if it isn't already open.

2. Click the Inbox icon in the Outlook Bar if it isn't already selected. You will probably only have one message, but it really doesn't matter.

3. Click the Inbox name in the folder banner (the title bar for the Inbox). The Folder
   List is displayed over the top of the Input window, as shown in Figure 2.2.

FIGURE 2.2.

*The Folder List is tem-
porarily visible.*

Folder Banner ⎯

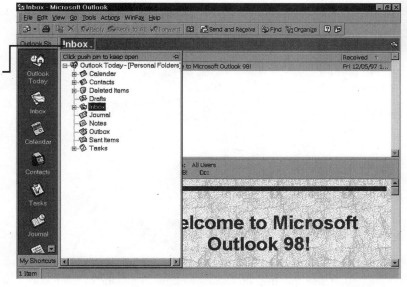

Using this method, the Folder List is only temporarily displayed. To revert to
the Inbox view, click the mouse anywhere outside the Folder List.

4. Right-click the first level folder (it may be called Personal File, Outlook Today,
   Internet Folders, or some other name). Click other folders. Nothing happens. You
   can't make any changes in the folder structure while it is not permanently opened.
   Click the push pin (using the *left* mouse button) to keep the Folder List open. The
   push pin changes to a Close box.

▼

> You can't make any changes to the folders when the Folder View isn't locked in. You can't change folder positions, rename them, delete them, or add new ones.

5. Right-click the Tasks icon (remember, don't click the word "Tasks"). From the pop-up menu, choose New Folder. The Create New Folder dialog box is displayed, as shown in Figure 2.3.

FIGURE 2.3.

The Create New Folder dialog box is used to create a subfolder beneath an existing folder.

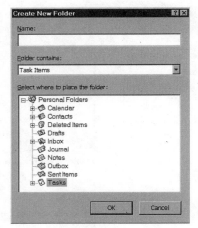

6. Click the drop-down menu on the right side of the Folder Contains dialog box. Notice that the folder can contain one of six item types: Appointment, Contact, Journal, Mail, Note, or Task. Click the Task option. In the Name text box, type Outlook 98 Tasks.

7. If you want to change the folder where the subfolder is attached, click the new position in the Select Where to Place the Folder display. Click OK. The Add Shortcut to Outlook Bar dialog box, as shown in Figure 2.4, is displayed. In this case, you don't want a shortcut, so click No (or just press Enter). If you don't want to view this dialog box again, click the Don't Prompt Me About This Again option.

> After you create a folder, you can make it a shortcut on the Outlook Bar by dragging it from the Folder List into the appropriate position on the Outlook Bar.

▼ FIGURE 2.4.

The Add Shortcut to Outlook Bar dialog box is used to automatically add a folder shortcut to the Outlook Bar.

2

8. Click the Outlook 98 Tasks folder icon in the Folder List. (If you click the right mouse button, a menu opens instead of displaying the new Task List.) The Folder Banner now reads "Outlook 98 Tasks." A new task list shows up in the right window, as shown in Figure 2.5.

FIGURE 2.5.

The Outlook 98 Tasks task list is displayed in the right window.

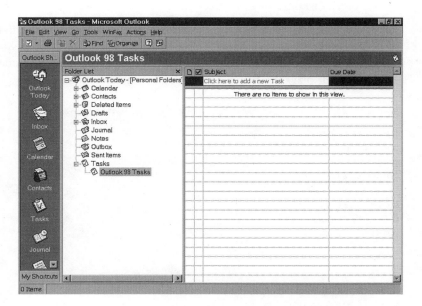

9. Click the Click Here to Add a New Task text box. Type `Learn to copy a folder.` Press Enter. The task appears in the Task List.

Copying or Moving a Folder

When you *copy* a folder from one place in the main folder to another, any items in the folder are also copied. When you *move* a folder, the items are also moved to the new position. Copying a folder is just like making a copy in a copy machine, you will have two folders. Moving a folder from one place to another means that the folder is no longer in the original location.

To move a folder, drag it from its current position into the new folder. If you want it to be a subfolder of the Mail folder, drag it onto the Mail icon. To copy a folder from one position to another, press Ctrl and drag the folder to the new position.

> If you move or copy a folder to a different folder, the original folder type and its contents remain intact. For example, if you drag the Outlook 98 Tasks folder into the Journal folder, it remains a task folder, even though it is located in the Journal folder.

You can also copy or move a folder by highlighting it and choosing Edit, Move to Folder, or Edit, Copy to Folder.

If you use the Edit, Move to Folder, or Edit, Copy to Folder method, the Move (or Copy) Folder dialog box, as shown in Figure 2.6, is displayed. Click the destination folder. If you want to create an additional folder as the destination folder, click the New button, which displays the New Folder dialog box (refer to Figure 2.3).

FIGURE 2.6.

The Move Folder dialog box is displayed when you choose the Edit menu and select Move. If you choose the Copy option, the Copy Folder dialog box is displayed.

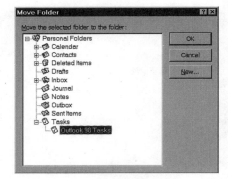

Renaming a Folder

The simplest way to rename an existing folder is to select the folder icon (so that the name is blue), and right-click to open the pop-up menu. Choose Rename <*Folder Name*>. Instead of a dialog box, the folder name text box is highlighted. Press any key to delete the current name and type a new name, or use the right or left arrow to position the insertion point and type additional information. (After the insertion point is positioned, you can use the Backspace and Delete keys to delete single characters.)

Adding a Folder to the Outlook Bar

In some cases, you may want to add a shortcut to the Outlook Bar. The easiest way to do that is to drag the folder icon onto the Outlook Bar. You can then drag it up or down to position it between existing icons, or move it to the top or bottom of the Outlook Bar.

Deleting a Folder

Deleting a folder may seem almost too easy. You can select the folder icon and press the Delete key (or click the Delete button on the toolbar or right-click and choose <u>D</u>elete *<File Name>*). Remember, if the folder icon isn't selected, you won't be able to delete the folder (or do anything else with it).

> If you delete a folder, you are not, repeat *not*, asked for confirmation. The folder and all its contents immediately disappears. (In the next section, you learn how to get it back, so don't worry too much.)

Recovering a Folder

Hold on, there! Microsoft is not mean enough to make you lose all your data when you accidentally delete a folder. Instead, the folder is sent to the Deleted Items folder, the shortcut for which is generally located at the bottom of the Outlook Bar. To recover a deleted item, click the Deleted Items shortcut in the Outlook Bar. A list of the deleted items is displayed. To recover a folder, expand the Deleted Items folder in the Folder List and drag the deleted folder's icon back onto the folder where you want it placed.

> Later in this hour, you learn to empty the Deleted Items folder on a regular basis. If you don't, there may be so many items in the Deleted Items folder that you won't be able to easily identify the one you need.

To Do: Manipulating Folders

1. The Outlook 98 Tasks folder should be highlighted. Right-click the icon (not the name of the folder), and choose <u>C</u>opy Outlook 98 Tasks. The Copy Folder dialog box is displayed.

2. Click the <u>N</u>ew button. Click the top level folder. In the Name text box, type `Priority Tasks`. Because the folder will contain tasks, just click OK. Press Enter or click No to bypass the shortcut dialog box. Your dialog box should be similar to the one shown in Figure 2.7.

▼ **FIGURE 2.7.**

A folder named
Priority Tasks has
been added to the top
level folder.

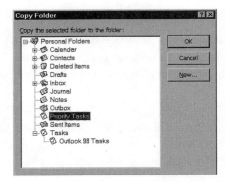

3. The Priority Tasks folder now has a plus sign to its left, indicating that there are subfolders that are not currently displayed. Click the plus sign. The copy of the Outlook 98 Tasks folder is now visible.

4. We have two folders with the same name, change the name of the copy. Right-click the Outlook 98 Tasks folder in the Priority Tasks folder. Choose <u>R</u>ename Outlook 98 Tasks. When the text is already highlighted, type January Priority Tasks and press Enter.

5. Add the January Priority Tasks folder to the Outlook Bar by dragging it into position. Position it between the Inbox and the Calendar.

6. Close the Folder List. Click Outlook Today in the Outlook Bar. Instead of using the Folder List to display a different folder, click the January Priority Tasks folder in the Outlook Bar.

7. To delete the folder from the Outlook Bar, right-click the icon and choose Re<u>m</u>ove From Outlook Bar. Confirm the removal. Click the Calendar icon. Display the folder list. Notice that the folder itself was not deleted, only the shortcut in the Outlook Bar.

8. If you opened the File List temporarily, click the push pin to lock it open. Right-click the January Priority Tasks folder icon. Choose <u>D</u>elete January Priority Tasks. The folder is removed.

9. To recover the folder, in the Folder List click the Deleted Items plus sign. Drag January Priority Tasks back onto the Priority Tasks folder. The deleted folder is
▲   now restored.

Changing Folder Properties

Each folder has specific properties. For example, a folder can be identified as containing Journal items or Task items. The folder name and its location are also properties. The *<Folder Name>* Properties dialog box has four tabs: General, AutoArchive, Administration, and Forms, as shown in Figure 2.8. To display the Properties dialog box, right-click the folder icon and choose Properties, or select the folder icon and choose File, Folder, Properties For *<Folder Name>*.

2

FIGURE 2.8.

The <Folder Name> Properties dialog box is displayed to change folder properties.

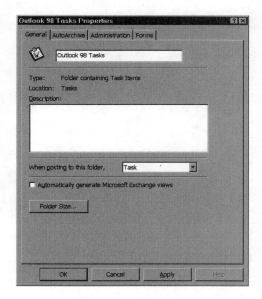

The only thing you may want to do from the General tab of the dialog box is to add a description. The description can only be viewed when the Properties dialog box is open, but when you have many subfolders, you may find it helpful to add a description.

Making Other Configuration Changes

Personalizing Outlook 98 is accomplished in the Options dialog box, as shown in Figure 2.9. This dialog box is displayed by choosing Tools, Options from the toolbar. As you can see, there are seven tabs used to set Outlook options. (If you have Exchange Services installed, you have an eighth tab: Delegates.)

Initially, you may find that most of the settings are acceptable. If you have previously setup Outlook 97, those configuration options will be automatically transferred to Outlook 98. In this section, only a few of the options will be covered. Others are seldom used. If you do need to use an option that isn't covered in this Hour, use the Outlook Help system, covered in Hour 3, "Help Me—I'm Lost."

FIGURE 2.9.

The Options dialog box is used to personalize Outlook to meet your needs.

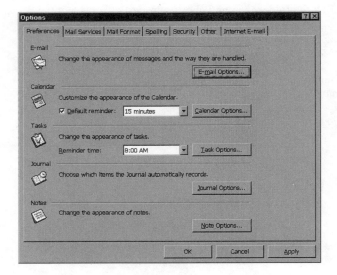

Setting the Preferences Options

The Preferences tab is used to set individual options for each of the five Outlook folders: E-mail, Calendar, Tasks, Journal, and Notes. We'll briefly look at each of the option screens. In some cases, you may have to ask your network administrator to help you decide on the specific settings. You will quickly notice that the options for Outlook are so plentiful, that it would take several hours to work through all the possibilities.

Setting the Email Options

The E-mail Options dialog box is shown in Figure 2.10. It is divided into two parts: Message Handling and On Replies and Forwards. After moving or deleting an open item, you can display the previous message, the next message, or return to the Inbox. You will probably want to keep copies of sent items and automatically save unsent messages. Automatically saving unsent messages will give you some protection in case of a power outage. The unsent messages are kept in the Draft folder. If you are always connected to your mail server (such as through a local network), you may want to turn on the mail notification option.

If you are notified as each message is received, you may find it very distracting; you may decide instead to simply check your mail on a regular basis.

FIGURE 2.10.

The E-mail Options dialog box assists you in determining how your email works.

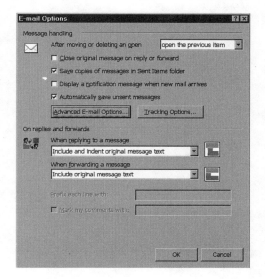

2

You can see the advanced email options in Figure 2.11. Normally, you won't need to change them, but to provide the maximum customization of Outlook, Microsoft has included them.

By default, messages aren't tracked. By opening the Tracking Options dialog box, as shown in Figure 2.12, you can control the tracking of the messages you send and receive.

Take a brief look through the On Replies and Forwards options in the main E-mail Options screen. Use the drop-down boxes to see the other available options.

Choosing Calendar Options

The Calendar options enable you to establish the days and times that you work. The Calendar Options dialog box is shown in Figure 2.13. Because the options are fairly self-explanatory, we'll leave it up to you to explore them. (Additionally, they are discussed in Part IV, "What Should I Be Doing Today?" so don't panic yet.)

FIGURE 2.11.

The Advanced E-mail Options dialog box enables you to set some of the more uncommon features of the Inbox folder.

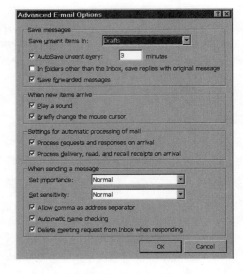

FIGURE 2.12.

The Tracking Options dialog box enables you to set the options for keeping track of messages that you have sent and received.

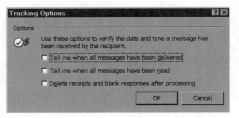

FIGURE 2.13.

The Calendar Options dialog box enables you to set information about how your personal schedule is kept.

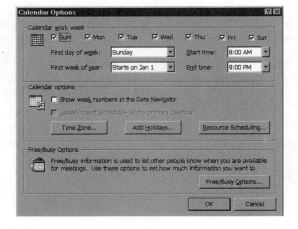

Selecting Task Options

The Task Options from the Preferences tab of the Options dialog box is very simple, as shown in Figure 2.14. Drop-down menus enable you to choose from one of twenty colors for displaying tasks that are either overdue or completed. (Only four colors will show at any time; you need to use the scroll arrows to see the rest of them.)

FIGURE 2.14.

The Task Options dialog box enables you to set the colors in which completed and overdue tasks are displayed.

2

Controlling the Journal

The Journal Options dialog box is considerably more complex than the other dialog boxes for setting options, as shown in Figure 2.15. Journal options are covered in detail in Hour 14, "The Journal: My So-Called Diary," and Hour 15, "Creating Your Own Point of View."

FIGURE 2.15.

The Journal Options dialog box is used to set which of your contacts, activities, or documents are tracked automatically.

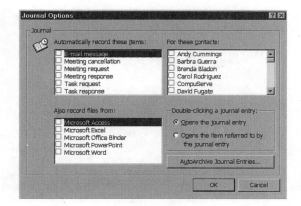

Setting the Options for Notes

The final option on the Preferences tab of the Options dialog box is controlling the Notes feature. As you experienced in Hour 1, notes are like sticky messages you can write as ideas occur to you, or as you stumble across non-priority information. The options for Notes, as shown in Figure 2.16, are very limited. You can choose the note color from five variations, one of three sizes, and the font used in the notes.

FIGURE 2.16.

You can set the color, size, and font used for Notes.

 The Mail Services, Mail Format, and Internet E-mail options are best left as they are until you are more familiar with the way Mail works in Outlook 98. These options are discussed in detail in Hour 7, "Back to Basics: Email Services," and Hour 8, "Setting Up the Mail Services."

Setting the Options for Spelling

Spelling options can be set to reflect your personal preferences. They are shown in Figure 2.17. The one option that is generally turned off that you will want to turn on is the Always Check Spelling Before Sending command.

FIGURE 2.17.

The spelling options are similar to those found in word processors, such as Microsoft Word.

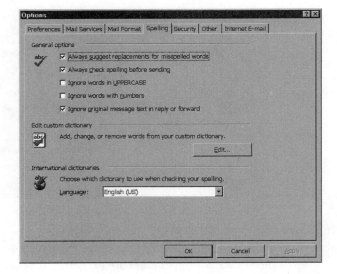

Securing Outlook

The Security options are beyond the scope of this book. If you need additional security for your messages, take a look at *Using Outlook 98* (published by Que Corporation, 1998).

Establishing Other Options

The Other options tab is divided into three parts: General, AutoArchive, and Preview pane (see Figure 2.18). We'll take a look at each of these, since they are simple to use and can be very important. The only option that can actually be set from the Other options tab is whether or not the Deleted Items folder is emptied each time Outlook is exited. You will need to establish a routine for emptying the Deleted Items folder, or it will grow to be a very large file and make it difficult to find recently deleted items.

FIGURE 2.18.

The Other tab of the Options dialog box enables you to control when the Deleted Items folder is emptied, the frequency of AutoArchive, and the look of the Preview pane.

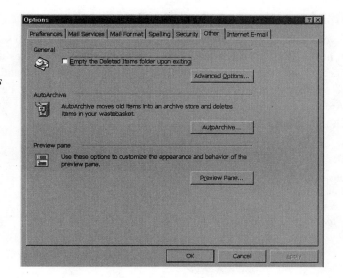

Setting the Advanced General Options

Clicking the Advanced Options button in the General area displays the dialog box shown in Figure 2.19. From this dialog box, you can set the folder that is opened when Outlook is started, the way Calendar items and Tasks are displayed, and additional options, which are beyond the scope of this book.

FIGURE 2.19.

The Advanced Options dialog box is quite complex, enabling you to control the way that Outlook actually works.

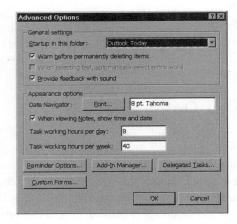

Establishing the AutoArchive Rate

When you click the AutoArchive button on the General tab, you'll see the dialog box shown in Figure 2.20. The AutoArchive takes older data and places it in a file for future reference. This is the opposite of the Empty Deleted Items command, but in a similar way, keeps the working file at a manageable size. If you leave the default setting, a full AutoArchive is performed every 14 days. The age of the items to be AutoArchived is set in each individual folder.

FIGURE 2.20.

The AutoArchive dialog box enables you to set the frequency and other options for the feature that backs up your data.

Modifying the Preview Pane

The Preview pane is the lower window in the Inbox, where the actual message is displayed. (The upper window displays the titles of the messages, with each message occupying a single line.) The Preview Pane dialog box is shown in Figure 2.21.

FIGURE 2.21.

The Preview Pane dialog box enables you to make modifications to the pane in which the actual email message is displayed.

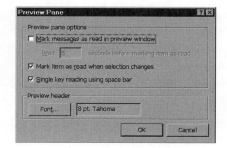

2

Summary

In this hour, you learned to control the configuration of Outlook 98. You learned to create new folders, delete them, rename them, move, and copy them, as well as looking at some of the configuration options available to you. In Hour 3, "Help Me—I'm Lost," you'll get a chance to use Outlook's Help features.

Q&A

Q **In this hour, we really covered a lot of options. You also said that other options will be covered in later hours. Does that mean all possible options will be explored in this book?**

A That would be nice. However, in an effort to enable you to make Outlook 98 exactly what you need, we don't even begin to explore the options that Microsoft offers. After you learn the basics, you may want to buy an advanced book to discover additional ways that Outlook can make your life easier.

Q **Do I have to create special folders?**

A No. Folders are simply a way of organizing your data. You can have as many or as few as you want. Of course, if you want to keep track of tasks, you must create a folder with the properties to handle task items.

Q **If I accidentally (or purposely) delete an item (rather than an entire folder), can I get it back, too?**

A Certainly. Click the Deleted Items icon in the Outlook Bar. All the deleted items will be displayed. Select the one you want to recover. Drag the icon back onto the folder where you want it stored. Be careful, if you set the Empty Deleted Items option to empty each time you quit Outlook, you must recover it *before* exiting.

When the Deleted Items folder is emptied (whether manually or automatically), all data is erased and not recoverable. If the Deleted Items folder is stored on a network drive, contact your System Administrator because it might be possible to recover the deleted material.

Q You didn't talk about changing the size of the viewing panes (windows). Can you change their size?

A All you need to do is drag one of the window edges to the new position, just as you would do with any other window.

HOUR 3

Help Me—I'm Lost

Few things are as frustrating as trying to complete a project under a tight deadline and not being able to solve a simple problem. Although Outlook 98 seems simple, learning to use its many features can be time consuming. In this hour, we examine various resources that can help you move down the road to becoming an expert Outlook 98 user. But first, some food for thought.

By this point in the book, you are familiar with many Outlook 98 features, but might not yet be fully comfortable with the program. Although you can't yet claim to be an Outlook expert, here's another perspective (from Saul Wurman's book, *Information Anxiety*): "…you don't have to know everything, you just need to know how to find it." Earlier this century, Albert Einstein also subscribed to the theory that it was wasteful to memorize anything that you could easily look up.

Few users are ever fully knowledgeable of all the features of Outlook (or any other computer program). In most cases, if you understand the basics of how to operate a program as well as how to find answers to your questions, you are well on your way to becoming an expert. Unless you dedicate your life to learning a single software package, you can never learn all of its features—and as soon as you become truly proficient, along comes an upgrade with new capabilities you have to learn.

This Hour provides some ideas for finding solutions to problems that you encounter. If you find something difficult to accomplish in Outlook, the chances are excellent that you can find an easier way to perform the task. With a little research, whether in books, online, or through human interaction, you can usually make the task a little easier.

Office Assistant: A Friend Indeed

You've already seen Office Assistant in action in Hour 1, "The View from the Outlook." Just in case you've forgotten what it looks like, it's shown again in Figure 3.1. Now you'll learn to have additional control over it. For a while, Office Assistant is cute. Later, you may find that it becomes annoying. If you don't like it, just turn it off.

FIGURE 3.1.

The default Office Assistant, Clippit, is waiting for you to type a question.

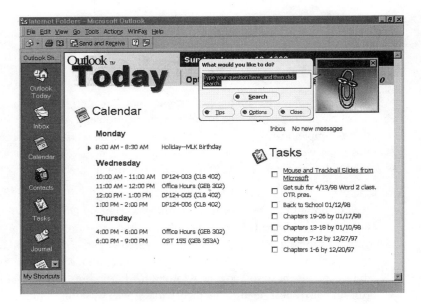

Office Assistant is designed to accept questions written in full sentences. For example, you could type "How do I print multiple copies of a document?" However, you don't have to type entire sentences. You could type "print multiple copies" and get the same answer.

If Office Assistant isn't displayed, click the Office Assistant button on the toolbar. It looks like a question mark in a cartoon balloon caption (always located on the extreme right end of the Standard toolbar). To ask a question, click Office Assistant. The help feature is generally context-sensitive. That is, Outlook examines what you are doing at the moment, and takes its best guess at what your question will be.

As you type your question, be sure to watch Office Assistant. If it appears as Clippit, the paper clip, notice that it takes notes on a clipboard while you type. Is Microsoft trying to tell us something? If your question is already displayed, click the button to the left of it to display the help topic.

> You don't even need to type consecutive words. You can just type the important words.

3

In the following exercise, you'll get a chance for some hands-on experience with Office Assistant. By the way, Office Assistant works the same (and uses the same *actors*) in all Office 97 or 98 applications.

NEW TERM *Actor*: A file (normally including both sound and animation) that is used for the picture in Office Assistant. Additional actors are available from your CD-ROM or from the Microsoft Web site (discussed later in this hour).

To Do: Using Office Assistant to Get Help

1. Open Outlook if it isn't already open. If Office Assistant isn't visible, click the Office Assistant button on the toolbar.
2. Click the Tasks icon in the Outlook Bar. Click in the Office Assistant box. Sample questions, as shown in Figure 3.2, are displayed.
3. Click the button to the left of the See More option. On the next screen, you see the option for several other questions, and at the top is the choice to return to the previous screen.

> You won't always have the option to see additional topics from the first screen. Also, you will never see more than two screens of questions.

▼ **FIGURE 3.2.**

*Office Assistant makes
its best guess at what
your question will be.*

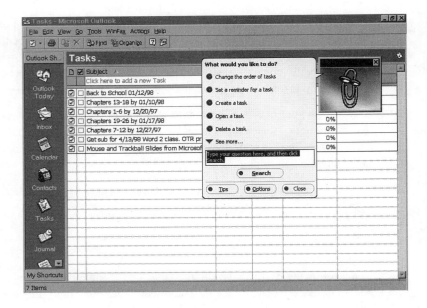

4. Highlight the area in which you will type a question. Type what do the icons
   mean. Click the Search button. Click About Symbols in Microsoft Outlook. Click
   the Symbols in Tasks button at the bottom of the help box. The Symbols in Tasks
   dialog box is displayed, as shown in Figure 3.3.

FIGURE 3.3.

*This Help dialog box
explains the meaning
of each symbol used in
Outlook 98.*

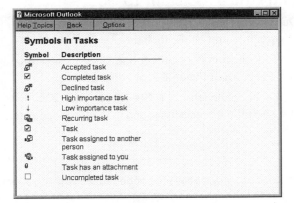

The Help dialog box remains on top of the screen until you close it. If you
want to move it out of your way, drag the title bar to the new position.

Office Assistant Options

Luckily, there are several options that can be set in Office Assistant. To see the options, click Office Assistant, then click the Options button. The Options tab, shown in Figure 3.4, is displayed.

FIGURE 3.4.

The Options tab of the Office Assistant dialog box is used to change the way Office Assistant operates.

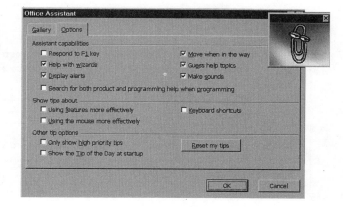

For my needs, the settings shown in Figure 3.4 are the best. You may find that your needs are different. Change the options as needed.

Getting New Office Assistants

After a while, you might want a little relief from Clippit. Luckily, from the Office Assistant dialog box you can click the Gallery tab, as shown in Figure 3.5, and choose to display different actors.

FIGURE 3.5.

The Gallery tab of the Office Assistant dialog box is used to change the appearance of the Office Assistant actor.

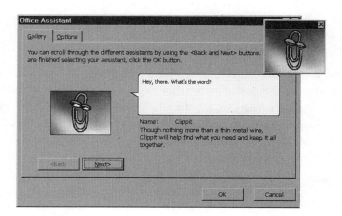

To see a new Office Assistant, click the Next button. The Dot will probably be the next displayed actor. Depending on your installation, you may only have a few actors. You will be able to see all of them in the Gallery preview window, but if you click the OK button, you may be prompted for the original CD-ROM. After you have installed an actor on your hard drive, it will be available from that time on.

> All actors have an *ACT* or *ACP* extension. You can use the Find command to find all the actor files on your CD-ROM; then, you can copy them to the actors folder on your hard drive. That way, all the actors are always available.

> Animated actors can take up a lot of space on your hard drive. The smallest is Hoverbot at 10K, and the largest is PowerPup weighing in at nearly half a megabyte.

You can get additional actors from the Microsoft Office Web site:

`http://www.microsoft.com/office/`

Using Help with Contents, Index, and Find

In many cases, you won't find the answer you need by using Office Assistant. At that point, you can move to the standard online help system built into Outlook 98. The help system is divided into three parts: Contents, Index, and Find. Each has its own advantages and disadvantages.

Understanding How Contents Works

In Hour 2, "Customizing Outlook 98 to Fit Your Needs," you learned to expand and collapse folders in Outlook. Now you get to put the same skills to use when working with the Help Contents. The Contents tab, as shown in Figure 3.6, is similar to the table of contents in a book, that is, it is arranged by topic, rather than alphabetically. Each topic may have one or more secondary topics. The Help dialog box is displayed by choosing Help, Contents and Index.

FIGURE 3.6.

The Contents tab in the Help Topics dialog box acts like a Table of contents in a book.

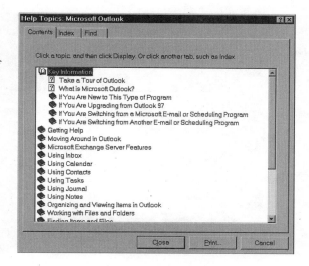

Notice in Figure 3.6 that the Key Information book now appears open. There are other books below the main topic that can also be expanded. Icons with a question mark represent a specific help topic, which can be reached by double-clicking the icon, or clicking the icon and then clicking Display.

The advantage of using the Contents feature is that it gives you a good overview of the topics covered in the Help feature. This is helpful if you want to get an overview of the topics covered by the online help feature. However, if you are looking for a specific topic, the Contents tab is not very helpful.

Double-clicking a book icon opens the book (expands the topic). After a book has been opened, it can be closed by double-clicking the icon again. Depending on the size of your screen, you may need to use the scroll arrows to see all the help topics.

Looking Up an Indexed Topic

The Index tab is shown in Figure 3.7. After the Help dialog box is opened, click the Index tab to display it. This tab functions just like an index in the back of a book: If you know the topic you want and if the Index is well developed, it's an easy way to find several references to a particular topic.

FIGURE 3.7.

The Index tab of the Help Topics dialog box can be used to look up more specific topics than the Contents tab.

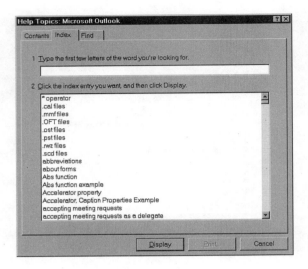

In the first text box, type the first word of the topic you are looking for. If you want to be more specific, you can type an additional word or words. As you type each letter, the display changes to show the first topic beginning with that letter. If you type the start of a word or words that are not contained in the index, the display jumps to the word in the index that is the closest alphabetically to what you are typing. You can press Backspace until you are back at the topic you want. When the relevant topic is highlighted, click the Display button to see it.

The disadvantage of using the Index tab is that if you don't know exactly what you're looking for, you might not find it in the Index. At that point, you need to use the Find tab.

Finding a Specific Term

The first time you click the Find tab, you see the dialog box displayed in Figure 3.8. You have three choices: minimize, maximize, or customize the search database. The first choice, usually the best, indexes all *keywords*, but leaves out some topics that don't have titles (such as pop-up definitions) and probably won't be of much help to you, anyway. The second option indexes every single word of every help screen. Although this may seem like a better choice, it usually results in a much larger database with slower search capabilities, and probably won't result in a more accurate search.

FIGURE 3.8.

The first time you use the find feature, help topics needs to build an index of the words in all the help screens.

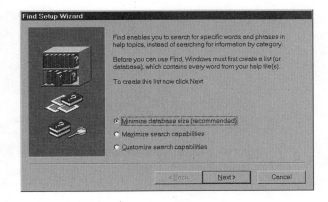

If you choose a customized search, you will see the screen in Figure 3.9. This enables you to choose one of the three generalized topic areas to index.

FIGURE 3.9.

This screen is used to customize the search capabilities of the Find Setup Wizard dialog box.

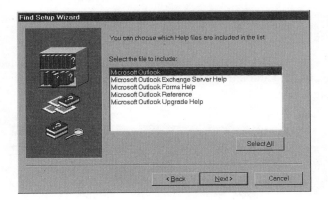

When you click the Next button, you see the second screen of the Find Setup Wizard regardless of the search type you selected. You can't really select anything here: You can only return to the previous screen, finish (and build the search database), or cancel the process.

After you have built the search database, the screen appears similar to the one shown in Figure 3.10. Type the word or words you want to find in the upper text box. All topics that contain all the words in the first box are displayed in the middle area of the screen. Highlight the topic you want, and click the Display button.

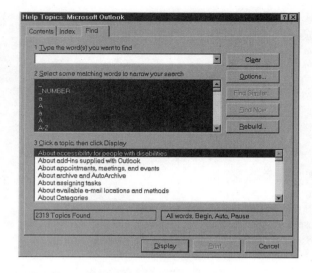

FIGURE 3.10.

When the topic you're seeking is highlighted, click the Display button to view it.

The Help Screen Options

Figure 3.11 shows a typical help screen. The Help Topics button takes you back to the Contents, Index, and Find screen. The Back button will be grayed out unless you have used a previous help topic.

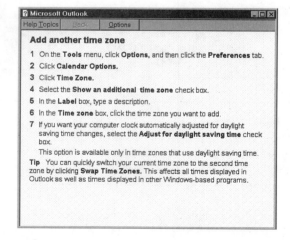

FIGURE 3.11.

A typical help screen in Outlook contains straightforward instructions for performing a procedure.

Clicking the Options button displays the menu shown in Figure 3.12. From here, you can choose any of eight options:

- *Annotate.* Use this option to add your own comments to any particular help screen. This is very helpful if you have problems finding a particular solution and think you might need it again. When a help topic is annotated, a paper clip appears to the left of the help screen title. Click it to view the annotation.

- *Copy.* This copies the entire help topic to the Clipboard. It can then be pasted into an Outlook note, or any other Windows application.

> If you don't want to copy the entire topic, simply select the text as you would any other text, then choose the Copy command.

- *Print Topic.* This sends the topic to the printer. This is helpful when you are going to be using complex instructions repetitively.

- *Font.* This enables you to change the relative font size of the help information to small, medium, or large.

- *Keep Help on Top.* The Keep Help on Top command offers three choices: Default, On Top, or Not On Top. The default is the setting for Windows Help. The other two specifically put the Help dialog boxes either on top of the current screen or beneath it. Generally, you will want to leave it at the Default setting.

- *Use System Colors.* If you have changed the color scheme on your computer, choosing this option uses the system colors for the help screens. If you change this option, you must reboot the computer for the color changes to take effect.

- *Bookmarks.* Enables you to choose from a list of markers that can be used to find a particular topic. This is helpful if you have had problems finding the answer to a specific question, or if there is a help screen you use often. To return to a bookmark, choose Options, Bookmarks and choose the desired marker name.

- *Define Bookmarks.* To use this option, display the help screen you want to mark, choose Options, Define Bookmarks, and name the bookmark.

3

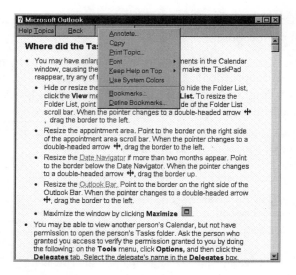

FIGURE 3.12.

The Options menu in the Help dialog box provides eight options that can make using Help easy and convenient.

A Few Words (or More) About Software Manuals

There is a saying among old computer users (and even those of us who are younger), "When all else fails, read the manual." Although this sounds silly, you would be amazed how many people would rather call Microsoft and stay on hold for some time (and *some time* may be a lot of time, depending on when you call), rather than try to find help in the manual or by using online Help.

With most of today's software—Microsoft Outlook 98 is no exception—the provided manuals tend to be skimpy and not very helpful. The full resources for help are found in the online Help feature, rather than in a printed manual. To put all the information found in online Help on paper would be costly, and the information couldn't be searched electronically, as it is with online Help.

Learning to use Outlook's online Help increases your effectiveness and your efficiency. By using this book in combination with the online Help, you can find answers to most of the beginning questions you may have on any Outlook subject.

What's This?

Another way to get help from Outlook is to select Help, What's This. Your cursor changes to a pointer with a question mark. Point to the button or command you need help with and click the mouse. For example, if you select Help, What's This and click the Find button on the toolbar, the screen display changes, as shown in Figure 3.13.

FIGURE 3.13.

The What's This option has been used on the Find button located on the toolbar.

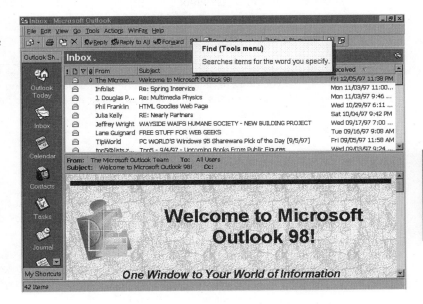

About Microsoft Outlook

The selection at the bottom the Help menu is About Microsoft Outlook. Selecting this option displays a dialog box similar to the one shown in Figure 3.14. To use Microsoft telephone technical support, you will need the information on this screen.

FIGURE 3.14.

The About Microsoft Outlook dialog box gives you information about the version of Outlook you are using. This information is required when using telephone technical support.

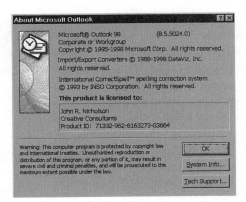

Microsoft on the Web

One of the more useful tools Outlook has for support is a built-in link from its Help system to the Microsoft Web site. Table 3.1 shows the Web pages directly accessible from the Help menu.

> If you don't have an active Internet connection, choosing one of the Microsoft on the Web options automatically begins the Internet logon procedure.

TABLE 3.1. ONLINE HELP OPTIONS.

Option	Result	URL (Web Address)
Free Stuff	Add-ons and bug patches are available from this Web site.	http://www.microsoft.com /office/enhoutlook.asp
Product News	Updated information about Outlook is available here.	http://www.microsoft.com /outlook/default.asp
Frequently Asked Questions	A list of Frequently Asked Questions about Outlook.	http://www.microsoft.com /office/astoutlook.asp
Online Support	Displays an area where you can access various support options.	http://support.microsoft .com/support/c.asp
Microsoft Office Home Page	Displays the Microsoft Office Home Page.	http://www.microsoft.com /office/update.asp
Send Feedback	The Microsoft Office Feedback page is displayed, enabling you to send messages to Microsoft technicians.	http://www.microsoft.com /office/update.asp
Best of the Web	Takes you to Microsoft's site of links to what's best on the Web. This page is updated often.	http://home.microsoft .com/exploring/exploring .asp

Option	Result	URL (Web Address)
Search the Web	Enables you to search for Internet topics by using one of over three dozen search engines.	http://home.microsoft .com/access/allinone.asp
Web Tutorial	Displays the Microsoft tutorial on how to use the Internet.	http://www.msn.com /tutorial/default.html
Microsoft Home Page	Displays the Microsoft Home Page (not the Office Home Page).	http://www.microsoft.com /microsoft.htm

3

Without doubt, the most thoroughly documented source of answers to Outlook problems can be found in the Microsoft Knowledge Base. This can be accessed through any Internet connection (including America Online and CompuServe).

When you call technical support with a question, if the technician doesn't know the answer, he or she searches the Knowledge Base (a computerized database containing all the known problems or questions about Microsoft software). If you have access to the Internet, you can find the answer to your question by directly accessing the Knowledge Base. Using the Knowledge Base as a source of information offers several benefits:

- The Knowledge Base is the largest and most complete source of Outlook information.

- If a user finds a problem that is not documented in the Knowledge Base, a technical support person reports it and creates an entry in the Knowledge Base to explain the problem to anyone who subsequently encounters it.

- You can access the Knowledge Base 24 hours a day, 365 days a year.

- The Knowledge Base is free (unlike a phone call to the 206 area code for most of us).

To complete the following exercise, you must have access to the Internet. If you don't, go to a friend and borrow a connection.

If you don't have an Internet connection and are friendless (or at least lacking in friends with a technical interest), you might find that your local library has a free connection for you to use.

To Do: Using the Microsoft Knowledge Base

1. Open an Internet connection, probably using Microsoft Internet Explorer or Netscape Navigator, and with America Online, CompuServe, or other service provider.

2. In the Address bar, type www.microsoft.com/kb. The browser displays the Microsoft Support Home Page, as shown in Figure 3.15. Make sure you enter the address with no spaces and all lowercase text. (You can omit http://. This is the default used if nothing is typed.) Press Enter.

   Because all Web sites are constantly evolving, the page you see might differ from the one shown in Figure 3.15, but it should still work basically the same way.

FIGURE 3.15.

The Microsoft Support Web site Home Page provides easy access to the Knowledge Base, Troubleshooting Wizards, and files that can be downloaded.

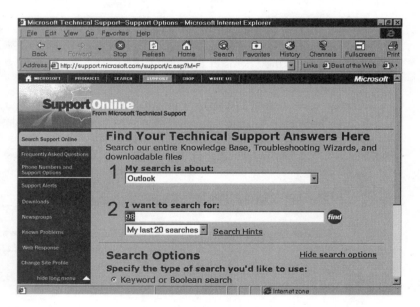

3. In the My Search Is About drop-down list, choose Outlook. Click in the I Want To Search For text box. Type 98 or any other term for which you need to find help. Click the Find button.

> You can also combine search terms, such as *symbol and trademark* or *symbol or trademark*. If you use the *and* command, only articles containing *both* words will be selected. Using the *or* command selects all articles that contain *either* term.

▼

▲
4. Take some time to explore the site. Type in some sample problems, and see what Microsoft provides for an answer.

Using Online Services to Get Help

Many users today subscribe to an online service provider, such as CompuServe, Inc. (CSi) or America Online (AOL). If you are a subscriber to either of these services, use the following methods for getting additional help with Outlook 98. If you don't have either one of the services, you might want to at least skim through the following information, so you know what the advantages to subscribing are.

CompuServe, although it is a separate entity, is now owned by America Online. (Of course, this could change before I finish typing this paragraph!) However, CSi and AOL have distinct "personalities." CSi is oriented to users with a technical interest, whereas AOL is family oriented, and the technical support for such programs as Outlook isn't nearly as strong as on CSi.

It's a tradeoff: People on CSi can tell you how to get a program to do things that Microsoft says it can't do, but sometimes it can be too technical an explanation to do you any good. Both services offer a free trial. If you are already on the Internet, you can get free trials at

`http://www.aol.com`

`http://www.compuserve.com`

Getting Help Using CompuServe

CompuServe forums are areas where people with similar interests can leave messages or comments. The CSi forum that deals with Microsoft Outlook can be displayed by clicking the Go button and typing mswga. This is the code for the Microsoft Mail and Workgroup Forum. Microsoft *doesn't* support this area. It's just a group of users who work with Outlook and other products.

To see the messages that others have left, click the Message Boards options and then select Outlook. The last time I was on, there were over 2,000 messages about Outlook, so it's an active area. Scan the messages to see if someone has already addressed your problem. If you want to see the files available (which will often include patches to fix bugs), look in the File Libraries area under Outlook.

If CSi reorganizes, and these commands don't work, just use the Find command and search for Outlook. Remember to keep your questions clear and concise. Usually, you will have several answers within 24 hours.

3

Using America Online to Get Help

When connected to AOL, you can use the keyword Microsoft. This gives you two options: Windows News and Knowledge Base. Both of these take you to the Microsoft Internet site, rather than to an area on AOL. The only advantage to using AOL in this situation is that you might find it slightly easier to navigate. You may be able to get individuals to answer questions by looking for the Home/Office area of AOL, but AOL doesn't support Microsoft products directly.

Using the Internet to Get Help

One of the most powerful sources of help is the Internet, and Outlook takes advantage of it at every step. Earlier, we discussed ways of getting help using the Internet. The following are three more parts of the Internet designed to help you get answers to your questions: newsgroups, Frequently Asked Questions, and search sites. Each of these has its own strengths. Learn to use them correctly, and you will be able to find the answer to nearly any question that might arise about Outlook 98 or any other computer-related questions.

Looking in Newsgroups

Think of a *newsgroup* as an extremely large, totally uncontrolled community bulletin board. That is, anyone can come along and thumbtack anything they want to it. Each bulletin board (newsgroup) has a theme or title that is displayed across the top of the screen. Because it is completely unmonitored, anyone can post anything. No censors monitor the board, and some people are more crude than others. Some stick to the topic; others post whatever they feel like. Opinions abound, with nobody to control them.

All newsgroups function similarly. First, you must access the newsgroup to read the information that's posted there. You can scan the headings for each entry, or you can plow through, reading all of them word for word. Anytime you see an entry that you agree or disagree with, you can post your own note, being as blunt or as tactful as you feel at the moment.

Newsgroups are wonderful places for getting answers to your questions. Just make sure you read the list of Frequently Asked Questions (FAQs), as discussed in the next section of this hour. If you search the newsgroup and can't find one or more FAQs, leave a note asking where you can find them. Usually, you get a polite answer because the users of the newsgroup *really* want you to use the FAQ, as it makes wading through the messages easier for them. In small newsgroups, you may see only a half-dozen or fewer postings a week; in larger newsgroups, you may see hundreds or thousands of messages posted daily.

Two newsgroups that you might be interested in are `microsoft.public.outlook97` and `microsoft.public.outlook98`. (The second one may not be available immediately upon shipment of Outlook 98, but keep checking back. It is an excellent beginning source for you to use.) You can also search the Microsoft Web site for the term *newsgroup*.

Getting the FAQs (Frequently Asked Questions)

When working with the Internet, you should avoid posting a message before reading the associated FAQ (list of Frequently Asked Questions). Nearly every newsgroup on the Internet has a FAQ so that people don't ask the same questions over and over. (And sometimes, over and over and over.) The regular readers of an Outlook newsgroup (or any newsgroup, for that matter,) can be very direct (and sometimes downright nasty!) if you ask questions without first checking the FAQ.

Check these sites for listings, explanations, and search tools for Frequently Asked Questions:

`http://www.cs.ruu.nl/wais/html/na-dir/.html`

`http://www.ii.com/internet/faqs/`

`http://www.yahoo.com/Reference/FAQs/`

Searching for Web Sites

You may not find exactly what you are looking for in a particular newsgroup. Luckily, the Internet has thousands of other Outlook resources (and a few of them are actually useful). To search the Internet, you use a *search engine*, a software program designed to find information on the Internet.

Each search engine monitors and indexes different material. If you don't find something on one search engine, don't conclude that it's not out there, only that the particular search engine didn't find it. The Internet is so large, no single search engine can cover it all (although some try). Most search engines are free: They make their money by selling advertising on the site.

Getting Help via Faxback Services

If you have fax capability, you can get information from most large computer companies 24 hours a day. Microsoft is no exception. Call 800-936-4100 for more information about its FastTips service. You can easily call and order a map of the particular area of the system (for example, Microsoft Outlook). From this map, you can order additional faxes that may help solve your problems.

Summary

In this hour, you learned about many ways to get additional help beyond the information supplied in this book. If you are going to use Outlook 98 on a regular basis, you will need an Internet connection—not only to get the described help, but to use all the features of Outlook.

Q&A

Q How can I get more information about getting services through America Online or CompuServe?

A For America Online, call 800-827-6364 for a free startup kit that includes software and a free trial of the service. CompuServe offers the same. You can reach them at 800-368-3343.

Q Getting help really sounds complex. Is it as hard as it appears?

A No, particularly if you've already used the help system in other Microsoft products. If you have problems finding help on the Internet, ask a friend or another Outlook user. Using other people as resources is a great way to get help, but remember that they have their own jobs to do, so try and find most of the answers on your own, saving friends and other users for the questions you just can't seem to find an answer to.

Q I don't want Office Assistant to pop up when I press F1. Can I stop it from doing that?

A Yes. Open Office Assistant and click it. Click the Options button. On the Options tab, turn off the Respond to F1 Key. From now on, pressing F1 displays the main help screen rather than Office Assistant.

Q I'm having problems understanding how to use newsgroups. What can I do?

A Access to newsgroups is through your provider of Internet services. If you are using America Online or CompuServe, look in the help areas under newsgroups. They are usually associated with the Internet menus because you must be on the Internet to access them. If you are using another service provider, call its technical support. Not all service providers (especially ones that offer only free email accounts) will provide access to newsgroups. That should be one of the questions you ask before signing up with a provider.

Any user with an Internet connection can access the Microsoft newsgroups by just pointing a newsreader (such as Outlook 98's version of Outlook Express) at msnews.microsoft.com. It's free and open to all, even to those whose Internet service providers don't provide any news services.

PART II
3-2-1 Contact

Hour

Hour 4

Establishing First Contact

Who are your contacts? Your boss? Your family? Your baby sitter? That guy at the mall who gave you his business card in case you decide to purchase a 200-pound drum of peanut butter? All of the above? Yes! Contacts are any people or businesses that you encounter. Some may be friendly, such as family and friends; some may be businesses—both the people you work with and those you use for service (the dishwasher repairman); and some may be not-so-friendly, such as the neighbor with the obnoxious dog that barks at three o'clock in the morning.

Now that you know who your contacts are (basically anyone on Earth), why do you want them in your Outlook 98 database? Well, the friendly contacts are easy to explain; these people are important to you—you don't want to lose contact with them. You may want to send them holiday greetings, birthday wishes, or family newsletters telling about your daughter's great swim meet. Until Outlook, you have probably kept their data in your personal address book (either electronic or paper).

For your business contacts, you may have a Rolodex™ of business cards and phone numbers, or you may have a photographic memory and be able to impress your business associates by always remembering your previous conversations with them (never forgetting to ask about the spouse and kids by name). A third way to keep track of business contacts is to amass business cards in a billfold or purse, periodically culling the ones that you have no idea who they are or why you kept them.

As for those not-so-friendly contacts, they are often relegated to sticky notes, scribbled on the front of the phone book or written on the backs of junk mail envelopes. A far better system (Outlook) enables you to keep track of each time you call asking them to quiet their dog, just in case it ever goes to court.

Outlook 98 gives you the opportunity to organize all those different phone numbers, addresses, and demographic data into an easy-to-handle database. You can add a new friend, business associate, or the school nurse in a matter of a few keystrokes, categorizing them so you can easily recall the data in the future.

Putting Contacts into Action

The Contacts folder is a good place to start when you first begin using Outlook. Entering all your contacts' information should be your first task because so many other features interact with the Contacts database. If you want to send an email or fax, schedule a meeting, or send a task request to someone, it is easier to do if you have an entry in your Contacts database for that person.

You can view your contacts in a number of different ways, but the most common view is the Address Card view, as shown in Figure 4.1.

With over 70 different fields for keeping track of contacts, your biggest challenge may be managing and updating your database. You learn the basics in this hour and more advanced techniques in Hour 5, "Manipulating Contacts." Outlook offers the usual business card and Rolodex™ fields, such as addresses, phone numbers, and email addresses. It also offers some not-so-common fields, such as Anniversary, Government ID Number, and ISDN Number. In this hour, you'll learn the basics of using Contacts in Outlook: adding, deleting, opening, and importing contacts. In addition, you learn to view your contacts in different formats.

FIGURE 4.1.

*The Address Card view
in the Contacts folder
enables you to see the
partial information for
several contacts at
once.*

New Contact button ⌐

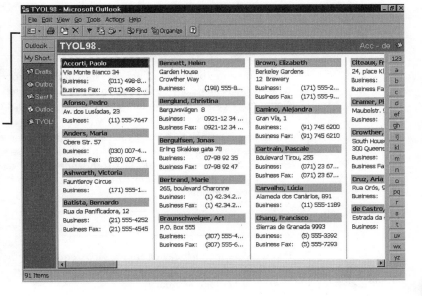

Managing Your Contacts Database

You can access the Contacts area of Outlook 98 either by clicking the icon in the Outlook Bar (it looks like a manual card filing system) or by choosing <u>G</u>o, C<u>o</u>ntacts from the menu.

Adding a Contact

Entering a new contact is a very simple procedure and will help you become acquainted with the way Outlook works. Information you enter here is usable in other areas of Outlook, as well as in other Office 97 applications.

There are several ways to add a new contact to your database:

- When in any folder other than Contacts, choose <u>F</u>ile, <u>N</u>ew, <u>C</u>ontact.
- When in the Contacts view, choose <u>F</u>ile, Ne<u>w</u>, <u>C</u>ontact from the menu.
- To use a keyboard shortcut, press Ctrl+N when you are in the Contacts view.
- Press Ctrl+Shift+C to display a new Contact form from any other area of Outlook.
- Double-click a blank area of the Contacts desktop.
- Click the New Contact button in the upper-left corner of the toolbar (refer to Figure 4.1).

After Outlook displays a new Contact form, you can enter all the information that you have about that person or business.

When you enter birthdays or anniversaries in the appropriate fields, those dates will automatically be entered in the Calendar component of Outlook. No more excuses for missing important dates! They appear on your calendar as recurring events.

If you want Outlook to remind you to buy a gift or send a greeting card, just place the cursor on the reminder in the calendar, select it, and drag it onto the Tasks icon. When the Task form appears, you can set an alarm for yourself. Click the Save and Close button. You can also click the appointment and set the reminder.

If you delete the birthday or anniversary from the Contacts database, it is also deleted from the Calendar. However, it is *not* deleted from the Task List: That must be done manually.

Name Notes

As we have already said (and will no doubt repeat as the hours progress), it is not possible to tell you (at least, in a book this size) all the different ways to accomplish any specific task in Outlook. But on occasion, we will show multiple options when it seems helpful. Adding a name to the Contacts list is just such a situation.

In the Full Name text box, enter the name as you normally would. If I enter John R. Nicholson in the Full Name text box, it is automatically stored in the File As text box as Nicholson, John R. when I press Tab to move to the next field.

In most cases, this filing method is fine. But what happens when you enter Dr. James E. Smith, Jr., in the Full Name text box? Outlook 98 is smart enough to store it as Smith, James E, but what happened to the rest of the information? Now for the really clever part. So far, text has been entered into the Full Name text box, but notice Full Name is also a button. Clicking on the button displays the Check Full Name dialog box, as shown in Figure 4.2.

FIGURE 4.2.

The Check Full Name dialog box enables you to add a title and suffix if needed.

In the following exercise, you create a new contact for yourself and learn the purposes of the most common fields. Before you begin entering the names of coworkers and friends into your Contacts database, work through the following exercise to enter data for yourself as the first of your contacts. This will save you a lot of time later.

To Do: Adding a New Contact

1. Open Outlook if it isn't already open. Click the Contacts icon in the Outlook Bar. Click the New Contact button on the left edge of the toolbar. A blank Contact form is displayed, as shown in Figure 4.3. When a new Contact form is first displayed, Outlook names it Untitled - Contact.

2. When the new Contact form is first displayed, notice the blinking insertion point in the Full Name text box. To enter your name, just type it (First, MI, and Last, no commas).

3. Complete the rest of the information on the General tab.

4. When you have entered the data about yourself, click the Save and Close button on the toolbar to close the Contact form and return to the Address Card View. Your information is now entered in the Contacts database.

▲

FIGURE 4.3.

A new Contact form is displayed.

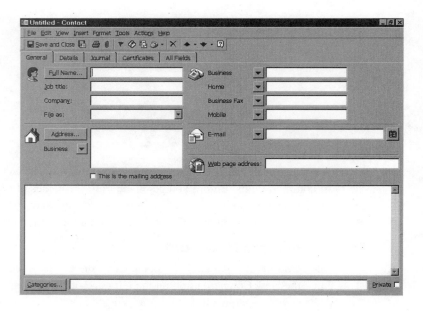

As shown in Figure 4.4, an example contact has been entered. There are five tabs on a typical contact entry form: General, Details, Journal, Certificates, and All Fields. Each of these tabs represents a form for the contact that is used to store specialized information. In Hour 5, "Manipulating Contacts," and Hour 6, "Customizing Contact Forms," you learn to use the other tabs.

> If you are entering information and decide you don't really want the contact entered, press Escape or click the Close button in the upper-right corner of the window. When asked if you want to save the changes, click No.

Deleting a Contact

You can delete a contact in several different ways. The method you choose will probably depend on what you are doing at the moment. You can use any of the following methods. All methods assume you are in the Address Card view (where you can see multiple entries at once).

FIGURE 4.4.

A completed sample Contact form is displayed.

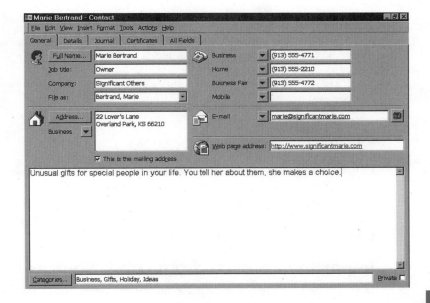

- Select the contact, right-click it, and choose Delete from the drop-down menu.
- Select the contact and choose Edit, Delete.
- Select the contact and press Ctrl+D.
- Select the contact and press the Del key.
- Drag and drop the contact into the Deleted Items folder.
- Select the contact and click the Delete button on the toolbar (it looks like an X).

If you delete a contact, you aren't asked for confirmation. It just disappears from the screen. It's stored in the Deleted Items folder (in the Outlook Bar), and will remain there until the folder is emptied.

Know when your Deleted folder is going to be emptied. You can check by choosing Tools, Options and clicking the Other tab in the Options dialog box. If there is a check mark in the Empty the Deleted Items Folder upon Exiting option box, the folder is emptied every time you exit Outlook. You can use the Advanced Options button to select other times to empty the folder.

4

Opening a Contact

You can also display the Contact screen in several ways. Again, the method you choose will probably depend on what you're doing. Here are two ways of opening a contact.

- Right-click the contact you want to open, and choose Open from the drop-down menu.
- Select the contact and press Enter.

Modifying a Contact

Contact information can be modified from either the Address Cards or the Contact screen. Simply drop the insertion point at the position where you want to change the information, and make the change. Many of the fields are not available from the Address Cards view, so if you want to make changes to one of these fields, you will need to use the Detailed Address Cards view.

Importing Contacts from Other Sources

In some cases, you may already have information stored in a database or other file. Using Outlook, you can import contacts stored in many formats, including the following:

- Comma separated (DOS)
- Comma separated (Windows)
- dBASE
- Lotus Organizer 1.0, 1.1, 2.1
- Access
- Excel
- FoxPro
- Personal Address Book (PAB)
- Schedule+ 1.0 and 7.0
- Tab separated (DOS)
- Tab separated (Windows)

The following exercise will take you through importing a database from Access. If you would like to work through the exercise at your computer, you can use the sample database in Access named Northwind.mdb.

To Do: Importing Data

1. Because you will not want to keep this information, begin by creating a new folder. Choose File, New, Folder. The Create New Folder dialog box is displayed, as shown in Figure 4.5. In the Name text box, type TYOL98. The Folder Contains box is already set to Contact Items, so click OK.

FIGURE 4.5.

The Create New Folder dialog box is used to create a new folder in which to store information.

2. When prompted to create a shortcut on the Outlook Bar, click Yes. The My Shortcuts icon in the Outlook Bar blinks for several seconds, indicating that an icon has been added.

3. Click the My Shortcuts icon. It moves near the top of the Outlook Bar. Click the TYOL98 icon. An empty Contact screen is displayed.

4. Choose File, Import and Export. The first step of the Import and Export Wizard is displayed, as shown in Figure 4.6. Several options are available. Highlight Import from Another Program or File.

5. Click Next. The next step of the wizard, as shown in Figure 4.7, is used to select the type of file you want to import or export. Use the scroll arrows *if* necessary and select Microsoft Access.

6. Click Next. Click the Browse button to locate the file called Northwind.mdb. It is probably located in the C:\Program Files\Microsoft Office\Office\Samples folder.

7. Choose the option Do Not Import Duplicate Items and click Next.

8. TYOL98 is already selected as the destination folder. Click Next.

4

▼ **FIGURE 4.6.**

The first step of the Import and Export Wizard is displayed.

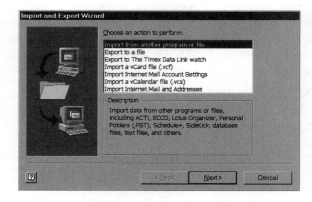

FIGURE 4.7.

The Import a File dialog box enables you to choose the exact type of file you want to import.

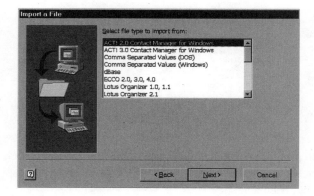

> If the option you want isn't available from the Import a File dialog box, you may not have installed all the components when you installed Outlook 98. Rerun the Setup procedure, and either choose to install all of Outlook 98 or do a custom installation and select the file types you may want to import and export in the future.

9. The next screen, shown in Figure 4.8, enables you to choose which table or tables you want to import. Click the Import "Customers" into the "TYOL98" folder. A
▼   check mark appears next to the option.

FIGURE 4.8.

Use this dialog box of the Import and Export Wizard to select the tables to be added to the TYOL98 folder.

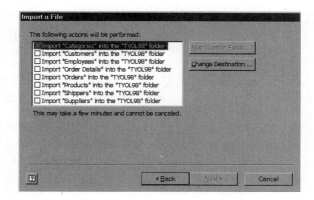

10. Click the <u>M</u>ap Custom Fields button. This dialog box, shown in Figure 4.9, is used to match the field names used in Outlook with the appropriate field names in the Northwind database. Because you are importing the table into an empty folder, you don't need to worry much about this. However, when you already have field names established in Outlook, you will need to match the field names.

If you double-click the table name, the Map Custom Fields dialog box is automatically displayed.

FIGURE 4.9.

This dialog box is used to match the names of the fields in the Access table with those in the Outlook folder.

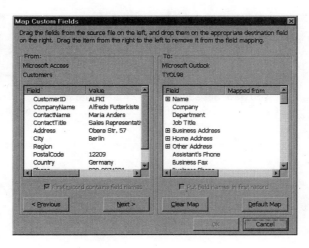

In this exercise, you are going to import the file in a less than optimal manner. This is to demonstrate what happens if you don't plan your strategy before beginning to import data. At the end of this exercise, you delete the entire TYOL98 folder, and will import the data correctly in a later exercise.

11. In the Map Custom Fields dialog box, drag the five fields from the database table (in the left pane) onto the matching field in the Contacts database in Outlook, as shown in Figure 4.10. Also drag the Phone and Fax numbers from the table into the right pane.

FIGURE 4.10.

Five fields have been matched between the Access table and the Outlook folder.

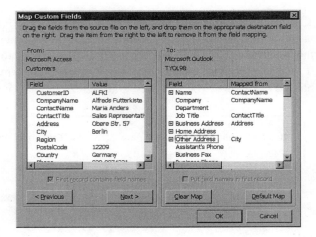

If you have already worked with this database in Outlook, it remembers the fields previously specified. You won't need to drag them unless you want them in a different position.

To clear the mapped fields, click the Clear Map button.

12. After you have finished matching the fields, click OK.

13. On the final screen, click the Finish button and wait for the database to be imported. It may take from several seconds to a few minutes to import the information, depending on your computer's speed, RAM, and other factors. When the computer is finished, your screen should be similar to the one shown in Figure 4.11.

FIGURE 4.11.

The data has been imported.

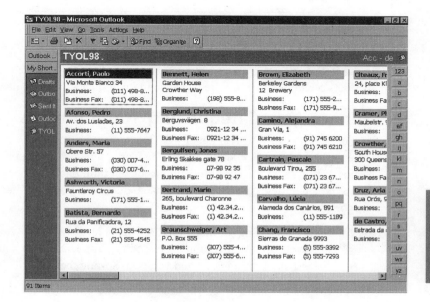

14. Double-click the record for Pedro Afonso. Notice that the city name is not displayed in his record. Click the down-pointing arrow to the left of the Address field. Notice that if you select the Other category, the city is displayed (but the address is not).

> You may find it easiest to create a dummy (fake) record in the database you are going to import with only the required fields before starting the import process. This ensures that you have an appropriately named field in the Outlook folder for each field of information in the database table you will import.

▼   15. Click the Close button to close the record.

> If you reopen the individual address card, the address is again displayed
> (even though you closed it with the city showing). Later, you learn to control
> which fields are displayed.

▲

More Control of Your Contacts

In the rest of this hour, you will get an overview of some of the helpful Contacts features.
In Hours 5 and 6, you will have a chance to input data and manipulate it.

General Tab: Categorizing Your Contacts

At the bottom of the General tab of the new Contact form, there is a place to list categories applying to each contact. When you work on many different projects or with many
groups of people, the category function is a great tool. Each contact can belong to many
groups or categories. As your Contacts database grows, you can filter your contacts by
categories.

 Filter: According to Microsoft, "A filter is an easy way to view only those items
or files that meet conditions you specify." You learn more about filters in Hour 5,
"Manipulating Contacts" and Hour 9, "Sorting the Mail."

As you can see in Figure 4.12, when the Categories button (in the Detailed Addresses
view) is clicked, a check list of available categories is displayed. You can use one of
these categories or create your own categories by going into the Master Category List at
the bottom of the list box and adding your own. You learn more about customizing categories in Hour 5.

Details Tab: Keeping Track of the Small Stuff

A sample Details tab is shown in Figure 4.13. As with the General tab, it isn't necessary
to fill out all the fields. For that matter, you don't even need to use the Details tab.
However, if you like to add a personal touch to your phone calls, using this can really
impress your customers. For example, on your next call, you might ask, Isn't your
anniversary next week? Are you and Molly doing anything special?

FIGURE 4.12.

The Categories dialog box enables you to choose from prede- fined categories or to create your own.

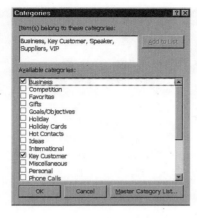

FIGURE 4.13.

The Details tab of the Contact dialog box can be used to keep addi- tional information about your clients.

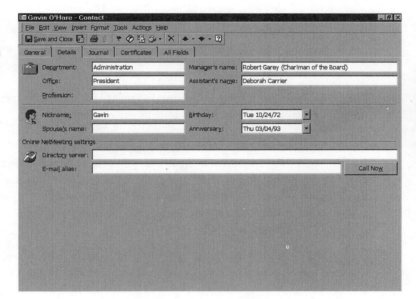

Journal Tab: Journal Entries with Your Contacts

By clicking the third tab in the Contact entry form, you can add information in the Journal about your contacts. Figure 4.14 shows an empty Journal tab.

FIGURE 4.14.

A blank Journal tab in the Contact entry form

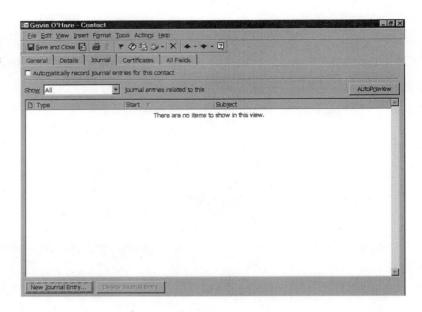

NEW TERM | *Journal*: Journal entries are used to record contacts with specific individuals. The Journal feature can work automatically or manually.

Automatic Journal Entries

You can make Journal entries manually, or you could choose to have Outlook automatically record Journal entries whenever you use Outlook to perform an activity involving one of your contacts. These activities include sending an email message, a fax, or a letter written in Microsoft Word. It can even record the duration of phone calls if you use the automatic dialing feature of Outlook.

For Outlook to automatically record Journal entries, click the tab marked Journal and enable the Automatically Record Journal Entries for This Contact check box.

> You can automatically record Journal entries only for contacts in the primary contact folder. If you try to set this on one of their sample contacts that you imported into the TYOL98 subfolder, the Automatically Record Journal Entries for This Contact check box is disabled (grayed).

You can set the Journal options by clicking Journal Options from the Preferences tab of the Options dialog box. You learn to control these options in Hour 14, "The Journal: My So-Called Diary," and Hour 15, "Creating Your Own Point of View."

> When Outlook automatically records Journal entries, your Outlook database increases in size. If you are concerned about saving hard drive space, you may want to record most of your entries manually and choose only a few, important contacts for whom you record all activities.

Manual Journal Entries

Some Journal entries need to be recorded manually, such as conversations you have with a contact. For example, if you place a phone call to Gavin O'Hare, clicking the New Journal Entry button at the bottom-left corner of the window opens the New Journal Entry dialog box, as shown in Figure 4.15. To place a call and have the dialog box automatically opened, open the Contact form for your contact, click the Autodialer icon on the toolbar, and select the phone number from the list. Outlook dials the number.

You can enter notes from the conversation as you speak. This really makes it easy when someone disputes what was said at a specific time. If you can state the date and time the call took place, and exactly what was said, you can save yourself a tremendous amount of frustration due to miscommunication.

> Another excellent application for manual Journal entries is being able to keep notes during a meeting. If you have your computer at the meeting (such as a laptop or the desktop computer in your office) you can open the other person's contact record and make meeting notes in the Journal.

Certificates Tab: May We See Some ID, Please?

Certificates (also called digital IDs) are files which are issued by a certified security authority, such as VeriSign, or from your administrator. These certificates are used to send security-related information over the Internet. For the Certificates to work, both the sender and the receiver must have a valid certificate.

4

FIGURE 4.15.

The Journal Entry dialog box is used to record contacts with specific individuals.

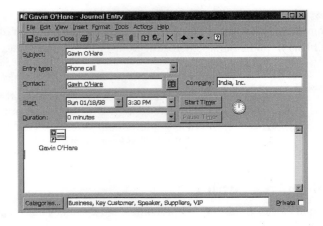

For more information about VeriSign, use Outlook's Online help to search for the topic. Even more information can be found in *Using Outlook 98* by Gordon Padwick (Que, 1998). You can also go to the "horse's mouth" at

www.verisign.com

All Fields Tab: Seeing the Whole Picture

The final tab on the Contacts form is All Fields. On this form, you can choose the fields you want to view from a drop-down list. As shown in Figure 4.16, the different fields and their corresponding entries are shown in a table format. You can enter information about a contact in this window, and you can select fields and copy information, as well. When you copy cells from this view and paste them into a Word document, for example, the information is separated by tabs.

You can also use the All Fields tab to create new fields for a Contact. Click the button marked New at the bottom-left corner of the form. Before you create a new field, remember that Outlook already offers four user fields that you can customize to meet your needs. View these user fields by choosing Miscellaneous fields from the drop-down list. Although you can add any information to the four User fields, you can't change their name or properties.

FIGURE 4.16.

All the fields for the Contact forms are displayed. You can modify, add, or delete fields using this dialog box.

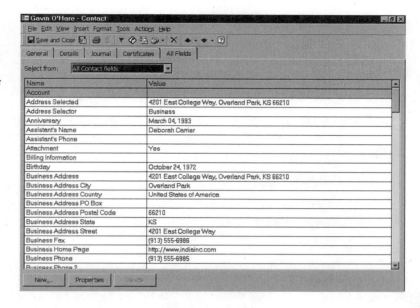

Displaying Contacts in Different Views

4

The default view for Contacts is the Address Card view. Both the Address Card view and the Detailed Address Card view are easy formats to work with, especially if you have many blank fields within each contact entry. These two views do not display blank fields unless you specify otherwise and modify the views.

As your Contacts database grows or as you begin to categorize and group your Contacts, experiment using views other than the Address Card view so that scanning through the list of names is as efficient as possible. You learn more about custom views for the Contacts database in Hour 6.

The Address Card view is the only format in which you cannot group your contacts. In other views, you can group contacts by fields, such as State or Category.

Creating Custom Views

If none of the predefined views offers what you need, you can create your own view and save it so that it appears in the drop-down list of views. To create a custom view, either modify one of the predefined views or create your own view from scratch. The following example shows you how to create a custom view using each method.

If you plan to update your list to include home phones, change to Phone List view, as shown in Figure 4.17. You want the following fields to be visible on your screen:

- Flag Status
- Full Name
- Company
- Business Phone
- Business Fax
- Home Phone

FIGURE 4.17.

In the Phone List view of the Contacts folder, you can control which fields are displayed. The sample is sorted by Company.

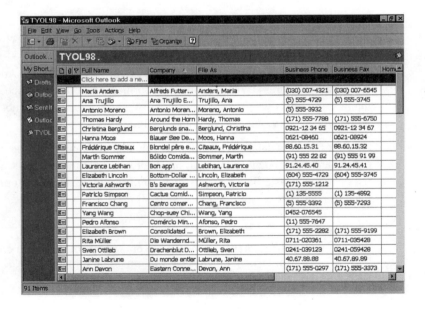

Switching Between Views

Besides the two predefined Address Card views, you can also switch between different table views. In the Contacts folder of Outlook 98, there are seven predefined views.

To choose a different view, choose View, Current View from the menu, and select one of the views in the drop-down list. The list offers different views that have already been defined by the creators of Outlook. However, you may want a different view from those listed. The Phone List view is close to meeting your needs. With just a few changes, it can be perfect.

To Do: Modifying a Current View

1. Click the TYOL98 Contact folder icon (it's located under the My Shortcuts group). Choose View, Current View, Edit Current View. The View Summary dialog box, shown in Figure 4.18, is displayed. Notice that there are many options for customizing a view. In this exercise, though, we'll keep the changes simple.

FIGURE 4.18.

The View Summary dialog box is used to modify a view.

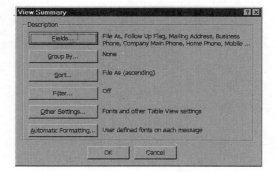

2. Click the Fields button. The Show Fields dialog box, as illustrated in Figure 4.19, is displayed. The fields in the left pane are those available in the current view. The fields in the right pane are those already shown in the current view.

FIGURE 4.19.

The Show Fields dialog box enables you to select the fields you want displayed in your modified view.

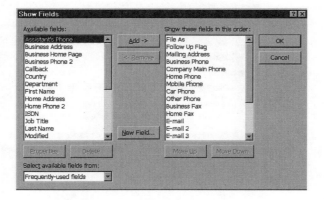

▼   3. Click in the left panel on Full Name. Press Ctrl and click Company and Primary
       Phone fields. Click the **A**dd button. Select the File As field, and click the
       <-**R**emove button. Click the Follow Up Flag in the right panel, press Shift, and
       click the last field (E-mail 3). Click the <- **R**emove button again. Click the Full
       Name field. Click the Move **U**p button. Your dialog box should now be similar to
       the one shown in Figure 4.20.

FIGURE 4.20.

*The Show Fields dia-
log box is set to show
only the fields Full
Name, Company, and
Business Phone (in
that order).*

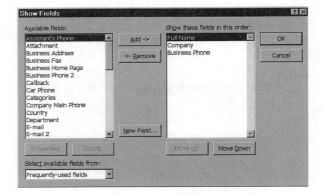

   4. Click OK to return to the View Summary dialog box, and OK again to close it.
       Your screen should be similar to the one shown in Figure 4.21.

FIGURE 4.21.

*The Address Card view
has been modified so
that only the three
desired fields are
displayed.*

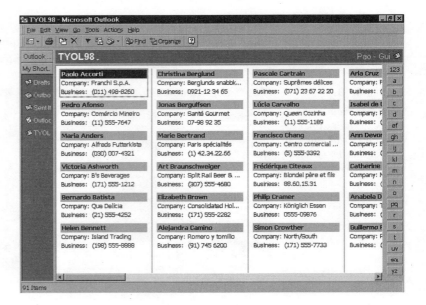

▲

A Few Helpful Hints

The following are a few miscellaneous hints that you will find useful:

- Notice that the entries are filed in alphabetical order by last name. (In this example, the records are actually sorted in File As order, but in another file, they might be sorted by company name or other field).The indicator on the TYOL98 Folder Banner shows Pao-Gui. This is because although the records are in last name order, they are displayed with first name prior to last. If you want to index them by last name, use the Last Name field.

- How many items are in the current database? Look in the bottom-left corner of the screen (in the Status bar). There are currently 91 items (records).

- If you want to return to the original view, choose View, Current View, Define Views. The Define Views for *<Folder Name>* dialog box is displayed, as shown in Figure 4.22. Click the original view, and then the Apply View button.

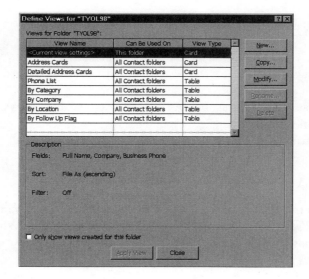

- If you want to see a group of records where the names begin with a specific letter, click the letter tab on the right side of the window.

- Remember, you can double-click any item and have the Contact screen displayed.

> Another fast way to get to a group of records that start with a particular letter is to just type that letter on the keyboard.

Deleting an Outlook Folder

Deleting a folder is a two-step process. First, you must delete the file itself and then delete the shortcut that points to the deleted file.

To Do: Deleting an Unwanted Folder

1. Click the Folder Shortcut and choose File, Folder, Delete Folder for <*File Name*>.
2. Right-click the Shortcut and choose Remove From Outlook Bar in the drop-down menu. When asked for confirmation to delete the shortcut, click Yes.
▲ 3. If necessary, display the new folder you want to view.

Summary

In this hour, you learned what the Contacts component can do for you. You read about how to manage your contacts and perform the basic tasks associated with the Contacts feature, such as adding, opening, deleting, and importing contacts. You also learned how to assign your contacts categories. As your Contacts database grows, you can easily locate specific groups of people for mailing, faxes, phone calls, and anything else you want to do with Contacts.

Q&A

Q I was trying to import a contact file from another program and I wanted it in a separate folder, but all the names are mixed together. What did I do wrong, and how can I fix it?

A Well, there's good news and bad news. The good news is that all you did was forget to create a new Contact folder (or chose the wrong one) before you ran the Import/Export Wizard. Just create a new Contact folder, and run the wizard again. The bad news is that there is no way to undo what you did. The only recourse is to delete the records one at a time. Of course, if you have backed up your data files, you can simply revert to the saved version. To see how to back up information, look in the online help under *backup*.

Q **I created a new folder to store my Contacts in, but when I exited and restarted Outlook, they were all gone. What happened?**

A When you created the folder, it was placed under the My Shortcuts group on the Outlook Bar. Click it once, and you will see the folder you created.

Q **I entered data into a Contact folder I created, and then changed the Address Card view to display only a few fields. When I went back to my original Contact folder, its view had also changed. How can I get back the original fields?**

A From the menu, choose View, Current View, Define Views. Click Address Cards and click Reset. Confirm the reset command. This changes the view for all Address Cards in all Contact folders.

Q **If I didn't do a complete installation of Outlook 98 the first time, how can I add import and export filters?**

A Click Start, Settings, Control Panel. Click the Add/Remove Programs icon. Select Microsoft Outlook 98. Click the Add/Remove button. The Installation Wizard automatically runs. Just follow the instructions.

Q **One of my contacts has a pager, but that isn't an option on the Detailed Address Card. How can I enter a pager number?**

A Click the down arrow next to the Business phone number. From the drop-down list, select Pager and enter the number.

Q **We didn't really discuss the Notes field very much. What can I use it for?**

A You can use the Notes field for virtually any information that doesn't fit easily into other fields, particularly information that is lengthy. For example, if you are conducting a simple phone survey, you can record the Contact's answers in the Notes field.

4

Hour 5

Manipulating Contacts

After you have entered all your contacts into an Outlook folder, you can do many things with them. You may want to sort them according to city, find contacts that meet specific criteria, or use them to communicate. A list of contacts that is just an alphabetical group of data isn't a lot of good, so you need to learn how to manipulate your contacts to make your life easier. After all, that's the reason you bought Outlook in the first place, isn't it? (Well, maybe it was because it came with Office 97, but because you already have it and you've bought this book, you must want to learn how to use it).

If Hour 4 was Contacts 101, then Hour 5 is Contacts 102. It's still a beginners' course, but now you can build on what you already know to see how Outlook 98 can be truly useful and save you time. In Hour 4, "Establishing First Contact," you learned to create and modify contacts. In this hour, you learn to manipulate contacts to give you exactly what you need.

You'll begin by creating a new Contacts database so that we'll all be working with the same information. Then you'll enter ten sample contacts to give you a starting place. You'll learn to add contacts from the same company without having to type duplicate data.

Of course, communicating with your contacts is the main purpose of the Contacts database, so you'll also get some hands-on experience in using various communication features.

Creating a Contacts Database

So that you can have a Contacts database to work with, you'll create a new Contacts folder and add 10 contacts in the next exercise. After you have the basic information in your Contacts database, we'll be able to further explore some of the intermediate levels of Outlook 98.

To Do: Creating a New Contact File

To Do

1. Open Outlook if it isn't already open. Click the Contacts shortcut in the Outlook Bar. Choose File, New, Folder. The Create New Folder dialog box, as shown in Figure 5.1, is displayed.

FIGURE 5.1.

The Create New Folder dialog box is used to create a place for storing the India Customers contacts.

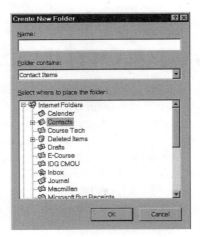

2. In the Name text box, type India Customers. Make sure that the Folder Contains text box reads Contact Items. The Contacts folder should be selected in the Select Where to Place the Folder window. Click OK. When asked if you want to add a shortcut to the Outlook Bar, click Yes.

3. Click the My Shortcuts icon in the Outlook Bar. Click the India Customers icon. No data is currently contained in this folder.

Adding the First Contacts

In the following exercise, you'll enter ten contacts, all from different companies. Besides the basic data, you'll also enter some keywords and other information that you can later use to examine Outlook Contacts capability.

To Do: Creating a New Contact Item

1. Click the New Contact button in the Toolbar. (It's the one on the left end of the toolbar.)

2. Enter the data shown in Table 5.1. After you enter the data for each contact, click the Save and New button on the toolbar (just to the right of the Save and Close button). That saves the current contact and displays a blank form.

> When entering the first phone number, you don't have to worry about formatting. Just type 8505556784. As soon as you press Tab or click the next field, it is automatically formatted as 850-555-6784.

TABLE 5.1. DATA FOR THE INDIA CUSTOMERS FOLDER.

Full Name	Company	Business Address	Business Phone	Business Fax
Matthew Adams	Florida Flippers	3256 South Grape St. Pensacola, FL 32502	850-555-6784	850-555-6701
Robert Allen	Art Time	13558 Anteres Court Englewood, CO 80111	303-555-7415	303-555-7488
Heidi Climber	Dane Printing Supplies	1801 Stratford Santa Rosa, CA 95404	707-555-8800	707-555-8701
Ashley Dollton	Artful Manufac- turing	7314 Booth Klamath Falls, OR 97602	503-555-6991	503-555-9898

5

continues

▼ **TABLE 5.1.** CONTINUED

Full Name	Company	Business Address	Business Phone	Business Fax
Deborah Garey	Holiday Supplies	8654 Sleepy Hollow Road Leavenworth, KS 66048	913-555-1122	913-555-1213
Jessica German	Sisters and Others	524 Hargis Lane St. Louis, MO 63105	314-555-2288	314-555-9881
Joanie Griffith	Paint, Inc.	12322 Main Street Hollywood, CA 90028	213-555-2224	213-555-7841
Kristopher Griffith	By-The-Numbers	6300 Owensmouth Aurora, CO 80013	303-555-3369	303-555-8433
Molly Kiowa	ArtFirst	244 Nicobar Lancaster, CA 93534	805-555-9898	805-555-7461
Charles Roberts	Felt Artist Supplies	84 North Oak Parkway Mission, KS 66202	913-555-9355	913-555-5000

▲
　　3. When you have entered the last contact, click <u>S</u>ave and Close on the toolbar. This
　　　　returns you to the Address Card view.

Adding a Contact from the Same Company

If you are building a large contact database, you will probably be entering several people
from the same company. Rather than having to repeatedly enter the same data, you can
tell Outlook that you want to enter a contact from the same company by selecting a

contact that represents the company and choosing Actions, New Contact from Same Company. You can do this from the Address Card view or from the Opened Card view.

To Do: Adding a New Contact from the Same Company

1. From the Address Card view, click the contact for Joanie Griffith. Choose Actions, New Contact from Same Company. Another Contact form, not quite blank, is seen in Figure 5.2. Notice that the Name and Job Title have been removed. All the other information is left the same. (You may need to change the phone number or extension.)

FIGURE 5.2.

A Contact form with the company information intact and the personal information removed is displayed when you choose to add a new contact from the same company.

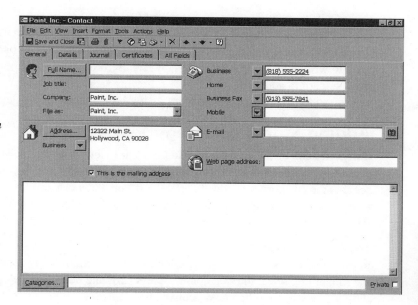

2. Type Jessica Stites in the Full Name text box.

3. Click the Save and Close button. As you can see, it's much easier to make a few changes to a contact than to type all the information again.

Understanding Categories and Items

In this hour, we are concentrating on adding categories to contacts. However, categories can be added to any item: email, task, journal entry, and others. These items can then be grouped. For example, if you are working on the Snail Foundation project (which you create in Hour 6, "Customizing Contact Forms"), you can group all the contacts connected with the project, any tasks you have assigned them, memos, and other related items, into subfolders beneath a single folder. Adding categories to contact items is only the beginning of a powerful process that enables you to quickly look at all items in a specific category.

Adding Categories to the Contacts

You can assign numerous predesignated categories to each contact. Outlook provides nearly two dozen categories for Contacts. Also, in the Master Category dialog box, you can create as many additional categories as you need.

Categories are important for grouping and filtering contacts. When you filter contacts, you tell Outlook to display only the contacts that meet specific criteria. For example, if a dozen contacts are participants in a committee you chair, you can tell Outlook that you want to write a memo to only those contacts. Before you learn to filter the contacts, you need to learn to add categories. In the following section, you learn to add standard categories and to use the Master Category dialog box to create new categories.

Adding Standard Categories

Categories can be added from the Address Card view, or to any open contact. Usually, you will find it best to add categories to an open contact because you can immediately see that the category was added correctly. If you add a category or categories to a contact from the Address Card view, you probably won't be able to see it (unless you have modified the view to include the Category field).

To add a category to a contact from the Address Card view, begin by clicking the contact to select it. If you want to add the same category to multiple, nonconsecutive contacts at the same time, select the first contact, press Ctrl, and continue clicking all other contacts desired. To select multiple consecutive contacts (for example, if you have sorted your contacts by company name), click the first to select it, press Shift, and click the last contact. All contacts between the first and last are automatically selected. Choose Edit, Categories to display the Categories dialog box, as shown in Figure 5.3.

To add a category or categories to selected contacts, click the check box next to each category name. When you have finished, click OK. Each selected category is added to the selected contacts.

Categories can also be added from the opened Contact view. Double-click the contact to open it. Then, to open the Categories dialog box, click the Categories button in the lower-left corner of the window. When you select the category or categories and click OK, they are added to the text box at the right of the Categories button.

FIGURE 5.3.

The Category dialog box is used to choose from predetermined categories.

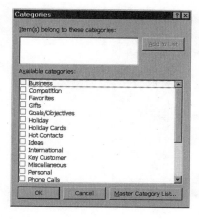

You don't have to use the Categories dialog box to enter a category. Click the text box to the right of the Categories button and just type the categories. For example, you could type Competition, VIP and the contact would be automatically listed in both categories.

Generally, try to use the Categories dialog box. From there, you can select predefined categories. If you misspell a category, such as *Compitition*, Outlook assumes that is a separate (and new) category. When you filter or group on the Competition category, the records in the misspelled category will not be included with the records in the correctly spelled category.

Adding and Deleting Custom Categories

You aren't limited to the categories offered by Outlook. To create a new category, open the Categories dialog box and click Master Categories List. The Master Category List dialog box, as shown in Figure 5.4, enables you to create new categories and use them in grouping your contacts and other items.

To create a new category, simply type the name in the New category text box and click Add. You can create as many categories as you need. When you are finished, click OK to return to the Categories dialog box. In the Categories dialog box, all the new categories are displayed. You can now select any of the new categories.

5

FIGURE 5.4.

The Master Category List dialog box is used to create new categories.

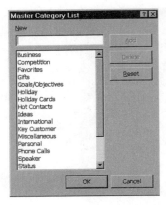

If you want to get rid of the Custom categories and return only to the original predefined categories, click Reset in the Master Category List dialog box.

You can also delete any categories in the Master Category List dialog box (including the predefined categories). Select the category to be removed and click Delete.

In the following exercise, you will add both single and multiple standard and custom categories to selected contacts. You also learn to delete a category, and find out what happens if you do.

To Do: Assigning and Adding Categories in Contacts

1. From the Address Card view, click the contact for Matthew Adams. Press Ctrl and click the contacts for Heidi Climber, Jessica German, and Molly Kiowa.

2. Choose Edit, Categories. The Categories list is displayed. If necessary, scroll down until the VIP category is visible. Click it to place a check mark next to the category. Notice that the category is now listed in the Item(s) Belong to These Categories text box.

3. Click OK. Double-click the contact for Molly Kiowa. Notice VIP is listed in the Categories text box at the bottom of the contact. Check the other contacts to make sure the VIP category was added to them. Return to the contact for Molly Kiowa.

4. Click the Categories button. Remove the check mark from the VIP category. Click OK. Notice the category has been removed from the contact. Close the contact by clicking the Save and Close button.

5. Select the contacts for Matthew Adams, Robert Allen, Heidi Climber, and Joanie Griffith. (Remember, click the first contact, press Ctrl, and click the other contacts).

6. Add a category called Speakers Bureau to each of the contacts. Choose Edit, Categories. Click the Master Category List button. In the New category text box, type Speakers Bureau. Click Add. Notice that Speakers Bureau has been added to the list of available categories. Click OK. Use the scrollbar if necessary, and place a check mark next to the Speakers Bureau category. Click OK.

7. Open the contact for Heidi Climber. Notice the categories now read *VIP, Speakers Bureau.* Close the contact.

Deleting Categories from the Master Category List

Categories are easily deleted from the Master Category List dialog box, but it isn't quite as straightforward as it might seem (until you think about it). To delete a category, display the Master Category List dialog box, highlight the category to be deleted, and click Delete. The category is deleted. The problem comes when you take a look at a contact that still contains that category. In the next exercise, you'll learn to fully delete a category.

To Do: Removing Contact Categories

1. From the Address Card view, choose Edit, Categories. Click Master Category List. Click the Speakers Bureau category. Click Delete. The category is deleted. Click OK twice.

2. Open the contact for Heidi Climber. Notice Speakers Bureau is still a category. Click Categories. Use the down scroll arrow, if necessary, to see the Speakers Bureau category, as shown in Figure 5.5. Notice that the category is no longer contained in the Master Category List (because you deleted it in the previous step).

FIGURE 5.5.

The Categories dialog box shows that the Speakers Bureau category is no longer in the Master Category List.

5

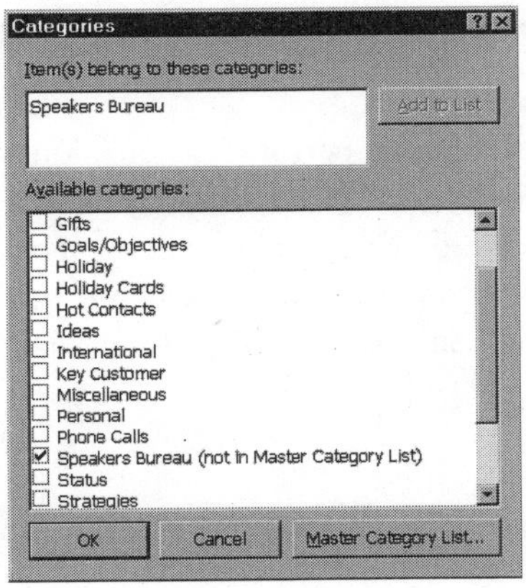

▼ 3. To permanently delete the category, you must remove it from all contacts containing the category. Click OK and close the contact.

4. In the Address Card view, select the contacts for Matthew Adams, Robert Allen, Heidi Climber, and Joanie Griffith. Choose Edit, Categories. The Categories dialog box will look similar to Figure 5.5. Highlight Speakers Bureau in the Item(s) Belong to These Categories text box, and press Delete on the keyboard. The text is deleted from the Item(s) Belong to These Categories text box, but not from the list below. That's OK. Click OK to close the dialog box.

5. Open the contact for Joanie Griffith. Notice Speakers Bureau is no longer in the Categories text box. Click the Categories button. Scroll down. Notice that the Speakers Bureau category is gone. Check the other contacts. All traces have been removed. Close the Categories dialog box and the contact.

Later, you will learn to filter contacts. When filtering contacts, you can display only the contacts with the category to be deleted. Then you can complete the deletion process for the category.

▲

Providing Additional Information About a Contact

Although we won't do a lot with the Details tab, you need to be aware of it because you can use it to your advantage, particularly in cases where you need to recall personal information about a contact.

To view the Details tab, open any contact and click the Details tab. It is shown in Figure 5.6.

Although this tab contains fields for some personal information, it may not be all you need. In Hour 6, you learn to modify the Contact form by adding and deleting fields. Unfortunately, Microsoft will not allow you to redesign this tab in any manner. You are stuck with it exactly like it is. The good news is that Outlook offers six extra pages when you design the Contact form, and you can add multiple fields (such as children's names) to any of the other tabs.

FIGURE 5.6.

The Details tab of a contact is used to record personal information about a contact.

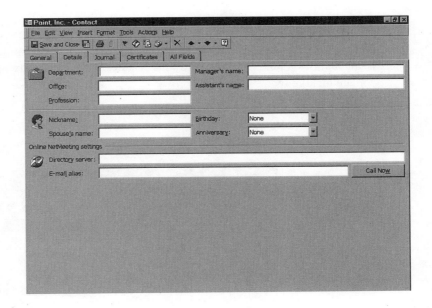

Manipulating the Contacts

The current India Customers database is very small. Without putting a lot of work into expanding a fictional database, it's difficult to imagine the power of the contacts feature of Outlook. Keep in mind that most of your databases will contain dozens or even hundreds of entries. In the India Customers database, you can easily scan the contacts to find the contact or contacts you need. However, as your database grows, this method of finding contacts becomes unrealistic.

As you work thorough the following exercises, remember that in real life you'll be applying the skills to larger databases, and your work will be simplified. If you already have a larger database created, you may want to work with it during the exercises rather than the small contact list we created.

In this section, you'll learn to locate a contact by various methods, sort the contacts by different fields, filter the contacts so that only ones meeting specific criteria are showing, and place the contacts into groups. After learning these skills, you'll be well on the way to mastering the Contacts folder of Outlook 98.

5

Finding a Contact

Finding a contact can be a big challenge when you are working with a large database. Using Outlook's Find and Advanced Find features, you can quickly find the information you are looking for.

From the Address Card view, choose <u>T</u>ools, Fi<u>n</u>d to open the Find dialog box, above the Address Card view, as shown in Figure 5.7. In this basic Find dialog box, only the Name, Company, and Address fields are searched.

FIGURE 5.7.

The Find dialog box is opened above the Address Card view.

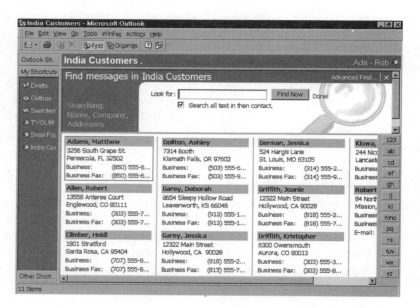

>
>
> You can also click the Fi<u>n</u>d button on the toolbar to open the Find dialog box.

To Do: Using the Basic Find Command

1. Make sure the Address Card view is displayed. (If you are looking at an open contact card, the Find command is not available). Choose <u>T</u>ools, Fi<u>n</u>d to open the Find dialog box.

2. Notice in the lower-left portion of the Find dialog box, Outlook notifies you that it is only searching the Name, Company, and Address fields. In the Look For text

box, type art. Make sure that it is all lowercase. Click Find Now. The view changes to a table view of all contacts that include the word *art* anywhere in the searched fields, regardless of case, as shown in Figure 5.8.

FIGURE 5.8.

The Find command has located all contacts containing the word "art" anywhere in the Name, Address, or Company fields.

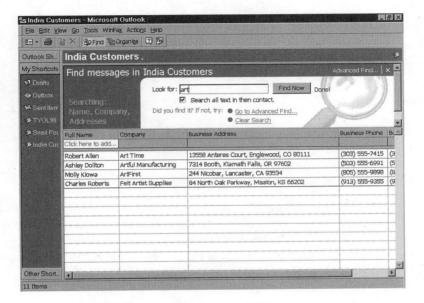

3. To display all contacts again, click the Clear Search command in the Find dialog box. Close the Find window by clicking the Close box in the upper-right corner.

Using the Advanced Find Feature

At this point, we can't do much with the Advanced Find feature because it is often used with email, tasks, and other features not yet covered in this book. However, we'll take a brief look at it so that you at least know what it is, and what it can do for you.

> This field can be used with contacts if you remember only a portion of the information (such as the spouse's name).

Figure 5.9 shows a sample Advanced Find dialog box. From here, you can search for information contained nearly anywhere in Outlook. Take a few minutes and explore some of the find options on the Contacts, More Choices, and Advanced tabs.

FIGURE 5.9.

The Advanced Find dialog box enables you to search many additional features and modules of Outlook 98 to find exactly the information you need.

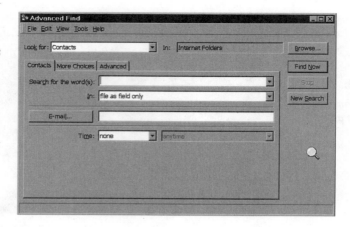

Sorting the Contacts

By default, contacts are filed by the contents of the File As field. To sort by another field, choose View, Current View, Customize Current View. The View Summary dialog box is displayed. Clicking the Sort button opens the Sort dialog box, shown in Figure 5.10. Using the Sort dialog box, you can sort up to four different fields at one time, although by default only the File As field is used to sort.

FIGURE 5.10.

The Sort dialog box is used to determine the field (or fields) used for sorting, as well as the direction of the sort (ascending or descending).

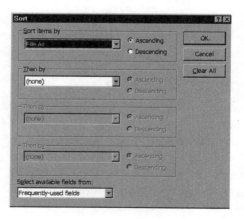

If you sort by multiple fields, all contacts are sorted by the first field. If the first field is identical in multiple contacts, those contacts are sorted by the next fields. For example, if the sort order of fields is Zip Code, Last Name, First Name, and Middle Initial, all the contacts are sorted by Zip Code. All contacts of the same code are further sorted by Last

Name. In a case where both the Zip Code and Last Name are the same, *those contacts* are sorted by First Name. In the unlikely event that all three fields are the same, the Middle Initial field is used for the final sort.

Each of the four sort orders can by sorted in ascending or descending order. In ascending order, the contacts are sorted 0 to 9, then A to Z. In descending order, the contacts are sorted from Z to A, then 9 to 0.

Removing a Sort

To remove a sort, display the Sort dialog box again and click Clear All. This returns the sort to None. The contacts are returned to the order in which they were originally entered.

In the next exercise, you learn to conduct a sort on single and multiple fields. When finished, you return the contacts to their original order by removing the sort.

To Do: Sorting the Contacts

1. Make sure you are in the Address Card view. Notice that the contacts are in File As order. Choose View, Current View, Customize Current View. The View Summary dialog box is displayed. Click the Sort button.

2. In the top Sort As dialog box, drop-down the list of fields. Choose Company. Drop-down the Then By box, and choose Last Name. Notice the next Then By box is now available. Choose First Name. Choose Descending for the First Name field. Your Sort dialog box should be similar to the one in Figure 5.11.

FIGURE 5.11.

The Sort dialog box is set to sort by Company, Last Name (both in ascending order), and First Name (in descending order).

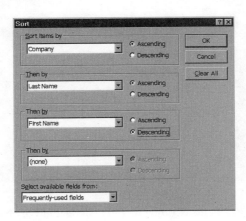

▼   3. Click OK to perform the sort. You are notified that the field Company is not cur-
        rently shown in this view and asked if you want to display it. Click Yes. Next, you
        receive the same message about Last Name. (This is because First and Last names
        are not displayed, only the File As field, which lists Last Name followed by First
        Name.)

     4. Look carefully at the Company Name fields. Indeed, they are sorted by Company
        Name, but some of the companies are not displayed. That is because you are look-
        ing at just part of the database. Click the scroll arrow until you see the other con-
        tacts.

     5. Return the view to its original order by choosing View, Current View, Customize
        Current View. The View Summary dialog box is displayed. Click the Sort button.
        Click Clear All. Click OK twice. The contacts are not back in their original order,
        and the extra fields are still displayed.

     6. To return the View to its original order, choose View, Current View, Customize
        Current View. The View Summary dialog box is displayed. Click the Sort button.

     7. In the Sort Items By drop-down list, choose File As. Click OK twice. The contacts
        are back in their original order (see Figure 5.12).

FIGURE 5.12.

*The Define Views dia-
log box can be used to
return a view to its
original order.*

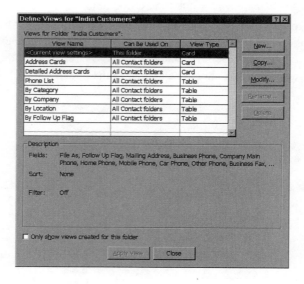

     8. Notice that the extra fields (Company, First Name and Last Name) are still there.
        To delete them, choose View, Current View, Customize Current View. Click the
        Fields button. In the Show Fields in This Order pane (on the right side of the dia-
        log box) select Company, press Ctrl, click First Name and click Last Name. Click
▼   the <-Remove button.

> Notice that there are many extra fields in the Show Fields in This Order
> pane. By default, Outlook doesn't show empty fields. If you put information
> in any of those fields, it would be displayed in the Address Card view.

9. Click OK twice to return to the Address Card view. Notice that Company, First
   Name, and Last Name are no longer displayed.

Filtering the Contacts

Filtering the contacts is also done from the View Summary dialog box (displayed by
choosing View, Current View, Customize Current View). Filtering displays only contacts
that meet the specified criteria. In the most basic mode, the Filter acts like the Advanced
Find command. To open the Filter dialog box, click the Filter button. On the Contacts tab
of the Filter dialog box, as shown in Figure 5.13, you can enter the text you are looking
for, and define the field in which to look.

FIGURE 5.13.

*The Filter dialog box
is used to display only
contacts that meet spe-
cific criteria.*

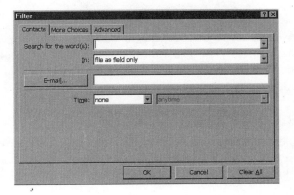

5

To Do: Applying and Removing Contact Filters

1. Make sure you are in the Address Card view. Notice that the contacts are in File As
   order. Choose View, Current View, Customize Current View. The View Summary
   dialog box is displayed. Click the Filter button. The Filter dialog box is displayed.

2. In the Search for the Word(s) text box, type art. In the In box, choose Company
   Field Only. Click OK twice. The results are shown in Figure 5.14. Notice two differences between this and the earlier Find exercise. The order is not changed, and
   the selected field (Company) is not displayed.

▼ **FIGURE 5.14.**

The results of the applied filter are displayed.

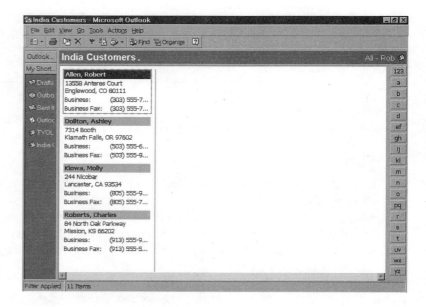

3. To remove the filter and display all contacts again, choose View, Current View, Customize Current View. The View Summary dialog box is displayed. Click the Filter button. Click the Clear All button. Click OK twice to display all the contacts ▲ in the Address Card view.

Dialing a Contact

If you want to have Outlook dial the phone for you, right-click the contact you want to dial and choose AutoDialer. The New Call dialog box is shown in Figure 5.15. To start the call, click Start Call. When prompted, take the phone off the hook, click Talk, and begin your call.

FIGURE 5.15.

The New Call dialog box is used to have Outlook dial a contact's telephone number.

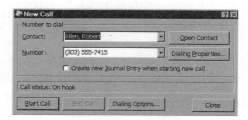

If the number you want to dial isn't displayed in the <u>N</u>umber box, use the drop-down list to display all other phones assigned to the contact.

Displaying Different Printing Options

There are several default ways to print your contact list.

Card   All cards one at a time from top to bottom on the page, two columns wide, with blank cards printed at the end, and with letter tabs and headings.

Small Booklet   All cards on two sides of a sheet of paper with eight pages per sheet, landscape orientation. You can cut and staple to make a booklet.

Medium Booklet All cards on two sides of a sheet of paper with four booklet pages per sheet, portrait orientation. You can cut and staple to make a booklet.

Memo   Selected items are printed one at a time in the form of a memo. Attachments print as graphics.

Phone Directory   Names and phone numbers for all contact items from top to bottom on the page, with letter tabs and headings. If you have enough records, the Phone Directory view is printed in two columns.

To print your contact list, choose <u>F</u>ile, <u>P</u>rint. In the Print Style panel, choose the method for printing. For customized print styles, view the online help files. Search for Print Style.

Summary

Communication is the hub of most office activity. Using Outlook to track your contacts can mean an increase in productivity, accountability, and accuracy. Many of the things you can do with using Outlook to control your communication were not covered in this hour due to limited time. Further research, either through the online Help system or advanced books on Outlook, will increase your productivity even more.

Q&A

Q Sometimes I delete a filter or change a view, and everything looks fine. When I exit and restart Outlook, it goes back to the way it was before. What am I doing wrong?

A Nothing. Every once in awhile, Outlook forgets what it's doing and reverts to an earlier version of your views. Don't worry about losing data, though. All it does is forget the views.

Q When adding a contact from the same company, is it always easiest to use that option?

A No. If the addresses, phone numbers, departments, and other information are all different (such as if two contacts are working in different offices) it may be faster to start a new Contact form.

Q Is it really necessary to assign categories to each contact?

A Necessary? No. Important? Yes. Later, as you expand your Outlook skills, you will want to send messages to specific groups of contacts. Using filters and categories, you can easily customize any list you need to create.

Q What is the difference between finding and filtering?

A Filtering is slightly easier to use, but less powerful. When you use the find feature, you can be more specific in the criteria that your records must meet to be displayed. You can use the And command, meaning that the record must meet all criteria to be selected, or the Or command (it must meet any single criterion to be selected).

Q What if my AutoDialer doesn't work?

A Your modem is probably not set up correctly, or you are using a network server rather than an individual phone line. Check with your system administrator for further help. If you are working from a regular (analog) phone line, you may need to call the modem manufacturer to help set it up correctly.

HOUR 6

Customizing Contact Forms

As you learned in Hour 4, "Establishing First Contact," and Hour 5, "Manipulating Contacts," Outlook offers a comprehensive Contact form with many general information fields. However, as you begin to work with Outlook and enter your contacts, you may find that you want to customize your forms to better meet your specific needs. Modifying the basic Contact form is not as difficult as you may think. Outlook makes it easy for you to drag objects onto a form and format them.

Microsoft doesn't instinctively know all your friends and associates or the type of information you need to keep. However, they have designed a simple-to-use and simple-to-modify way to help you track those special people in your life.

During this hour, you learn to customize the basic Contact form in Outlook. When you become more familiar with Outlook, you may decide to design your own forms from scratch.

This hour contains several new vocabulary words. If you have worked with databases previously, many of them will be familiar to you. You'll learn the options for formatting your forms and why you may want to use those options.

Why Customize a Form?

If you enter many people into your Contacts database, you'll probably find that you don't need some of the fields included on the basic form, and perhaps other fields are missing. For instance, you may need to keep more personal information about your friends than you do for your coworkers or other business contacts. If you design your contact forms correctly, they should prompt you to gather the proper information about each person.

The standard Contact form is fairly complex and may not be the best form for entering information about your contacts. For your friends, you might want to keep track of additional information, such as birthdays, anniversaries, hobbies, and the names of children and spouses. You certainly don't need to use all the fields on the standard form, such as Assistant's Name, Department, and other business-related fields.

Doing the Two-Step

Customizing a form can be a two-step process. The first is to actually make the changes to the form and the second is to publish it. After the form is published, it is available for use as the *default* form, rather than the standard Contact form that comes with Outlook.

 Default: The value or object that a program uses unless otherwise indicated. For example, in most word-processing programs, the default top and bottom margins are one inch.

Building a New Contacts Database

Creating your own Contact form gives you the opportunity to add the specific fields you need for collecting information about friends, family, businesses, coworkers, or social groups; you can also delete unneeded fields. For instance, if you are a proud member of the world famous Adopt a Snail Foundation, you may want to have a roster of all the members. In addition to personal information about each human member, you may also want to collect information about each person's snail, its type, and its distinguishing marks. In the following exercise, you create a new folder to hold your information, and then customize the basic Contact form to fit your needs. Folders and file management are covered in greater detail in Hour 9, "Sorting the Mail."

To Do: Creating a New Contact File

1. Open Outlook if it isn't already open. Click the Contacts shortcut in the Outlook Bar. Choose File, New, Folder. The Create New Folder dialog box, as shown in Figure 6.1, is displayed.

FIGURE 6.1.

The Create New Folder dialog box is used to create a place for storing the Snail Foundation contacts.

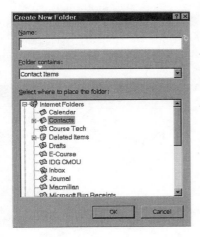

2. In the Name text box, type Snail Foundation. Make sure that the Folder Contains text box reads Contact Items. The Contacts folder should be selected in the Select Where to Place the Folder window. Click OK. When asked if you want to add a shortcut to the Outlook Bar, click Yes.

3. Click the My Shortcuts icon in the Outlook Bar. Click the Snail Foundation icon. Currently, no data is contained in this folder.

Displaying the Contact Form

The first step in customizing a Contact form is to display the current form. After the form is displayed, you can begin to make changes to it.

If you are planning to make a lot of changes, or design a form from scratch, you may find it a lot faster if you design your form on paper before sitting down at the computer. If you already have a paper data form from which you will be entering data, make your electronic form look as much like the paper one as possible. This greatly enhances productivity.

6

To Do: Displaying the Contact Form

1. Press Ctrl+Shift+C to create a blank Contact form.

2. Choose Tools, Forms, Design This Form. The Untitled Contact (Design) screen is displayed, as shown in Figure 6.2. It looks similar to the normal Contact form except for the addition of tabs marked (P.2) through (P.6), (Properties), and (Actions). The tab names in parentheses are hidden and won't normally show. Also, notice that the form is filled with equally spaced dots. The dots form a grid that is used to automatically align fields so your form remains neat.

FIGURE 6.2.

The Contact Form Design Screen enables you to make changes to the current form, rather than having to start from scratch.

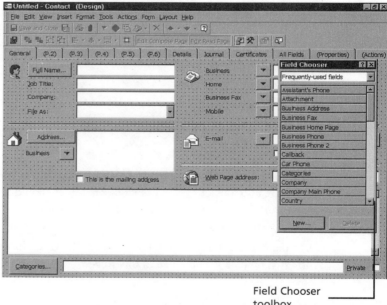

Field Chooser toolbox

3. The Field Chooser toolbox should be displayed. If not, choose Form, Field Chooser. This toolbox lists all the predefined fields available in Outlook. The fields are organized into groups, such as Frequently-Used fields, Address fields, and All Contact fields. Now that you've seen the Field Chooser, close it by clicking the Close button (the x to the right of the Field Chooser title bar).

Learning New Concepts

Before we move ahead with customizing the form, there are a few additional terms you need to understand. We'll be talking about *bound* and *unbound controls,* discussing exactly what a control is and what it does, and making reference to Visual Basic for Applications (VBA), an application language.

Binding Boxes and Buttons

Most box and button types can either be bound or unbound. A *bound* box or button is tied to a specific field, while *unbound* objects are simply placed on the form (like a form title, which appears in the same position on every record). Bound objects store user information in the field to which they are bound. You can bind an object to an existing field, or to a field you create. When you bind a box or button, you are simply telling Outlook where to store the information entered by the user.

Visual Basic for Applications Buttons

Shortly, we'll be discussing controls. Some controls are easy to use, and you simply drag them onto the form and modify them as needed. Other controls, however, can only be used in conjunction with Visual Basic for Applications (VBA) scripts. *Scripts* are simple programming codes, and are beyond the scope of this book. They are described here to give you some ideas of things you might want to learn to do in the future. To find out more about VBA, see some of the Sams Publishing titles, such as *Visual Basic for Applications Unleashed* by Paul McFedries.

Basic Form Modifications

The General tab is displayed as soon as you open the Design screen for a form. To see the other tabs, click the tab heading. In the next exercise, we'll work with the General tab, adding, deleting, and moving fields so that they better fit the needs of the Snail Foundation.

To Do: Modifying the Contact Form

1. Click the Job Title label. Press Shift and click the Job Title field (the blank box to the right of the label). Both objects are now selected. Press Delete. The two objects are removed from the form.

2. To delete a single object, click it and press the Delete key. To select multiple adjacent objects, select the first, press Shift, and click the other objects to be selected. To select multiple non-adjacent objects, click the first, press Ctrl, and click each of the others. When the appropriate objects are selected, press Delete to remove them. Use this method to remove labels, fields, and one horizontal line until your form is similar to the one shown in Figure 6.3.

▲To Do

▼

6

▼

FIGURE 6.3.

Here is the basic Contact form with several objects deleted.

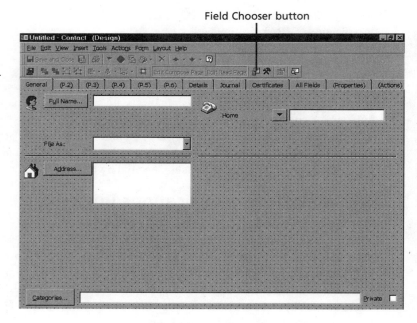

3. Select both the Home label and the Home text box (below and to the right of the telephone icon) by moving the cursor above and to the left of the Home label and dragging it down and to the right to include the Home field. When you release the mouse button, the objects are selected. All objects are now enclosed in a *marquee*; this is called marquee selection.

If you select too many objects, or not enough, repeat the procedure. It is somewhat exacting, but once learned serves you well in nearly all Windows-based application programs.

4. Point to the outside border of the Home label (not to one of the square sizing handles). The cursor changes to a four-headed arrow. Drag the label up, until it is lined up with the telephone icon. Notice that the telephone text box (field) moved with

▲   the label (because it was also selected).

Using the Field Chooser

The Field Chooser is a simple method for adding predefined fields to your form. With over 100 contact fields available, you should have no problem finding exactly what you need. However, Microsoft may not have a predefined field for identifying marks (for the snails), so, anticipating your needs, they also enable you to create new fields.

To display the Field Chooser, you can press the Field Chooser button on the toolbar (the fourth button from the right) or choose Form, Field Chooser from the menu. The Field Chooser, with the most frequently used fields displayed, is shown in Figure 6.4. In the next exercise, you'll take a look at the Field Chooser and get a little better idea of how to use it.

FIGURE 6.4.

The Field Chooser is used to place fields on a custom form.

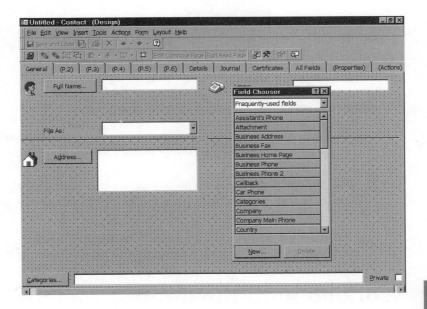

To Do: Exploring the Field Chooser

1. Use the scroll arrows on the right side of the Field Chooser toolbox to see a listing of the most frequently used fields.

2. Click the drop-down arrow to the right of the Frequently-Used Fields box. Select All Contact Fields. Now scroll through these fields. As you can see, there are a great deal of predefined fields for you to use. Select Frequently-Used Fields again.

6

▼   3. Use the scroll arrows until you can see the Notes field. Drag it onto the form and position it beneath the Address area. The field takes up a significant portion of the screen, as shown in Figure 6.5.

FIGURE 6.5.

A Notes field has been added to the form; it may be larger than you want it to be.

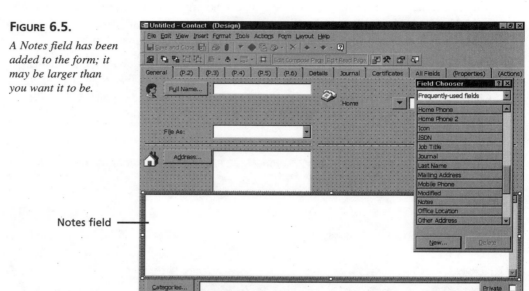

Notes field ────

▲   4. Close the Field Chooser toolbox to get it out of your way. Notice that the notes box has a border with sizing handles. Use the left scroll arrow at the bottom of the screen until you can see the left edge of the Notes box. Drag the center-left handle to the right, until the left edge of the Notes box is aligned with the Address box. Then, resize the box so that it is similar to the one shown in Figure 6.6.

Working with the Control Toolbox

Using the Field Chooser is very simple, as you discovered. You simply drag the field onto the form, reposition it, and resize it if necessary. Although the Notes field does not have a label, most fields that you choose have both a label and a text box. In those cases, both the label and the text box are added to the form at the same time. If you simply want to enter data into fields, it is easiest to build your custom form using the Field Chooser. You have some minor control over the field size, but basically, many fields are the same size, and are balanced nicely on the page. However, there is another feature that offers much more flexibility in designing fields: the Control toolbox.

FIGURE 6.6.

The Notes box has been resized.

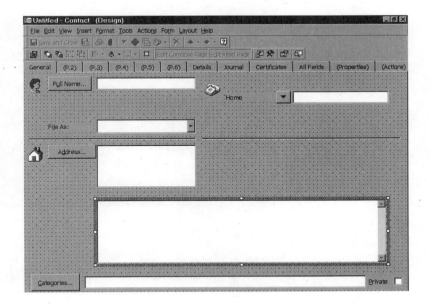

Differences Between the Field Chooser and the Control Toolbox

The Control toolbox contains a set of tools that enables you much more flexibility in the types of objects you can create, in setting defaults, or by creating pick lists.

Controlling Controls

A *control* is an object on a form enabling the user to more easily input data and more accurately display the output. Fifteen control tools are available in Outlook.

The Control Tools

The Controls toolbox, as shown in Figure 6.7, has icons representing the fifteen controls available for building your form. If you have designed forms in other Microsoft applications, such as Access or Excel, these controls may look familiar to you.

The fifteen control tools in the Outlook Controls toolbox and a brief description of their uses are listed in Table 6.1. The most commonly used controls are also presented in the exercises.

6

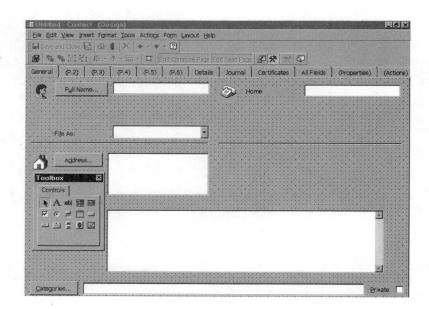

TABLE 6.1. THE 15 AVAILABLE CONTROLS.

Control	Description
Select Objects	Used to select single or multiple objects that can be formatted, moved, deleted, copied, and otherwise manipulated.
Label	Creates a box that either acts as information about some portion of the form, or as a label for a text box.
TextBox	Creates a box that can be bound or unbound. Bound text boxes are linked to a specific field where the input data is stored.
ComboBox	Creates a box with a drop-down list of choices. The user can select from a previously defined choice, or enter information not available as a choice.
ListBox	Creates a box with a list of choices. The user must select from one of the available choices, and cannot enter other information.
Checkbox	Creates a small box, normally bound to a True/False or Yes/No field. A check mark in the box indicates one state (usually True or Yes), and no check mark indicates the opposing state. These are also called option boxes. If they are grouped, as many can be selected as desired.
OptionButton	Option buttons are always grouped. Only one button can be active in each group. For example, a person's uniform size can't be Small, Medium, and Large. Only one of the options can be selected. These are also commonly called *radio buttons*.

Control	Description
ToggleButton	Similar to a check box, the toggle button appears recessed when active, and raised when inactive.
Frame	The Frame tool enables you to place a border around related objects on the form, and it allows multiple sets of option buttons on the same form. You can title the frame and size it to fit your needs. This is a good tool to use if you want to separate a field or a group of fields on a form.
CommandButton	Used to execute a procedure or function. An example of a command button is the Send button on an email form. When the user clicks the Send button, a VBA script is run and the message is sent to the recipient.
TabStrip	Used for organizing controls and buttons on numerous tabs. Just as the tabs show at the top of a form, you can add multiple tabs to a single page. They can contain multiple bound or unbound controls.
MultiPage	The MultiPage control essentially creates a form within a form. You can drag a MultiPage control onto your workspace and put fields on each page.
ScrollBar	A ScrollBar control works the same in all Microsoft applications. Scrollbars can be found at the bottom and/or on the right side of a window. ScrollBar controls can be used when there is more information contained in a box than is visible on the screen. The ScrollBar option can be used to scroll vertically or horizontally in a box. VBA scripting is required to use this feature.
SpinButton	The SpinButton control can be used for anything that you want to increase or decrease incrementally. Like the CommandButton, this control works only if you program it using VBA.
Image	The Image control is a frame in which you can place a picture file. For example, you might place your company's logo in the Image control for company forms. A bound image frame can display a different picture for each contact. An unbound image frame displays the same picture for all contacts.

6

All controls requiring VBA intervention are beyond the scope of this text. Unlike in other Microsoft applications, Outlook does not provide wizards to step you through setting up the more complex controls. After you have mastered Outlook in 24 Hours, and want to create more complex forms, refer to Gordon Padwick's *Using Outlook 98* from Que Corporation.

Selecting Objects

The Select Objects tool is the simplest tool; use it to select objects on the workspace. It is the default tool. When an object is selected, handles appear around the edges of the object. You can resize a selected object by dragging one of its handles. To move a selected object, drag anywhere on the outline of the object *except* the resizing handles. To select more than one adjacent object, click the first, hold down the Shift key and click the last object, or press and hold the mouse button while you drag across all the objects you want to select.

To select non-adjacent items, click the first, press Ctrl, and click the others you want to select. You can also edit a label by clicking the object once to select it and then clicking inside the text to make it available for editing. When the insertion point appears, you can begin editing.

Making Labels

The Label control enables you to create a label anywhere on your form. When you choose this tool, you can draw a box using your mouse. Then, click inside the box to type the desired caption. Clicking the Properties icon on the toolbar or right-clicking the label enables you to set the font, size, and color of the label. In most cases, labels are used to identify a group of items on a form—such as the label Special Dates to Remember, which can be placed above a group of date fields. Labels are also used next to text boxes (fields) on forms to instruct users to type the proper information into the text box.

The Plain Vanilla Text Box

The TextBox tool is used to draw text boxes (blank boxes where you can enter information). When you use the Field Chooser list box to drag a field onto your workspace, both the label and the text box generally appear. When using the Controls toolbox, you must drag the label and text box separately.

Place as many fields as you can using the Field Chooser because you can place the label and text box at the same time. Otherwise, by using the Controls toolbox, you have to drag and align twice as many objects.

Labels are for *identifying* fields (text boxes) and remain the same from record to record. Text boxes, however, are placeholders (fields) where variable data is entered for each record.

I'll Take the Combo(Box)

The ComboBox enables you to create your own drop-down list so that you can list possible entries for a particular field. For example, if you create a new field on your contact form for eye color, you can set up a ComboBox specifying green, blue, brown, and hazel as the values in the drop-down list. The user then just clicks the down-pointing arrow and clicks a choice of eye color. Some of Outlook's predefined fields are already set up as ComboBoxes, such as the Sensitivity field for which Normal, Personal, Private, and Confidential are predefined choices.

ComboBoxes have numerous advantages. Two key advantages to using a ComboBox are an increase in productivity (the data entry person doesn't have to type an entire line of text) and accuracy. For example, is the city Shawnee Mission entered exactly as shown, or Shawnee/Mission, Shawnee-Mission, SM, or yet some other variation? Accuracy is critical when using a database, such as the Outlook Contacts database. If you want to list all the people who live in Shawnee Mission, Outlook ignores any variation of that name.

Categories for ComboBoxes should be discrete. That is, no entry can fit into more than one category. For example, if you are entering age groups, *0–21* and *21 or over* are not discrete because a person who is 21 years old could fit into either group. Make sure your categories don't overlap.

In the following exercise, you learn to create a drop-down list on your form. You'll find that it requires quite a few steps to set up, but after the initial work it will save time and improve the accuracy of input, so you'll probably find it's worth the effort.

To Do: Adding Basic Objects to the Form

1. Click the Label tool. Drag a box to the right of the Address field. This box will contain the text "Age Category," so make it approximately the right size. You will be able to adjust it shortly. Notice that as soon as you have outlined the box and released the mouse button, the Select Object tool is automatically activated.

6

To Do

▼

▼   2. Click inside the new label box. Delete the current text (it probably says Label1 or some variation). Type `Age Category`. Adjust the size of the box as necessary.

3. Click the ComboBox tool icon in the Controls toolbox. As you move the cursor back onto the page, it changes to an icon of a ComboBox with a cross in the upper-left area.

4. Drag a box to the right of the Age Category label. Don't worry about size; you'll learn to modify it later.

5. Right-click the new ComboBox and choose Properties. The Properties dialog box, as shown in Figure 6.8, is displayed. Notice there are three tabs in this dialog box.

FIGURE 6.8.

The Properties dialog box for a ComboBox is used to specify categories and other information.

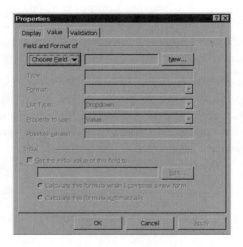

 You may need to drag the Controls toolbox to another position to make the Properties dialog box more accessible.

6. Drop down the Choose Field list by clicking the button. These are the major field groupings. Pointing at any one of them displays another drop-down menu with additional choices. In this case, though, you don't want to use an existing field. Click any blank area of the Properties dialog box to close all the menus.

7. Click the New button. The New Field dialog box, as shown in Figure 6.9, is displayed. In the Name text box, type `Age`.

▼ **FIGURE 6.9.**

The New Field dialog box is used to give the field an identifying name, set the type of field, and, if necessary, select the format for the data.

8. Change the Type to Keywords by dropping down the related menu. Leave Format set to Text. Click OK. Several new options are now available on the Value tab of the Properties dialog box, as shown in Figure 6.10. The List Type is already set to Dropdown. For this type of field, it is the only choice. Leave the Property to Use set at Value. The other options here are beyond the scope of this lesson.

FIGURE 6.10.

The Value tab has been changed to enable you to input additional information.

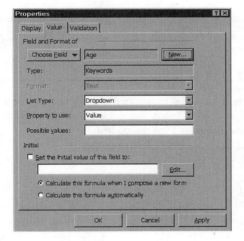

9. Move the insertion point to the Possible Values text box. Type the possible values, each separated by a semicolon. Type 0-20;21-40;41-60;61-80;81-100; Extraordinary.

Always assume that all your information is available for public consumption. Don't think that it's secure, even if you have password protection on your computer. For example, if you were keeping a Contacts database for potential employees, tracking ages might be grounds for a lawsuit.

▼

6

▼

In the previous instruction, I was going to use *Older than dirt* for the final category, but realized some readers might be offended. Just remember as you enter your Outlook information, although it may be password protected, no system is foolproof, so keep the data appropriate for anyone to read. Better safe than sorry. This advice makes sense for anything you enter on your computer. In these days of open journalism, anything you write is fair game for publishing—no matter how private or embarrassing.

If you wanted a default value in the field (information that appears in the field if you do not specify otherwise), you would enter it into the Initial Value area of the Value tab.

10. Click OK to close the Properties dialog box. The field is currently blank. To check your choices, click the drop-down arrow to see the available information. Click any blank area of the design screen to close the menu.

To modify the choices, return to the design screen for the form, right-click the field, and select Properties. Click the Value tab. Make the required changes and then exit the dialog box.

▲

List Boxes

The major disadvantage of list boxes is that the user is limited to the choices offered. In the earlier eye color example, the choices were green, blue, brown, and hazel. But what if an employee has gray eyes? In that case, the design properties for that field must be changed to include the new option. Another way to get around this is to include an *Other* category. Generally, this isn't a good idea because it may group people with totally dissimilar traits.

Gender is another common use for a list box. People are either Male or Female, right? If you put the two choices in a list box, no other options are possible. What happens if you don't know the gender? Big problem! You need to add a third choice, Unknown. For example, the contact name may be Leslie Baber, Shawn Severin, or Chris Svoboda.

Check Yes or No

Check boxes are also called *option boxes.* If check boxes are grouped, you can generally select as many as apply, unlike OptionButtons, where you can only select one from each grouping. The CheckBox tool can be used for any field for which the entry is either Yes or No, True or False, or On or Off. One of Outlook's predefined fields that uses the CheckBox tool is the This Is the Mailing Address check box found on the General tab on the New Contact form.

The advantage to using a check box is the capability to divide your contacts into *have* and *have not.* For example, you can design a check box for employees who have or have not attended orientation. A check mark means that the item is Yes, True, or On. The lack of a check mark means the opposite. You can set the *default* value to Yes or No, True or False, or On or Off.

Check boxes are bound to a Yes/No field. They can only be in a selected or not-selected state.

Editing a Label or Caption

Sometimes a predefined field does not clearly explain what type of information should be entered in the text box. You can edit any label to make instructions more clear. Click once inside the label to select it, and then click a second time to drop the insertion point. (Labels are also called *captions.*) To edit a caption, right-click the field and click Properties to display the Properties dialog box, change the caption, and click OK.

> For multiple changes to a field or a label, it's easier to use the Properties and Advanced Properties dialog boxes instead of the menu. The Properties dialog boxes are simply tables that enable you to go down the list and make many different changes within one dialog box.

6

Adding Another Page to the Form

The tabs (P.2) through (P.6) are extra pages where you can store additional information. Tab names that are enclosed in parentheses are hidden. You can hide any page that is displayed by entering the Design view, clicking the tab to be hidden, and choosing Form, Display This Page. This doesn't delete the data, only hides the page.

In the next exercise, you'll have a chance to add a few more fields to a different page. Feel free to experiment with adding even more field types when you have completed the exercise.

To Do: Adding Basic Objects to the Form

1. Click the (P.2) tab. This is where you will keep the information on the snail that is adopted. Take a look at Figure 6.11 so that you can see how the finished page should look.

FIGURE 6.11.

The completed Snail Information design page should look similar to this.

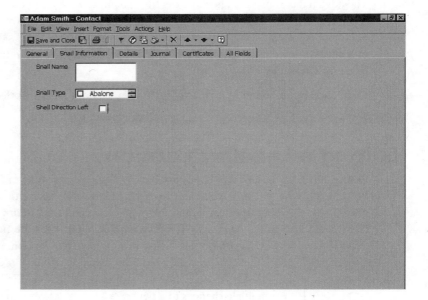

2. Change the name of the tab. Choose Form, Rename Page. Change the Page Name to Snail Information. Click OK.

3. Drag a label, and name it Snail Name. Adjust the size of the box if necessary. Drag a text box to its right. Right-click and choose Properties. The Value tab is already selected (it is the default for new items). Click New to create a new field to which the text box will be bound. Type Snail Name in the Name field. Leave the Type and Format set to text. Click OK twice.

4. Using the skills learned in the previous exercise, add a label named Snail Type. Add a list box (not a ComboBox) named Snail Type. Use keywords for the list box type. Although there are as many as 50,000 species of snails (according to the *Deluxe Microsoft Encarta 98 Encyclopedia*), you only need to enter the eight basic

▼ groups—lucky you! Possible values are `Abalone`, `Conch Cone`, `Drill`, `Giant African Snail`, `Periwinkle`, `Sea Hare`, and `Whelk`. Click OK.

> Notice that a check box appears to the left of each name. Placing a check mark in the box enters the information into the field.

5. Add a check box. If it is selected, the shell circles left; if not checked, it circles right. Right-click the check box and choose Properties. Click the New button on the Value tab. Name the new field `Shell Direction Left`. Use the drop-down list to set the Type to Yes/No. Leave the Format set to Icon. Click OK twice. Adjust the width of the box as required.

> If you were using VBA, you could program two option buttons, one for Left, one for Right. You could also use a list box, a ComboBox, or even a simple text box. However, as long as you get the information, it doesn't really matter what form the collection takes, although you want to minimize data error whenever possible.

> If you try to save a custom form based on a contact form, and don't include data in the File As field, you get an error if you try to save the file. If you have information in the File As field, the form is saved under that name. Rather than saving a form at this point, it is best to publish it.

NEW TERM *Publish*: To save a form as a template. A template is a file already containing basic layout information. You can use a template to create multiple new files. Another use for a form template is to send the form to others to electronically collect information.

6. Publish the form by choosing <u>T</u>ools, <u>F</u>orms, Pu<u>b</u>lish Form As. In the Look In text box, make sure it says Outlook Folders. If not, select it from the drop-down list. In the Display Name box, type `Snail Foundation`. The name is automatically mirrored in the Form Name box. This is a more advanced feature and is not discussed here. Click Publish. You are returned to the design screen. Close it. When asked if

▼ you want to save the changes, click No.

6

▼   7. Choose File, New, Choose Form. There are several Form Libraries from which to
        choose. If necessary, drop down the Look In box and choose Outlook Folders.
        Make sure Snail Foundation is highlighted and click Open. A blank Contact form
        is displayed.

     8. Fill out the General Page, as shown in Figure 6.12.

FIGURE 6.12.

*The completed General
page should look simi-
lar to this.*

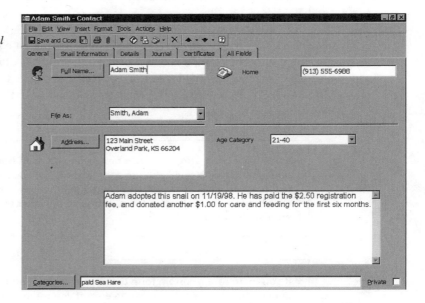

     9. Fill out the Snail Information page, as shown in Figure 6.13.

    10. If part of the text is cut off for any of your categories, you need to go back to the
        design page (Tools, Forms, Design This Form) and make the appropriate changes.

▲   11. Close and save the contact information.

Arranging the Tab Order

Although it might not occur to you when you are first designing your form, the order of
your labels and text boxes is important. When you are filling out a form and you press
the Tab key after each entry, you expect your cursor to go to the next blank box on the
form. This happens because the person who designed the form dictated the order of the
tabs during the design process.

FIGURE 6.13.

The completed Snail Information page should look similar to this.

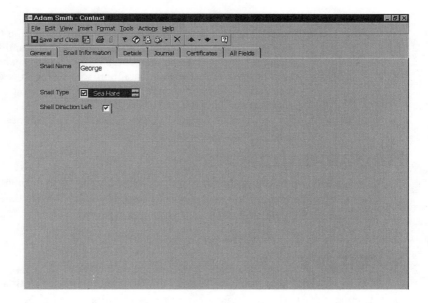

In Figure 6.14, the names of the labels and text boxes can be moved up and down the list so that when someone completes the form and presses the Tab key, the insertion point will move down the form in order of the blank boxes. The Tab Order dialog box is displayed by right-clicking any blank area of the design form screen and selecting Tab Order.

FIGURE 6.14.

Before you save a form, remember to arrange the order of your labels and text boxes using the Tab Order option.

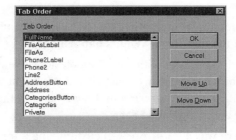

To control the tab order, click the tab you want to move and use the Move Up and Move Down buttons until it is correctly positioned. Continue with the other tabs until all tabs are in the correct order.

6

If you have used a default form, you may notice that the fields have such names as Label1 and TextBox1. If you have many fields, this can be very confusing when trying to change the tab order. You can change the name of each box (without changing its caption) in the Properties dialog box. In the long run, it's faster to change the names of the boxes so that you can more easily control how the tabs are ordered.

Finishing the Form

You probably don't have the time to complete an entire form during this hour, but at least you have some idea of how one is constructed. If you have more time, add additional fields or even create a new form for your specific use.

Summary

During the last hour you have learned how to shorten your work time by customizing Contact forms. These options may take a little while to set up, but in the long run they can save you a lot of time. In addition, a well-constructed form prompts you to collect all the information you need for each entry. Although you have learned a lot about working with Contacts in the last few hours, you have barely covered the depth of features available in Outlook 98.

Q&A

Q I imported some names from another file, but when I modified the form, only new records used the new form. What's happening?

A Unfortunately this is a problem with how Outlook stores the data. If Outlook were to apply the new form automatically, many data fields might be lost. So if you are going to import data, it's always easiest to design the form first and then import the data, matching the appropriate field names.

Q It seemed like there was a lot of work to customizing a form. Is it really worth it? Is there anything else I can do to further customize my forms?

A If you are going to use a form to register many contacts, customizing your form can save you a great deal of time. You may find it easiest to use the Field Chooser, rather than the Control toolbox to place the fields, but the choice depends on how much control you want over the data that is entered. As to the second part of the question, you only scratched the surface of what you can do to design forms. See the online Help or advanced books on Outlook 98 to get more information on customizing forms.

Q **I know that we started with the Contacts database in Outlook because it is so often connected with other areas in Outlook. Will the skills I gained in this hour carry over to modifying forms in other modules?**

A Absolutely. You'll find that the skills learned in this hour not only carry over to other Outlook modules, but also to other Microsoft products, including Word, Excel, PowerPoint, and Access.

Q **Can I change the font characteristics on a Contact form?**

A Yes. In the design screen, right-click what you want to change, and choose Properties. Click the Font button and make whatever changes you want. You may need to resize and reposition the field after you have made formatting changes.

6

PART III
The Postman Knocks: Mail and Faxing in Outlook

Hour

HOUR 7

Back to Basics: Email Services

The development of email is one of the most significant advances of the computer age. No longer do you have to wait two to three days for the post office to deliver your letters to a friend or associate just so you can wait two or three days *more* for the response. (This is the reason that the United States Postal Service is often referred to as *snail mail*.) Now, with a few keystrokes and a click of your mouse, you can send messages that are delivered within seconds (depending on how well your mail server or the Internet is working), and you can receive a reply within a matter of minutes.

In the past, however, many email programs have been clumsy and awkward to use and have often given users more frustration than help. Outlook's email function, however, has continually offered users an easy-to-use, graphically-oriented program that speeds you through the email process. Outlook 98 added many new features that make sending email to friends and business associates even simpler and (at times) more fun.

In this hour, you'll be introduced to many of Outlook 98's email components. In addition to other activities, you'll learn to use the Inbox, to create, send, and read email messages, and to print and file your messages. So, get out your address book, dig up those email addresses that your friends and family have been giving you, and get ready to send email!

> As you develop new contacts and add them to your contact list (covered in Part II, "3-2-1 Contact"), be sure to include email addresses in the contact information. This enables you to use the contact list as your online address book and speeds the email process.

What Is the Inbox?

Essentially, the Inbox is just like the mailbox attached to your house or the "In" tray on your desk. People put things in the box or tray, and, at your convenience, you take them out, read them, and respond as desired. Outlook 98's Inbox, however, does more than just provide you with a pile of stuff to read. It organizes your information, tells you what is high (or low) priority, and can even tell you when one of your meetings has been canceled or moved.

To Do: Customizing Your Inbox

1. Open Outlook 98 if it is not already open.
2. On the Outlook Bar, select Inbox. As shown in Figure 7.1, the Inbox is displayed. Notice that the Inbox screen is divided into two parts. The top half displays summary information about each piece of email. The bottom half of the screen displays the full text of the selected email message.

> If you have not previously used your Inbox, there is a single message from Microsoft welcoming you to Outlook 98. If, however, you have used a previous version of Outlook, any email messages that were stored in the previous version are displayed.

▼

▼ **Figure 7.1.**

The Inbox lists all email messages that you have received in the top box, and displays the text of the selected email messages in the bottom box.

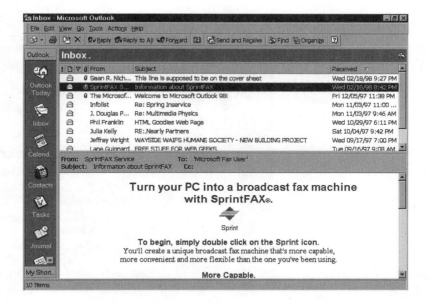

3. On the Column Heading bar, as shown in Figure 7.2, click the From box. This directs Outlook 98 to sort your email messages alphabetically, based on the name of the sender.

Notice that Outlook has placed a small arrow in the From column heading. This arrow tells you whether Outlook is alphabetizing the information in ascending (*A* to *Z*) or descending (*Z* to *A*) order. If the arrow is pointing up (as in Figure 7.2), the email is sorted in ascending order. To change the order to descending, simply click the From column heading again. The arrow points down, and the email will be reorganized in descending order.

4. Click the Received column heading. This sorts your email by the date of receipt rather than by the sender's name, as shown in Figure 7.3. Also notice that you can organize your mail by importance, icon, flag status, attachment, or subject, simply by clicking the appropriate column heading.

▼

7

▼

FIGURE 7.2.

*Click the From col-
umn heading to sort
your email alphabeti-
cally by the sender's
name.*

From column heading   Column Heading bar

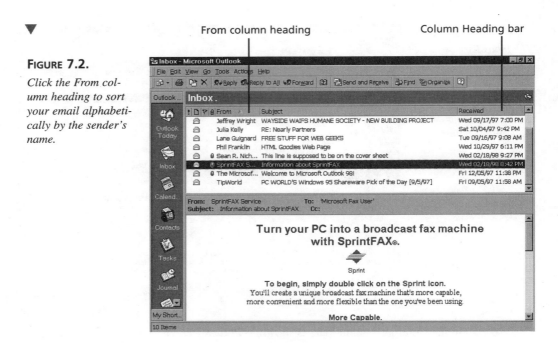

Subject

FIGURE 7.3.

*Outlook 98 offers you
many ways to organize
your Inbox.*

Importance ⎯

Icon ⎯

Flag status ⎯

Attachment ⎯

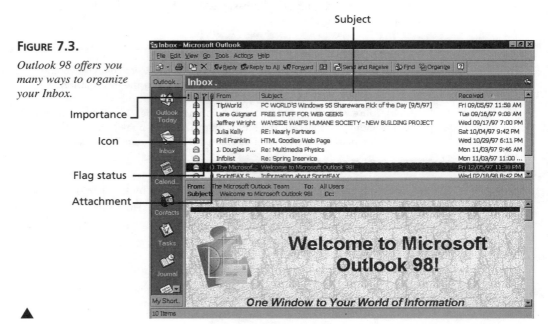

▲

Inbox Symbols

Understanding the various symbols in the Inbox enables you to organize your email effectively and understand the general nature of the email even before you read it. For instance, some symbols indicate whether the email is of high priority, while others tell you whether there is a file attached to the email. Figure 7.4 shows a list of the various Inbox symbols and their descriptions.

FIGURE 7.4.

The various symbols used in the Inbox.

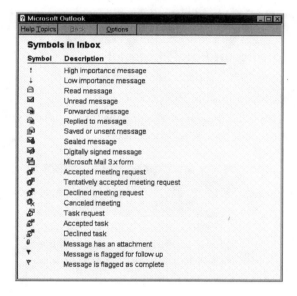

You can access this symbol description at any time by choosing <u>H</u>elp, <u>C</u>ontents and Index, clicking the Index tab, typing Inbox, and double-clicking Symbols in the lower window pane. In the Topics Found dialog box, double-click Symbols in Inbox.

Composing a Mail Message

Take a moment to think about a conventional "snail mail" letter. Each letter needs a delivery address, a return address, the body of the letter, and, of course, a signature. Email composed using Outlook 98 has many of the same elements and a few more to make the email more effective.

7

For instance, email includes a *subject* line that cues the recipient to the subject matter of the email. In addition to the standard components of an email message, email created with Outlook can also tell the recipient whether the message is of high or low importance and whether a file has been attached to the message. Finally, an Outlook email can tell the sender when the email was received, and even when it was read. Gone are the days of "I never got your letter" or "It must have gotten lost in the mail."

This section takes a look at each component of Outlook email and shows you how to create, address, and send email. Additionally, you'll learn to modify several of Outlook 98's that enable you to track your message to its final destination.

To Do: Beginning an Email Message

1. Open Outlook 98 if it is not already open.
2. Select the Inbox if it is not already displayed.
3. Click the New Mail Message button on the toolbar. The Untitled-Message dialog box, as shown in Figure 7.5, is displayed.

FIGURE 7.5.

The Untitled-Message dialog box is used to create a new piece of email.

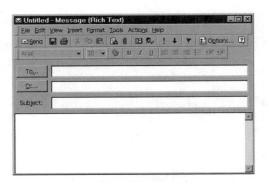

▲

Using Your Contact List to Address Email

Who you send your message to is often as important as the message you send. Sending a copy of your personal email to your boss is usually not a good idea, and emailing documents to the wrong client can be equally disastrous. It is very important that you carefully address your message.

Replying to email can also be dangerous if you are not sure exactly who sent the message. Carefully review the sender's address and the original recipient list of each message you receive so that you know who you are replying to (the sender or the sender and all the recipients). In addition, if you only want to reply to the person who sent the original message, make sure that his address is the only one to which you reply.

In the following exercise, you learn to address the new email message. You also find out how to send a "carbon" copy, and even a blind "carbon" copy to other users.

To Do: Addressing Your Message

1. Click the To-> button so that you can specify an address for your mail. The Select Names dialog box, as shown in Figure 7.6, displays all the email addresses that Outlook has in the Contacts database.

FIGURE 7.6.

The Select Names dialog box lists all the names with email addresses in the Contacts database.

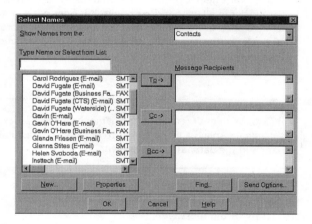

2. In the Select Names dialog box, you see the names of your contacts and their email addresses. (You might also have some fax numbers or other information in the list.) You may have to scroll up or down to find the desired name. Highlight the name and click the To-> button. As shown in Figure 7.7, Outlook places that name in the Message Recipients box. Click OK.

7

▼ **FIGURE 7.7.**

Simply point and click to choose your recipients.

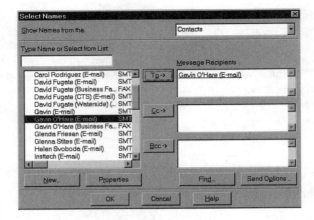

You can also type the names of the recipients directly into the blank boxes next to each field. Outlook then attempts to match the names you type with the entries in all your address books. If it does not recognize a name from an address book or determines that the address is not a proper Internet address, Outlook notifies you of the problem and asks you to select a name from the address list or enter a new address.

If Outlook doesn't recognize the name, it underlines it in red. Right-clicking the name displays a list of names to choose from (assuming *any* of the names in the database are a match).

3. Click the Cc-> button and select another recipient to whom you would like to send a "carbon" copy of the message.

You can also designate recipients to receive blind copies of your message by placing their name in the Bcc-> box. When recipients receive a blind copy, their names and email addresses are not visible to the other recipients.

▲   4. Click OK to close the Select Names dialog box.

Formatting Your Message

Outlook 98 enables you to format your email in the same way you format a document created in Microsoft Word. Text can be formatted using different colors, fonts and font sizes, and styles (such as bold, italic, or underline) simply by choosing the appropriate buttons on the toolbar. Remember, however, that the recipients of your message may lose the formatting if they are using an email editor that does not support formatting. Therefore, before sending your message, be sure it accurately conveys the information regardless of your formatting.

In the next exercise, you learn to add formatting to your message.

To Do: Formatting Your Message

1. In the Subject field, type `email is handy`. Press Tab to move the insertion point into the message window.

2. Type `It's nice to know how to create email using Outlook 98.` in the text message area, as shown in Figure 7.8. Press Enter.

FIGURE 7.8.

Type the body of the text.

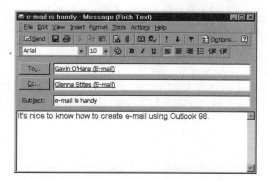

3. Highlight the phrase `Outlook 98`, and click the Bold button.

4. Highlight the entire sentence, and click the Font Color button. Choose Lime as the text color. (You won't see the color change until you deselect the text.)

Adding a Custom Signature to Your Message

Another way to customize your email is to add a custom signature to your message. Although this option is not actually your signature, it is a custom-formatted version of your name, which adds some personality to your messages. In this exercise, you learn to create and format a signature.

7

To Do: Adding a Custom Signature

1. Press Enter to place an empty line between your text and your signature.
2. Choose Insert, Signature, More. Outlook displays a message telling you that you don't have any signatures set up. Click Yes to create a custom signature.
3. In the New Signature text box, type a name for your new signature, as shown in Figure 7.9. Make sure that the Start with a Blank Signature radio button is selected, and click Next.

FIGURE 7.9.

Type a name for your signature file.

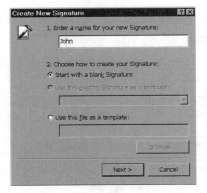

4. In the Signature text box, type your name as you want it to appear in your message (see Figure 7.10). You can then format the text with any font, size, and style you want. The signature in the figure was formatted with a handwriting font and sized at 12 points.

FIGURE 7.10.

Format your new "signature" to your taste.

Be sure that the text of your signature is highlighted when you change the font, size, or style. If the text is not highlighted, Outlook assumes that you don't want to change the format.

If you want to get really fancy, you can add a favorite saying beneath your signature. For example, "I started with nothing, and still have most of it left." Or, "You can't have everything, where would you put it?" Keep your signatures to three or four lines maximum; otherwise, readers get annoyed. You can also type your complete URL (such as `http://www.johnco.cc.ks.us/~jnichols`) to add a hyperlink to your home page.

5. When you finish formatting your signature, click Finish. Outlook inserts your new signature into your message.

Enabling Outlook's Tracking Features

After you send your message, wouldn't it be nice to know when it has been received on the other end and when the recipient has read the message? Outlook 98 provides you with such a capability. When enabled, Outlook's advanced tracking feature sends you an email message when the recipient's mail server receives the email, and another message when the recipient opens the mail.

To Do: Tracking Your Messages

1. Click the Options button on the toolbar. The Message Options dialog box is displayed, as shown in Figure 7.11.

2. In the Message Options dialog box, select both the Tell Me When This Message Has Been Delivered and the Tell Me When This Message Has Been Read check boxes.

3. Click Close.

When your email has been delivered or read, Outlook will notify you via email.

7

FIGURE 7.11.

Checking the two tracking boxes tells Outlook to notify you when the message has been delivered and read.

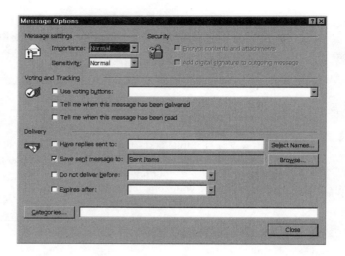

The tracking works in limited fashion over the Internet. Not all servers support sending delivery receipts and not all mail readers support sending *read* receipts. Generally speaking, your chances of getting a delivery receipt back are probably 50-50 at best. For read receipts, the odds are much worse.

Checking the Spelling in Your Message

The final step that you should take before sending your email is to run Outlook's spelling checker. This ensures that your message is as professional looking and as easy to understand as possible.

To Do: Checking the Spelling in Your Message

1. Choose Tools, Spelling.

2. If Outlook finds misspellings or words that are not in its dictionary, it prompts you to replace or ignore the spelling of the word.

3. If, however, Outlook does not find any misspellings, it will confirm that there are no misspellings in your document and tell you that the spelling check is complete.

If you're like me, you might forget to check the spelling in every message you send. If you want Outlook to automatically do it before sending the message, choose Tools, Options and click the Spelling tab. Click Always Check Spelling Before Sending.

▼

▲

Another way to accomplish the same thing is to click the Options button at the bottom of the Spelling dialog box when the spelling checker finds a word that is misspelled. A new dialog box appears with several options. Check the box marked Always Check Spelling Before Sending.

Sending the Message

After you have chosen your recipients, created the message, added your files and signature, and checked the spelling, you are ready to send your message. To send the message, simply click the Send button and away it goes (maybe).

Although you may have sent the message, it first goes to your local mail server. If you don't have a connection to your server (that is, you have to use a modem to dial up your server), the message sits in your Draft folder until you establish an Internet connection. The server may send your message immediately, or it may be programmed to send at various intervals.

Depending on Internet activity, the message may be delivered to the server immediately, or it may take several minutes. Then the receiving server has to decide when it has time to post your message to the recipient. Normally, you won't notice a delay, but you should be aware of what happens when you click the Send button.

Checking for New Mail

It's a good idea to check your email account fairly frequently so that you can have all the up-to-date news from friends, family, and business colleagues.

To check for new mail, simply click the Send and Receive button on the toolbar. This command instructs Outlook to check all the services specified in the Options dialog box under the Mail Services tab.

You can also choose the Send and Receive command from the Tools menu, and choose All Accounts. With this command, you can also choose to log on to only a specific account if you have more than one.

Opening the Mail

Now that you know how to create and send email, it is highly likely that soon you'll start receiving replies. Therefore, it's a good idea to familiarize yourself with the process of reading, printing, and managing the email that you receive.

7

Reading Your Messages

Reading a message in Outlook 98 is simple. Just highlight the message that you want to read in the top portion of the Inbox, and scroll through the text that is displayed in the bottom portion of the Inbox. What could be easier?

> If you want to open the message, select it and press Ctrl+O (the letter O, as in Open). The message opens, and you can choose to reply to the sender, replay to all addressees, forward the message, or select from a multitude of other options.

Printing a Message

Printing an email with Outlook is almost as easy as reading your mail. There are two ways to print an email message:

- Select the mail message and choose File, Print. In the Print dialog box, you can choose to print not only the message, but any attachments as well. To print the attachments, find the option at the bottom left of the Print dialog box, and place a check mark in the check box for printing the attachments.
- From the Inbox, right-click any mail message, and choose Print from the drop-down list of options.

Saving a Message as a File

There are times when you may want to save an email message as a file. Doing this does not remove the message from Outlook; it simply creates a file with the format you choose in the Save As dialog box. Your choices for formats are Text Only (*.TXT), Outlook Template (*.OFT), Message Format (*.MSG), or HTML (*.HTM). If you are using Word as your email editor, you can also save any message as a Word document (*.DOC).

Replying and Forwarding

Replying to messages and forwarding them are similar tasks. Forwarding a message means you send it to someone who wasn't originally listed as a sender or recipient of the original message. Replying means answering the email.

To reply to a message, simply highlight the message and decide whether you want to reply to just the original sender or to everyone who received the original email. If you want to reply only to the original sender, click the Reply button on the toolbar. If, however, you would like to reply to everyone that was on the original sender's recipient list, click the Reply to All button.

> Reply to All doesn't send to those who was blind copied (Bcc) on the original sender's list.

To forward a message to someone who was not on the original recipient list, simply click the Forward button, and choose the person to which the message is to be sent.

Deleting Messages

Be sure to go through your messages regularly, and delete those that are no longer needed. Deleting messages with attached files saves room on your hard drive or your network's mail server. There are a couple of ways to delete items from your Inbox:

- In the Inbox, right-click the message, and choose Delete from the drop-down list of options.
- Highlight the message you want to delete, and click the Delete button on the toolbar.

Troubleshooting Email Messages

There are a number of things that can go wrong when you try to send or receive an email message. The following are the three most common problems:

- A message will sit in the Outbox and not leave, in which case something may be invalid in your Outlook Services setup or the network setup. Check the Services setup under the Tools menu. Check the properties of each of the mail services that you have set up in Outlook. Is the phone number or network location correct? Contact your administrator or service provider to get help with the problem.

> The order that the services are listed on the Tools, Services, Delivery tab can cause this problem. Internet e-mail should be listed *first* to ensure that it is sent properly.

7

- Outlook will return a message as undeliverable, which also may indicate problems with your setup information. Another explanation is that the service provider may be overloaded, and you need to try to resend the message.
- The Internet returns a message to your Inbox as undeliverable, in which case the recipient's address is probably incorrect or the recipient's system may be malfunctioning.

If you have considered each of these measures but still cannot send or receive mail messages, try exiting Outlook and restarting Windows. Sometimes you will have a MAPI error (don't worry about what MAPI means) that can be corrected by simply logging off and logging back on to the system.

Resending a Message

On occasion you may want to resend a message, such as when it has been returned to you as undeliverable (see Figure 7.12). The message will have quite a bit of extra information, which really won't mean much to you. You can delete the message, because sending it again from here returns it to the postmaster that returned it to you.

FIGURE 7.12.

When a message is returned, it contains extra information that probably won't make much sense to you.

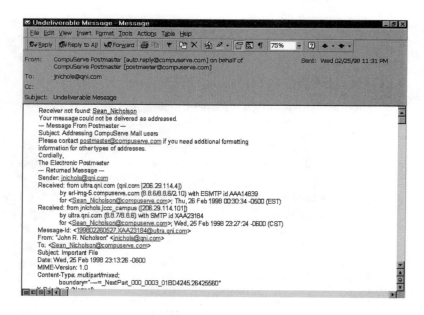

You can open the returned message by double-clicking it in the upper pane. Usually there is some type of explanation in the message box regarding the problems delivering the message. In the case of an Internet mail message, sometimes you may send a message to a proper address, but when the message reaches its final destination, the recipient's mail server may not be available or the recipient cannot be located by the mail server. If the message states that "no transport was available," try resending the message to the recipient.

> To resend the message, click My Shortcuts in the Outlook Bar, click the Sent Items folder, and double-click the message that was returned to open it. Correct the address (or leave it if you know it is correct), and choose Actions, Resend This Message.

Summary

Learning to create, send, and manage your email can open up a whole new avenue of communication for you. Just think: no more stamps, no more paper cuts, and no more licking of envelopes. Understanding the most effective way to create and manage your email can also increase productivity by cutting down on the amount of time you spend waiting for replies.

The basic skills you've learned in this hour have made you familiar with the fundamentals of email messages and have prepared you for the more advanced email hours that follow.

Q&A

Q How do I find someone's email address?

A The easiest way is to ask the person. If you can't do that, however, there are various *search engines* on the Internet that can help you find addresses registered with those services. Check out the following Web sites for help:

```
http://www.altavista.digital.com
http://www.yahoo.com
http://www.four11.com
```

Q Can I set up Outlook 98 so that it automatically checks for new mail at specific times or intervals?

A To automatically check for email, choose Tools, Options, and click the Internet E-mail tab. Set the automatic check time, or turn it off if you want to check only manually.

7

Q If I delete a mail message, can I undelete it?

A Yes. Outlook maintains a Deleted Items folder that acts like your Windows 95 Recycle Bin. Just scroll down the Outlook Bar and find the Deleted Items folder. If the Deleted Items folder is AutoArchived, the deleted items remain available until the Deleted Items folder is emptied in the AutoArchive folder.

Q Why can't I use my Contact folder for email?

A If you don't have the Outlook Address Book service installed, you won't have the ability to use the contacts folder for an email address book. You can check this by choosing Tools, Services. In the Services dialog box, make sure that the Outlook Address Book is installed. If not, click Add and follow the instructions.

You might also want to check the properties of the Contacts folder. Right-click the Contacts folder and choose Properties. Click the Outlook Address Book tab, and make sure that Show This Folder as an E-mail Address Book is checked.

HOUR **8**

Setting Up the Mail Services

As email has become more and more popular in the business world, many business are setting up mail servers so that their employees can email one another without having an Internet service provider. In the past, however, these email systems have been costly and cumbersome and were only cost-effective for large businesses.

Outlook, as an integral part of Windows 95, has simplified the email process by creating a network interface that enables small businesses and home computer users to join the corporate world in having cost-effective and easy-to-use email systems. This hour concentrates on the Outlook/Windows 95 network interface, and will show you how to create a simple, manageable email network using Microsoft Mail.

Installing and Configuring Microsoft Mail

Over the last few years, network computing has become popular for even small businesses and home computer users. With the costs of computers falling and the need for
increased productivity rising, many small businesses and home computer users have
opted to connect their computers for the benefits that networks offer, including file-
sharing and email.

Networks of the late 1990s are much easier to use and set up than the networks of the
past. No longer do you need a dedicated server with complex software. Now you just
need two or more computers running Windows 95 with network cards, and your network
can be set up in a matter of minutes.

To facilitate the boom in network computing, Microsoft created a program called
Microsoft Mail, which enables you to send and receive email messages over your network (often called a *LAN* or *Local Area Network*). Microsoft Mail is easy to set up and
use, and meshes well with Outlook 98.

Before starting this section, find out what version of Windows 95 you are
running. Different versions of Windows 95 have distinct methods of setting
up Microsoft Mail. To determine the version that you are using, right-click
the My Computer icon on your desktop and choose Properties. If the
General tab shows that your Microsoft Windows 95 version is 4.00.950 a,
then you have revision a of Windows 95 (see Figure 8.1). Likewise, if it says
you have version 4.00.950 b, then you have revision b.

To Do: Setting Up and Configuring Microsoft Mail

▲ To Do ▼

1. Close Outlook 98 if it is open.

2. Open the Control Panel by selecting Start, Settings, Control Panel.

3. Double-click the Add/Remove Programs icon to open the Add/Remove Programs
   Properties dialog box.

4. Select the Windows Setup tab, as shown in Figure 8.2. If you are using Windows
   95 revision a, find the box marked Microsoft Exchange, and click the box to select
   it. If, however, you are using revision b, find the box marked Windows Messaging,
   and place a check mark in the box to select it. If Microsoft Exchange *or* Windows
   Messaging is already installed, skip the rest of this To Do section.

FIGURE 8.1.

The System Properties dialog box shows which version of Windows 95 you are running.

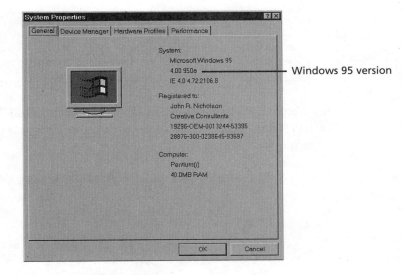

Windows 95 version

FIGURE 8.2.

Use the Windows Setup tab of the Add/Remove Programs Properties dialog box to install the necessary software.

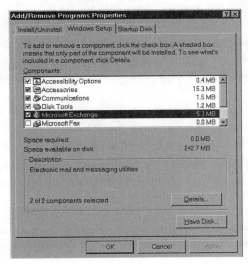

5. Click OK. If your Windows 95 CD-ROM is not in the drive, you may be prompted to insert it.

Depending on who you purchased your computer from, your Windows 95 compressed files may already be on your hard drive. In that case, you will not be prompted to insert the Windows 95 CD-ROM.

6. After Windows 95 finishes installing the files from the CD-ROM (or your hard drive), the Inbox Setup Wizard, as shown in Figure 8.3, opens to guide you through the configuration process.

FIGURE 8.3.

The Inbox Setup Wizard steps you through the configuration process.

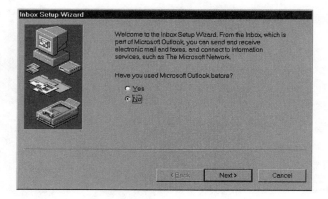

7. Outlook offers a tutorial to those users who are not familiar with its features. If you would like to view this tutorial, click No and choose Next. If, however, you are familiar with Outlook, choose Yes and click Next.

8. Next you are asked to specify which information services you want Outlook to use. Make sure that all services are selected (indicated by check marks) and click Next.

It isn't necessary to install all the services. If you don't want one or more, make sure there is no check mark next to the services you don't want installed.

9. Outlook now prompts you for the directory of your Mail Postoffice. If you know the directory, enter it; otherwise, simply enter c:\ and click Next.

8

You will be setting up your Microsoft Mail Postoffice in the next section. Although it seems strange, you have to install the Mail services *before* you are able to create a Postoffice, even though, as you see in the next step, Outlook assumes you already have set up a Postoffice. Don't worry about this; you will reconfigure Outlook to look in the right Postoffice after you set it up.

10. Outlook now tells you that it was unable to connect to your Postoffice. Because you already know that the Postoffice is incorrect, click Next.

11. Next, Outlook asks the name of your mailbox on the Postoffice. If you know the name (and you entered the path to the mailbox earlier), then enter it. If not, simply type your name and a password *(don't forget it),* and click Next.

12. At this point, you don't want to set up an Internet account (you will do that in the next section), so click Cancel.

13. Outlook displays a message stating that you can reconfigure Outlook at another time by double-clicking the Inbox icon. Because you have finished configuring Outlook, click Yes. Microsoft Mail is now installed and configured.

Setting Up a Postoffice

Now that you have installed and configured Microsoft Mail, you need to set up a Postoffice so that you can take advantage of Mail's network features. When you have set up the Postoffice, sending messages to others on your LAN is just a mouse click away.

So, what is a Postoffice and what does it do? Well, a Microsoft Mail Postoffice acts just like a real Postoffice. Messages are sent there and are then directed to the recipient. In addition, as administrator of the Postoffice (that makes you the postmaster), you will be able to configure the mail system to your own specifications.

To Do: Setting Up and Configuring a Postoffice

1. Before you can create and configure a Postoffice, you must create a folder where the Postoffice will be maintained.

You must create a Postoffice folder *before* you proceed with creating a Mail Postoffice. Although the folder does not have to be named Postoffice, it must exist *before* starting the Postoffice creation process.

▼   2. Open Windows Explorer by choosing Start, Programs, Windows Explorer.

     3. Highlight the C: drive and choose File, New, Folder. Name the folder Postoffice.

     4. Close Windows Explorer.

     5. Open the Control Panel by choosing Start, Settings, Control Panel.

     6. Double-click the Microsoft Mail Postoffice icon, as shown in Figure 8.4.

FIGURE 8.4.

The Postoffice icon enables you to create and configure your mail Postoffices.

Postoffice icon

     7. Windows 95 now offers you the choice of either administering an existing Postoffice or creating a new one. Choose Create a New Workgroup Postoffice and click Next.

     8. Now you are asked to select a location for your Postoffice. Type `C:\Postoffice` and click Next.

     9. As shown in Figure 8.5, Windows 95 has created a Postoffice named wgpo0000 in the C:\Postoffice directory. Click Next to confirm the creation of the Postoffice.

> If you create multiple Postoffices, you can create them in the Postoffice directory, and Windows 95 names them wgpo0001, wgpo0002, and so on.

    10. To administer your new Postoffice, you must enter some information about your-self. Type your name in the Name field. Next choose a Mailbox name for yourself.
▼   Finally, type a password for your mailbox.

▼ **FIGURE 8.5.**

*Confirm that you want
to create a new
Postoffice.*

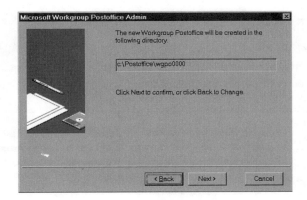

Do not forget your mailbox name or your password. If you do, you won't be
able to gain access to the administration controls to add or remove mail
users from the system. If you forget your mailbox name or password, you
will have to create a new Postoffice and add all users again.

11. When you complete this form, click OK and Windows 95 confirms the creation of
your Postoffice and explains that you must share the directory for others to have
access to it, as shown in Figure 8.6. Click OK again.

FIGURE 8.6.

*Outlook displays a
sharing notification.*

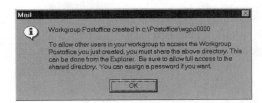

For the File and Print Sharing button to be available in the next step, the
Client for Microsoft Networking must be installed. To install it, double-click
the Network icon in the Control Panel and click Add. Click Client and Add
again. In the Manufacturers panel, click Microsoft. In the Network Clients
panel, choose Client for Microsoft Networks. Click OK. Close the window.

▼

▼   12. To share your Postoffice, open the Control Panel and double-click the Network icon. Click the File and Print Sharing button. Make sure there is a check mark next to the I Want to Be Able to Give Others Access to My Files box. Click OK. Click OK in the Network dialog box. Windows 95 will require you to restart your computer before the changes take effect.

> Checking this box merely gives you the *capability* to share your files. No one else on the network is going to be able to access your files unless you specifically share the folder where the file is located—as you are going to do in the next step.

13. After restarting your computer, open Windows Explorer and right-click the C:\Postoffice folder. From the drop-down menu choose Sharing. From the Sharing tab of the Postoffice Properties dialog box, click Shared As, select Full under Access Type, and click OK (see Figure 8.7). Notice that Window 95 has now placed a little hand icon on your Postoffice folder to indicate that it is shared.

FIGURE 8.7.

Sharing your Postoffice enables others to send and receive mail.

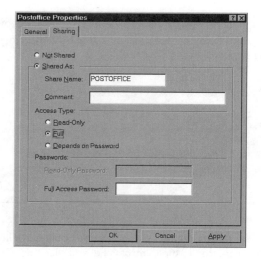

▲   14. Close Windows Explorer.

Configuring Your Postal Services with Outlook

Although you have set up a Microsoft Postoffice, you still have to configure Outlook to recognize it. If you don't, you will be unable to use the mail services in Outlook. In the next exercise, you learn to configure Outlook to meet your needs.

To Do: Configuring Outlook for Postal Services

1. Start Outlook.

2. In the Inbox Setup Wizard box, select each service that you want to use. Internet Mail enables you to get mail from an Internet service provider, CompuServe mail lets you get mail from CompuServe, and Microsoft Mail lets you get mail from your Postoffice. Click Next.

3. As shown in Figure 8.8, Outlook should now recognize your Postoffice. If it doesn't, simply type C:\Postoffice\wgpo0000. Click Next.

FIGURE 8.8.

Outlook now recognizes your Postoffice.

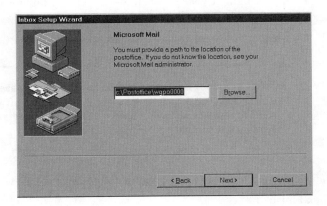

4. Select your name from the list of people on your Postoffice list (right now there should only be you). Click Next.

5. Type your mailbox password and click Next.

6. If you chose to use Internet Mail, then you will be asked to set up your email account, as shown in Figure 8.9. Additionally, if you chose CompuServe mail, Outlook asks you to configure your CompuServe account.

FIGURE 8.9.

You can set up Outlook to get mail from your Internet email account.

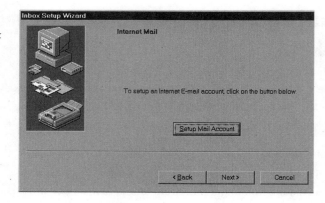

7. After you have set up your Internet or CompuServe accounts, Outlook asks you to specify the location of your personal address book. The default directory is usually satisfactory for new users, so click Next.

8. Specify the location of your personal folders. Once again the default is fine. Click Next.

9. Choose whether you want Outlook to start up when you start Windows 95.

 If you use Outlook on a regular basis, go ahead and have it start when you start Windows 95. (Normally, it's a good idea to turn off your computer once a week to reset it, otherwise leave it on.) If you don't have much RAM, you may not want Outlook running in the background.

10. Outlook confirms the successful configuration of your Inbox.

11. Click Finish.

Creating a Mail Account with an Internet Service Provider

Rather than using a Microsoft Mail account (or in addition to it), you might have an Internet service provider (ISP) for which you need to configure Outlook. Before adding the ISP, you need to know some basic information from your provider. You can get it by calling it or sending an email message. The following is a list of what you need to complete the next exercise.

8

- A name for your account.
- Your personal information, including your email address.
- The address of the mail server for incoming and outgoing mail.
- Your name and password.
- The method of connection (local area network, phone line, or Internet Explorer or third-party dialer).

To Do: Configuring Outlook for an ISP Mail Account

1. Open Outlook if it isn't already open. Choose Tools, Services. You may not have all the services shown in the Services dialog box (see Figure 8.10).

FIGURE 8.10.

The Services dialog box is used to add and remove items from the Outlook configuration.

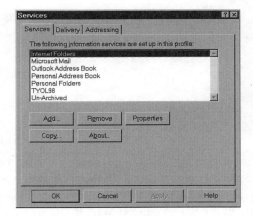

If Internet E-mail already appears on this list, select it, click Properties, and skip ahead to step 3.

2. Click Add to open the Add Service to Profile dialog box, as shown in Figure 8.11. Make sure Internet E-mail is highlighted, and click OK to continue.

FIGURE 8.11.

The Add Service to Profile dialog box is used to add a new email account to Outlook.

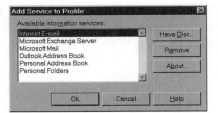

▼   3. Click OK to open the Mail Account Properties dialog box. As shown in Figure 8.12, the dialog box contains four tabs: General, Servers, Connection, and Advanced. We'll look at each of these in turn.

FIGURE 8.12.

The Mail Account Properties dialog box contains four tabs for setting up the mail server.

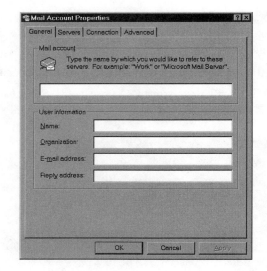

4. The Mail Account Properties dialog box is used to specify mail server information. The General tab consists of two panels. In the upper one, type a name that you want to use for the service. The server I am setting up in this example is qni.com. In the Mail Account panel, I typed QNI Mail. If you are following along, type the name of your mail provider. In the lower panel, I typed personal information. Enter your name, organization, and email address. If you receive replies to email at a different account, type its address in the Reply Address text box; otherwise, type the same address for Reply Address.

5. Click the Servers tab. The display changes to that shown in Figure 8.13. The Servers tab is divided into three panels. In the top panel, enter the name of the Outgoing Mail (SMTP). Normally, this is *mail* followed by a period and the name of the server, but check with your Internet service provider to be certain. The name of the Incoming Mail (POP3) server is usually the same. In my QNI example, both addresses in the Server Information panel would be mail.qni.com. Type your

▼   Account Name and Password in the Incoming Mail Server panel.

8

FIGURE 8.13.

The Servers tab of the Mail Account Properties dialog box is used to list information about the server you are using.

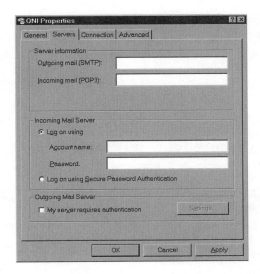

6. Click the Connection tab. The Connection tab has two panels, as shown in Figure 8.14. If you choose to connect using a LAN, Internet Explorer, or a third-party dialer, the Modem panel is grayed out (you don't need it). If you choose to connect using a phone line, you need to select the Dial-Up Networking connection you are going to use in the Modem panel.

FIGURE 8.14.

The Connection tab of the Mail Account Properties dialog box is used to supply information about how you will log on to the account.

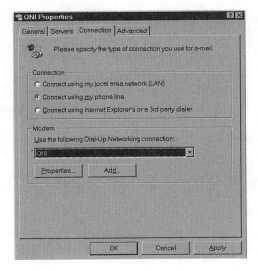

7. Click the Advanced tab. As shown in Figure 8.15, the Advanced tab contains options you will probably not need to use. Ask your Internet service provider if there are any special settings that need to be made on this tab.

 If you are accessing the same email account from multiple computers and want to have the mail available from all machines, click the Leave a Copy of Messages on Server option. This downloads the message to the local hard drive *and* leaves a copy of the message on the server.

FIGURE 8.15.

The Advanced tab of the Mail Account Properties dialog box is not normally needed. Ask your ISP about specialized settings for this page.

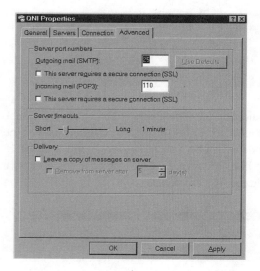

8. When the information is complete, click OK to continue. You will see the message displayed in Figure 8.16, telling you that you need to restart Outlook.

FIGURE 8.16.

When you are finished setting the mail configuration, you need to restart Outlook for the changes to take effect.

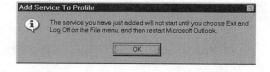

 9. Click OK twice to return to the main Outlook screen. Exit and restart Outlook.

8

▼ 10. To define which mail accounts you want to check, click <u>T</u>ools, <u>O</u>ptions. Click the Mail Services tab. As shown in Figure 8.17, mail accounts are listed in the Mail Services tab of the Options dialog box. Place a check mark next to the accounts you want Outlook to normally check for mail.

FIGURE 8.17.

From the Mail Services tab of the Options dialog box, you can select any or all of the mail accounts that Outlook should check.

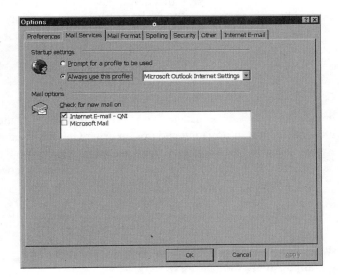

11. To actually check your mail account, click the Send and Receive button on the Standard toolbar. Outlook will check for incoming messages, download them to your computer, send any outgoing messages, and sign off the server.

> If your mail service doesn't disconnect when finished, click <u>T</u>ools, <u>O</u>ptions, and the Internet E-mail tab. Make sure the If Using a Dial-Up Connection Hang Up When Finished Sending and Receiving Mail option is checked.

> To check only one account on an intermittent basis, choose <u>T</u>ools, S<u>e</u>nd and Receive, and select any or all accounts to be checked.

▲

Using Other Mail Services

You may be connected to the Internet via an information service, such as CompuServe or America Online. As we saw in the last section, Outlook 98 is fully compatible with CompuServe, and provides users with a quick, easy setup process. At this time, Outlook is not able to directly retrieve email from your America Online account, although America Online has announced that it will be moving to an Outlook-compatible mail system soon.

Summary

Although this hour does not concentrate on specific features of Outlook, it does provide you with some helpful information and tips on using Outlook in conjunction with a local area network and with Microsoft Mail. Understanding how to use these features can provide you with the capability to set up and maintain a local area network that supports email.

Q&A

Q Wow! This was a lot to digest in an hour. Are there any good books that can explain local area networks to me?

A Yes. Take a look at Greg Newman's *Sams' Teach Yourself Networking in 24 Hours* (Sams Publishing).

Q Can I send attachments with email using Microsoft Mail just as I can with Internet email?

A Sure. Microsoft Mail supports all aspects of Outlook just as though you were sending an Internet email message.

Q Can I use the Address Book to address my messages to the people in my Postoffice?

A Yes. All the members of your Postoffice are listed in an address book called the Postoffice Address List. When creating a new message, click the To: button and drop down the Postoffice Address List. You can then select any member of your Postoffice as a recipient.

Q Can I send a message to someone who has an Internet email message *and* to someone who is on my Postoffice at the same time?

A Yes. When you send the message, Outlook will send one, then the other.

Hour 9

Sorting the Mail

Have you ever looked at a big pile of mail, either at work or at home, and wished that someone would go through it and sort it? Outlook 98 can do just that with your email. In fact, you can have Outlook sort your email by the name of the sender, the date the message was received, or in a number of other ways. Just think of how much time that can save you.

In this hour, we begin by looking at the Organize command, which enables you to sort information in many different ways. Following this, we'll take a brief look at some of the other features that can be used to better organize your work.

Organizing Your Inbox

One of the most powerful features in Outlook 98 is the Organize command. Figure 9.1 shows the Inbox with the Organize box displayed. Notice that in the top-right portion of the Ways to Organize box there are commands for creating a New Folder and accessing the Rules Wizards.

New Folder   Rules Wizard
command   command

FIGURE 9.1.

The Organize command can be used to arrange your email.

Unlike most dialog boxes, the Organize box has four tabs down the left side (rather than arranged across the top of the box, as in most tabbed dialog boxes).

A Theory of Organization

According to Richard Saul Wurman, author of *Information Anxiety*, there are only five ways to organize information:

- Category
- Time
- Location
- Alphabet
- Continuum

When you are planning the organization of your workload, be aware of how different items can be organized. For example, employees can be grouped by any of the five categories. All the people organized by department might be considered in a *category*. If arranged by their length of employment, *time* is the deciding factor. If they are grouped in different offices, you might have a list by *location*. Another list might contain all the employees *alphabetized* by last name. Finally, you might rank the employees in your department on a *continuum* from most effective to least effective.

You can combine the groupings so that you have a list of people by office (location) that is arranged by last name (alphabet). The reason this is important is because you need to understand exactly how you are going to organize your information. After you decide that, Outlook can help you get things in order—creating information out of data.

Creating a New Folder

As you learned in earlier hours, folders are used to group similar items. For example, all email messages are, by default, placed in the Inbox folder, while all contacts are filed in the Contacts folder. One of the ways to organize Outlook items is by working with folders, which is discussed shortly.

Although the default folders might be acceptable to some Outlook users, the chances are good that you might want to organize your information differently from those suggested by the creation of default folders. For example, you might want to group your items by project. Although you are still limited to the six basic folder types used by Outlook, you can be creative in your management of folders to organize your items.

Clicking New Folder in the Organize box is the same as choosing File, Folder, New Folder. The Create New Folder dialog box, as shown in Figure 9.2, is displayed.

FIGURE 9.2.

Use the Create New Folder dialog box to create additional folders for item management.

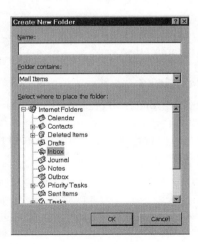

The creation of new folders was covered in depth in Hour 2, "Customizing Outlook 98 to Fit Your Needs," so if you need additional information on creating them, refer to the earlier discussions.

Accessing the Rules Wizard

The Rules Wizard is covered in depth in Hour 22, "New and Fun Outlook Features." However, because it has an impact on the way items are handled, we'll take a brief look at it here. A sample rule is shown in Figure 9.3. This rule is very simple: If a message arrives that is marked High Priority, a notification is to be immediately displayed on my desktop.

FIGURE 9.3.

The Rules Wizard dialog box is used to configure Outlook to handle items in a way that best suits your needs.

As you will learn in Hour 22, you can create many complex rules. This helps sort and prioritize important items, so you aren't distracted by junk mail.

Organizing Using Folders

Outlook offers two options for using folders to organize your information by using folders. First, you can move a selected message into an existing folder. In reality, it is probably easier to simply drag the message onto the receiving folder in the Outlook Bar. You can also create simple rules from there.

The rules are based on who sent the message or whom it is addressed to, and what you want done with it. For example, if Bill Collins is a pesky salesman, constantly sending you email you don't want to read, you can select a message from him and create a rule that states, "Move messages *from* Bill Collins (the sender's name is automatically entered based on the selected message) into *Deleted Items* (or other folder of your choice)."

Organizing Using Colors

You might want to sort messages by color. The Using Colors portion of the Organize box is shown in Figure 9.4.

FIGURE 9.4.

*Another organizer fea-
ture is the capability to
color code mail that
meets specific criteria.*

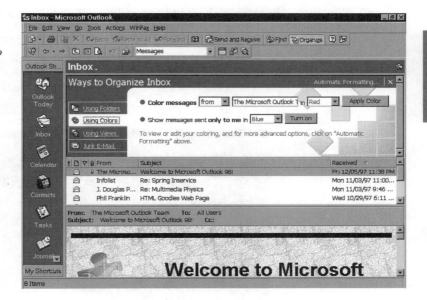

Outlook 98 also offers you two choices for organizing messages by color. You can color code messages sent either from or to specific people. Each person can have his or her own color. (You can choose from 15 colors.) You can also choose to color code messages sent only to you in a specific color.

Organizing Using Views

Changing your view is just a quick way of doing the same thing you can do from the menu. It is in the Organize box because this enables you to quickly change the way your messages are displayed.

Setting Junk Email Options

Options for junk email in the Organize box are broken down into only two groups, as shown in Figure 9.5. Outlook can automatically look for junk email and mail with adult content and color code it for you.

Notice the little warning at the bottom of the Organize box that says this feature is not 100% effective. In fact, one recent study found that it correctly identified junk mail and mail with adult content about 80% of the time. Some was missed, which isn't terrible, but some email was flagged as junk mail when it really wasn't. If you really want to make full use of this feature, refer to Hour 22 for more information on the Rules Wizard.

Outlook can even automatically delete color coded mail for you. If you click the Color drop-down list you'll see a Move To option that enables you to move specific colors to a separate folder—including the Deleted Items folder.

FIGURE 9.5.

Junk mail can also be color coded.

Organizing Folders Other than the Inbox

The Organize command is available from all folders with the exception of Outlook Today. You might want to click each of the folders and click the Organize button to see the ways the items can be organized.

The other folders work similarly to the Inbox folder when organizing items, so you shouldn't have any difficulties in figuring out how each option works. If you do, use the online Help system for more information on organizing your folders.

Changing the Way Your Messages Are Sorted

As discussed in Hour 7, "Back to Basics: Email Services," messages can be sorted by any of the fields visible in the Inbox view. In the example shown in Figure 9.6, all messages have been sorted by the date they were received in descending order. The down arrow next to the word *Received* indicates that they are sorted in descending order, with the most recent messages at the top of the list.

You can also sort your messages by any of the mail headings by clicking the desired heading. By clicking the heading a second time, you can reverse the order from ascending to descending or vice versa.

FIGURE 9.6.

Outlook can sort your messages by any of these fields.

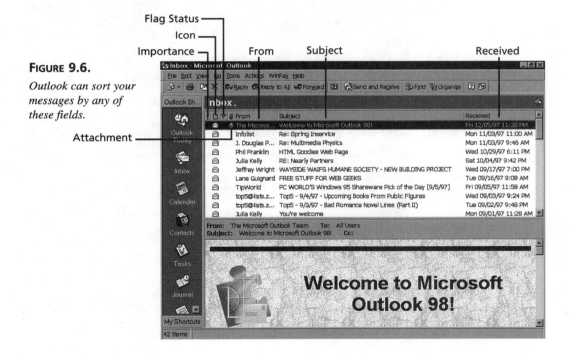

To Do: Sorting Your Messages

1. Open Outlook 98 if it is not already open.
2. Select the Inbox folder from the Outlook Bar.

This exercise steps you through sorting your messages by some of the available fields. If you don't have any messages in your Inbox, wait to do this exercise until you get some mail. That way you can see the results of your sorting.

3. Click the From heading. Outlook sorts your mail in ascending order by that field. Notice that there is an up arrow in the From heading to indicate that the messages are sorted in ascending order, as shown in Figure 9.7.

FIGURE 9.7.

You can sort your messages in either ascending or descending order.

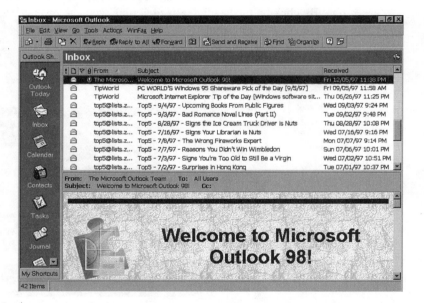

Although sorted, the message selected before the sort was applied remains visible. The scroll box may now be located anywhere on the scrollbar, rather than at the top.

4. To change the sorting order from ascending to descending, click the From heading again. A down arrow now appears in the From heading box and the message order is reversed.

5. Practice sorting your messages by each of the different fields in your Inbox. Choose a sorting method that best suits your needs. (Normally, most users prefer the Received field in descending order.)

▲

Previewing Your Messages

Another way Outlook helps you save time is by enabling you to AutoPreview your email messages before reading the full text. When you enable the AutoPreview feature, Outlook places the first three lines of the message in the top part of your Inbox along with the sender's name and the information about the email. This enables you to see what the sender has typed in the first three lines and can help you determine the importance of the message. If the entire message appears in the first three lines, Outlook adds "<end>" at the end of it to indicate that there is no more to the message.

The AutoPreview feature works only on *unread* messages. After a message is marked as read, the AutoPreview (for that message) is off. You can mark the message as unread and AutoPreview will again appear for that message.

Often the first lines of text in the message is the *routing information.* This information tells you who the sender is and what servers processed the message before it got to you. Unfortunately, if your message has routing information in it, the routing text will be displayed as the first few lines of text. This usually isn't helpful in determining the content of the message.

To Do: Previewing Your Messages

1. Choose View, AutoPreview. As shown in Figure 9.8, Outlook has added the first three lines of each unread message to the top portion of the Inbox.

2. To turn off the AutoPreview, choose View, AutoPreview again and the feature is disabled.

▲

Customizing the Fields in Your View

Microsoft has shipped Outlook to you with the most commonly used fields as the default in your Inbox. It realizes, however, that some people like to see additional information about their messages, so it enables you to customize your Inbox. With this feature, you can set up your Inbox in a manner that best suits you.

FIGURE 9.8.

The AutoPreview feature gives you an idea of what each message is about.

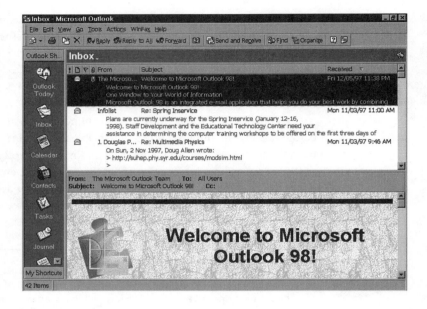

To Do: Customizing the Fields in Your Inbox

1. Select <u>V</u>iew, Current <u>V</u>iew, <u>C</u>ustomize Current View. As shown in Figure 9.9, Outlook summarizes the fields and options currently available in your Inbox.

FIGURE 9.9.

The View Summary dialog box offers a variety of ways to customize your Inbox.

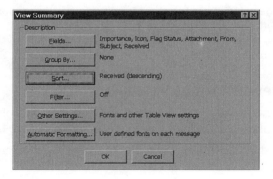

2. Click the <u>F</u>ields button. Outlook displays the Show Fields dialog box, as shown in Figure 9.10. This box is divided into two sections. The A<u>v</u>ailable Fields panel lists the names of all the fields available for your Inbox. The Sh<u>o</u>w These Fields in This Order panel displays the fields *currently* used in your Inbox in the displayed order.

▼ **FIGURE 9.10.**

*The Show Fields dia-
log box enables you to
determine which fields
are displayed and to
specify their order.*

Available fields —

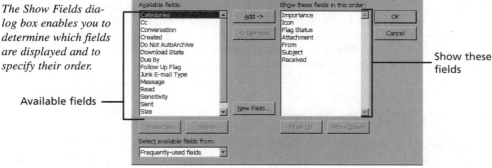

Show these
fields

9

3. From the Available Fields box, highlight Sent and click the Add-> button. Outlook
   places the Sent field after the Received field. Click OK.

4. In the View Summary box, click OK.

5. As seen in Figure 9.11, Outlook adds the Sent field to your Inbox. This tells you
   what date the sender posted the message.

FIGURE 9.11.

*The Sent field is added
to the current view.*

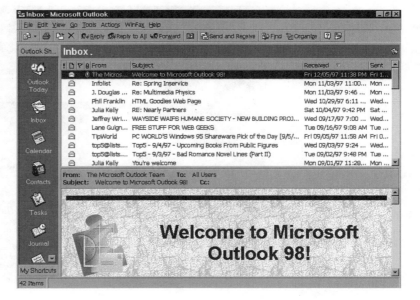

▼

▼

> If you are not able to see all the Sent field, decrease the amount of space
> available for the Subject field by dragging the divider bar between the
> Subject and Received headings to the left until the space used for Subject is
> smaller. Now drag the divider bar between Received and Sent to the left.
> You should be able to see the full view of each field.

▲

Filtering Information

Although you may prefer all your messages to be visible most of the time, there may be
times when you want to view only the messages that meet certain criteria. By using filters, you can tell Outlook which messages to display.

Outlook offers ten predefined views. Choose View, Current View, and select Messages,
Messages with AutoPreview, or any one of the other eight predefined views. As shown in
Figure 9.12, viewing your email by the Follow-up flag allows only the messages for
which you have set the Follow-up flag to be displayed. Set the flag by right-clicking the
message and clicking Follow-up Flag.

FIGURE 9.12.

*Filters enable you to
view only those mes-
sages that meet specif-
ic criteria. In this case,
they are grouped by
follow-up status.*

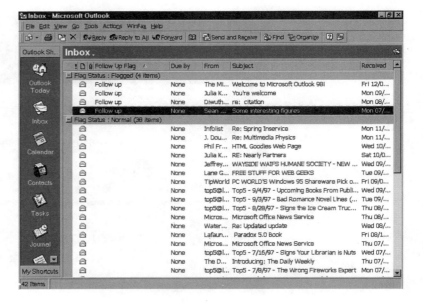

Defining Filters

There are 33 individual fields that apply to mail messages. You can design a filter to match criteria from one mail field or narrow the filter even further by designating that the messages match information in a combination of fields. To define a filter, open the Filter dialog box by choosing View, Current View, Customize Current View and clicking the Filter button in the View Summary dialog box. The Filter dialog box has three tabs where you can enter information to designate the criteria for your message display, as shown in Figure 9.13.

FIGURE 9.13.

The first tab in the Filter dialog box, Messages, is shown.

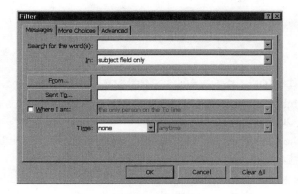

The first two tabs, Messages and More Choices, help you define your criteria by offering ways of categorizing information. The third tab, Advanced, is the most flexible for defining exactly what you want to filter, but it is also the most difficult to construct.

Categorizing Your Messages

You can display your messages using views other than Outlook's predefined views. To categorize a message, right-click the message in the Inbox, and choose the Categories option on the drop-down menu. You can then categorize your message using any of Outlook's 20 predefined categories (see Figure 9.14), by the 32 included fields, or by a category that you create.

Sometimes you may want to set up a display other than one of Outlook's predefined views. Follow these steps:

FIGURE 9.14.

Outlook offers you a wide variety of predefined categories.

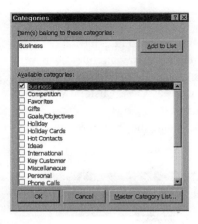

To Do: Categorizing a Message and Creating a Simple Filter

1. In the Inbox, right-click any message. Choose Categories from the drop-down menu. Outlook opens the Categories dialog box.

2. From the Categories list, choose Business and click OK. Outlook now displays the selected message as a business message.

3. Choose View, Current View, Customize Current View and click the Filter button. In the Filter dialog box, select the More Choices tab and click the Categories button.

4. Choose Business to select that as your filter, and click OK until you are back at the Inbox. Outlook now shows only records with Business as the category. Click OK.

5. As shown in Figure 9.15, Outlook has filtered out all messages except the one you classified as a business message.

> To show only messages that contain a specific word in the subject or message body, choose View, Current View, Customize Current View and click the Filter button. In the Search for Word(s) text box, type the word or phrase you want, and in the In drop-down list, choose Subject Field Only, Subject Field and Message Body, or Frequently-Used Text Fields. Click OK twice to return to the Inbox and display only the messages meeting the criteria you have established.

▼ **FIGURE 9.15.**

Unwanted messages are now filtered out.

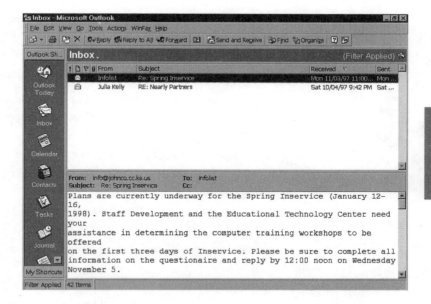

▲

Removing a Filter

After you apply a filter, that filter stays in effect until you change it. To remove a filter, choose View, Current View, Customize Current View, and click the Filter button. In the Filter dialog box, click the Clear All button.

To Do: Removing a Filter

1. Choose View, Current View, Customize Current View, and click the Filter button.

2. Click the Clear All button.

3. Click OK twice to return to the Inbox. All the messages are again displayed. The single message you chose before, however, still has the Business category attached to it. This is important, as it will be a part of the next exercise.

Creating a More Complex Filter

The results of the first filter left only one message showing in the Inbox because only one message was classified in the Business category. Imagine, however, that you have been categorizing all your messages for the last year, and your simple filter has left 50 messages in your Inbox. You might want to narrow your filter further to display only those messages meeting even more strict criteria.

In the following exercise, you set the filter to find only the business messages that were sent by a specific person. To complete this exercise, you must have at least two mail messages. The one used in the exercise to set a simple filter and an additional one.

To Do: Increasing Filter Complexity

1. Choose another message. Using the skills learned in the earlier exercise, assign it to a Business category. Remember, a filter has not been reapplied, so all the messages are still visible.

2. Write down (if you need to) the name of the person who sent the second message.

3. Open the Filter dialog box by clicking View, Current View, Customize Current View and clicking the Filter button.

4. Set the Categories box to Business. Click OK until you are at the Inbox. Notice that you now have two messages displayed.

5. To narrow your Business search even further, reopen the Filter dialog box, and click the Advanced tab.

6. Click the Field drop-down button, choose the Frequently Used Fields, and select the From field. Make sure the Condition field is set to Contains.

7. In the Value field, type one or more of the words in the From box, as shown in Figure 9.16.

FIGURE 9.16.

The fields in the Define More panel narrow the selection of messages.

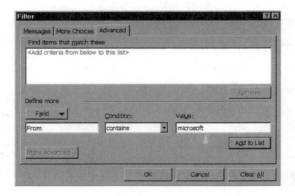

8. Click OK to return to the Inbox and filter out any messages that are in your business category that are not from someone with the name you typed in the Value field.

9. Remove all filters from the view by clicking the Clear All button in the Filter dialog box. You should again have all messages displayed.

> The Clear All button clears all tabs, not just the one that is displayed.

Sorting Messages by Group

Another handy way to sort your messages is to sort them by group. Grouping your messages, like filtering, places messages with common criteria together. You can group your messages by sender, by date sent, or by any of the other fields available in your Inbox. Doing so allows you to look over just the messages you received yesterday, or enables you to quickly glance at all the messages you've received from a specific coworker.

Making a Group

An easy way to group messages by a mail field is to right-click the desired column heading and choose Group By This Field from the drop-down menu.

To Do: Grouping Your Messages

1. Right-click the From heading in your Inbox.

2. From the drop-down menu, select Group By This Field.

3. As shown in Figure 9.17, Outlook has now grouped all the messages by sender's name.

FIGURE 9.17.

Each message is placed in a group.

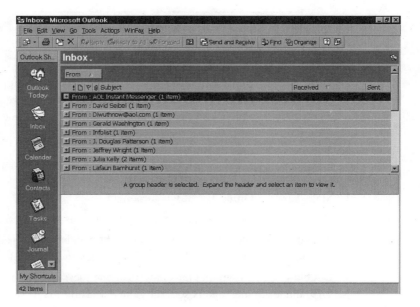

▼   4. To the right of each group name is the number of items in that group. If you have
        many messages, scroll through until you find a group with more than one message.

     5. Click the plus to the left of the sender's names. The list of messages from that
        sender is displayed. To view a message, click it.

     6. To turn off the grouping feature, choose <u>V</u>iew, Current <u>V</u>iew, Customize Current
        View, and click the Group By button. In the Group By dialog box, select (none)
        from the Group Items By drop-down menu.

> You can also turn off grouping by right-clicking the button in the Group By
> box and choosing Don't Group by This Field. You can also drag the button
> off the Group By box and drop it back on the headers area where it was
> originally.

> After you have used the group feature, Outlook places a box at the top of
> your Inbox that says Drag a Column Header Here to Group by That Column.
> This is called the Group By box. This is another quick and easy way to group
> your messages.
>
> To turn off the Group By box, right-click any of the field headings (such as
> From or Subject), and click the Group By Box option.

▲

Grouping by More than One Field

If you receive many messages each day and want to organize them even better, you can
group them by multiple fields. Suppose you want to group all your messages by the
From field, as we did in the last exercise, but you also want to group each message within each group by the date received. This enables you to view all messages received from
a certain person or business on a specific day. In the next exercise, you'll have an opportunity to group messages by multiple fields.

To Do: Grouping by Multiple Fields

     1. Make sure the Group By Box is turned on.

     2. Drag the From heading into the Group By box, as shown in Figure 9.18.

     3. Now that your messages are grouped by the Sender, drag the Received heading
        into the Group By box. Outlook now organizes each group by the date sent.

     4. Double-click a group that has more than one message. Notice, as shown in Figure
        9.19, that each message is sorted by the date and time it was received, as well as
▼   by the name of the sender.

FIGURE 9.18.

Grouping is as simple as drag and drop.

Group By Box

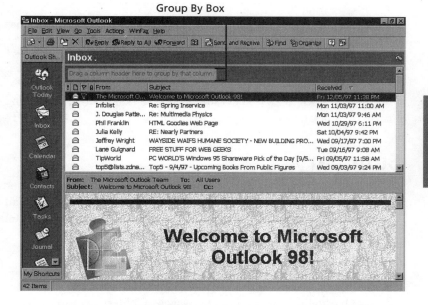

FIGURE 9.19.

Each group now has a subgroup. The Microsoft group has three items, and they are arranged in date order.

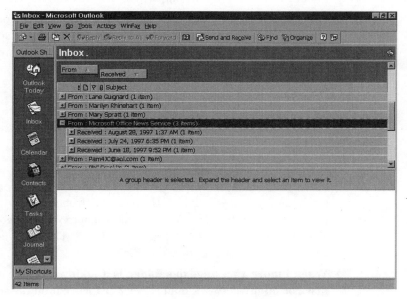

5. Turn off the grouping feature by choosing View, Current View, Customize Current View. Click the Group By button. In the Group By dialog box, click the Clear All button.

An alternative way to ungroup messages is to drag the field names from the Group By box back onto the heading bar. You still need to close the Group By box.

6. The Group By box is still open. Right-click any field heading (such as From) and click the Group By box to turn it off.

Summary

Outlook offers many different ways to manage your mail. From sorting to personalized file folders, each feature is designed to help you organize your mail in the most effective manner possible. Take advantage of these features to reduce the time needed to sort through unwanted messages or to find specific messages.

Q&A

Q Should I move all my messages to folders instead of deleting them?

A Remember that email messages take up space just like any other file. If you neglect to delete old, unnecessary messages, you will be taking up space on your hard drive. Therefore, when a message is no longer useful, be sure to delete it.

Q Is there a *right* way to sort my messages?

A Different people sort their messages in different ways. Some like to have it sorted by when it was received, while others like to have it sorted by sender. The choice is completely up to you. Try a few different sorting methods and then choose one that suits you.

Q Are the filters really useful?

A When you read the filters section of this hour, you probably didn't have very many email messages in your Inbox. However, think about how useful the filters would be if you needed to find a single message sent to you by a coworker on January 10, and you had 300 email messages in your Inbox. The more messages you receive, the more important your filters become.

Q When I move a message to a folder, is it taking up space on my local hard drive or on my network mail server? If I leave it on the server, the system administrator says it's taking up too much hard drive room, but I don't have a lot of storage space available on my hard drive.

A Some companies set aside a certain amount of space for each user on their network servers for the storage of mail. Others, however, set the computers up so that the messages are stored on the local machines. It is a good idea for you to check with your email administrator so that you know where your messages are being stored and how much space has been set aside for you. This is important if you have a limited amount of free hard drive space.

Q **When categorizing my mail, can I place a message in more than one category?**

A Sure. You can specify as many categories as you like.

9

Hour **10**

More than Email: Faxing and Attaching

In addition to sending and receiving email messages, Outlook 98 can transfer complex files, such as spreadsheets, databases, and just about any other type of file that you use, across your local area network or the Internet. In this hour, we examine Outlook's attachment and faxing features. You will then be able to provide friends and colleagues with documents and files in a flash.

Attaching a File to Your Email Message

Outlook 98's Inbox capabilities extend far beyond basic textual email messages. Using Outlook's attachment feature, you can send virtually any file to a recipient with a few keystrokes. Simply attach the file to an email message and send it. The recipient will receive it just as though you had handed it to him on a floppy disk.

Although Outlook does not limit the size files you can attach to your email, some mail servers may have difficulty processing large files. Therefore, if you plan to send an attached file that is greater than 1 megabyte (MB) in size, check with your mail administrator to confirm that your mail server can handle it.

If the mail server is not able to process your file, consider using compression software, such as PKZip, to reduce the size of your file. This technology is further discussed later in this hour. Just make sure that the recipient has access to identical or compatible compression software to access your file.

The recipients may also have a limitation on the file size that can be received. Have them check with their network administrators before sending the email; otherwise, it may get bounced back to you with a very cryptic message as to the reason for the return.

To Do: Attaching a File

1. Open Outlook 98 if it is not already open.
2. Click the Inbox, and create a new mail message.
3. Select a recipient for your message.
4. In the Subject line, type Important File.
5. In the text box, type Here is the file I promised you. Press Enter to place the cursor on the line below your text.
6. Outlook 98 enables you to place your file anywhere in your text message. You will place it below your text. As shown in Figure 10.1, click the Insert File button on the toolbar.
7. In the Insert File dialog box, select the C:\Windows directory and highlight the file called Waves.bmp., as shown in Figure 10.2. Click OK.
8. As you can see in Figure 10.3, Outlook attaches the file to your message and places a small preview of the image in your message. If you insert other file types than BMP, you will see various icons representing the files.
9. To send the message and the attached file, click the Send button.

FIGURE 10.1.

The Insert File button enables you to quickly attach a file to your message.

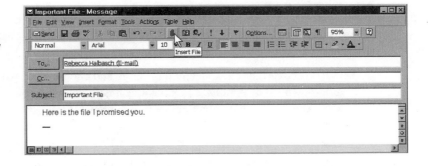

FIGURE 10.2.

Choose the file you want to attach to your message.

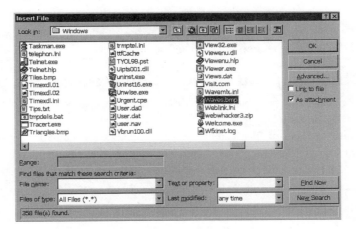

10

FIGURE 10.3.

Outlook attaches the file to your message.

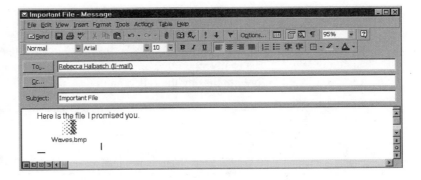

You must be connected to the Internet or your local mail server before mailing the file.

Saving an Attachment

When you receive a message with a file attached, there are a few ways to save the attached file to your local drive:

- In the Inbox, right-click an email message and choose View Attachments from the drop-down list of options. Click the attachment you want to save. At the Opening Mail Attachment dialog box, make sure the Save It to Disk option is selected and click OK. In the Save As dialog box, choose the folder where you want the attachment saved.

- Open a mail message with an attachment, and choose File, Save Attachments. A dialog box appears in which you can specify a location for saving the file.

- With the message open, right-click the attachment and choose either Open or Save As from the drop-down list of options.

Obtaining and Using a Compression Program

As noted in the previous section, it is usually not a good idea to send files larger than 1MB over a mail server unless you know the server can handle it. Unfortunately, this limits the types of files you can send to colleagues via email. To solve this problem, several software developers have created programs that compress your file (thus making it smaller) so that it can be sent across an email server. These programs are easy to use and, when used properly, have no negative effects on your file.

The most popular compression program available is PKZip and its companion product WinZip. These products are easy to use and easy to install, and make sending large files much easier.

You can obtain a copy of WinZip at your local software store or you can download a copy of WinZip at www.winzip.com. At this Web site, you can either download the full version of WinZip or a trial version that allows you to evaluate the product for 30 days to see if you like it before purchasing the full version.

> Make sure that the recipients of your file have identical or compatible compression software so that they can uncompress the file when it is received. It is a good idea to confirm that the recipient has compression software *before* you send the message so that he can obtain the software prior to receiving your message.

When you have obtained a copy of WinZip, you can compress your file by clicking the New button, selecting a new filename for your compressed file (files compressed using WinZip usually use the .zip extension), and adding whatever files you want to be included in the *zipped* file.

You can add numerous files to a zipped file. Remember, however, that the more files you add, the larger the file becomes, and the reason for using compression technology is to reduce the file size to less than 1MB.

If you are connected to the Internet through a local area network that uses a dedicated high-speed connection, file size is generally not a problem. If either you or the recipient is using a modem, file size becomes much more of a concern.

10

After you have created your zipped file, attach it to your email message, and send it like you would any other file.

Installing Microsoft Fax Software

Before you can begin faxing with Outlook 98, you must make sure Microsoft Fax and Outlook's fax service are installed. You can do this by choosing Tools, Services. If Microsoft Fax is not listed as one of your installed services, such as in Figure 10.4, then you must install Microsoft Fax by following the steps in the next exercise. If, however, you already have Microsoft Fax installed as a service, skip the upcoming To Do section, and proceed directly to the next section, "Configuring Microsoft Fax."

To Do: Installing Microsoft Fax Service

1. To set up the Microsoft Fax service, close Outlook 98 and open the Control Panel by choosing Start, Settings, Control Panel.

2. In the Control Panel, double-click Add/Remove Programs.

3. Click the Windows Setup tab, as shown in Figure 10.5. In the Components box, make sure that Microsoft Fax is installed. If not, click the box next to Microsoft Fax so that there is a check in the box, and click OK.

▼ **FIGURE 10.4.**

Check to see whether the Microsoft Fax service is installed in Outlook 98.

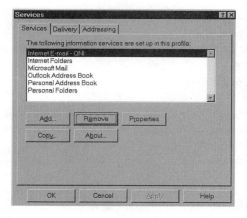

FIGURE 10.5.

See whether Microsoft Fax is installed on your computer.

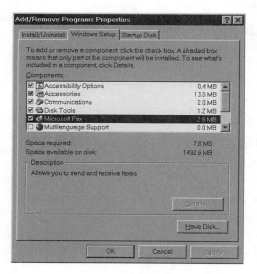

> You may be asked for your Windows 95 CD-ROM to complete the installation.

4. After Microsoft Fax is installed, close the Control Panel.

5. Open Outlook 98, choose Tools, Services, and click the Add button.

6. As seen in Figure 10.6, Microsoft Fax is available to be added as a Service. Select Microsoft Fax and click OK.

▼

FIGURE 10.6.

You can now add Microsoft Fax service to Outlook.

 If you don't have the latest version of Microsoft Fax installed, you will see a warning like the one in Figure 10.7. You need to close Outlook (and any other open programs) at this point. When you have the latest version installed, move ahead to step 7. Because the update is done from the Microsoft Web site using Internet Explorer, make sure you have an active Internet connection before beginning the update procedure.

10

FIGURE 10.7.

If you don't have the latest version of Microsoft Fax, you will see this notification. Follow the instructions to update Microsoft Fax to the latest version.

7. When you see the Install Complete message box, close all the windows.

8. Open Outlook. Choose Tools, Services, Add. Click Microsoft Fax and click OK. You now need to set up (configure) Microsoft Fax. Leave the display as it is.

Configuring Microsoft Fax

After the Fax software has been installed (and updated, if required), you need to configure the program so that it meets your needs. In the following exercise, you learn to configure Fax settings.

To Do: Configuring Microsoft Fax

1. When you add Microsoft Fax, Outlook asks you to enter some basic information regarding your faxes. To do this, click Yes.

▼   2. In the Microsoft Fax Properties page on the User tab, as shown in Figure 10.8, enter your fax number and personal information.

FIGURE 10.8.

Customize your faxes with your personal information.

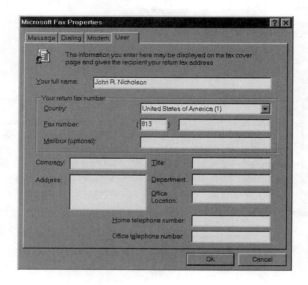

3. After you have entered all the necessary information, click the Modem tab.

You must provide a Fax number. If you don't have a dedicated fax line, type your voice number. Outlook won't allow you to continue until a valid number is in the Fax Number box.

4. From the Modem tab of the Microsoft Fax Properties dialog box, select the modem that you want to use as your fax, and click the Set as Active Fax Modem button. Click OK.

FIGURE 10.9.

Set your modem to be an active Fax Modem.

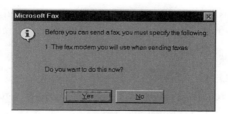

▼

▼   5. Outlook informs you that your fax settings will not become active until you close
         Outlook and restart the program. Click OK.

      6. In the Services dialog box, notice that Microsoft Fax has been added. Click OK.

▲   7. Close Outlook and reopen it; your fax service is ready to use.

Faxing with Microsoft Fax

Before you begin faxing with Outlook, you should have an overview of how it works and
how it differs from sending a fax from a fax machine or from using fax software from
other companies to send a fax using the modem.

- If you send a fax with an attachment to another computer, the fax arrives in the
  Inbox. When the recipient reads the fax, he or she can choose to save the file to the
  local hard drive.

- If you send a fax from within a word processing program, such as Microsoft Word,
  the receiving computer receives it as a regular fax, which can be read from the Inbox.

- If you send a fax with an attachment to a real fax machine, the fax machine is not
  able to store the attachment. It is lost. Therefore, know your recipient before
  including an attachment.

- If you receive a fax in Outlook that has been sent using Microsoft Fax Services, it
  appears in your Inbox as email. If there is an attachment, you can save it as a file
  on your hard drive.

Sending Faxes

Sending a fax is similar to sending an email message. Almost all the skills you learned in
the preceding section on email apply to fax messages. Addressing the message involves
the same steps; however, when you choose the recipient from the Address Book list, you
need to choose one with the word *fax* in parentheses next to the name.

> To display the Contacts list where you have stored the fax numbers of all
> your various colleagues, you *must* have either Microsoft Fax or Microsoft
> Mail installed and then you must add the Outlook Address Book to your list
> of services. To do this, select Tools, Services.
>
> If Outlook Address Book is already listed, then you should be able to access
> your Contacts under the Address Book option. If, however, you don't have
> the Outlook Address Book installed, choose Add and select it.

10

To Do: Sending a Fax with Attachments

1. Open the Inbox if it isn't already open. You see a new message concerning Sprint Fax services. Ignore this for now. Choose Actio<u>n</u>s, New Fa<u>x</u>.

2. The Compose New Fax Wizard guides you through the process (see Figure 10.10). If you have properly set up your fax services, you should see Default Location in the text box under the statement I'm dialing from. Otherwise, you may need to click the <u>D</u>ialing Properties button and fill in the information for your location. Click <u>N</u>ext.

FIGURE 10.10.

The Fax Wizard makes faxing easy.

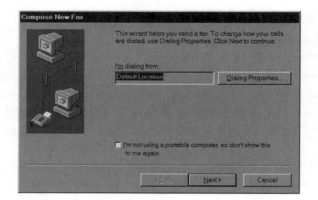

3. On the next screen, you must enter the recipient information. If you are sending to a fax number already listed in your Contacts database, click the Address Book button to locate the recipient. Otherwise, you can enter the recipient's information manually. Click <u>A</u>dd to List to add the number as a recipient. You can add as many recipients to the list as you need. Click <u>N</u>ext.

4. This screen asks if you want to use a cover page and, if so, what kind of cover you want. You can also click the <u>O</u>ptions button to set formatting options, dialing instructions, and security. After choosing a cover page, click <u>N</u>ext.

> The <u>O</u>ptions button also enables you to add a custom cover page to your fax. This cover page, however, must have been created (using a program like Microsoft Word) prior to the sending of the fax. Then, to use your custom cover page, click the <u>O</u>ptions button and click Browse in the cover page box. Specify the location of the cover page that you want to include with your fax.

▼ 5. On the next screen, enter the subject of the fax message and type a brief note.

6. The final screen asks you if you want to include any files with the fax message, such as a Word document or an Excel spreadsheet (see Figure 10.11). If you decide to add a file, you will need to designate the directory where the file is stored. Click <u>A</u>dd File to browse the files.

FIGURE 10.11.

You can even attach files to your faxes.

10

7. Click <u>N</u>ext, and the ready-to-send screen of the Compose New Fax dialog box is displayed, as shown in Figure 10.12. Click Finish to begin sending the fax.

FIGURE 10.12.

Click the Finish button to begin sending your fax.

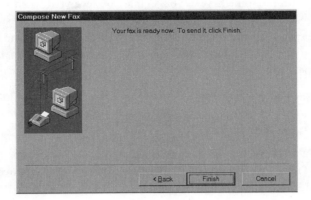

You can send a fax in the exact same way that you send an email message. Simply choose the recipient's fax address from the Address Book instead of the email address. This process, however, is slower than using the Fax Wizard, and you won't have the option of using a cover page and attaching a file, as you do when using the Fax Wizard.

▲

Sending Faxes as Word Processing Pages

You can also send a word processing document as a fax. This is truly among the simplest things you can do.

- From within the word processing program with the document you want to fax open, choose File, Print.
- Choose Microsoft Fax as your printer. Press OK.
- The Fax Wizard is run. Fill in the information. Complete the Fax Wizard and click the Finish button.
- The document is automatically sent as a fax.

> Don't forget to reset your printer to the default printer. Otherwise, the next time you try to print the document, Microsoft Fax tries to fax it for you.

Scheduling a Fax

Another convenient faxing feature offered by Outlook 98 is that you can schedule the time and date that you want a fax sent. For instance, suppose your colleague works on the East Coast and you work on the West. He starts work three hours earlier than you, and he wants to fax something to you so that you receive it when you go to work for the day, but doesn't want it to sit around the office for everyone to see. He does not, however, want to spend his morning checking his watch to see if it's time to send the fax. All he has to do is schedule Outlook to deliver the fax at 8:00 a.m. Pacific time, 11:00 a.m. Eastern time.

Another reason to schedule faxes is to save money. If you send a lot of long-distance faxes, you can tell Outlook to wait until the long-distance rates are discounted (usually after 10 p.m.) to send the faxes.

To schedule a fax, follow the steps outlined previously for creating a new fax. Follow the Fax Wizard until you come to the page where you specify your cover page, as shown in Figure 10.13. Note the Fax Options panel, which says Click This Button to Change the Time When the Fax Is Sent and Set Other Options.

FIGURE 10.13.

You can customize the options for each message.

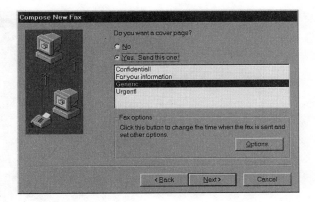

Click the Options button. Outlook opens the Send Options for This Message dialog box where you can specify the time you want Outlook to send your fax. When you are finished setting the options, click OK and continue with the Fax Wizard.

Sending Faxes to Groups

In the past, sending the same fax to multiple recipients was a cumbersome task that either required an expensive fax machine or someone to stand at a regular fax machine and send the fax to each individual number. Now, Outlook enables you to send the same fax to as many people as you want.

For instance, suppose you want to send a fax to all the department heads in your company. To do this, create your fax following the steps outlined previously, and when you are prompted to enter the names of the recipients, choose Address Book. In the Address Book dialog box, make sure you select Contacts as the Address Book to be shown (see Figure 10.14). Highlight the name of each person who is to receive the fax and click the To-> button. When you have added each recipient, click OK and continue with the Fax Wizard.

Recipients don't have to be in your Address Book to receive a group Fax. You can type their Fax numbers directly, and click the Add button.

10

FIGURE 10.14.

The Address Book makes it easy to choose recipients.

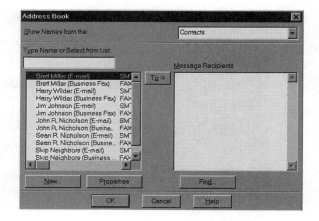

Receiving Faxes

All incoming faxes are placed in the Inbox along with your email. To set Outlook to receive a fax, click the Inbox and choose Tools, Microsoft Fax Tools, Options. Click the Modem tab and click the Properties button. If your Answer Mode properties are set to Don't Answer, choose the Manual option or the option to automatically answer after a specified number of rings. If you choose the Manual option, you need to click Answer on the screen when the sender's fax modem calls. If you make a change here, be sure to restart the computer for the changes to take effect.

When a fax has been successfully received, it appears in your Inbox among your email messages. To read the fax message, either scroll down through the text in the preview box or double-click it to open it as you would an email message.

> If the fax is sent from a fax machine, the fax doesn't appear as text in your Inbox. Instead, it appears as an attachment that you have to open— generally using the Imaging viewer that comes with Windows 95.

Converting Faxes

Even though your faxes resemble email messages, each page of a fax is not text, unlike a document or an email message. Instead, a fax is made up of pages of pictures. Essentially, when you send someone a fax of your document, you are sending them a picture of the words on the page. Therefore, if you want to open a fax document with your word processor, you would have to open the file as a graphic. When you want to open a fax and alter the contents, you must convert the pictures of the words into actual words. Fortunately, Outlook offers a quick and easy way to do this.

To do this portion of the hour, you must have a fax in your Inbox. When you set up Microsoft Fax, Outlook placed a sample fax in the Inbox, so if you haven't yet deleted it, use this fax. If you already deleted the sample fax, have a coworker or friend send you a fax. If you don't know anyone who can send you a fax, call Microsoft's faxback system at 1-800-936-4100 using your telephone (not your fax machine) and order a document to be faxed to you.

10

To Do: Converting a Fax to a Word Processing File

1. Open Outlook if it is not already open.

2. In the Inbox, double-click any fax item.

3. As you can see in Figure 10.15, Outlook opens the fax message just as it would an email message.

FIGURE 10.15.

Outlook displays a fax just as it does an email message.

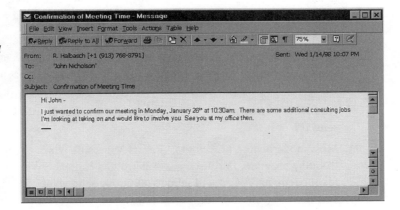

4. To convert a fax message to text, choose File, Save As. In the Save As Type box at the bottom of the Save As dialog box, select RTF Text Format. This is a format that is easily readable by most word processors, such as Microsoft Word.

5. After you have saved the file, you can then open it in your word processor and modify it as necessary.

Summary

This hour covered many of the features Outlook includes for attachment and faxing. Faxes and attachments offer a great way to reduce the piles of paper that come across your desk each day. Because each file or fax is in electronic form, you can quickly organize it and even reply more quickly than if it was sent to you on paper. Plus, you don't even have to worry about recycling because everything is electronic.

Q&A

Q I have a paper fax that I want to send to someone. How do I get it into my computer.

A Unfortunately, the only real drawback of fax/modems is that you can't send a paper fax with them. That is, unless you have a scanner. Scanners have become very popular over the last few years as their prices have fallen below $100 for a good quality scanner.

   If you find that you need to fax a large amount of paper documents, consider investing in a good scanner with an Optical Character Reader (OCR), which is a software program that "reads" your fax and converts it into a word processing document that you can then fax. OCR software is not necessary if you just want to scan and send a fax. Most new scanners come with scan and fax software.

Q How easy is compression software to use?

A Compression programs, such as WinZip, are *very easy* to use and are widespread in their use. With the average size of a file growing each day, compression technology enables us to transfer files not only via email, but on floppy disk.

Q Do I have to import my word processing document into Outlook before I can send it?

A Most modern word processors, such as Microsoft Word, enable you to fax directly from the program. For instance, in Word you can choose Print and select your fax/modem, and Word will guide you through the process of sending the document as a fax.

Q When I get a fax message, will Outlook notify me just like it does when I receive email?

A Yes. Outlook places a small envelope in the task tray on your toolbar to let you know that you have new faxes.

Q It seems that Microsoft Fax is a little difficult to use. Is there a better option?

A Yes. Buy a commercial faxing package. I use WinFax Pro for Windows 95 from Symantec. I highly recommend it.

PART IV
What Should I Be Doing Today?

Hour

HOUR 11

Time Is on My Side: The Calendar Feature

In this hour, you're going to take a look at what may be Outlook's most attractive feature: the Calendar.

Calendars have been around for quite some time. Civilized man has always been interested in keeping track of time for agricultural and religious reasons—not to mention starting the odd war or two. However, early time-keeping devices were more than slightly cumbersome. No one really used Stonehenge as a personal information manager. And, although sundials are a lot more portable, getting the correct time on cloudy days is quite a chore.

It wasn't until 46 B.C. that Julius Caesar said "enough," and set up the 365-day Julian calendar. Finally, those clever Romans could calculate just how many shopping days were left until Christmas (after Christmas was added to the calendar, of course).

In 1582, Pope Gregory XIII took the advice of his calendar commission and designed a more accurate calendar that mirrored the 365.25 day solar year. However, it was only as international commerce expanded that people outside of Europe adopted the Gregorian calendar. Today, most of the Western world uses it. However, Greece held out until 1923, and there are still many different calendars in use throughout the world.

> Do you think you know what day it is? Here's a Mayan date; try converting it. The first correct email answer proves that you have too much time on your hands.
>
> 12 baktun, 16 katun, 11 tun, 16 uinal, and 6 kin

Even the Gregorian calendar is not perfect. Because the solar year is not exactly 365.25 days long, another adjustment of one day is needed every 2,500 years. This will surely be designated as another sale day at the mall.

For the purposes of this book, let's stick with the Gregorian calendar, which is the one that Outlook uses. Also to remain consistent with Outlook, let's use the seven-day week and the 24-hour day. However, if you misbehave, it's right back to the Mayan calendar.

An Overview of the Calendar Features

Besides its capability to display the nifty calendar put together by Pope Gregory XIII, Outlook's Calendar tool also helps you keep track of your time by setting appointments, holidays, and meeting dates. Calendar can

- Set detailed appointments for any time of day. These appointments can be categorized by the criteria you set (business meeting, school event, or in-law interaction). You can easily set Calendar to remind you of impending appointments with an onscreen message and/or a reminder sound that you choose. (This can range from a bell ringing to a cow mooing—you can import any sound to remind you of important events.)

- Create all-day events on your schedule. Similar to appointments, scheduling events enables you to quickly block out days of time, rather than just hours. You can even indicate how reachable you are (free, busy, or out of the office), and whether the time and date are firm or tentative.

- Plan meetings with associates in your office who also use Outlook. Calendar's Meeting Planner can search each person's calendar and automatically set a meeting time that is convenient to all, and can even notify everyone who needs to attend the meeting.

- Enhance your déjà vu by making recurring appointments, meetings, and events a snap. If you have to go to the gym every Monday at noon, Calendar can set reminders for you with just a few clicks.

In this hour you learn to set and modify appointments, schedule events, and set recurring meetings.

Starting Calendar

Like so much of the Microsoft get-there-from-anywhere paradigm, there is more than one way to access Calendar. You can even enter data into Calendar without starting Outlook.

The main way to start Calendar is within Outlook itself. From any part of Outlook, start Calendar by clicking the Calendar icon in the Outlook Bar or the Calendar folder in the Folder list, depending on the view you have displayed. From the menu, choose Go, Calendar.

Taking the Grand Tour

Once Calendar is displayed, you see the default Calendar screen, as shown in Figure 11.1. Your screen may look slightly different; for example, your Calendar will probably just be named Calendar, and the date will be different.

11

FIGURE 11.1.

The default view of the Calendar screen.

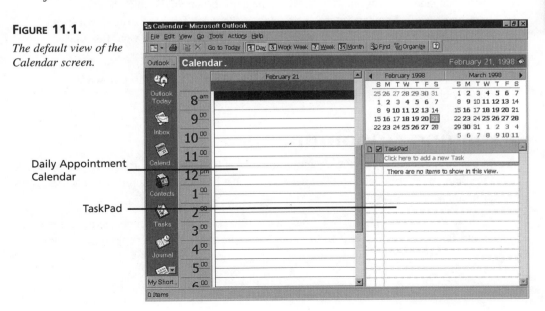

Daily Appointment Calendar

TaskPad

Calendar, like all the other Outlook tools, has dynamic menus and toolbars. As the situation changes, so do the tools available on the toolbars and menus. The display is actually dictated by two criteria: first, the Outlook module that you are using, and second, the view that you are in. In Calendar, there are seven possible views, with the toolbars varying slightly for each view. This hour and Hour 12, "Power Calendaring," exclusively cover the Day/Week/Month view for setting appointments, events and meetings. In later hours, you will see more complex views and create custom views.

In the default Day/Week/Month view, the Information Viewer has three panes: the Daily Appointment Calendar, the Date Navigator view of the current and next month, and the TaskPad. The TaskPad activities are covered in Hour 13, "Getting Things Done."

Customizing Calendar

Outlook defaults the workday to 8 a.m. to 5 p.m., Monday through Friday. But, what do you do if your workday is 7 a.m. to 4 p.m.? Or third shift Sunday through Thursday from 11 p.m. to 7 a.m.? You can customize Calendar to define when your workday and work week begins and ends.

To change the workday parameters, choose Tools, Options, Calendar Options.

In the Calendar work week section, click the appropriate days' check boxes to match your work week. You can enter the first day of the week from the drop-down list or directly type the day. You can also designate the first week of the year, just in case you work a fiscal year rather than a calendar year.

Enter the Start times and End times of your day using either the drop-down lists or directly entering the times into each field.

Managing Appointments

In pre-computer days, setting an appointment was fairly straightforward. If you were important enough to need appointments, you most likely had a secretary to handle scheduling for you.

In these technically enlightened times, we still have support personnel to make appointments, but there never seems to be enough of them to go around (support personnel, not appointments; there's always more than enough appointments!). More and more, it's the Average Joes and Josephines who are setting their own appointments and trying to get the work done in the "group mentality," which is so pervasive in Western business.

Sometimes making appointments and tracking dates yourself is a challenge. The old standby of writing it down on a slip of paper is good—until you lose the paper. Desk calendars are better, and day planners even better. Unfortunately, they are all hard to update, especially for recurring meetings. And they can't show much detail or block out time for you. These are just a few of the things that Calendar can easily do for you.

Creating a New Appointment

There is (naturally) more than one way to begin the process of setting an appointment. However, all roads lead to the same place—the Appointment tool.

The easiest way is to click the New Appointment button on the far left side of the standard Calendar toolbar. The menu command is Actions, New Appointment. And, if you like to use shortcut keys, Ctrl+N activates the New Appointment tool.

The Ctrl+N shortcut key access the New Item tool for whatever module of Outlook you are currently in. For instance, if you are in the Inbox, Ctrl+N activates the New Message tool. If you are in Contacts, Ctrl+N activates the New Contact tool.

11

If you are in Outlook, but not in Calendar, and you need to set an appointment, select the Appointment command in the standard toolbar's New Items drop-down box. Figure 11.2 shows the New Item drop-down menu from the Contacts folder. This also displays Ctrl+Shift+A as the shortcut key for activating the New Appointment tool.

If you are not in Outlook and you need to quickly set an appointment, you can do so without opening the Outlook program. When you installed Office 97, you had the option of creating the Office Shortcut Bar. If you created it, then in addition to the buttons that access all your Office 97 modules, the installation also generated a New Appointment button (see Figure 11.3).

FIGURE 11.2.

The New Item drop-down list viewed from the Contact folder.

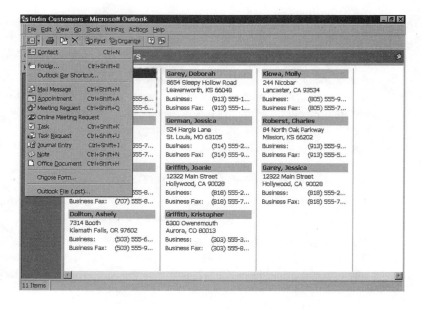

FIGURE 11.3.

You can make a new appointment from the convenient Office 97 Shortcut Bar.

New Appointment

Your startup bar may not look exactly the same as the one in Figure 11.3. It may be longer or wider, and positioned anywhere on the screen. Regardless, the New Appointment button is in the same relative position (unless you have moved it).

A Quick Look at the Appointment Tool

As shown in Figure 11.4, the Appointment Tool screen offers menu commands and tool-bar functions to help you easily set appointments.

Oops: An Error

When you first create a new appointment, you will probably see a warning (located just above the Subject line) that states the appointment occurs in the past. This is because by default, Outlook assumes that the appointment you want to schedule is at 8:00 a.m. on the current date. If the current time is after 8:00 a.m., then the appointment occurs in the past. Don't worry about this error message; you'll learn to fix it shortly. Actually, although this may seem like an extra step, it keeps you from accidentally scheduling appointments in the past.

FIGURE 11.4.

The Appointment Tool screen enables you to enter appointment information.

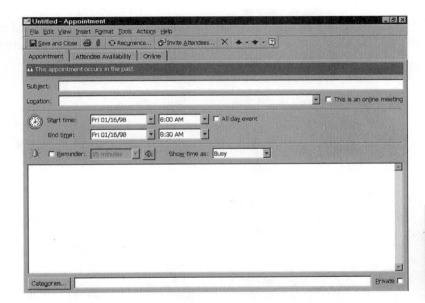

Defining the Meeting Subject

Keep the subject short and to the point. Save detailed explanations for the Note box near the bottom of the Appointment tool.

Entering the Location

If you have a large office building, it is always good to note where meetings and events will be held. This field is especially helpful for off-site events. The nice thing about the Location field is that it is actually a drop-down list box that remembers the last seven locations you have entered into this field. This is great for office appointments, as these tend to occur in the same places.

Entering a location here automatically displays it on the calendar page. This saves time when viewing your calendar and trying to recall where a particular appointment will be held.

Entering Dates

To save you from typing in dates and times, Calendar's drop-down boxes in these fields enable you to use the mouse to set up the appointment's date and time. Click the drop-down arrow next to the date field in the Start time line to see a calendar of the current month. Click any day in the displayed month to choose the day for your appointment. The current date always appears enclosed in a red box. If you want to move to a different month, click the back (left) or forward (right) arrows in the top corners of the calendar. Also, anytime you want to quickly move back to your present position, simply click the Today button on the bottom of the calendar.

You can also type dates in the normal format, for example:

12/12/98

12/12/1998

December 12, 1998

However, to make things even easier, Outlook can also understand many natural date commands. The following are examples of entries that Outlook can translate:

December twelfth	Dec 12	Next Friday
Tue	Tomorrow	Yesterday
Christmas	Christmas next year	Fourth Monday in December
Three weeks ago	90 days	Friday of next week
3 weeks	2 months	4 years

Outlook understands major holidays that occur on the same date each year (such as Christmas), but not variable holidays (such as Easter and Hanukkah).

Setting Times

The Start time drop-down box displays times in one-half hour intervals starting at 8 a.m. By default, Outlook assumes that appointment duration is one-half hour.

Set the appropriate date and start time for the appointment. Generally, you can skip the End Time *date* field (appointments generally last less than one day), and click the drop-down arrow for the End Time field. A list of half-hour intervals is displayed with duration notations next to them. If you know the specific time that your appointment will end, you can click that, or if you just know the duration of the appointment, you can search for the correct duration without mentally calculating the actual end time.

In the next exercise, you set an appointment to surprise one of your office workers, Andy, with a 40th birthday party tomorrow. The party is at 2 p.m. in the cafeteria. You are the person who is responsible for getting Andy there.

To Do: Creating a New Appointment

1. Open Outlook if it isn't already open. Click the Calendar folder in the Outlook Bar.
2. Press Ctrl+N to display the Appointment tool.
3. In the Subject text box, type Andy's Birthday Party.
4. In the Location text box, type Cafeteria.
5. Display the calendar for the Start date and click the next business day.
6. Click 2 p.m. to set the start time. As soon as you finish entering the date and time, notice that in the End Time fields, the end date and end time changes to the same date and a half-hour later than the time in the Start Time fields. This saves steps setting up the end time.
7. If the party is scheduled to last only a half-hour, this appointment's times would now be set. However, Andy and his coworkers are a bit more fun than that, and plan to party about an hour and a half. This party will last 1.5 hours, so click that duration. Outlook displays the end time of 3:30.
8. Your Appointment screen should be similar to the one shown in Figure 11.5. With the subject, location, date and time completed for Andy's party (the minimum amount of information you need to set up an appointment), click the Save and Close button.

> In the Date Navigator, notice that the next business day is now boldfaced. Any day with an appointment is boldfaced.

More Ways to Set Appointments

There are other ways to set your times and to create a new appointment. Instead of using the Appointment tool to set the dates and times, you can use Calendar itself.

- Move to the day and time you wish to set up the appointment by clicking the new date on the Date Navigator.
- Double-click the half-hour block of time in the Daily Appointment Calendar when the appointment will begin.

• The Appointment tool pops up with the correct date and time for a half-hour appointment already entered. Change the duration if necessary.

FIGURE 11.5.

The basic appointment information for Andy's party has been entered.

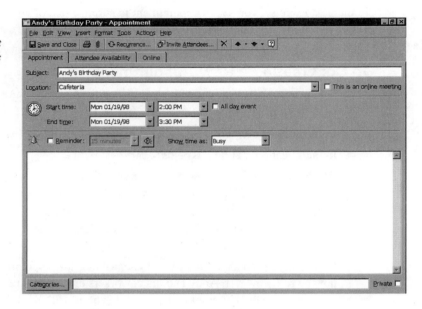

Another method is to select the complete time you want for the duration of the appointment in the Daily Appointment Calendar view. Then, right-click the selected time, and choose New Appointment from the pop-up menu. This fills in the beginning *and* ending time in the New Appointment tool.

If you use the Appointment Tool and enter a subject and location in the Daily Appointment Calendar view, it appears, for example, as "Andy's Birthday Party (Cafeteria)" directly in the Daily panel. If you enter the information in the hourly panel, it looks identical, but when you open the Appointment Tool, you will see that the information is all contained on the Subject line.

Outlook doesn't automatically move the location into the location field, and therefore, you won't be able to sort by location later (if you need to do that).

In the following exercise, you enter several appointments. The dates you enter should be based on today's current date, not the date shown in any figures.

To Do: Creating Appointments Using the Calendar

Enter the following appointments for practice:

- Dr. Appt For Sinuses at Seifert Family Practice on next Thursday at 8–9 a.m. (Hint: type next thu as the date.)
- Sales Staff Meeting in the Executive Conference Room on next Wednesday at 1–4 p.m.
- Conference Call with Tokyo Office in your office on next Thursday at 1–2 p.m.
- Plant Tour in Sri Lanka at the Sri Lanka Plant on next Friday at 10–5 p.m.
- Editing Manuscripts in your office on Wednesday at 3–5 p.m.
- Time Management Seminar at Radisson Hotel, Ballroom A, on next Wednesday at 9 a.m.–Noon.
- Lunch with Barb at Spaghetti Factory on next Wednesday at 11 a.m.–1 p.m.

Editing Appointments

In a perfect world, when you set an appointment, that would be it: no changes and no conflicts. But call it Murphy's Law, entropy, or chaos theory, we all know that unforeseen problems arise. Look at Figure 11.6 for a case in point.

FIGURE 11.6.

This day has some scheduling conflicts.

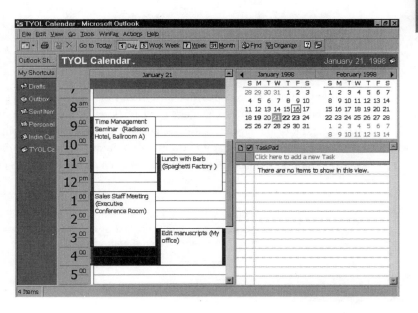

This schedule, which easily could have been created over a number of different days, has some conflicts that need to be resolved. If the creator had been paying attention as these appointments were made, this might not have happened. When an appointment is created, Calendar warns you when the appointment conflicts with another or when it is immediately adjacent to another (see Figure 11.7).

FIGURE 11.7.

Conflicting appointments generate this warning message.

Conflict warning message

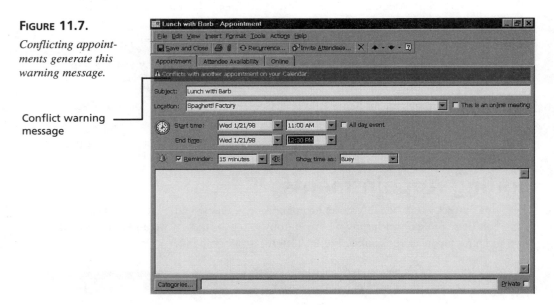

Selecting Appointments

To do any editing to an appointment, it must first be selected. To select an appointment in the Daily Appointment Calendar view, click it. Three sides are outlined in blue. The move handle is the bar that always appears at the left of the appointment item. Thinner blue bars appear at the top and bottom of the item. These can be dragged to change the start or ending time of the appointment. To open an appointment, double-click it.

Once you've selected an appointment, you won't be able to double-click to open it unless you deselect it first or double-click the move handle. An alternative way to open a selected appointment is to press the Enter key.

You can select and open more than one item at a time. For items that are consecutive, click the first item, press Shift, and click the last item with the mouse. To select nonconsecutive items, click the first, press Ctrl, and click each of the other items you want opened.

When all items are selected, right-click the mouse, and choose Open Selected Items from the pop-up menu. One appointment is displayed, but all are open and can be viewed. To view another appointment, click the Next Item or Previous Item buttons in the right portion of the Appointment toolbar. The open appointments are also displayed in the Task Bar at the bottom of the screen, or you can use the keyboard shortcut Alt+Tab to move among open appointments.

Changing Appointment Start and End Times

An appointment's beginning or ending time can be changed by opening the item and changing the time in the Start time and End time boxes. An easier way is to select the item and drag the top or bottom boundary to the new starting (top boundary) or ending (bottom boundary) time.

Although the item is *not* selected, just point anywhere inside the item, and drag and drop the item on the new time block. If the item is already selected, you can do the same thing by "grabbing" the small move handle located between the appointment text and the appointment time, and dragging and dropping at the new time.

11

Changing Appointment Dates

Date conflicts cannot be resolved quite as easily as time conflicts, although they really aren't difficult either. In the example shown in Figure 11.7, the seminar is mandatory, and Barb cannot change her lunch time. She can, however, have lunch at the same time on Thursday. You could simply double-click the item (or the item's move handle if it is already selected) to open the Appointment tool and type in the new date.

However, there is an easier way to do this. Click the move handle on the item to be changed (remember, the move handle is the thicker blue line along the left edge of the item). Drag the item onto the correct date in the Date Navigator (above the TaskPad).

The item is automatically moved from the current date to the new date. All other information, including time and location, remains unchanged.

Changing the Subject

During the course of rechecking the schedule shown in Figure 11.7, you become aware of another error: the teleconference call is to London, not Tokyo. This is good to know because you have to consult a completely different set of notes for the London meeting. Subjects can be changed by using one of the following methods.

- Double-click the item (or the item's move handle if it's already selected) to open its Appointment tool and change the subject.
- Change the subject by clicking once on the appointment item. All but the subject information disappears, which enables you to directly edit the item. As soon as any other part of the screen is clicked, the new information is saved.

Moving to a New Location

As you have seen, when a location is initially added to an appointment, it is displayed in the Daily Appointment Calendar view in parentheses, directly following the Subject. If you click the item in the Daily Appointment Calendar view, the location disappears. It cannot be edited there. If you find an error in the location, there is only one method to change the location of an appointment: You must open the item and change the location in the Location text box.

In the following exercise, you have an opportunity to make changes to the schedule created in the previous exercise. Although you will only practice one way to make the changes, you might want to practice making changes to other items using different methods you learned earlier in this hour.

To Do: Fixing Scheduling Errors

1. Click the date that contains the conflicts. (It should be the next Wednesday on your calendar.)
2. The 3–5 p.m. block of time spent in the office editing manuscripts can be adjusted because it is your time to work alone. Drag and drop the item on 4–6 p.m.
3. Save and close the item.
4. Drag the Lunch with Barb item (using the Move handle) to the following day. It should disappear. The view automatically switches to the next day. Click the previous day.

▼   5. Change the location of the Time Management Seminar by double-clicking the item to open it, and changing the location to `Ballroom C`. Save and close the item.

   6. To cancel the Sales Staff Meeting, right-click it to open the pop-up menu. Click Delete.

   7. Click the date to which you moved the lunch with Barb. Notice that the conference call is adjacent to the lunch date. Click the lunch date item to select it. Drag the bottom border up, so the lunch is from 11:00 a.m.–12:30 p.m.

   8. Open the conference call item. Change the location to `Jenny's office`. Change the Subject to `Conference Call with London office`.

   9. Save and close the item. You should be in the Daily Appointment Calendar view.

   10. Change to Wednesday. Drag from 1:00–2:30 p.m. Type `Executive Staff Meeting`. As soon as you type the first letter, Outlook displays its editing mode.

   11. Click any open area to deselect the item. Double-click the Executive Staff Meeting item. Notice there is no location. Add Executive Conference Room as the location by clicking the pick list (located at the right edge of the Location text box). Save and close the item.

   12. As shown in Figure 11.8, you have worked out your Wednesday schedule so that it no longer contains conflicts.

11

FIGURE 11.8.

Now the conflicts are resolved, and there is a little breathing room between appointments.

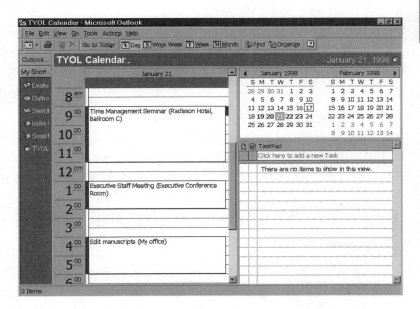

▲

Deleting an Appointment

If you decide that you do not have to go to your doctor's appointment because you are feeling much better, you can delete the appointment. (Just make sure you call the doctor's office to actually cancel the appointment.) You can delete an appointment in one of several ways:

- Double-click the item's move handle to open its Appointment tool. Click the Delete button on the Appointment's toolbar.
- From the Daily Appointment Calendar view, single-click the item and then click the Delete button on the Calendar toolbar.
- From the Daily Appointment Calendar view, single-click the item, and then press the Delete button on the keyboard.
- From the Daily Appointment Calendar view, single-click the item, right-click, and choose Delete.

Handling Events

Outlook refers to any appointment that lasts 24 or more hours as an *event*. Scheduling events is much the same as handling appointments. In fact, the procedures are virtually identical, except for one thing.

In the Appointment tool just to the right of the Start Time and End Time fields, you see the All Day Event check box. When this is checked, the start and end times disappear because the event now stretches over the entire day. Display the date for your Sri Lanka tour. Click the item and change this to an all day event by putting a check mark next to All Day Event. The time shows as Free, which is the default. Change it to Out of Office. Click the Save and Close button.

Figure 11.9 shows how an event looks in the Daily Appointment Calendar. Notice that the event is displayed as a fixed banner at the top of the Daily Appointment Calendar. To edit, move, or delete an event, use the same techniques used for appointments.

Déjà Vu All Over Again: Recurring Items and Events

Often you will find that certain events occur over and over again, such as that pesky Friday afternoon team meeting or the quarterly staff meeting. If your events have a specific pattern (the second Thursday of the month, for example), you can make them recurring.

FIGURE 11.9.

An event is not scheduled for a specific time.

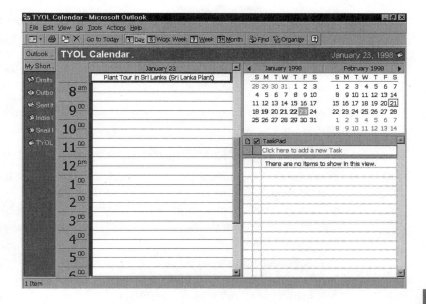

The Appointment Recurrence dialog box, as shown in Figure 11.10, is displayed by choosing Actions, New Recurring Appointment. If you selected the starting date and time in the Daily Appointment Calendar view before opening the dialog box, the start date and start and end times are already inserted.

FIGURE 11.10.

The Appointment Recurrence dialog box enables you to schedule regular items, such as weekly meetings.

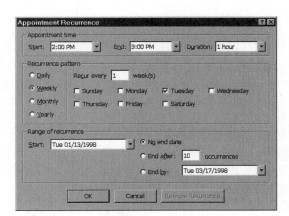

You can choose to have the appointment recur daily, weekly, monthly, or yearly. You can set the Recur Every text box to define the frequency of the appointment. You can select the day of the week the appointment is to occur.

In the lower area, you can specify the start date, and whether or not there are a specific number of meetings before the item ends (for example, in the case of a six-week class). If the appointment recurs indefinitely, then choose the No End Date option button. If a specific number of recurrences is known, this value can be entered in the End After: <X> Occurrences field. If a specific end date is known, enter this value in the End By field.

In the following exercise, you learn one way to create a new recurring appointment in Calendar.

To Do: Creating a New Recurring Appointment

1. In the Daily Appointment Calendar view, highlight the time for your recurring appointment. Click the *next* Tuesday in the Date Navigator. Highlight 2:00–3:00 p.m. in the Daily Appointment Calendar view. Choose Actions, New Recurring Appointment to open the Appointment tool, along with the Appointment Recurrence dialog box.

2. The Appointment time section is at the top of the dialog box. You can set the beginning and ending times for the recurring appointment, just as you would a regular appointment. Because you highlighted the time on the calendar before opening the Appointment Recurrence dialog box, the time is already entered.

3. Make sure that Weekly and Tuesday are chosen and 1 is entered in the Recur Every 1 Week(s) box.

4. At the bottom of the dialog box in the Range of Recurrence panel, the Start date defaults to the date you first entered for this appointment. No End Date is the default.

5. When finished, click OK and you are returned to the Appointment tool.

6. Fill in the subject (Staff Meeting), location (Conference Room), and any other items, just as you would for a regular appointment. When finished, click Save and Close.

Adding Holidays and Other Recurring Events

When entering a recurring event, the steps are almost identical to entering a recurring appointment. The only difference is that you need to click the All Day Event check box before you Save and Close.

Holidays are one form of recurring event. Adding them to your Calendar is a snap.

To Do: Adding Holidays

1. Choose Tools, Options, Calendar Options to display the Calendar Options dialog box.

2. Click the Add Holidays button. The Add Holidays to Calendar dialog box appears (see Figure 11.11).

FIGURE 11.11.

The Add Holidays to Calendar dialog box makes it easy to keep track of a wide variety of holidays.

3. Locate the United States and place a check mark next to it. (It is probably already checked.) You may want to add other countries or holiday sets. Click OK. Calendar imports all the holidays for the countries you select.

> If you do business with companies in other countries, make sure to add their holiday sets to your calendar.

4. Click OK to exit Calendar Options and OK again to exit Options and return to the Daily Appointment Calendar view. ▲

Making an Existing Appointment or Event Recur

Once in a while, the need arises to make an appointment repeat indefinitely or for a number of consecutive days. Remember your appointment in Sri Lanka? Well, unless you are a visitor from another planet, there's no way you can get there and back in one day. So, let's repeat the all-day event and stretch out your travel time. This technique works for any appointment.

11

To Do: Making an Existing Appointment Recur

1. Open the Appointment tool for the Sri Lanka trip on Friday by double-clicking the event item's move handle.
2. In the Standard toolbar, click the Recurrence button (the one with two arrows in a circle). This opens the Appointment Recurrence dialog box.
3. Click the Daily Recurrence pattern option button and then the Every 1 Day(s) option button.
4. In the Range of Recurrence section, set the End By date to be one week after your departure date. The settings should be similar to those in Figure 11.12.

FIGURE 11.12.

It's easy to make a scheduled item recur.

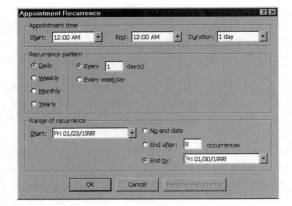

5. Click OK to close the Appointment Recurrence dialog box; then click Save and Close.
6. Click the other days you will be gone. Each is now blocked out as a recurring event.

Editing a Recurring Item

Editing a recurring item is much the same as editing any item in Calendar. But when you first double-click the item's move handle in the Daily Appointment Calendar view, Calendar displays an exclamation dialog box, asking you if you want to edit the entire series or just that item (see Figure 11.13). Use caution here because if you only want to edit one occurrence of the appointment, you could inadvertently change the entire series' information.

FIGURE 11.13.

The Open Recurring Item warning box.

Proceed to edit the item or series as you normally would edit a single item. Entering the occurrence results in a change being made only to that specific item. If you edit the series, changes made are applied to every single occurrence of the appointment or event.

Removing a Recurring Item

When an appointment that was supposed to repeat changes to a one-time-only event, Calendar gives you a way to make this change. Double-click the single appointment you wish to keep. Choose the Open the Series option button and click OK. Click the Recurrence button once more to open the Appointment Recurrence dialog box. The Remove Recurrence button is displayed. If you click this, all other occurrences of this series except the date currently showing will be removed.

> Be careful when removing an occurrence; there is no undo command for this action.

Deleting All Occurrences of a Recurring Item

If you want to get rid of all or one occurrence of a recurring series, do the following:

- Double-click the item's move handle, open its Appointment tool, and click the Delete button on the Appointment's toolbar. Choose to Delete All Occurrences or Delete This One.
- Click the item and then click the Delete button on the Calendar toolbar. Choose to Delete All Occurrences or Delete This One.

Summary

By now, you should be able to see just how easy it is to set and edit appointments and events. Recurring appointments and events, the bane of anyone with a non-electronic day planner, are simple to create and manage as well.

Calendar also gives you the ability to set up meetings. As you'll see in Hour 12, "Power Calendaring," Calendar can let you view schedules for other people on your network, choose the best time for everyone to meet, and even invite the attendees to the meeting using Outlook's messaging tools.

Q&A

Q When entering a date and time, how specific do I have to be?

A When selecting the start and end times for appointments, Outlook offers you a function called AutoDate. If you type in text, such as "next Friday" or "noon," Outlook is smart enough to know what it means and will create your appointment correctly.

Q If there is a personal holiday (such as a religious holiday that isn't included), can I add it?

A Not as an actual holiday, but you can use the recurring event to identify the holiday. You can also enter your vacation time in the same manner.

Q When my calendar is placed on the network, others have access to it. There are some items I do not want anyone to be able to see. How can I do that?

A At the bottom of the Appointment Tool dialog box is a small check box marked Private. Place a check mark in that box to keep others on the network from viewing that item.

Q Exactly what is the difference between an appointment and a meeting?

A In this hour, you only worked with appointments. These are items that don't require an invitation. In Hour 12, you'll take a look at meetings, and learn to issue invitations and track the acceptance or denial of the request.

Q What happens if I have an appointment scheduled and I need to put something else in that time slot?

A Obviously you can't be in two places at the same time, so you must move or cancel one of them. If you are moving or canceling a single appointment, drag it to the new position, or select it and delete it, as described earlier in this hour. If you want to change a recurring appointment, open it and tell Outlook you want to edit only the single occurrence. Then, move it by changing the time and date, or delete it altogether.

Hour **12**

Power Calendaring

When people meet, they share ideas, someone doesn't get it, and the process starts over again. Of course, some meeting topics do take hold. If they didn't, we'd still be hanging out in caves.

It is that glimmer of hope that keeps the business world always coming back for more. Today, meetings occur in record numbers. No one wants to make any decisions by themselves. Businesses find group contributions valuable, and like to build consensus for important decisions. You can actually get a job as a meeting coordinator whose work description includes arranging meetings, setting up the rooms, getting any audio-visual equipment ready, and ordering the bagels.

In most offices, however, there may not be a big enough budget or large enough staff to employ a full-time meeting coordinator, so you have to make do on your own. Calendar can give you a lot of help with meetings, from initial scheduling to inviting the attendees. Calendar can even help you make sure there's an available room.

In this hour, you learn to set meetings, both with and without Exchange Server. After you understand the meeting process, you'll learn more advanced Calendar manipulation: how to view and print the calendar.

The Virtues of Exchange Server and Microsoft Mail

> This hour is based on the requirement that your office or organization has networked email, such as Microsoft Mail, Microsoft Exchange, or cc: Mail, which is configured to work with Outlook. If it does not, the Meeting Planner functions simply will not work, and you'll be forced to contact people the old-fashioned way—either personal contact or by phone.

Many of the group capabilities in Outlook, including the Meeting Planner, can be taken advantage of only if *every* user is connected to a server using Microsoft Exchange Server or are using Microsoft Mail to send and receive mail over a network.

In this hour, however, we discuss the ins and outs of setting up a meeting with *and* without the capabilities of Exchange Server or MS Mail. So if you are connected to a Banyan or Novell network or are simply using Outlook to schedule a meeting via Internet mail, don't panic. The process is, however, much simpler and enables you to take advantage of the goodies if you have Exchange Server or Mail, so if your office doesn't have it yet, go pester your Information Technology (IT) person.

With that in mind, suppose that you need to meet with some coworkers to discuss a new training program for your staff. To do this, you'll learn to use Calendar to set up a meeting.

To Do: Setting a Meeting with Exchange Server or MS Mail

1. Open Outlook. Click the Calendar icon in the Outlook Bar.
2. In the Calendar view, click the date in the Date Navigator for which you want to schedule your meeting.
3. Choose Actions, Plan a Meeting to display the Plan a Meeting dialog box, as shown in Figure 12.1. It reflects your personal schedule for the day you have selected and blocks those times when you have appointments scheduled.
4. Invite the other people to your meeting by clicking the Invite Others button. The Select Attendees and Resources dialog box is displayed, as shown in Figure 12.2. Because you are setting up the meeting, your name is already displayed in the Required field.

▼ **FIGURE 12.1.**

The Plan a Meeting dialog box shows your schedule as a grid to help you avoid conflicts.

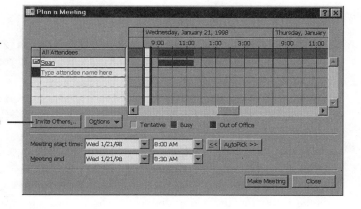

Invite Others button ——→

 Most of the time, a meeting involves a number of people who have very different schedules. Unfortunately, there may be no one time that every person can attend. With this in mind, the Calendar enables you to designate the Attendees as Required or Optional so that you can make certain you select a time that is convenient to all the essential participants.

FIGURE 12.2.

Use the Select Attendees and Resources dialog box to organize your meeting.

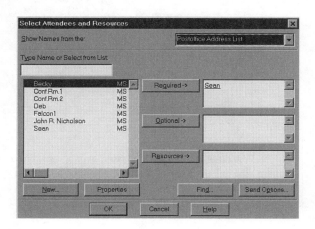

12

5. You can also place more people in the Required or Optional fields by typing each name and then clicking either the Required or Optional button. When you are connected to the Exchange Server, a drop-down list of all others on your network, sometimes called the *Global Address List,* is displayed. You can click the desired name instead of typing it in the text box.

▼

▼   6. Additionally, if Exchange Server or MS Mail is configured to enable you to choose resources, such as conference rooms, you will see these resources listed in the Global Address List in Exchange or the Post Office Address List in MS Mail. To choose one of these resources, select it and place it in the Resources box.

7. After you have selected all the desired people and added them to either the Required or Optional field text box, click OK to return to the Plan a Meeting dialog box.

Click the AutoPick button, and Calendar will select the first available start time (10 a.m.). The half-hour default interval is probably not enough time for you to cover all the new training options, so enter 11 a.m. in the End Time field. (You can also click the vertical red End Time bar and simply drag it to the right until it is even with the 11:00 time line.) Your dialog box should look similar to the one shown in Figure 12.3.

FIGURE **12.3.**

The Plan a Meeting dialog box shows the attendees' schedules.

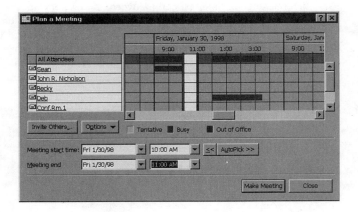

   If the first time automatically chosen isn't acceptable to you, click AutoPick again and get the next available time. Keep AutoPicking until you find an acceptable time.

8. You need to invite each person by sending an invitation. Click the Make Meeting button to display a modified Appointment tool with your attendees listed in the To: field. As shown in Figure 12.4, the Save and Close button has now been replaced

▼   with a Send button.

FIGURE 12.4.

The modified Appointment tool enables you to send meeting invitations.

Send button —

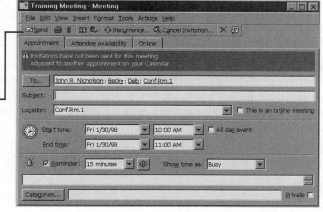

9. Type `Training Meeting` in the Subject text box. Type `Conference Room 1` in the Location text box. After you have filled in the pertinent information, click the Send button. This automatically notifies your colleagues that you are requesting a meeting.

Creating a New Meeting Request

As with most Microsoft applications, Outlook 98 gives you several options for setting a meeting. Instead of creating the meeting and setting up everything, you can also make a request for input from the people you invited regarding the meeting.

To display the Meeting Appointment tool, choose Actions, New Meeting Request (or press Ctrl+Shift+Q). The Appointment tab is displayed by default.

The same basic steps you used in the previous exercise are followed here to create the meeting, except instead of using the Plan a Meeting dialog box, you use the tools on the Attendee Availability tab (which are identical).

Setting the Meeting

Setting a meeting without using Exchange or MS Mail is also possible. However, because Calendar can't see the other attendees' schedules, you have more difficulty setting a time that is convenient to all because you do not know when the others are free.

12

To Do: Setting the Meeting Without Exchange Server or MS Mail

1. Display the Plan a Meeting dialog box by choosing Actio<u>n</u>s, <u>P</u>lan a Meeting. Add the desired names to the attendees list.

2. This time, when you click Invite Others, you see that all the people in the Select Attendees and Resources dialog box now have (email) after them. This is because without Exchange, the only way Outlook can contact these people is through email.

3. After you have finished inviting the other potential attendees, you will notice that the Plan a Meeting dialog box will not show you the available times of the other invitees (see Figure 12.5). Therefore, you will have to pick the meeting time based only on your schedule. As you can see, this tool is of limited value without Exchange Server.

FIGURE 12.5.

Choosing a time without Exchange Server is a chancy proposition.

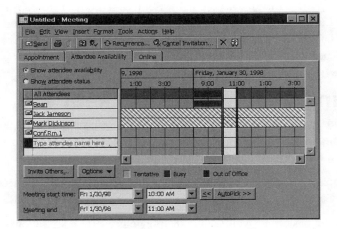

4. Without Exchange, even though you are still using the old-fashioned method of throwing the party and hoping everyone will come, using Calendar still saves you the hassle of contacting each person to confirm a time, then calling again if someone finds the time unworkable. With Calendar, you can email everyone at once, and if there are any conflicts, you can make a change and resend the meeting request to all the attendees. Nonetheless, using the Meeting Planner addresses everyone for you and then updates your schedule, thus saving you steps.

▼   5. With the hope that 10 a.m. to 11 a.m. on Thursday will work for everyone, click
       Make Meeting. The Appointment tool is displayed. Fill in the subject of the meet-
       ing and location information and, in the Note box, write a note requesting atten-
       dance. Click Send.

> When Exchange sends a meeting request that the recipient accepts, Outlook
> automatically sets a new appointment in that person's Calendar. However,
> when one of the attendees does not use Outlook for email, you won't have
> the automatic response/scheduling capabilities.

▲

Changing the Meeting

Even when using Calendar and Exchange to organize your meeting, sometimes circum-
stances dictate change. Perhaps someone was inadvertently left off the guest list or the
conference room was flooded or the CEO suddenly announced that he will be at your site
that particular day or one of the recipients hates cream cheese. (The list of possibilities is
endless.) Here you learn how to adjust a meeting that you have scheduled.

To Do: Changing a Meeting

1. From your daily calendar, double-click the meeting item's move handle (the box
   surrounding the appointment) to open the Appointment tool so you can change
   information for a meeting.

2. After making your modifications, click the Save and Close button. Outlook
   prompts you to send the changes to the other invitees.

3. Sometimes you may discover that more (or fewer) people need to be invited to a
   meeting, or that your resource needs have changed because you need a larger meeting room.

   To make these adjustments, open the meeting item by double-clicking its move
   handle.

4. Click the Attendee Availability tab.

5. Click the Invite Others button. After selecting additional attendees or removing
   them, click OK.

6. Change the meeting location by clicking on the Appointment tab and making the
   changes to the Location field.

▲   7. Click the Send Update button to be sure everyone is aware of the changes.

Canceling the Meeting

If you want to cancel a meeting, open the meeting item and then choose Acti<u>o</u>ns, <u>C</u>ancel Meeting. Before you close the window, be sure to click the <u>S</u>end button so that the attendees are notified that the meeting has been canceled.

> Outlook does *not* prompt you to send notices of cancellation if you cancel a meeting. You must remember to send them.

Creating a Meeting from an Appointment

When you have an appointment scheduled for which you really need to include other associates, Calendar can easily set this as a meeting from the appointment. Open the appointment by double-clicking it and selecting the Attendee Availability tab. Follow the steps in the preceding exercise to set up the meeting time and to invite attendees. After you invite your first attendee, you will notice that the <u>S</u>ave and Close button changes to the <u>S</u>end button on the toolbar. After you have listed all personnel, you can click the <u>S</u>end button and notify everyone.

Creating a Meeting from a Contact

Outlook's AutoCreate feature also enables you to create a meeting from a Contact listing. There are two ways to begin this action:

- Open a Contact item, and choose Acti<u>o</u>ns, New Meeting with Contact (see Figure 12.6).

> You can accomplish the same thing *without* opening the contact if you select the contact in the Address Cards view and take the same steps.

- In Contacts, drag-and-drop a contact item onto the Calendar icon in the Outlook Bar or the Calendar folder in the Folder list. This immediately opens an Appointment tool with the contact already listed as an attendee. Add other names, set times, and send the meeting request just as you would for any other meeting.

FIGURE 12.6.

You can create a meeting from a contact listing.

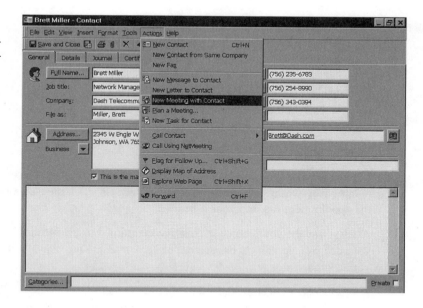

Creating a Recurring Meeting

Any meetings that you have on a regular basis at the same time on the same day of the week or month are called *recurring* meetings. For instance, the staff meeting every Friday from 9–11 a.m. is a recurring meeting. Outlook can schedule each one of these meetings in one action so that you don't have to schedule them individually.

To Do: Creating a Recurring Meeting

1. From the Calendar view, choose Actions, New Recurring Meeting. An Appointment tool appears, quickly covered up by the Appointment Recurrence dialog box.

2. Using the techniques for setting recurring appointments from Hour 11, "Time Is on My Side: The Calendar Feature," set the recurrence pattern for this meeting. Click OK when finished.

3. Fill in all pertinent information in the Appointment and Attendee Availability tabs. Click Send.

If you want to make an existing meeting recurrent, perform the following steps:

1. Open the meeting item by double-clicking its move handle.

2. Click either the Recurrence button on the toolbar or choose Actions, Recurrence. Complete the necessary fields in the Appointment Recurrence dialog box.

12

▲ To Do

▼

▼   3. Click the Send Updates to Attendees button before you click the Close button to be
      sure everyone is aware of the changes. If there are already other people invited to
▲   your meeting, the Send Update button is displayed.

Getting Meeting Requests

By now you should be a real pro at creating meetings. But what do you do if you're on
the receiving end of one of those meeting requests?

Meeting requests are received as messages in your Inbox.

Like many choices in life, you have the option of saying yes (Accept), no (Decline), or
being wishy-washy (Tentative). Before you decide, click the Calendar button to see how
the appointment fits into your schedule.

After you make your choice, a message is returned to the meeting's organizer stating
your decision. If you choose Accept or Tentative, the meeting is automatically added to
your calendar.

If you receive a meeting cancellation notice, as shown in Figure 12.7, click the Remove
from Calendar button to remove the meeting from your schedule and acknowledge the
message's receipt to the meeting organizer, both with one mouse click.

FIGURE 12.7.

A cancellation notifi-
cation is received like
a meeting request.

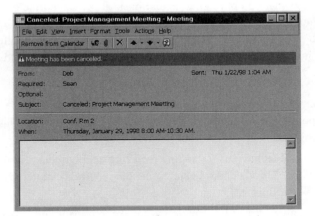

Automated Processing of Meeting Requests

There is a way to automatically process cancellation and meeting requests. Choose
Tools, Options, and select the Preferences tab. Click the Calendar Options button and the
Resource Scheduling button. Choose one or more of the following options as needed:

- If you are an easy-going individual and would like to automatically accept all non-conflicting meeting requests and automatically remove any canceled meetings from your schedule, check the Automatically Accept <u>M</u>eeting Requests and Process Cancellations check box.

- If you hate conflict and decisions, and don't even want to know about conflicting requests, click the Automatically Decline <u>C</u>onflicting Meeting Requests check box.

- If you hate repetition (and redundancy), click the Automatically Decline <u>R</u>ecurring Meeting Request check box.

Allowing Others to Access Your Calendar

Why would you allow other people to have access to your calendar? Because they'll know whether or not you really do have an appointment at the same time they want you to attend their meeting, and you won't be able to bow out gracefully with a little white lie about a conflicting meeting. However, giving colleagues access to your calendar also means they don't have to call you every time they need to set up a meeting. You have to balance privacy with convenience to make this decision regarding the accessibility of your schedule to others in your office.

Your administrative assistant should always have access to your calendar so that your life can be properly scheduled and you can be located in meetings in case of an emergency.

To control how much of your calendar is published for viewing by others, select <u>T</u>ools, Options and choose the Preferences tab. Click the <u>C</u>alendar Options button and click the Free/Busy Options button. In the Free/Busy Options dialog box, as shown in Figure 12.8, you can set the number of months between zero (to publish none of your calendar on the network) and twelve (to publish the entire year).

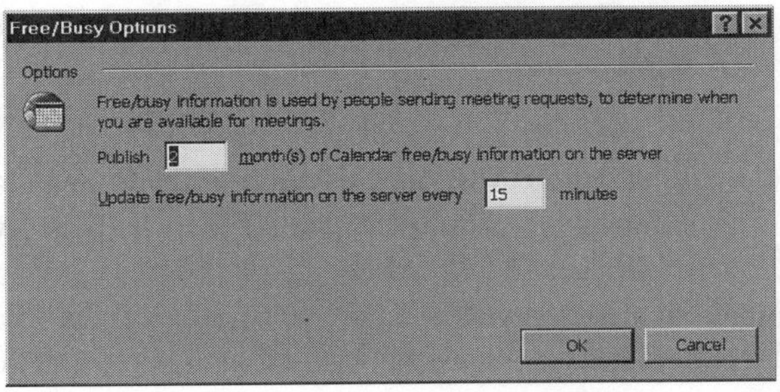

12

FIGURE 12.8.

You can restrict how much of your calendar is made available to others.

By default, even though you give permission for others to view your calendar on the network, they don't have permission to make any changes to it. If you have an administrative assistant who needs to make changes, you may want to give that person permission to change your calendar (or answer your email). You cannot do this for a personal folder file (.PST) stored on your hard drive. The folder must be stored on the server, and the server must be running Microsoft Exchange Server. For additional help with this feature, see the online help topic "About Delegate Access." This offers a full explanation of Delegate services, adding them, and setting the permissions.

Setting a Reminder

When you create an appointment, you can also have Outlook remind you on the day of the appointment, an hour before, or just about any time you would like. When it's time to remind you of your appointment, Outlook flashes a message on your screen and plays a sound if your system has sound capability.

> Do you have a certain time of day you would like to be reminded about appointments? Maybe you'd like to see your reminders when you first get into the office, or when you get back from lunch. You can set the default reminder duration in Calendar by choosing the Tools, Options command. In the Default Reminder field in the Appointment defaults section, use the drop-down list to set your preferred Reminder time (not the physical time for the reminder, but the number of minutes, hours, or days of advance warning you want).

To Do: Setting a Reminder

1. In the Calendar view, open an existing appointment by double-clicking the Move frame of the appointment.

2. Click the Reminder check box. The default time displayed should be 15 minutes.

3. Click the Sound button. This opens the Reminder Sound dialog box (see Figure 12.9). This contains the path to the sound file (usually in .WAV format) that will activate when the Reminder time begins. This can be any sound you like, from a bell ringing to a Tarzan yell or a baby crying. Windows 95 and Office 97 have default sounds, such as Reminder.wav, but you have to get the silly ones from an outside source, such as the Internet. If you're in an office (particularly one with cubicles), try to choose a sound that is not too obnoxious.

▼ **FIGURE 12.9.**

The Reminder Sound dialog box enables you to determine the sound that Outlook uses to remind you of appointments.

For a really good index to sound sites on the Web, try surfing to this site:

`http://www.yahoo.com/Computers_and_Internet/Multimedia/Sound`
`/Archives/WAV/`

4. Click the Browse button to find a sound for your reminder. (There are normally many options if you go to C:\Windows\Media). I've chosen the Jungle Exclamation.wav file.

The Jungle Exclamation.wav file may not be available to you. This is part of the Plus kit add-on. If it isn't available, choose one you like.

5. Click Open. This takes you back to the Reminder Sound dialog box.

6. Make sure the Play This Sound check box is checked, and click OK.

▲ 7. Click Save and Close.

12

When you set up a Reminder, a dialog box similar to the one shown in Figure 12.10 appears at the appropriate time. (If you are using Office Assistant, a dialog balloon with the same information appears.) There are three buttons in this dialog box that you can use to either dismiss the reminder, snooze the reminder, or open the appointment information.

FIGURE 12.10.

The Reminder dialog box contains a drop-down list for postponing the selected time.

The Dismiss button dismisses the Reminder so it never appears again. Use this only when you are sure that you won't forget the appointment because after you dismiss a Reminder, it won't appear again.

The Snooze button turns the Reminder off temporarily, to return at a later time. The drop-down list opens to show some of the available choices for delay times. The default is 5 minutes. Choose a time shorter than the amount of time left to the actual appointment so that another Reminder will go off before the appointment.

The Open Item button opens the Appointment box to show all the information associated with the item. This is a great way to scan the list of attendees or see the topic of the meeting. The specific appointment Date and Time appears in the title bar.

Rating and Hiding an Appointment

Next to the Reminder settings in the Appointment screen is a field labeled Show Time As. This field is a drop-down list box with four choices: Free, Tentative, Busy, and Out of Office. Your selecting one enables anyone with access to your schedule to see when you are available. This is handy when someone is setting up a meeting and wants you to attend. If your appointment is tentative or is something that can be interrupted and is marked Free, then the meeting organizer will be able to count on you as a potential attendee.

Each one of these choices is graphically shown in the daily calendar by color-coded status bars that surround the items. Busy time is marked by dark blue, tentative appointments by light blue, free time by white, and out of the office by purple.

One other field in the Appointment tool is used to set your availability and keep your privacy: The Private check box in the lower-right corner of the toolbox makes an appointment's contents invisible to those looking at your schedule. The time, however, is still blocked off, so people will know you are busy doing something even if they don't know what it is. This is a great way to look busy even though your appointment is actually a tee time (or tea time, depending on your desired level of activity).

In the next exercise, you'll learn to set privacy. In this example, you don't want Andy, your coworker, to know that a surprise birthday party is being held at 2 p.m., so you mark it as private.

To Do: Gaining Some Privacy

1. Open the appointment created for Andy's birthday party in Hour 11.
2. In the lower-right corner, click the check box next to Private.
3. Click Save to prevent the network from publishing this appointment.

Looking at Calendar a Whole New Way

There are seven different views packaged with Calendar. You can change them by adding or subtracting the amount of information displayed, removing the view altogether, or creating your own view from scratch. We will look at the most common views in this hour.

Daily/Weekly/Monthly

The first three views are grouped into one category, the Daily/Weekly/Monthly (D/W/M) view set.

So far, all the work we have done in Calendar has been completed in the Daily view. There are, however, two variations of the Daily view we haven't seen: the addition of time zone information and reformatting of the time intervals.

Just to the left of the daily calendar box are time intervals. Calendar defaults these intervals to 30 minutes. However, when you right-click anywhere in the time interval area, a pop-up menu appears that enables you to set the intervals anywhere from 5 to 60 minutes (see Figure 12.11).

FIGURE 12.11.

You can reset your time intervals.

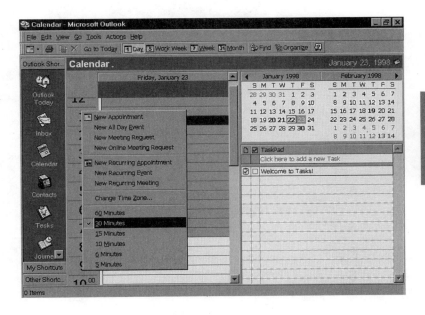

Changing or adding time zone information is a little more involved. By default, Calendar displays times based on the time zone specified when you first installed Windows 95.

Suppose, however, that your office is in New York and there is a branch office in London that you contact daily. It would be handy to be able to see two time zones on your calendar to ease the scheduling of teleconference meetings that fit the hours of both locations.

To Do: Working with Time Zones

1. Choose Tools, Options, Calendar. Next click the Time Zone button. The Time Zone dialog box appears, as shown in Figure 12.12.

FIGURE 12.12.

You can configure time zones in the Time Zone dialog box.

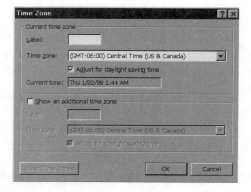

2. Open the Time Zone drop-down box by clicking the arrow to the right of the Time Zone field. Your time zone should already be highlighted and correct.

3. Click the Show Additional Time Zone check box. Before you click it, everything is a lighter shade of gray and cannot be selected.

4. Type London Office in the Label field.

5. In the Time Zone drop-down box, choose London's time zone, which is (GMT) Greenwich mean time.

6. Click OK. When your daily calendar is displayed, you have two time displays on the left side, similar to those shown in Figure 12.13.

A quicker way to access the Time Zone dialog box is to right-click anywhere in the Time interval area and click Change Time Zone.

FIGURE 12.13.

Now you can be sure that meetings don't intrude on tea time.

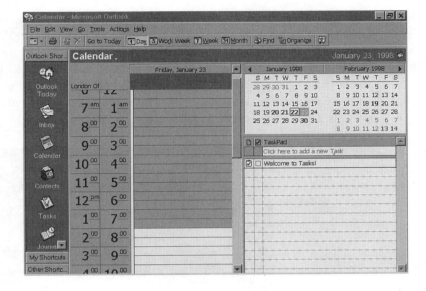

A Different View

Outlook 98 has added a view to its Daily/Weekly/Monthly view. The new view is called Work Week. This view can be selected by choosing View, Work Week. As shown in Figure 12.14, the work week view shows only the days that you have set up as your official work week.

FIGURE 12.14.

You can configure the Work Week view in Calendar to conform to your work schedule.

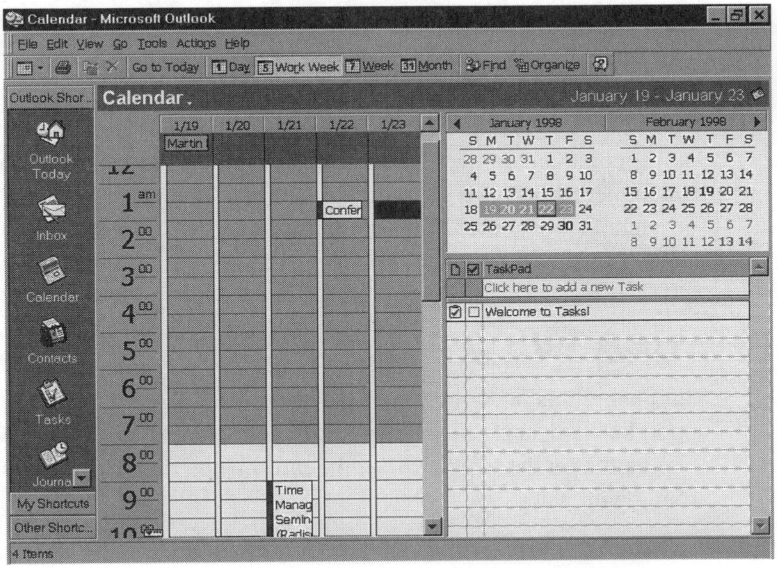

12

The next view in the D/W/M set is the <u>W</u>eek view. By clicking the Week button in the toolbar or selecting <u>V</u>iew, <u>W</u>eek, you can see the entire week instead of a single day. Notice in Figure 12.15, however, that the Folder Area (also called the Calendar Page) on the left-hand side of the screen is the only part that changes. The toolbar, the TaskPad, and Date Navigator remain the same. The daily calendar has been replaced with the weekly calendar. Each appointment is still marked by times and reminder and privacy symbols, but the color-coded appointment status bars are missing.

FIGURE 12.15.

The Week view helps you plan your week.

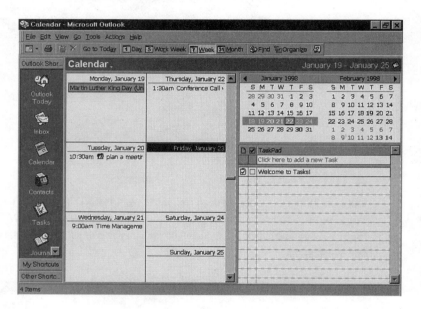

When you select the Month view, the Calendar page gets a more dramatic makeover, as shown in Figure 12.16. Now, only the current month is visible and only the subject of each appointment or event is shown. No times, locations, or symbols are used. If the appointment labels don't fit entirely within a single day's cell, a tiny yellow arrow/ellipsis symbol (shown in the margin) is used to indicate a continuation of the day's appointments. Clicking this symbol returns you to the Daily view for that day.

Printing What You've Got

Throughout this hour you may have been wondering how you can keep track of your appointments when you are away from your computer. At any point, you can click the Print button on the toolbar to get the information down on paper so that you can carry it around with you.

FIGURE 12.16.

The Monthly view displays an entire month at a single glance.

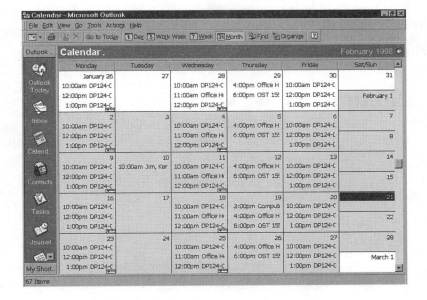

The Print dialog box, as shown in Figure 12.17, is similar to the standard Windows Print dialog box; however, you can choose to print a daily, weekly, or monthly calendar, as well as a tri-fold calendar. A tri-fold calendar prints in three columns for each day. In the left column is an hourly view of the day, the Task List is in the middle column, and the right column shows a seven-day calendar.

FIGURE 12.17.

The Print dialog box provides options for printing your calendars.

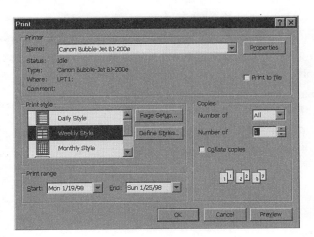

12

Print the view by either clicking the Print button on your toolbar or choosing File, Print. The Print dialog box is displayed.

Summary

Now that you have finished this hour's look at Calendar, you can see that it can be a simple or very complex tool. What determines Calendar's functionality, like any other part of Outlook, is how you want to use it.

In Hour 13, "Getting Things Done," you'll start organizing your work as well as your time using Outlook's Task tool.

Q&A

Q How much will Microsoft Exchange Server cost me or my company?

A That depends on several factors. There are upgrades from previous versions, upgrades from competitive products, several versions, and multiple licenses for users (each person on your system has to have a license to use the server software). Basically, it will cost somewhere between $250 and $5,000. (How's that for a nice, definitive answer?)

Q Do I have to always show seven columns when printing monthly calendars?

A No, you can suppress Saturday and Sunday by clicking File, Page Setup, Monthly Style, Don't Print Weekends.

Q What if I can see someone else's calendar, but can't access it?

A It probably means that he has forgotten to allow read (and/or write) access to it. Remind him that he needs to change the permissions.

Q When in the Calendar folder, can I see a specific variety of tasks in the TaskPad?

A Yes. Choose View, TaskPad View, and select from All Tasks, Today's Tasks, Active Tasks for Selected Days, or several other views.

HOUR 13

Getting Things Done

We have become so busy that almost everyone has *to-do lists* floating around their offices and homes. At work your projects are broken down into specific tasks in addition to your daily and weekly routines that seem to pile up overnight. At home there are the family-related tasks, such as the Monday night Scout meeting, the patches that need to be sewn on the shirt before that meeting, the field trip permission slip to return to the school, and trying to find a sitter for Saturday night. You also have the home-related tasks, such as mowing the lawn, fixing the toilet, grocery shopping, and picking up the dry cleaning.

Sometimes people (like my mother and other Type-A persons) go a bit over-board when it comes to making lists. My mother went away for a weekend and the family was left with hundreds of sticky notes everywhere. They were on the front door, back door, refrigerator door, bedroom doors, and bathroom doors with all the instructions on what needed to be done. She even left a sticky note on the bird cage! I was kind of surprised there wasn't a note on the dog saying "Feed Me!" (then again, I guess the dog could have eaten it). Of course, it was always nice finding a note that just said "Smile" or "I Love You."

Even with to-do lists and sticky notes, how do we manage to find time to get it all done? Despite being scheduled down to our last fifteen minutes, we recognize the need for variety, social interaction, and family life. However, the more efficiently we manage our time and our tasks, the more quickly we can move on to the next challenge or reward.

Task management and time management are the focus of this hour. You learn new ways to use Outlook 98 to track your time, your projects, and those tasks you've delegated to colleagues (or family members). You can even track all those sticky notes your mom leaves you.

Time Management and You

There are many tried-and-true methods of time management out there, as well as a crop of new ones each year. Just wander over to the Business section of the local bookstore, and you will see a variety of books on how to organize your life, your time, and your files, not to mention every other thing you can possibly organize (even your closets).

Although we don't recommend any specific time management system, the following are some basic ideas that always seem to work:

- First, do the tasks that accomplish the most with the least energy.
- Be accessible, but firm. Don't let a lot of minor interruptions sidetrack you from your tasks.
- Set aside a few minutes at the beginning of each day (or the end of the previous day) to set each day's goals. They don't have to be big, just some things to accomplish each day.
- Do similar tasks together. For instance, return all your phone calls at the same time and schedule another time to do all your computer work. When you leave the office or your home, combine as many errands as you can to avoid needless retracing of your steps later.
- Always make time for yourself and your family. No matter how much you love your job, it's only one part of your life. If it becomes all your life, you're missing out. If you haven't talked to your spouse, parents, kids, friends, or other significant people in your life today, put this book down right now and go do that.

What Is a Task?

If you are among the many skeptics of time management and personal organizers, the Tasks feature of Outlook 98 can make a believer of you by:

- Enabling you to create and maintain lists of things to do, as well as track tasks by project, by the people involved, and by priority.
- Letting you maintain lists of recurring tasks that occur either on set dates, or a certain time after the previous occurrence of the task is completed.
- Enabling delegation of tasks and task management to other people for those times when you're too busy to do it yourself.
- Accepting task assignments from others. This is certainly not fun, but at least Tasks makes it easy by enabling you to integrate a new incoming task into your list of things to do.

Starting the Tasks Screen

Accessing the Tasks screen in Outlook is much the same as using any of the other tools.

You can start Tasks by

- Clicking the Tasks icon in the Outlook Bar
- Clicking the Tasks folder in the Folders list
- Choosing Go, Tasks; Ctrl+Y is the shortcut command

And on Your Right, You Can See...

The Tasks screen is not flashy. As you can see in Figure 13.1, the Information Viewer section of the Outlook screen is filled with a simple-looking table. But you know by now that in Outlook, such things are never quite as simple as they look. If they were, this book would be very short.

This particular view of Tasks is the Detailed List view. Actually, there are two views even more compact than this: the TaskPad you see in the Calendar view and the Simple List view, which is very similar to the Detailed List except it contains only columns for Sort by: Icon, Sort by: Complete, Subject, and Due Date.

The Icon column shows the type of Outlook item. Most of the time, the Task icon will be present here, although assigned tasks are symbolized in this column as well. We'll take a closer look at assigning tasks later in the hour.

The Complete column is merely a check box that indicates when a task is complete.

13

FIGURE 13.1.

The Tasks screen is one method of inputting tasks.

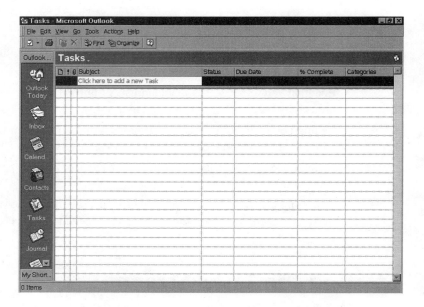

The Subject column describes the task: "Take out the trash. Get Dave the Top Ten List by 5:30. Launch the Mars probe." These are all good examples of task subjects. Just make sure you don't go overboard, because you can add more information to the Note box at the bottom of the Tasks screen.

Finally, the Date Due column displays the date the task should be completed. Not all tasks need due dates (my favorite task, `Earn a million dollars`, is pretty much ongoing). Tasks that do not have due dates are indicated by `None`.

Creating a Task

Tasks can help you out with things in both your business and your personal life, especially in our upcoming example in which your family is soon to be enlarged.

In the following example you are going to be a working parent-to-be. For all you men out there, play along. In light of the recent Family Leave Act, fathers, too, are assuming more active roles in planning for a new family member.

Over the next few months you are going to be very busy preparing for the new arrival. To be able to get everything done without waiting until the last minute, you make a long list of tasks.

To create a task list, there are several ways to activate the New Task tool.

- Click the New Task button on the far-left end of the Standard toolbar.
- Use the shortcut keys Ctrl+N.
- Choose Actions, New Task.
- Double-click the Click Here to Add a New Task in the Task Entry Row button.

 If you single-click the Click Here to Add a New Task, it places the insertion point in the Subject box, and doesn't open the New Task screen.

- Double-click an empty line in the Task List or right-click and choose New Task.

After choosing any one of these methods, where do you end up? With the New Task screen displayed, as shown in Figure 13.2.

FIGURE 13.2.

The New Task tool is used to enter more thorough data than can be entered from the simple view.

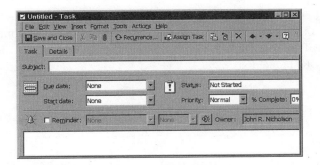

Besides its similarity in style to all of Outlook's other tools, notice the small number of fields to fill out. This makes creating tasks quick and painless.

The subject line should be simple and to the point. You can add extra information in the Note box at the bottom of the Task tool as you need it.

The next information group are the Due Date fields. The default is None. By clicking the drop-down arrow, you see the Date Navigator box (see Figure 13.3). The current date is highlighted. Select the date you want to complete the task or leave it at None. For the current date, either click the Today button, or click the date on the Date Navigator. To choose another date, use the Date Navigator to click the appropriate date. Also, you can just type the correct date directly over None.

13

You can also use the other date formulas, such as Today, Tomorrow, Next Wed, as discussed in Hour 12, "Power Calendaring."

FIGURE 13.3.

The Date Navigator in the Task Tool can be used to specify a date.

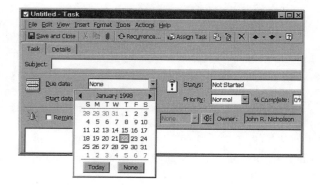

The Start Date field works in much the same way as the Due Date field. It is used to establish the date that the task will begin. Sometimes this can be immediately or other times it will be some time in the near future. If the task is already in progress, the Start Date may be in the past.

The Start Date field is totally optional. You may not even find a need for it.

The next field is the Status field. How is the project going? Has it begun? This is what Outlook means by status. In the Status field, there are five choices: Not Started, In Progress, Completed, Waiting on Someone Else, and Deferred.

Another drop-down list box lists three priority choices: High, Normal, and Low.

The next field, % Complete, is optional. There are certain situations for which pinning down a percentage value is tricky. When the task is more segmented or can be easily measured, then it's helpful to use this field. For instance, when writing a specific number of chapters in a book, an author could change the percentage of chapters completed and submitted to the editor through either directly entering the percentage or using the spin buttons to the right of the field to increase or decrease the percentage.

If you mark the task as complete, the Status and % Complete field are automatically adjusted.

In the following exercise, you enter several tasks that are of concern to your expanding family. Later, you learn to edit them and add additional ones.

To Do: Entering a New Task

1. Using one of the recently discussed methods, open a blank Task tool.
2. Type Purchase baby crib in the subject line.
3. Insert the date three months from now as your due date.

You can just type 3 months and press Tab.

4. Enter today as the Start Date.
5. Choose the In Progress option for the Status field.
6. Leave Normal as the Priority for now. (Normal is the default priority.)
7. Click Save and Close.
8. You may need to drag the column headings so that the width is similar to that shown in Figure 13.4.
9. Over the course of the next few months you are going to have a lot of other tasks that need to get done before the new arrival comes home. Take the next few minutes and enter the tasks noted in Table 13.1.

You can enter the tasks from the TaskPad rather than opening the Task tool for each entry.

13

Input dates by typing 1 mo (or the appropriate number of months). Enter status by typing the first letter of the status code (Not Started; In Progress; Completed; Waiting on Someone Else; or Deferred). Priority codes can also be entered by typing the first letter (High; Normal; or Low). The percent complete spin buttons are set to 25% increments, so you will need to type the 10% entry.

▼ FIGURE **13.4.**

A single task has been entered and the column widths adjusted.

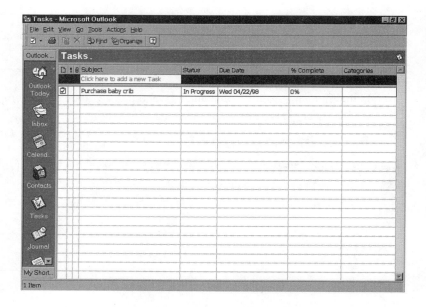

TABLE 13.1. DATA FOR TASK ENTRY.

Subject	Due Date	Start Date	Status	Priority	% Complete
Arrange for diaper service	3 mo	None	Not started	Normal	0
Decorate baby room	3 mo	Today	In progress	Normal	10
Time off work, HR Paperwork	1 mo	Today	In progress	High	25
Choose a pediatrician	1 mo	Today	Waiting on Someone Else	High	25
Select a baby name	3 mo	Today	In progress	High	25

Your tasks should look similar to the ones shown in Figure 13.5.

When you are not in Tasks but are still in Outlook, you can also create a new task by clicking the Task command in the Create New drop-down list in the Standard toolbar or by using the shortcut keys Ctrl+Shift+K.

Even if you do not have Outlook running, you can still create a task using the Microsoft Office Shortcut Bar. Click the New Task button to open the New Task tool.

FIGURE 13.5.

The tasks in Table 13.1 have all been entered.

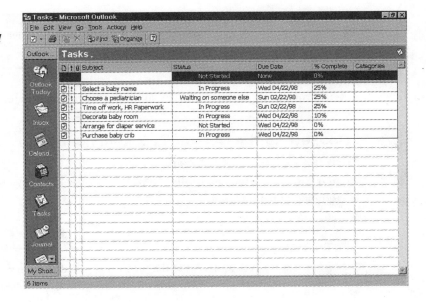

As in Calendar, the Tasks feature enables you to set reminders for any task you want. However, there are some differences between reminders in Tasks and reminders in Calendar.

When you click the Reminder check box, the date field next to it activates, with the default data value as the due date of the task. If there is no due date, the date field will default to the current date. The next field is the Reminder time field with a default of 8:00 a.m.

Usually setting the reminder by date is enough unless you are on a tight schedule. For example, you might have to have a report ready for the Quarterly trustees meeting and because it contains up-to-the-minute stock prices, you will be working close to the exact time that it is due.

13

At this point, you may be asking yourself, what's the difference between Calendar and Tasks items? On the surface, not much. They handle different things in a similar way.

What makes Tasks different is that it does not focus on a certain point in time as does a meeting or an appointment. After you set a reminder and that date is reached, Tasks will keep reminding you each day until the task is complete (unless you dismiss the reminder).

> If you are using task subfolders, reminders are not active. Reminders only activate from the primary Tasks folder.

If a certain time of day is better for you to receive task reminders, change the default time.

To Do: Setting the Default Task Reminder Time

1. In Tasks, choose Tools, Options.
2. In the Reminder time field, either directly enter or use the list box to set the Reminder time to 7 p.m.

3. Click OK.

> In the Task tool, next to the time field is a little button with a speaker icon on it. Click this button to open the Reminder Sound dialog box. This contains the path to the sound file (usually in WAV format) that will sound when the Reminder time begins.

Learning More About the Task Tool

The Owner field is not editable because it shows the user who owns it. When a task is assigned, the creator of the task gives up ownership to the person he is assigning it to.

The large note box that dominates the lower third of the screen lets you enter as many details about the task as you need. You can keep track of the names as you and your spouse narrow the choices by putting the top six baby names for each sex in the Note box.

To Do: Updating a Task

1. Open the Task tool for `Select a baby name` by double-clicking the task. Maximize the window so that you can see the other fields at the bottom of the screen.
2. In the large note box beneath the Reminder field, enter `Girls' names: Jessica, Ashley, Kristen, Emily, Holly, Traci` and `Boys' names: Kristopher, Scott, Jason, Jonathon, Zachary, James`.
3. Change the % Complete to `50%`. Your screen should be similar to the one shown in Figure 13.6.

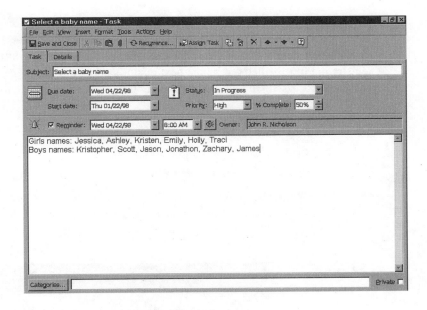

FIGURE 13.6.

The maximized Task Tool window shows additional fields at the bottom of the screen.

▲   4. Click Save and Close.

The final field in the New Task tool is the Private check box. This is used when a task is created that not everyone needs to know about, such as any information in your personal folder. After all, you don't want everyone to put in their two cents' worth regarding baby names.

Creating a Task Automatically

If you are like me, you get a lot of email that contains urgent matters that you must efficiently deal with to keep the world safe for democracy. You know, things like, "Could you get me a copy of that report? Or, Can you find a way to deal with that knucklehead Lex Luthor?" Such messages can be converted to a task quite easily.

- Click Inbox and select the appropriate message. Drag and drop the message onto the Task icon (or into the Task folder).
- When the New Task tool appears, fill in the appropriate information (priority, due date, and so on).
- Click Save and Close. The world is now safe for another day! (Well, it will be if you complete the task.)

13

Calendar offers another clever way to automatically create a task. For instance, if you have an appointment or meeting that you need to prepare for, associating a task with the Calendar item is a great idea. For example, you need to have all the hospital pre-registration forms filled out by the next doctor's appointment, so the doctor's office can get them processed. To help you remember this, create a task from the appointment on the Calendar.

To Do: Creating a Task from a Calendar Item

1. Click the Calendar icon in the Outlook Bar.
2. Create an appointment for next Friday at 9:00 a.m. with Dr. Roberts and save it.
3. Highlight the appointment item in the Calendar.
4. Drag and drop it onto the Task icon, into the Task folder, or onto the TaskPad.
5. A New Task tool appears with the appointment in the Note box (see Figure 13.7).

FIGURE 13.7.

Make sure you're prepared for an appointment.

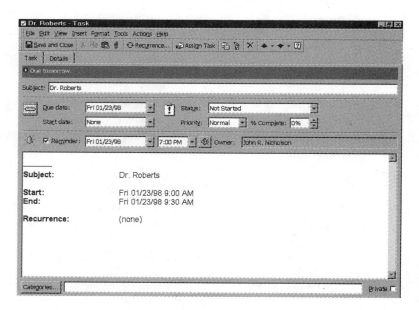

6. The Reminder time is set for 7 p.m. (because you changed the default). You need to change it to 7:30 a.m., or you may be late.
7. Click Save and Close.

Finishing a Task

There's no greater satisfaction than a job well done, but how do you tell Tasks that you're done? There are four ways:

- When the Complete column is in view, as in Tasks' Simple List view, click the check box next to the finished task to mark that task as completed.

- When the Status field is in view in the Information Viewer (the Detailed List view), enter Completed in the Status field to tell Tasks the job is done. You can also enter this value within a Task's Task Detail Screen.

- In the Task tool, enter 100% in the % Complete field. Or, enter 100% in the % Complete field for Tasks' Detailed List view.

- In the Task tool, click the Mark Complete button on the toolbar.

After you have marked a task complete, it does not disappear from the Simple List view. Rather, it changes to a lighter, strikethrough text. This helps you keep track of the recent things you've accomplished.

In the Active Tasks view, however, tasks disappear as soon as they are marked complete. Although the tasks are still in the folder, to see them you must switch to the Simple List view. Later you will learn to completely delete a task.

Editing a Task

Editing a task is not difficult at all. If the item you want to edit is visible in the Information Viewer, you can edit it directly without opening the Task tool. In the next exercise, you learn to add a reminder date.

When you want to do more detailed editing, double-click any task in the Information Viewer. This opens up that task's Task tool. Editing any of the fields on the Task tab is the same as creating the task.

To Do: Editing a Task

1. In any of the Information Viewer views, open the Time off work, HR paperwork task.
2. Add a reminder date of one week prior to the due date.
3. Click Save and Close to exit this item, and the change is saved.

After the Doctor appointment, you and your spouse have found out that you are having a baby boy. Delete all the girls' names and add two more boys' names.

To Do: Editing a Task Using the Task Tool

1. Open the Task tool for `Select a baby name`.

2. Delete the girls' names and add two more boys' names: Gavin and Ryan. Your screen should be similar to that in Figure 13.8.

FIGURE 13.8.

The girls' names have been removed, and two boys' names are added.

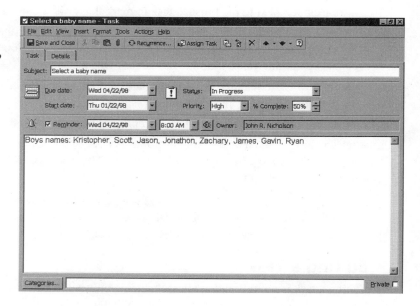

▲   3. Click <u>S</u>ave and Close.

There are also other fields that can be edited—fields on the Details tab that deal with many things that come up during a particular job. Take a look at the Details tab, as shown in Figure 13.9. There's lots of room for information here! Let's look at what each field can record for you.

The Date Completed field is automatically filled when a task is marked complete. This is helpful when the task is part of an overall project and you need to know who finished what and when it was completed.

The Total <u>W</u>ork and Act<u>u</u>al Work fields are sort of misnomers. At least, the Total <u>W</u>ork field is. It should be called the Estimated Work field because you enter the *estimated* number of hours you think a task will take to finish here. In the Act<u>u</u>al Work field, you enter the number of hours the task really took to complete. (If this task had been assigned, this would be a great way of monitoring someone's performance level.) The values of the field automatically change to day or week values if you enter more than eight hours.

FIGURE 13.9.

The Details tab in the Task tool can be used for tracking additional information.

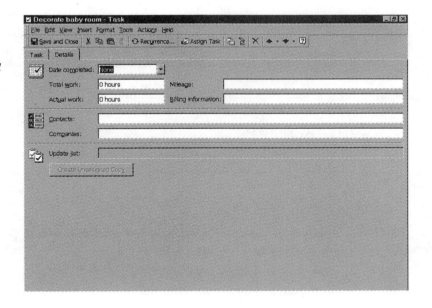

You might find the value changes somewhat confusing. 8 hours changes to 1 day, 9 hours stays as 9 hours. The conversion only happens in certain major increments (10 hours=1.25 days, 12 hours=1.5 days, and so on); 4 hours changes to .5 days. Other increments (like 11 hours) stay displayed in hours.

When hours are converted to days and weeks, the formula used is based on values you can set. The default values are eight hours equal one work day, and 40 hours equal one work week. If your office has a different schedule, change these conversion values by choosing Tools, Options, Calendar Options. Set your own work hours.

13

The next four fields are self-explanatory: Mileage, Billing Information, Contacts, and Companies. If you need to track any of this type of information, here's where to do it. For the tasks associated with the baby, you could use the Mileage field to record your mileage to and from the doctor's office, which is tax-deductible.

Instead of just typing names into the <u>C</u>ontacts field, highlight the contact in Contacts, then drag and drop the information over to the Task tool's <u>C</u>ontacts field. However, to do this, the Task tool window should not be maximized.

Copying a Task

If you need to create a task that is nearly identical to another, you can make a copy. Try this with Purchase a Baby Crib because you've decided you also need a new bed. A copy is born!

To Do: Copying a Task

1. In any of the task lists shown in the Information Viewer, click the task (or tasks) you need to copy: Purchase a Baby Crib.
2. Click the <u>E</u>dit, <u>C</u>opy menu command.
3. Click the <u>E</u>dit, <u>P</u>aste menu command.
4. Open the newly copied task and change the subject to Purchase a Bed.
5. Click <u>S</u>ave and Close when you are finished.

An even faster way of doing this is to highlight the task, press Ctrl, and drag the task somewhere else in the Information Viewer. As soon as you release the mouse button, the task is copied to the new location.

Keep the CTRL key pressed until you release the mouse button; otherwise, you merely move the task rather than copy it.

Deleting a Task

As I've mentioned, when tasks are completed, they do not just vanish into the air. They stick around, reminding you of all the work you've accomplished.

You can keep tasks around until they are autoarchived, but you may want to clean house and sweep out these old tasks sooner than that. You may even need to delete a current task if someone else has taken it over, and you are no longer responsible for its completion. In any case, to delete a task, highlight it, then click the Delete button on the Standard toolbar in Tasks or on the Task tool toolbar if the Task Detail screen is open.

Checking Task Status

Usually the status of tasks is best used at work because work tasks tend to be more segmented and easier to track. If your boss has access to your calendar, he can use the status section to check the progress of a task he has assigned to you without having to call you into his office.

Delegating and Tracking a Task

In the past you may have asked a coworker to do a project and then forgotten that you gave it to him. It doesn't happen often, thankfully, but it always tends to happen at the worst times.

With Outlook you can create a task that needs to be done, assign it to someone to be completed, and be able to find out the status of it at any time without having to call repeatedly. In the following exercise, you Assign a task to another person.

To Do: Assigning a Task to Another Person

1. Open the Task tool to arrange for a diaper service using one of the methods you've learned this hour.
2. Click the Assign Task icon on the toolbar. This brings up a page for you to complete. When you are finished it will be emailed to the person you are assigning it to.
3. Click the To: Button to bring up the Select Task Recipient dialog box.
4. Choose the person you are assigning the task to, and click the To-> button.
5. Click OK. You are now back at the Task tool with the recipients name in the To: field.
6. Make sure the check boxes are marked where it says Keep an Updated Copy of This Task on My Task List and Send Me a Status Report When This Task Is Complete.

> The first option keeps a copy of the task on your Task list, and updates it automatically. The second option sends you a message when the new owner completes the task.

7. When finished click Send.

Summary

During this hour you learned some ways to manage your time and your life better. You will find that tracking all your tasks will become a habit and you will be much more organized after using it for a while. Not only will you know what you need to complete and what you have already done, you will also be able to keep a close eye on all those tasks and projects you ask other people to take care of.

Q&A

Q **When editing a task, do I lose the information if I accidentally close the tool?**

A If you have made any changes to the task and click the close button instead of the <u>S</u>ave and Close button, Outlook will prompt you, asking if you would like to save your changes.

Q **I have 10 items included in a task and have completed one of them. Do I automatically have to enter 25%?**

A No, you can manually enter 10% into the percent completed field.

Q **How can I see additional tasks in the TaskPad list?**

A Use the scrollbar to scroll through the tasks. Double-click a specific one to open it.

PART V
Journals and Notes

Hour

HOUR 14

The Journal: My So-Called Diary

When many people think of a journal, they think of the secret diaries of their youth. These tiny books, kept under lock and key, contained thoughts and feelings that could never be shared with anyone else. (And then there were the rest of us, trying to sneak a peek at them.)

People have kept journals ever since writing began. At first, they were probably just used to keep track of daily activities. Then, along came publishers and lucrative book contracts for interesting and historical journals, and suddenly "Spent day shopping for blender," became "For the entire day, I searched for that one perfect item to complete my kitchen."

Outlook's Journal is not quite as flowery as that (although it can be if you want). However, it is doubtful that anyone will offer you huge sums of money for these chronicled memoirs. It is a very utilitarian tool that gets back to the real roots of journal keeping. In other words, it helps you and your faulty memory keep your work straight.

To do this, Journal automatically records any activity you perform with Outlook or Office 97. It also enables you to manually record other accomplishments or activities. This may not sound like a big deal. Think about it this way: Try to recall the actual file-names of all the files you worked on the day before yesterday. Can you? If you can, you're good—really good. Now think of the files you worked on a week ago Tues-day.Aha! No one is that good!

If any of these questions stumped you, don't let it bother you. Some days I can't remem-ber what I worked on that morning. But sooner or later, you will need to locate that file you sent to your boss last week, and darn if you can remember the filename.

Or, how about this scenario? What if you need to find the next-to-last version of the doc-ument because the most recent version's changes are unsatisfactory?

Tracking your activities by filename and version would take a lot of time. Journal enables you to look at your workday—not only by your appointments and meetings, but by the files you worked on and the time that you last opened them. For a lot of us, this is a much easier way to perceive our workday.

Starting and Configuring Journal

To start Journal, click the Journal icon in the Outlook Bar. When you start Journal the first time, you see the dialog box shown in Figure 14.1. Journal tracks the email you send and receive from any contact you specify, and tracks the Office documents you work on. You are asked if you want to turn the feature on. If you don't want to see the dialog box again, place a check mark in the Please Do Not Show Me This Dialog Again option box. Click Yes to turn the journal feature on.

If you have previously installed any version of Outlook, you will not see this dialog box.

After choosing to turn the Journal features on, the dialog box shown in Figure 14.2 is displayed. This is where you enable those items you want to track automatically.

Three of the four sections in the Journal Options dialog box are used to set recording configurations. The two at the top are directly related to each other. The section on the left, Automatically Record These Items, gives you a choice of what kind of Outlook transaction you want Journal to monitor.

In the For These Contacts section, pick the contacts whose transactions Journal will record. For example, I might want to record all email messages between my brother Sean and me.

FIGURE 14.1.

The dialog box is for turning the Journal feature on the first time.

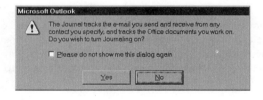

FIGURE 14.2.

The Journal Options dialog box enables you to specify items for Journal to track.

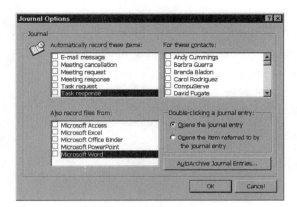

One thing to keep in mind is that you can't monitor one kind of Outlook transaction for one set of people and another transaction type for another group. If you choose email, tasks, and so on, those transactions will all be recorded for all the contacts you choose.

In the Also Record Files From section, the Journal Options dialog box enables you to set which Office 97 document types you want to record. This is pretty straightforward. You can record any combination of Office documents.

The remaining section in this dialog box is discussed later in this hour. In the next exercise, you'll set the options telling Journal what to record for you.

To Do: Telling Outlook What to Record

▼ **To Do**

1. Start Outlook if it isn't already running. Choose Tools, Options, Journal Options to open the Journal Options dialog box.

2. In the Automatically Record These Items section, place a check mark next to the items you want to record in your journal. For now, place a check mark next to each category.

3. In the For These Contacts section, Outlook has listed all your contacts. Place a check mark next to the contacts for whom you want to record *all* interactions.

▼

14

> Do not automatically include everyone that is in your Contacts list. You could end up with a huge Journal filled with meaningless and trivial information. You can create a Journal entry from any tool in Outlook, so anytime you interact with a contact, you can add that activity to Journal manually.

4. In the Also Record Files From section, place a check mark next to Microsoft Access, Microsoft Excel, Microsoft PowerPoint, and Microsoft Word.

5. Click OK. At the Options dialog box, click OK.

6. Open Word and create a new document. Type Learning Outlook is a snap. Then, save the document as Journal Demo. Close Word.

7. Maximize Outlook. Look at the timeline entry.

> If Outlook is your only installed Office 97 product, you will find Journal's AutoRecord record feature extremely limited. All events will need to be manually recorded.

Exploring the Journal Screen

The Journal screen seems quite a bit different from the other tools in Outlook. Figure 14.3 shows Journal in its default view. There are other views in Journal, of course, but this hour addresses this one.

This view of Journal is called a *timeline* view. All the Journal items appear on a specific date and time of the timeline. This view reflects when the item was created or when the last version of the item was saved. Of course, we can't see some items because some of the group boxes in this view may be collapsed.

Group boxes enable you to group Outlook items by any criteria you want. Here, the Entry type is the grouping criterion. *Type,* in this case, is the kind of Office 97 document.

Depending on the way you configured Outlook, Journal automatically records three types of activities:

- Any Office 97 documents created from an Office 97 program. This includes any future releases of the Office 97 products.
- All email, message requests and responses, and task requests and responses.
- Any phone calls that you make from Outlook.

Collapsed Group boxes

FIGURE 14.3.

The beginning Journal screen is shown in its default view.

Expanded Group box

Journal

January 1998

| 21 | Thu 22 | Fri 23 | Sat 24 | Sun 25 | Mon 26 | Tue 27 | Wed 28 | Thu 29 |

Entry Type : Microsoft Access

Entry Type : Microsoft Excel

Entry Type : Microsoft Word

C:\My Documents\TY_OL98\Hour14\ch_14pam.doc
C:\My Documents\TY_OL98\Hour09\12883_09.doc
C:\My Documents\Journal Demo.doc
C:\My Documents\TY_OL98\Hour14\ch_14pam.doc
C:\My Documents\Choosing Fonts.ppt

65 Items

Email items and phone calls are tracked only if they are initiated from within Outlook.

Entries in Journal are often grouped. Similar to group boxes in other areas of Outlook, those in Journal can be expanded or collapsed using the small plus/minus sign box on the left side of the group box. Clicking a plus sign expands the group, while clicking on a minus sign collapses it.

In the expanded groups, you see icons with one-line tags next to them. These tags can either be a filename and its full directory path, or the subject of a mail message or meeting request. Also, notice the icons. They resemble the icons of their parent programs—Word icons for Word documents and Mail icons for Outlook's Inbox items—except for one difference: In the lower-left corner of each icon (squint now) is a tiny clock. This additional symbol is Journal's clever way to indicate that this item is not a Word or Excel document. Instead, it is a Journal entry *for* that document.

The distinction here is important to understand. If you double-click one of these items expecting to open the actual document, you will get a surprise. A Journal entry for a document (or Outlook item) contains information about when the document was created, who created it, and the duration of its most recent use, among other things. Figure 14.4 shows an open Journal entry and the kind of information it displays.

14

FIGURE **14.4.**

A Journal entry for a Word document includes a shortcut icon to open it.

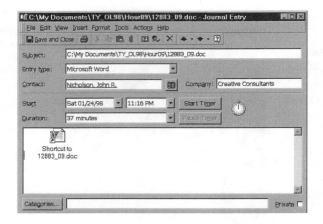

Navigating around the timeline view in Outlook is fairly simple. You can either use the scrollbars at the bottom of the information viewer to move forward and backward in time, or (even better) use the Date Navigator.

In a timeline, the Date Navigator is hidden in a rather sneaky way. See the little black triangle next to the month heading? When you click it, the Date Navigator appears, as shown in Figure 14.5.

FIGURE **14.5.**

The timeline Date Navigator can be used to display another date.

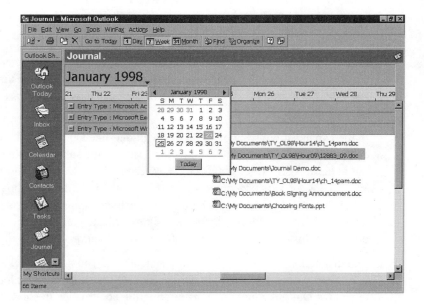

If you want to see what's in today's Journal, simply click the Today button in the Date Navigator or the Go To Today button on the Standard toolbar.

Is This Thing On?

At this point in an hour, I would usually tell you how to create a new item in whatever part of Outlook that's being discussed. This time, however, I'll show you how Journal can create new entries for you.

When you enter a new contact, you may want to go ahead and tell Outlook that you want all actions with this contact recorded. Instead of spending a lot of time going back and forth between the Contact Tool and the Journal Options dialog box each time you enter a new contact, you can easily take care of it in the Contact Tool.

To Do: Recording Contact Interactions

1. Click the Contact folder in the Outlook Bar.
2. Click the New Contact button to open a blank Contact form. Fill in the demographic information (name, phone, address, and so on.) on the General tab.
3. Click the Journal tab.
4. Place a check mark next to Automatically Record Journal Entries for This Contact.

 You can automatically record only those Journal contacts that are in the *primary* Contacts folder. If you've created a subfolder for some Contacts, those won't be recorded by the AutoJournal feature.

5. Click Save and Close. From now on, Outlook automatically records all Office 97 and Outlook interactions that you have with that person.

 You can also open an existing contact and enable the automatic tracking feature.

I did say that you could also automatically record phone calls made from Outlook, and the Options dialog box appears to have made a liar out of me. After all, there is no phone call setting. This is one of Microsoft's hidden tricks for Outlook. Fortunately, we discovered it, so perform the following steps:

14

To Do: Automatically Recording Phone Calls

1. Click the Contacts icon on the Outlook toolbar.
2. Choose Actions, Call Contact, New Call, or press the Ctrl+Shift+D shortcut key combination.
3. In the New Call dialog box (see Figure 14.6), enter the name of the person or organization you want to call.

> If the number is in your Contact list, you can also click the Contact folder, select the Contact item, then click Actions, Call Contact and select the number to dial, or just click the AutoDialer icon on the toolbar. You can select the Contact and press Ctrl+Shift+D.

FIGURE 14.6.

The New Call dialog box is your vehicle for placing a telephone call.

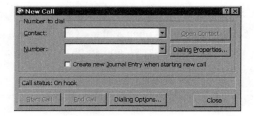

4. If the person is in your Contact list, click the correct phone number in the Number field. Otherwise, type in the phone number in the Number field.
5. If you want Journal to record this call, click the Create New Journal Entry When Starting New Call check box.
6. Click the Start Call button. The call will proceed, and an Entry will be added to the Journal.

Activating Manual Override

Journal is not limited to just recording the few things we have mentioned. Actually, Journal can record pretty much anything you do, both on and off your computer. This function is called manual recording, and it's simple to use. However, let's first examine the Journal Entry tool—the place where you will always end up. Figure 14.7 shows a Journal Entry tool for a Word document.

FIGURE 14.7.

The Journal Entry tool for a Word document includes the document's icon.

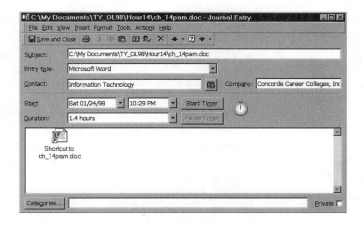

The Subject field contains a full DOS path to the file. It can contain anything, as long as it's related to the document. This is so you can easily determine the entry by the name with which it is listed in Journal. After all, you wouldn't label a wedding invitation "Recipe for Barbecue Ribs."

The Entry Type field consists of a large drop-down list that contains all the choices you should need to define this Entry (see Figure 14.8). If these selections do not exactly meet your needs, you are going to have to improvise, as direct entry to this field is not allowed. The only way you get more choices is when a new Office-compatible program is installed.

FIGURE 14.8.

Use the Entry Type field to choose a type of Journal entry.

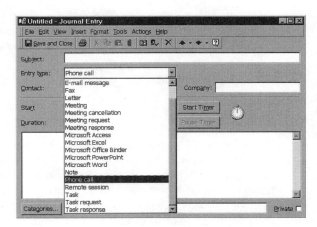

The Contact field contains the name of anyone associated with the document, whether the creator, a collaborator, or an editor. (For most Contacts, like phone calls, the Contact field contains the name of the person being called.) If the name is underlined, this means the person or company is in your Contacts list. Just to the right of the Contact field is an Address Book button. When you click this, the Select Names dialog box appears, as shown in Figure 14.9. By highlighting the names on the left and clicking Add, you can quickly add contacts. When you are finished, click OK, and all the contacts are added in the Contact field.

Using the address book to select the contact name can be a problem. Only people with email addresses and/or fax numbers will appear on that list. For example, if you were calling a "non-techie" friend who appears in your Contacts folder, but has neither a fax number nor an email address, he won't appear in your address book.

FIGURE 14.9.

The Select Names dialog box contains your Contacts list entries.

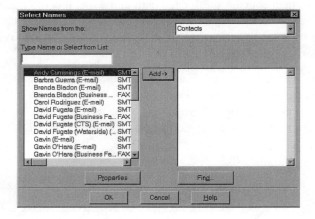

The Company field is a text-only field where you can enter a company associated with the Entry.

To limit the number of Categories needed in the Master Category List, you can use the Company field to record the name of a larger project the Entry may be a part of. When you view the Entries in one of Journal's table views, you can easily see the items associated with this project.

Just make sure you don't use the Company Name as the name of the project, or the records will be mixed with company records, and may cause a lot of confusion.

The next section of the Journal tool gives the time and date details for the Entry. The Start fields show the date and time the document (not the Journal entry) was last edited.

> Always remember that the Start time does *not* necessarily reflect the creation date of a document. If the Journal Entry is not for the original version of the document, the Start time shows the duration of the most recent editing session.

You can change these times, but it will have the effect only of moving the Entry on the Journal timeline. It will not change the document's actual times. So, although you can change the Journal to show this document was edited on December 9, anyone examining the document itself will know otherwise.

The Duration field shows the total time the document was last opened. It, too, can be changed manually, but this affects only the Journal Entry, not the document itself.

The neatest use for the Duration field is as a stopwatch. Do you want to time a meeting or a phone call? Click the Start Timer button. When you are finished, click the Pause Timer button. Now your event is accurately timed. This is great for keeping track of billable hours if you are a consultant!

The next three fields—the Notebox, Categories, and Private fields—should be familiar to you. They function the same way throughout all Outlook tools. Two things to note before we end this little tour: The Previous Item and Next Item buttons in the toolbar enable you to proceed through all the Journal Entries one at a time, either backward or forward, respectively. If you click the drop-down menus (next to the Previous or Next Item buttons), you can also move to the adjacent item, or to the very first or very last Entry in the Journal.

Entering a Document

At this point, you may be getting a bit nervous about all of this. There seems to be a lot of information to enter, so why would you even bother?

Well, you will soon see that manually recording something (for example, when Automatic Journaling of Office Documents is not enabled) is not quite as manual as you might think. As an example, let's record a document. Do you think you have to enter all the DOS path in the Subject field? Think again. To enter a document into the Journal, follow the steps in the next exercise.

14

To Do: Recording a Document

1. Close all applications other than Outlook.

2. Open your preferred file navigator (Windows Explorer will do nicely).

3. Arrange your screen so both applications are visible. Click the Outlook icon in the taskbar at the bottom of your screen. Both Outlook and Explorer should be active on the screen. Right-click an empty area in the taskbar. Choose Tile Vertically. Your screen should be similar to that shown in Figure 14.10.

FIGURE 14.10.

Outlook and Explorer are tiled vertically on the screen.

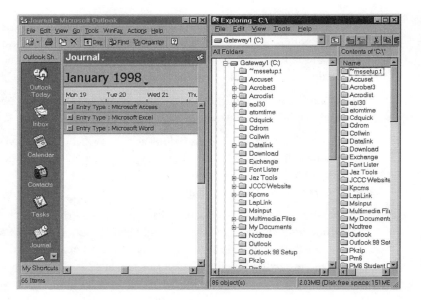

4. Click and drag a *file* (not a folder) over to the Journal icon on the Outlook Bar or the Journal folder in the Folder List.

5. A new Journal Entry tool appears, as shown in Figure 14.11. You can enter any pertinent information now.

6. Click Save and Close.

A Journal entry for this document appears in Journal. That was easy, wasn't it? The item appears each time you open Journal, and the file activity is automatically recorded.

Entering an Outlook Item

The procedure for entering an Outlook item is even simpler because you don't have to fuss with window positioning.

FIGURE 14.11.

The Journal Entry tool shows the icon for the file that you recorded.

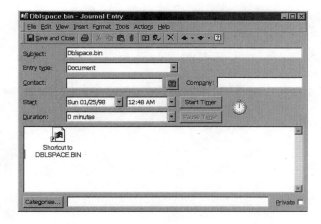

To Do: Manual Recording

1. Find the item in Outlook that you want to record in Journal (for example, an email message).

> If you don't have the email AutoJournal feature turned on for this contact, you'll have to drag an outgoing email message from the Sent Items folder.

2. Click and drag the item over to the Journal icon on the Outlook Bar or the Journal folder in the Folder List.

3. A new Journal Entry tool appears (refer to Figure 14.10). You can enter any additional information now.

▲ 4. Click Save and Close.

Again, this is not too difficult. Journal Entries are designed to be automated. In fact, they even show up in other parts of Outlook.

Entering a Contact Activity

Many activities that can be recorded in Journal often have a contact or two associated with them. After all, it takes two to tango, right? If you are the kind of person who remembers things by people association, you are in luck. Outlook enables you to assign Journal entries related to a contact from the contact item itself.

14

To Do: Activating the Tracking of a Contact

1. Open the desired contact item.

2. In the Contact tool, click the Journal tab. The tab should be similar to Figure 14.12.

FIGURE 14.12.

Click the Journal tab to begin recording a contact.

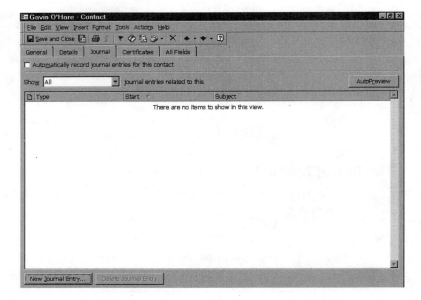

3. Click the New Journal Entry button at the bottom of the tab to display a new Journal Entry tool.

4. The information fields have default information already entered (see Figure 14.13).

> The phone call is the default activity because it is the most common task associated with Contacts. You can easily change this to another type of activity, such as email messages, by using the drop-down list in the Entry Type text box.

5. After making your desired changes, including timing the activity, click Save and Close.

▼ FIGURE **14.13.**

The Entry Type field shows that you are about to initiate a phone call to this contact.

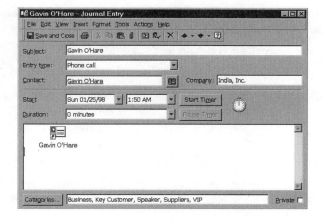

Taking notes during phone calls is the most common use of the Journal feature in most offices.

Entering Everything Else

Here is another example of the Journal's ease of use. Imagine that you're walking down the hall to your office, pondering a complex issue. Inevitably, you run into someone who immediately starts discussing an entirely different topic. You only half-listen—the perplexing issue has locked up most of your brain's processing power. You nod at the right places, mumble a departing comment, and then rush back to your office.

Perhaps your colleague was talking about something important. If you don't write it down quickly, you may forget all about it. This is where Journal can help you. You can briefly record the topic of the conversation, whom it was with, and when it occurred so that you can call him when you are able to give the topic more of your attention.

To do this, you need to open a new Journal Entry tool. Use one of the following methods to activate the tool:

- From anywhere in Windows, click the New Journal Entry button on the Office Shortcut bar.
- From any screen in Outlook, choose File, New, Journal Entry.
- From any part of Outlook, click the Journal Entry command in the New Item drop-down list on the Standard toolbar.
- In Journal, click the New Journal Entry button on the Standard toolbar.

14

- In the date timeline or in an empty section of the Journal field, right-click and select New Journal Entry.
- Also in Journal, choose Actions, New Journal Entry.
- Use the shortcut keys: Ctrl+N in Journal or Ctrl+Shift+J anywhere else in Outlook.

Fill in the pertinent information in the Journal Entry tool, then click Save and Close.

Using Journal

Journal can do more for you than just act as a memory jogger. It can also serve as a time-based file manager of sorts, letting you open files and items based on when the document was used. If you need to talk to the people who have been using a document, Journal can automatically link you to them.

Opening Files and Outlook Items

As stated earlier this hour, when you double-click any Journal item, that document does not automatically open. Instead, you see the Journal Entry for that item, which has an attached shortcut to the document. However, you can skip this middle step and go straight to the document. There are actually two ways: a fast way and an even faster way.

To use the fast way, perform the following steps:

1. Right-click the Journal item.
2. On the context menu (see Figure 14.14), click the Open Item Referred To command.

To use the faster way for all subsequent documents, perform the following steps:

1. In Journal, choose Tools, Options, Journal Options.
2. In the Journal Options dialog box, locate the Double-Clicking a Journal Entry section. Choose Opens the Item Referred to by the Journal Entry option button.
3. Click OK.

From now on, Journal acts just like a file manager because every item will open with just a double-click. Pretty nifty, eh? However, there's a trade-off. You no longer can open the Journal entry for the item by double-clicking it. However, you can access the entry if you right-click and choose the Open Journal Entry command on the pop-up menu. You need to decide whether you will want to access Journal entries or the original files most often.

Opening Contacts from Journal Entries

If you need to open any contacts associated with a document or recorded Outlook item, try the following simple two-step method:

1. Open the Journal entry.
2. Double-click any underlined names in the Contact field.

FIGURE 14.14.

You can directly access the document with this pop-up menu.

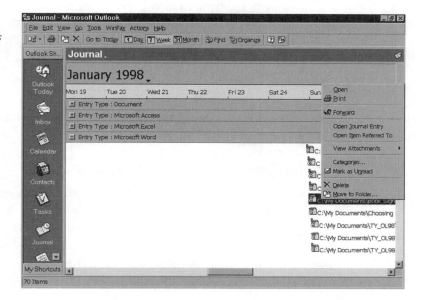

This calls up the Contact tool for that person. If the name is not underlined, that means this person is not on your Contact list. If you want to be able to automatically track Journal activities for a specific contact, or just be able to easily reach them, you should add the name to your Contacts list as soon as possible.

Sometimes names are not underlined, yet you know they are in your Contacts list. (Perhaps they were added to Contacts after the Journal entry was created, or they don't have a fax or email address.) To reconcile names in the Contact field, click the Check Names button on the toolbar. If the name still does not become underlined, check the spelling of the name for accuracy.

Summary

Journals have come a long way since those little lock-and-key diaries. In Journal, you have a very powerful tool that not only tracks your work and activities, but also calls up old work in a chronological fashion.

14

Q&A

Q I have a contact to AutoRecord who I know is in the Contacts list, but I can't see the name in the Options dialog box. What gives?

A The contact item is not in the main Contact list. If the contact is in a subfolder, it won't be read by Journal. Move or copy the contact into the main Contact folder, and all will be well.

Q Can I delete entries?

A Yes. Simply highlight the Entry and click the Delete button on the Standard toolbar. In fact, it's a good idea to houseclean on a regular basis. For more information on archiving, see Hour 2, "Customizing Outlook 98 to Fit Your Needs," and Hour 17, "Keeping House."

Q Can I safeguard my Journal with a password?

A Currently Outlook does not have the option for password protecting individual folders. If you have delegated access to others and want to secure some items, you need to mark them as private.

You can password protect individual .PST files by clicking Tools, Services and selecting the folder you want to protect. (It must be a folder, which is really a file with a .PST extension.) Click Properties. Click Change Password. Type the old password, the new one, and the new one again in the Verify box. Click OK. From now on, each time you try to open that folder, you are prompted for the password.

Q Do I have to have the Contacts tool open during the entire phone call to be able to record?

A It can be minimized, but it must remain open.

Q How do I find out when a document was originally created?

A To find out when the document was created, you need to access the document itself. When the document is open, choose File, Properties and look under the General tab. It will show you when the document was created.

Q Will Journal track items if Outlook is not running?

A That would be a really good trick, and if Microsoft learns how to do it, maybe it can pick up a few more billion dollars. Meantime, Outlook must be running (even though it can be minimized) to track any items. If you want to open Outlook every time you start your computer, add it to your Startup folder.

HOUR 15

Creating Your Own Point of View

Like snowflakes, no two of us are alike. We each interpret data or evaluate situations slightly differently. Not only are there "the glass is half full" and "the glass is half empty" people, but there are still others who believe the glass has the perfect amount because it contains all they need.

We all like being different. So much so that we shape the world around us to match our preferences. We decorate our homes, we accessorize our clothing, and we add personal touches at work that say this office (cubicle, desk) is mine! Microsoft recognizes your uniqueness and builds in options that enable you to customize computer programs, such as Outlook.

Therefore, in celebration of the diversity of human nature, this hour covers customizing the look of Outlook's Journal. Ultimately, the choice is yours to make, but in this hour you'll get to see a variety of options for viewing Journal information.

Using the Organize Dialog Box

The Ways to Organize Journal dialog box is one of the easiest tools for organizing information. Throughout this hour you learn organizational methods, but why not begin with the simplest?

> The Organize dialog box is actually available in every folder except Outlook Today. It varies in each folder, but the basics are the same, and what you learn during this hour applies to other folders as well.

To open the Ways to Organize Journal dialog box, as shown in Figure 15.1, click the Journal folder if it isn't already active, and click the Organize button on the Standard toolbar.

FIGURE 15.1.

The Organize dialog box has been opened in the Journal view.

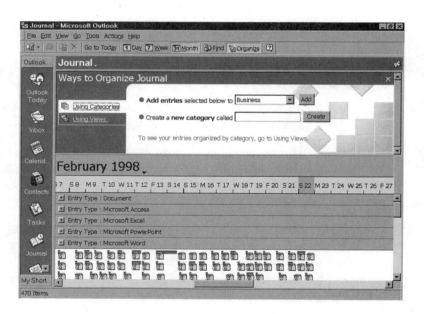

The Ways to Organize Journal dialog box is divided into two tabs: Using Categories and Using Views. You can select multiple documents by clicking the first, pressing Ctrl, and assigning them specific categories. You can also select multiple documents and create and assign a new category. After assigning predefined or new categories, you can then sort or filter them as needed.

The Using Views tab simply enables you to choose from any of the six views available when you choose View, Current View. To close the Ways to Organize Journal dialog box, click the Close button.

Viewing by the Month

Before diving into the techniques of customizing your journal, let's look at what Journal has to offer. In Hour 14, "The Journal: My So-Called Diary," you used the timeline view By Type to look around Journal. This view is shown in Figure 15.2.

FIGURE 15.2.

The By Type view shows a list of entry types.

Monthly scale bar ——

Daily scale bar ——

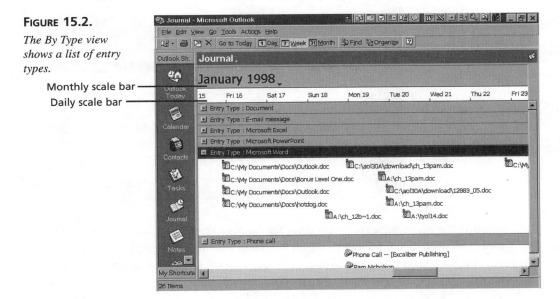

Remember: This is the default view of Journal, and it shows the Week view, one of the three types of timeline views. You can tell this by looking at the increments in the two scale bars above the groups and items. The lower scale shows the dates with the days of the week, and the upper scale shows the month and year.

Note that the items are stacked on top of each other, but are not quite aligned. This is because the items are arranged by the time they are created or opened on a particular day. Consequently, by looking at January 15, you can see that four Word documents were edited in the evening.

Journal Viewing by the Day Timeline

If a more detailed timeline is needed, click the Day button on the Standard toolbar to create a Day view, much like the one shown in Figure 15.3.

FIGURE 15.3.

The Day Timeline view provides detail by the hours of the day.

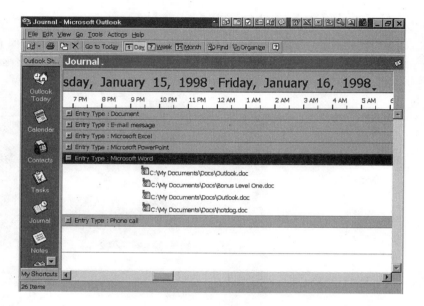

The timeline views have specific criteria for display: The entire label must be visible and cannot be overlapped. So, to display all the items without overlapping, items in the timeline are displayed farther and farther down the screen. This sometimes makes it difficult to read. If you would have used the scrollbar to move down the screen (refer to Figure 15.3), you would have come upon the three Friday evening documents. The afternoon documents have precedence, so they appear on the top of the group.

To Do: Cleaning Up Your Views

▼ To Do

1. Open Outlook. Click the Journal icon in the Outlook Bar.
2. Choose View, Current View, Customize Current View to open the View Summary dialog box.
3. Choose Other Settings. This opens the Format Timeline View dialog box.
4. In the Labels panel, change the number of characters that are displayed in the label to a smaller number. Try **20**.

▲ 5. Click OK. The View Summary dialog box again appears. Click OK again.

You may think this is silly, especially if your labels show file pathnames. After all, now they will be cut off and you won't be able to tell what they signify. There's another trick you can use here: Whenever labels have been *truncated* (shortened), you can move the cursor over an icon and a little pop-up label with the full name appears.

Viewing an Entire Month of Journal Entries

The third view of a timeline is the Month view, as shown in Figure 15.4. Because the increments in the daily scale bar are so narrow, Journal doesn't even try to show the items' labels, by default. The items look more aligned along the timeline, but they are not. It's more subtle at this scale, but the items still fall at the approximate time of day they were created or edited.

FIGURE 15.4.

By default, the Month timeline view shows less detail than the other views.

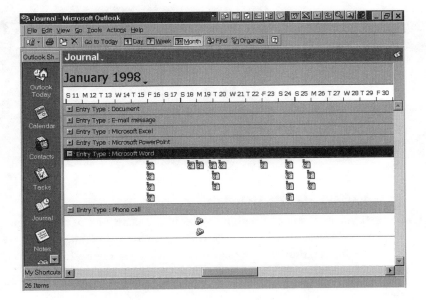

You just can't live without those labels? You don't like the little pop-up labels? Rest easy. Choose View, Current View, Customize Current View, and choose Other Settings. In the Labels section in the Format Timeline View dialog box, click the Show Label When Viewing by Month check box.

When you do this, your timeline expands vertically because items have to be stacked to avoid label overlap.

Less Common Views of Journal

You should be pretty familiar with the By Type view by now. Let's take a look at the other six views of Journal before learning how to customize your timeline. To display the list of view categories, choose View, Current View, as shown in Figure 15.5.

FIGURE 15.5.

The six types of Journal views are displayed in the menu.

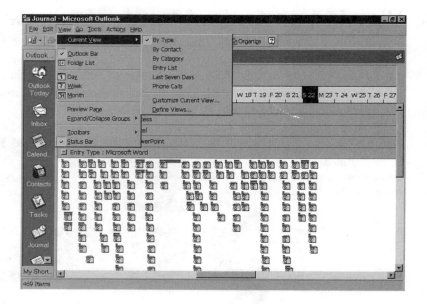

Viewing by Contact

If you communicate with many people or share a lot of files, be prepared to see a lot of group boxes in this view. The By Contact view is identical to the By Type view, except the Journal Entries are grouped by contact (see Figure 15.6).

It is imperative to understand just what is meant by *contact* in this context (working with documents). It is *not* those people with whom you talk or exchange email. Inside every Office document is Summary Information that contains the time of original creation, the *original author* of the document, the time of the last edit, and so on (this is true in both Office 97 and 95). If you want to manually change this information, choose File, Properties (except Access and Outlook) when the document is open. *It is the name in the Author field in the Summary Information dialog box that Journal uses as the contact name.*

FIGURE 15.6.

This view is organized by contact.

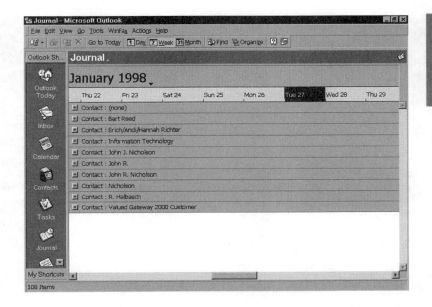

This is all very nice, but it can lead to problems. Some files carry a lot of summary baggage that can clog up your timelines with a lot of puzzling group boxes. If you really hate this kind of thing, you can select any group box and then click the Delete button in the Standard toolbar to delete that group.

In my opinion, this is a nearly worthless view. I haven't a clue how most of my group names were created. When you expand (click the plus on a category) and see a blank space, you need to use the left scroll arrow to see previous dates. You may want to forgo using this view.

The one potential use of this view is to see a timeline of phone calls, letters, faxes, or emails to a single contact (at least the ones entered in Outlook's Journal).

Displaying the By Category View

In contrast to the By Contact view, the By Category view groups by category. However, I suspect the first time you open it, you are going to find very few category group boxes (see Figure 15.7). Most if not all *documents* you have created will be assigned to the None category.

FIGURE 15.7.

The By Category view. All the listed files are in the "None" category.

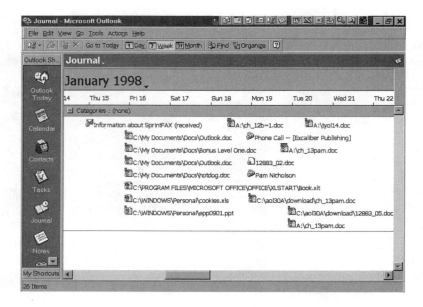

This is because, for all its cool AutoRecording, Journal does not automatically assign a category to anything it records for you. Therefore, a great majority of Journal's entries do not have categories. Only when you have manually recorded information in the Category or Keywords text boxes on the Summary Information tab of the Properties dialog box for the document will any categories be assigned. This limits the usefulness of this view, unless you are diligent in always assigning categories to your entries.

If you create a journal item from a contact, task, or other item that has a category assigned, the journal entry automatically inherits the item's category. This is most often seen when you're entering email messages and phone calls to contacts who have categories.

The following is a fast way to assign categories to Journal entries:

1. While holding down the Ctrl key, click all the items you want to assign to the same category (which selects all of them).

2. Right-click one of the selected items.

3. In the pop-up menu, click the Categories command to display the Categories dialog box.

4. Select all appropriate categories and click OK.

15

If you don't want to maintain this kind of organization, I recommend that you do not use this view very often. However, there is one positive use for this view. In the Categories: (none) group, you can easily see the order in which you last worked on the files, regardless of type or contact.

Displaying the Entry List View

The Entry List view is the first of the three table views in Journal. The information fields are displayed in a more familiar form, as shown in Figure 15.8. The data is displayed in descending order, with the most recent entries at the top.

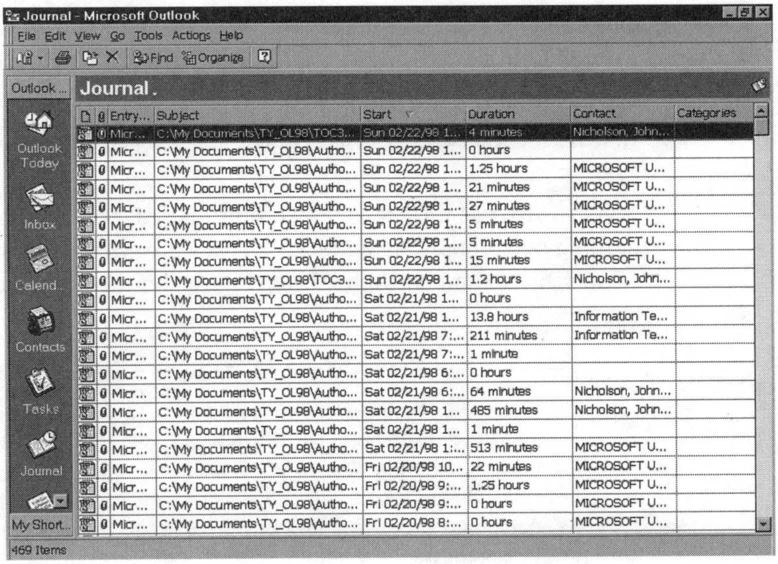

FIGURE 15.8.

In the Entry List view, the data is sorted by date.

The fields displayed in this view are the Icon, Attachment, Entry Type, Subject, Start, Duration, Contact, and Categories. They are probably sorted in descending order on the Start column.

> You can sort by any column. Clicking a column heading changes the sort to that column. Clicking the same column again reverses the sort direction.

The Icon and Entry Type columns show exactly the same information: what the Journal item is. One just uses icons rather than words. Such redundancy is usually not needed and also eats up acres of screen real estate. I recommend that you learn to recognize each icon and delete the Entry type column.

Hour 12, "Power Calendaring," showed you how to define a view in Outlook, including deleting a field from a view. There is a faster way to delete a particular column from a table view, as shown in the following exercise.

To Do: Deleting and Moving Columns from a Table View

1. Display the Entry List view by clicking View, Current View, Entry List.

2. Click and drag the Entry type column header up or down on the screen.

3. As soon as the header box leaves the heading area of the table, a large black *X* appears over it.

4. Release the mouse button. The header disappears, along with the entire column of data.

5. You can also use this technique to shift the order of columns. As you drag the heading horizontally, a pair of vertical red arrows appears at the leftmost position of the *new* column position. The change won't take effect until you release the mouse button.

> To return a deleted column to the view, make sure the Entry Level view (or whichever view you want to change) is displayed, and choose View, Current View, Customize Current View. Click the Fields button to open the Show Fields dialog box. Select the field you want to add in the Available Fields panel and click the Add-> button. Use the Move Up and Move Down buttons until the new field is correctly positioned. Click OK twice. You may need to change the field width by dragging the column heading boundary left or right.

Understanding the Columns in the Entry List View

We've already discussed Icon and Entry Type columns. The Attachment column tells the user whether a document or Outlook item is linked to an item. A paper clip icon denotes an attachment. This may seem superfluous because most things that are *automatically* recorded in Journal are documents. If you use Journal only to record Office documents, you should also delete this column from Journal's table views to save a little space.

15

The Subject field contains the same information as the icon labels in the timeline views. This view shows the complete information, even if you resized the label information in the Format Views dialog box.

The Start field shows the start date and the time the Entry was last updated. The Duration field indicates the length of time the document was edited, or the length of time for the journal entry that you manually recorded.

The last two fields, Contact and Categories, are no different from any other part of Outlook. This view has no groups or filters automatically applied; therefore, you can see all your data at once.

Last Seven Days View

The next table view in Journal uses the same columns as the Entry List view. However, a filter has been automatically applied to the data, as shown in Figure 15.9, restricting the view to only the entries that have been made during the previous week.

FIGURE 15.9.

The data has been fil-tered to show only the last seven days.

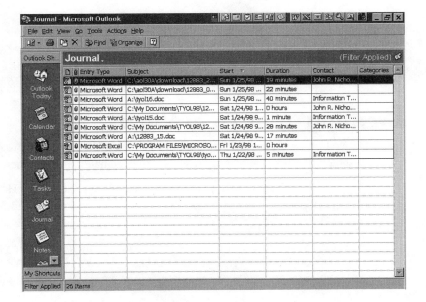

Phone Calls View

The final predefined table view in Journal is the most restrictive of the views. The filter applied to the Journal data displays only the phone call items. Unless you manually place a seven-day filter on this view, all calls—regardless of how long ago they were made—are shown.

In Figure 15.10, you can see the effect of this. Note the loss of one information field: the Entry Type column. Journal's designers recognized its redundancy with the Icon field and, at least in this view, chose not to display it.

FIGURE 15.10.

The data has been filtered to show only phone calls.

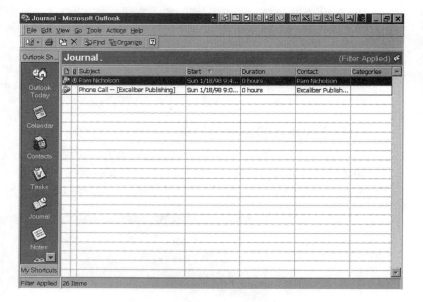

Creating Your Own Views

Did you ever get one of those model kits as a kid? Weren't they great? You'd break off all the pieces from the plastic "tree" and then cement them together, one by one.

Next, it was time for painting the model and applying the decals. However, for me, it was difficult to get the paints right. So, all my X-wing fighters and Starship Enterprises remained suspiciously white.

In Outlook you can leave the views as they are—plain vanilla—or you can do your own detailing, venturing into chocolate, strawberry, or even spumoni. You can give each of Outlook's tools your own personal look and feel—no need to settle for plain, vanilla views.

In previous hours, the methods for customizing your views are fairly well outlined. However, changing the look of a timeline view is a bit different than altering the day/week/month or table views. So for the rest of this hour, let's try out different configuration techniques as they apply to timelines in Journal.

Globally Configuring Views

When you want to create a new view in Journal, it is easiest to take a current view and modify it to meet your needs. Using the following instructions, you can modify any existing view by duplicating the steps and changing them as needed.

To Do: Changing All Views at Once

1. Choose <u>V</u>iew, Current <u>V</u>iew, <u>D</u>efine Views. The Define Views for "Journal" dialog box appears (see Figure 15.11). With this one dialog box, you can modify the display of every Journal view.

FIGURE 15.11.

The Define Views dialog box.

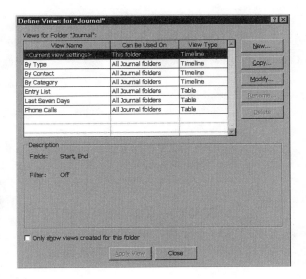

2. Use the down arrow to examine each of the View Names. Notice how the Description panel changes for each entry.

3. Highlight the Phone Calls view. Notice that the calls are sorted in descending order based on the Start field. This means that the newest phone calls are displayed at the top of the list.

4. Click Modify. The familiar View Summary dialog box is displayed. Click Sort to display the Sort dialog box. Drop down the Sort Items By list to see the various fields that you can sort by in this view. Choose Duration.

5. Click OK or Close until you are back to the current Journal view. Change to the Phone List view. Notice in the column heading for Duration that there is an up-pointing arrow, showing that the phone calls are sorted in ascending order by that category. (If you haven't entered any phone calls in Journal, the list is empty, but you can still see the sort icon.)

Shortcuts for Defining Views

If you want to modify just one aspect of a view in Outlook, you can save a step and go straight to the needed tool without using the Define Views dialog box. Table 15.1 shows the menu commands that will take you straight to the right tool.

 You need to be in the view you want to modify to use this trick.

TABLE 15.1. DEFINING VIEWS.

To define...	Use this command...	And this dialog box will appear
The displayed fields	View, Current View, Customize Current View, Fields	Show Fields
How data is grouped	View, Current View, Customize Current View, Group By	Group By
How data is sorted	View, Current View, Customize Current View, Sort	Sort
What data is shown	View, Current View, Customize Current View, Filter	Filter
The "cosmetic" look	View, Current View, Customize Current View, Other Settings	Format View Type View
What font to use	View, Current View, Customize Current View, Automatic Formatting	Automatic Formatting

 If you want to format more than one of these view aspects, it is better to use the Define Views dialog box, where the Description section can help you keep track of all the changes you have made. This is only true if you're going to modify multiple views. If you're changing multiple aspects of the same view, it's unnecessary to return to the Define Views dialog box after each change.

Modifying a Current View

To change the currently selected view, open the Define Views dialog box and click the Modify button on the right side. This displays the View Summary for the View dialog box, as shown in Figure 15.12. Like the Description section of the Define Views dialog box, this dialog box shows all the settings for the current view, and has six buttons that activate the dialog boxes to modify each setting.

FIGURE 15.12.

The View Summary dialog box.

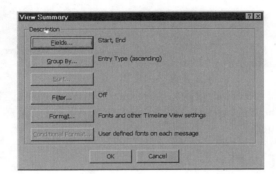

In this figure, two of those six buttons, Sort and Conditional Format, are grayed: the universal Windows symbol for a disabled function. This makes sense if you think about it. A timeline should only be able to sort chronologically, so Journal does not give you the option to change this.

Displaying Timeline Fields

When you click the Fields button in the View Summary dialog box, Outlook opens the Date/Time Fields dialog box (see Figure 15.13). Here you can designate the information that will be visible in the Timeline view. This does not seem to be a very powerful function. After all, there are only three available fields to choose from: End, Modified, and Start. By default, the Start field in a timeline is assigned the Start data, and the End field is assigned the End data.

Selecting Other Fields

There are more data fields available for use as a timeline's Start or End field than just the three mentioned in the preceding section. To access them, click the Select Available Fields From list box in the Date/Time Fields dialog box.

FIGURE 15.13.

Use the Date/Time Fields dialog box to determine the information that is shown in the Timeline view.

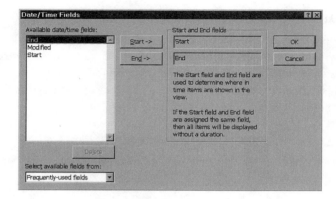

If you click any of the other options, the list in the Available Data/Time Fields box will reveal item-specific fields to use. This is handy if you are creating views that examine specific Outlook items.

Grouping Timeline Data

To change the grouping structure of a timeline, click the Group By button. To open the Group By dialog box, as shown in Figure 15.14, switch to the view you want to modify, and choose View, Current View, Customize Current View. Click the Group By button. You see that there are four nearly identical sections, each containing a drop-down list box and ascending and descending option buttons.

FIGURE 15.14.

The Group By dialog box enables you to modify the grouping of a timeline.

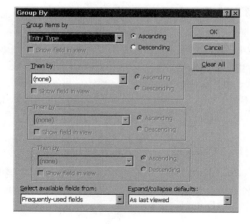

In the first panel, Group Items By, you see the current grouping criteria for the view you are in. For timelines, the Show Field in View check box is disabled because this applies to columns in table views.

The Then By drop-down list, which is expanded in Figure 15.15, enables you to establish a second level of timeline grouping criteria.

FIGURE 15.15.

You can group timeline data by several levels.

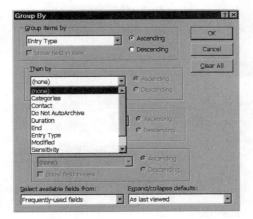

The rest of the sections enable you to group more specifically by third and fourth grouping levels. At the bottom of the dialog box is the Select Available Fields From list box, which enables you to choose which field set to use for grouping fields. Next to this is the Expand/Collapse Defaults list box, which sets the default view for any expandable group heading.

Filtering Timeline Data

If you want to restrict the data that is displayed, click the Filter button to open the Filter dialog box, as shown in Figure 15.16.

To use the Filter dialog box, enter the information value you want Journal to show. This filter performs the same as in any other Outlook view. Figures 15.17 and 15.18 show the More Choices and Advanced tabs, respectively, of the Filter dialog box to give you an idea of the different tools you can use to limit your data.

Remember: After you have applied a filter, you can once again view *all* your data by opening the Filter dialog box and clicking the Clear All button. All data in Journal will again be visible.

FIGURE 15.16.

Use the Filter dialog box to determine which data you want displayed.

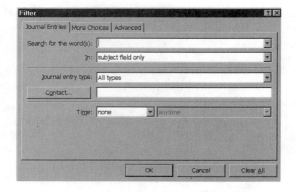

FIGURE 15.17.

The More Choices tab of the Filter dialog box provides additional filtering options.

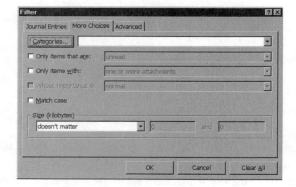

FIGURE 15.18.

The Advanced tab of the Filter dialog box enables you to define very specific rules for filtering data.

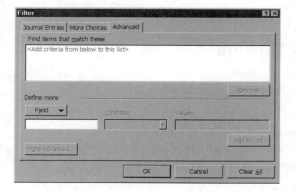

Changing a Timeline's Look

The last button in the View Settings dialog box, Other Settings, opens the Format Timeline View, as shown in Figure 15.19.

FIGURE 15.19.

The Format Timeline View dialog box enables you to choose the fonts for the time-line display.

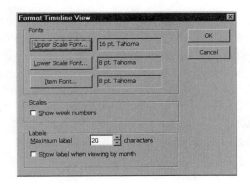

There are three areas of a timeline where you can modify the format: the Upper Scale Font, the Lower Scale Font, and the Item Font. The corresponding Font buttons each activate a standard Windows Font dialog box. After you change the font settings, samples of the new font appear next to the Font buttons.

The Scales panel has just one check box: Show Week Numbers. If this is checked, Week N (for which N is a number from 1 through 52) is displayed next to the date in the upper scale for the Day and Week views of a timeline, and as the only unit label in the Month view. To review the labels section, see "To Do: Cleaning Up Your Views" earlier this hour.

Summary

The evidence is in, and there is only one conclusion: Journal is much more than a simple record of the work you have done. It is part file manager, part version tracker, and, yes, part diary. When you have customized Journal and created exactly the views you need, Journal enables you to manage all your work in a focused, organized manner.

Q&A

Q **I thought only document attachments would show the Attachment icon. Why does it appear in some of my phone call and remote messaging Journal entries?**

A The Attachment icon applies to attached documents and Outlook items. If you have made a phone call, sent an email, or faxed someone in your Contacts list, the paper clip appears. You can use this to your advantage to update your contacts. Modify or create a new table view in Journal that will sort by Attachment and then by Entry Type. Look at the items you frequently send to someone not currently included in your Contacts list. These would be good candidates for addition.

Q **Is there any way to shorten the vertical size of some of the timeline groups? They get so tall that sometimes they're hard to manage.**

A Other than decreasing the font size of your items, no. This is a valid concern because it makes the timelines one of the more awkward parts of Outlook.

Q **Doesn't tracking all that information take up a lot of disk space?**

A It does indeed take up a great deal of disk space. Many people actually choose to turn off automatic journal recordings, and prefer to manually create their entries only as needed. If you do decide to use automatic tracking, pay close attention to Hour 17, "Keeping House," which addresses managing your journal entries and other files.

Hour **16**

Not-So-Sticky Notes

The next time someone tells you that we will one day live in a paper-free society, feel free to laugh in his or her face. We will probably never be totally free of paper or its influence—at least not for a very long time.

This is not just an author trying to justify the medium. The art of the written word will long survive the passing of paper. This isn't just an environmentalist ranting either. I like trees, and I recycle paper as much as possible. It's just that since computers became commonly used, more paper than ever is being consumed by the average office.

This argument is based on the physical concept of inertia. Paper, archeologists estimate, has been around since papyrus was first used in ancient Egypt over 4,700 years ago. That's a lot of staying power.

When an idea gets into our collective head, it is very difficult to expunge it. Money is a good example. Computers, bar-coded products, and plastic cards with magnetic swipe strips are sophisticated enough to handle almost any financial transaction, but we still like to have cash on hand. ATM cards are great, but it's also nice to have the real stuff once in a while.

Computers can also handle any kind of document you can think of. Indeed, the invention of the computer also brought about the development of quite a few new kinds of documents. However, even people who use computers every day still think in terms of paper. For instance, you are probably asked, How many pages is that Word document? But a more accurate question would be, How many bytes is that Word document? We are still wary of the reliability of computers and feel safer with a paper copy of our data.

Once in a while, however, a paper form can actually be improved in electronic format. The spreadsheet is a good example. The whole row/column/cell configuration didn't just appear in some programmer's head. Spreadsheets were huge, unwieldy sheets of paper with sometimes hundreds of rows and columns of financial data; accountants spread them out over big tables and checked them by hand. Spreadsheets were perfect for making the transition to the electronic venue. With cell-linking capabilities and formulas that can be directly entered into cells, their accuracy actually increases.

In this hour, we look at another kind of paper that has successfully made the leap to computers: the sticky note. Outlook has taken the entire sticky note phenomenon and created a new computer version of it—right down to the ubiquitous pastel color schemes.

Passing Notes

Electronic sticky notes are a novel idea, but what good are they? When *you* start using electronic sticky notes, you'll find they are as indispensable as their paper siblings.

Notes in Outlook are sort of a cross between a task, an appointment, and a contact. Notes let you jot down any kind of information you want—activities, reminders, phone numbers—and let you keep them indefinitely. If you use Outlook to its full potential, Notes can be one of your primary tools. As you see later this hour, when you save something in Notes, it's there to stay and can easily be transferred to a more functional part of Outlook: Tasks, Calendar, and even the Inbox.

Despite all this flexibility, Notes has some limitations. A note cannot be set to remind you of something with a beep and a message. Nor can a note be directly sent to someone else via email. Notes doesn't have a lot of fancy controls and display settings, and they cannot recur. However, just as paper sticky notes have limitations, they also have many practical applications. You can use Notes in most situations where you would use a paper sticky note.

By creating a new note, you'll be able to see just what a note can and cannot do for you.

Creating a Note

Five ways to start a new note are

- If you are not in Outlook, you can click the New Note button on the Microsoft Office Shortcut Bar.

- If you are in Notes, choose File, New, Note or click the New Note button on the Standard toolbar.

- If you are in a note item, click the Note icon in the upper-left corner, and then choose New Note from the menu.

- If you are in some other part of Outlook, you can click the New Note command on the New Item drop-down list on the Standard toolbar.

- Finally, if you like shortcut keys, press Ctrl+N if you are in Notes and Ctrl+Shift+N if you are anywhere else in Outlook.

Using any of these methods displays a little yellow box on your screen, as shown in Figure 16.1.

FIGURE 16.1.

A brand-new, empty, yellow note is created.

01/26/98 8:00 AM

Just a quick word about colors. Because all the money for this book was spent on exorbitant author royalties (ha, ha), this book was printed in black and white. Notes uses blue, green, pink, yellow, and white for background colors. Yellow is the default color, and that is what will be used unless otherwise noted. So, when referring to the figures, you'll just have to believe me.

To Do: Creating a Note

1. Open Outlook and click the Notes icon on the Outlook Bar. Click the New Note button to create a New Note.

2. Type Call home before leaving work!

3. Leave the Note open for now.

Setting the Note Options

Let's look closely at this note. The Note icon is in the upper-left corner, and the Close Window button is in the upper-right corner. At the bottom of the note is a bar containing the time and date the note was created with a resizing tool in the lower-right corner.

That's it: no menus, no save buttons—not even the ever-present Windows OK button. So, it's safe to move onto the next hour, right? Not exactly: You need to explore some of Notes uses.

To write a note, type the message you want into the note. When you have done this, you can save it as is or set some of the note's parameters so that you can organize it. Because you want to explore the full range of Notes, don't save the note yet.

Notes have two main parameters for organization: color and categories. You may use one, both, or none. When you start using Notes, one of the first things you want to do is to assign a category to each color. For example, you could use blue for personal notes, yellow for interoffice business, and green for business with other companies.

To Do: Changing the Note

1. Click the Note icon in the upper-left corner of the Note window to display the Note options menu, as shown in Figure 16.2.

FIGURE 16.2.

Use this menu to set Note options.

2. Choose Color. You have a choice of five different colors. Yellow is the default.
3. Choose Blue because this will be a personal reminder for you. As soon as you click Blue, the note changes color and you are returned to a normal view (see Figure 16.3).
4. Click the Note icon in the upper-left corner once again to open the options menu.
5. Choose Categories. This displays the Categories dialog box, as shown in Figure 16.4, where you can assign a variety of categories to the Note.

▼ **FIGURE 16.3.**

You can color-code your notes.

FIGURE 16.4.

Use the Categories dialog box to assign a note's category.

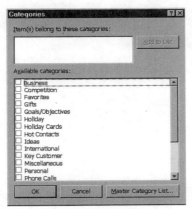

6. Choose Personal as the category and click OK. You'll see that the note has not changed in the slightest. Categories are only shown in selected views of the Notes' Information Viewer screen, as you will see later this hour.

7. Close the note by clicking the x in the upper-right corner, or by clicking anywhere
▲   outside of the note.

Saving a Note

After you have completed your note, click the Close Window button to instantly save it to Outlook's database. You can also save it to another format by using the Save As command you saw on the Note Options menu, but I do not recommend it because it's time consuming.

> Notes are automatically saved, even after their initial creation. If you open a note, make a change, and click outside the note, that change is reflected in all views of Notes' information viewer.

The Closed Note Icon

After closing the note, it appears in the Notes information viewer (see Figure 16.5). In Icon view (Notes' default view), the first several words of the note are visible when it is selected; otherwise, only a portion of each note is displayed.

FIGURE 16.5.

Notice that the selected note in Icon view displays more text than non-selected notes.

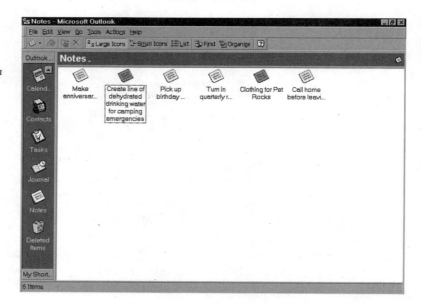

When you create a note, it is recommended that you keep the first paragraph of the note short, yet descriptive. If it is too long, too much screen real estate will be hogged by the note. However, beware of making it too short. Include enough information to convey the note's topic.

Editing a Note

If you see something in a note that needs to be changed, double-click the note item in any Notes view. The note opens, and you can make your changes in the note's text, color, or categories.

Notes can be assigned to multiple categories.

You can also resize an open note. To do this, move the mouse pointer to the lower-right corner of the note. When the mouse pointer changes to the diagonal resizing arrows (see Figure 16.6), drag the corner of the note to the desired size. This is a handy way to see all of a lengthy note's text at one time.

FIGURE 16.6.

You can easily resize a note to show more or less text.

Resizing arrows

16

In the next exercise, you'll create a few practice notes that will be used later in the hour.

To Do: Creating Practice Notes

1. Use the information in Table 16.1 to create several new notes.

TABLE 16.1. SAMPLE NOTES TO USE FOR THIS HOUR.

Note Color	Note Category	Description
Pink	Ideas	Clothing for Pet Rocks.
Yellow	Business	Turn in Quarterly Review to VP Sales.
Blue	Personal	Pick up birthday present for Mom.
Pink	Ideas	Create line of dehydrated drinking water for camping emergencies.
Blue	Personal, Phone Calls	Make anniversary dinner reservations.

▼ 2. Double-click the Anniversary note to open it. Right-click the Control menu in the top-left corner of the open note. Click Minimize. This moves the note onto the taskbar at the bottom of the screen.

3. Right-click the Note icon in the taskbar, and click Maximize.

4. The window can no longer be resized, and (more annoying) every subsequent note will appear like this. To return to smaller notes, use that same Control menu and

▲ click Restore.

Deleting a Note

When you no longer need a note, highlight it and click the Delete button on the Standard toolbar. If the note is open, you can open the Note Options menu and choose the Delete command.

Organizing and Configuring Your Notes

When I was in school, I had my notes all very organized. Notes to and from Lisa were in one side of the desk drawer, notes to and from Gretchen on the other, and notes to and from Aubrey in the middle. This may not seem all that important, but I still remember the trouble I got into the one time I goofed up this system. Fifth-grade girls can really punch.

Although your motivations may not be so necessary for self-preservation, it's still nice to be able to organize all your notes into some kind of pattern so that they can more easily help you.

To aid in this endeavor, Notes has five different views to see your notes. We have already seen the first: the Icon view. To change views, chose View, Current View, and choose any of the five available views.

The remaining four views of Notes are all table views, which should be familiar to you. A quick look at them will allow you to make a decision on which view you prefer.

Using the Organize Dialog Box

The Organize dialog box is similar to the one discussed in Hour 15, "Creating Your Own Point of View," for Journals. This one works slightly different. To open the box, click the Organize button on the Standard toolbar. You can use this box to move selected messages to a specific folder. You can create a new folder by clicking the New Folder option. You can also display the Rules Wizard, discussed further in Hour 22, "New and Fun Outlook Features."

As in the Journal Organize dialog box, the Notes Organize dialog box also has a second tab: Using Views. This tab enables you select from any of the five views available by choosing <u>V</u>iew, Current <u>V</u>iew.

Listing Notes

The Notes List view shows the Icon, Subject, Created, and Categories information fields. The icons are colored with the same color the note has been assigned. The Subject shows the first paragraph of the note. If it is too long, ellipsis points indicate that the Subject has been truncated. Created shows the date the note was first made. This is the default sorting column for the Notes List view, meaning that all the notes are sorted from newest to oldest. The Categories field shows the categories that have been assigned to the note, as shown in Figure 16.7.

16

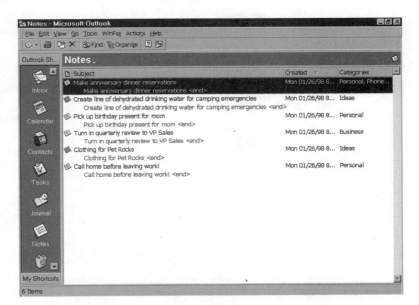

FIGURE 16.7.

The Notes List view provides important information about the notes, and enables you to read the first few lines of each note.

Another default setting for the Notes List view, as you can see in Figure 16.7, is the AutoPreview, enabling you to read the first few lines of the note's contents. This feature can be deactivated by selecting the Auto<u>P</u>review item from the <u>V</u>iew menu.

The Last Week View

The next view, Last Seven Days, also has a default AutoPreview setting. In fact, it is identical to the Notes List view in every way, except that now a filter has been applied to the data. The filter displays only the notes created or modified in the last seven days. This view is useful if you use a lot of notes.

Viewing Notes by Category

The By Category view displays only three information fields: Icon, Subject, and Created. This time, the notes are grouped into their respective categories.

The default view of the By Category view has all the groups closed (collapsed), but this can be changed by clicking the little box with the plus sign (+) in it on the left side of the group box. This expands the category, as shown in Figure 16.8. To collapse the category again, click the minus sign (–) in the group box.

FIGURE 16.8.

In the By Category view, you can see all the groups and their individual notes.

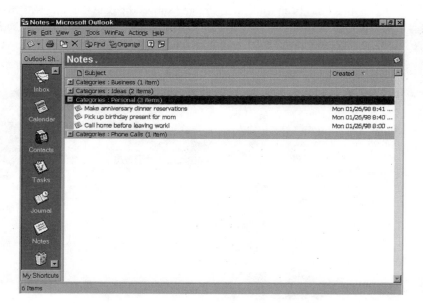

Coloring Your View

The last view is the By Color view. This view is identical to the By Category view, although now the notes are grouped by their color (see Figure 16.9).

Noting the Number of Items

Compare the number of items in Figure 16.8 with those shown in Figure 16.9. The first shows a total of seven items, while the second shows only six items, and yet you haven't added or deleted any notes. The answer is simple: In Figure 16.8, the number of items are grouped by category, and one of the items falls into two categories: personal and phone calls. Because a note can be assigned to multiple categories, the number of notes by category might be larger than the number of actual notes. In Figure 16.9, the grouping is by color, and each note can have only a single color assigned to it.

Figure 16.9.

In the By Color view, you see the notes grouped by color.

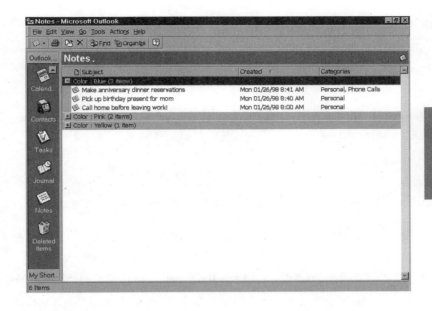

16

 Also worth noting is that the status line shows the correct total: six in each case.

Configuration Hints

For the sake of example, you saw notes that were organized both by color and category. In real life, this kind of detail would probably be counterproductive. This is especially true, given the presence of these last two views.

I recommend using the following organizational techniques, based on your needs:

Organized By	If
Color	You have five or fewer general groups to which you want to assign your notes
Category	You have five or more organized groups for your notes
Both color and category	You have a group that you want to subdivide

Like any other tool in Outlook, all these views can be customized to suit your needs. (See Hour 12, "Power Calendaring," for more information.)

Note Options

There is one other set of configuration parameters you can set in Notes: the note item itself. Choose Tools, Options, Note Options. This opens the Notes Options dialog box, as shown in Figure 16.10.

FIGURE **16.10.**

The Note Options dialog box enables you to set default values.

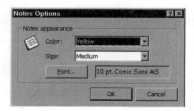

The Color drop-down list sets the default color of your notes when they are first created. You can set the default color to any of the five colors.

The Size drop-down list sets the default size of the note: Small, Medium, or Large.

The Font button opens the standard Windows Font dialog box (see Figure 16.11). You can set the size, appearance, and color of the Notes font. When you are finished, a sample of the font appears in the field just to the right of the Font button. After setting font options, click OK to return to the Notes Options dialog box.

FIGURE **16.11.**

Use the Font dialog box to set the font default values for new notes.

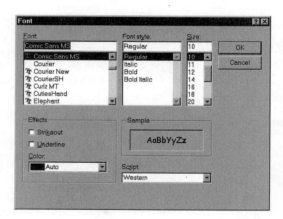

After changing any of these controls, click OK to apply the changes to subsequent notes that you create.

Putting Notes in Their Places

One nice feature of Notes is that its entries can be directed to other parts of Outlook, and even to other files on your computer. To be truthful, this feature is available with any Outlook item: a task, a contact, or whatever. However, with Notes, it's a lot faster (and therefore easier) to use because of the very small file size of a note.

The very nature of a note—sort of a sticky note slapped on a bigger document—also lends itself to this kind of use. In the following exercise, you learn to manipulate notes in various ways.

To Do: Manipulating Notes

1. To move a note to another part of Outlook, click once on the note item in any view, and drag the note onto any of the folders in the Outlook Bar or any of the folders in the Folder list.

2. To copy a note to another part of Outlook, begin the AutoCreate function. For example, copying a note to the Tasks folder AutoCreates a new task with the body of the note appearing in the note section of the dialog box (see Figure 16.12). Notice that the category for the note has been moved into the contact's category field.

FIGURE 16.12.

A copy of the note is now in the note box of the new Task.

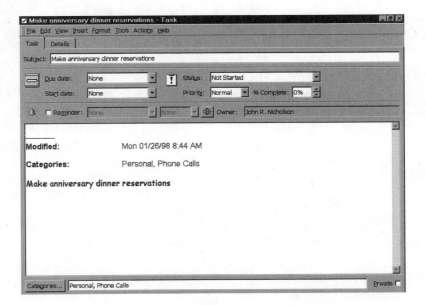

This action is repeated whenever you copy a note to any part of Outlook. If you want to have a note appear as an attached object inside an Outlook item, the procedure is slightly different. The following exercise shows you how to attach a note to any Outlook item.

To Do: Attaching a Note to an Outlook Item

1. To attach a note to an Outlook item (a contact for this example), first open that item.

2. Choose Insert, Item.

3. In the Insert Item dialog box (see Figure 16.13), navigate until the Notes folder is highlighted in the top panel, and you can see the contents of the Notes folder in the lower panel.

FIGURE 16.13.

Locate the note in the Insert Item dialog box to attach it to an Outlook item.

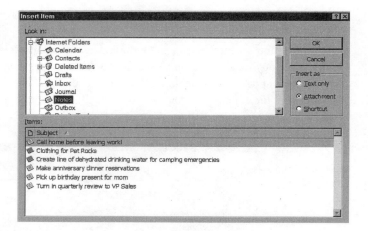

4. In the Insert As panel, Attachment is the default. Click OK.

A note is embedded within your contact item, as shown in Figure 16.14. To open this note, simply double-click it whenever the item to which it is attached is open.

When you attach a note to any Outlook item, its icon always appears yellow, despite any other color it has been assigned within Notes.

FIGURE 16.14.

The note is now attached to the contact.

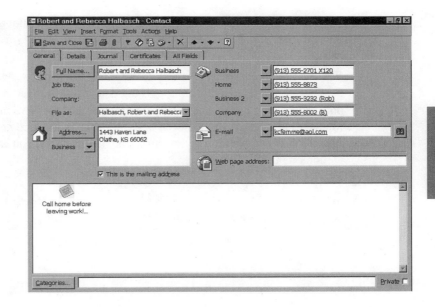

Summary

By now, you should have a good idea of how to quickly create and organize notes in Outlook. Use them for those in-between items that don't quite fit into the Tasks or Calendar components. If used in this manner, Notes will soon become indispensable as an integral part of Outlook.

Q&A

Q I really don't like any of the pastel colors of Notes. Can I change them?

A No. Unfortunately, there is no way (short of programming) to add more color choices to Notes.

Q Can I attach a Note to my desktop?

A With ease. Select the note, and drop it anywhere on the desktop. It will turn yellow, but that will be the only change to the note.

16

Q I have tried to drag and drop a note into my Word document, and all I get is text information. I can't find the note to attach it from Word, either. Can I do this?

A Yes, but first you have to get the note out into the open as a separate file. Notes are generally just data items in Outlook's big database. However, if you drag the note onto the desktop first, the note becomes a separate *.msg (Microsoft Mail Message) file, which you then can drag into your Word document as an embedded file, complete with a little yellow note icon. (By the way, you can do this with any Outlook item.)

Q Can I create new categories for notes?

A Yes. Using the Master Category List button in the Categories dialog box, type the new category name and click the Add button. Click OK.

PART VI
Improving Your Outlook

Hour

HOUR 17

Keeping House

If you are obsessive-compulsive about neatness and filing, this hour is critical to your use of Outlook. If you are just a normal person, then this is still an important hour for you to understand. Earlier in this book, you learned to make Outlook automatically record a journal entry of the files you use, the phone calls you make, the email you both send and receive, and a variety of other tasks. After using Outlook for an extended period, it will slow down without your employing some kind of file management.

Managing your file folders in Outlook is a very important task. By learning how to perform tasks, such as archiving your data and importing and exporting files, you can save time, make your data transferable, and conserve valuable hard drive space.

This hour helps you understand the structure of your personal folders and shows you how to archive old data and transfer files between computers.

Where Are My Personal File Folders?

All your Personal File Folders are stored in a single file. Therefore, to properly maintain your Personal File Folders, it is important that you know where this file is stored on your computer. To find its location, choose Tools, Services. In the Services dialog box, select the Personal Folders File and click the Properties button. The Personal Folders dialog box is displayed, as in Figure 17.1. The Path box specifies the location of the file (probably `c:\windows\outlook.pst`).

FIGURE 17.1.

The Personal Folders dialog box enables you to customize and protect your personal folders.

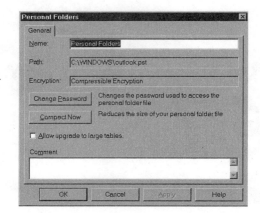

When you have located the file, you can reduce its size by compacting it, thus enabling Outlook to run much faster. From the Services dialog box, click the Properties button. Click Compact Now. You can also set a password from the Properties dialog box to prevent others from opening your file. This was explained in Hour 16, "Not-So-Sticky Notes."

Don't Lose It: Archiving

At times, you may need to remove old and seldom-used files from Outlook by archiving some of the information stored in your Outlook Personal Folders file. Archiving is a way of removing old data from your Outlook file in such a way that you can get it back anytime you need it. It's an operation that can be compared to filing old bills and receipts. You probably don't refer to them very often (if at all), but you have to keep them somewhere in case the IRS ever wants to audit you. Hopefully, you have filed and stored this data where you can easily access it, just in case Uncle Sam comes knocking.

Similarly, you may have Outlook files from past projects or previous years. You don't want to delete these files, but you also don't want Outlook to have to sort through the information every time you instigate a Search or Filter operation. The best way to take care of these files is to archive them. This removes old data from your Outlook database and stores it in an archive file, usually called archive.pst, which can be accessed by Outlook whenever you want to refer to the data.

Setting Up AutoArchive

Realistically, most of us don't have time to sit around and sift through our files to see what needs to be archived and what doesn't. Fortunately, we have Outlook to do this for us.

You can choose to allow Outlook to automatically archive your old files, based on a schedule that you designate. You can schedule an archiving session to take place as often as every day or as infrequently as every 60 days. This really depends on how you work and how much hard drive space you have available.

To Do: Setting Up AutoArchive

1. Open Outlook if it is not already open.

2. To configure the AutoArchive feature, choose Tools, Options, and click the Other tab, as shown in Figure 17.2.

FIGURE 17.2.

The Other tab offers a variety of options, including the capability to customize the AutoArchive.

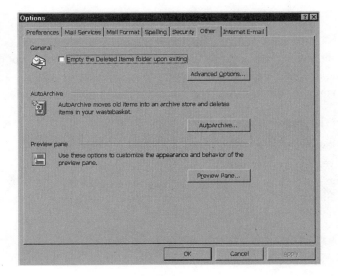

3. Click the AutoArchive button on the Other tab. As shown in Figure 17.3, the AutoArchive dialog box provides you with the capability to customize AutoArchive's settings.

4. When you have specified the desired frequency of your AutoArchive, the location of the archive file, and the various other options, click OK. Click OK again to close the Options dialog box.

17

▼ FIGURE 17.3.

*You can
customize
AutoArchive's various
settings.*

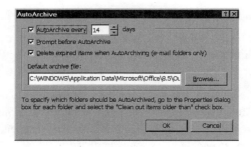

The Journal module in Outlook is the only one that is set up for AutoArchive from the Preferences tab of the Options dialog box by choosing Tools, Options and clicking the Journal Options button. Click the AutoArchive Journal Entries button. A dialog box appears where you can specify how often, if at all, you want Journal entries to be removed.

▲

Before Outlook performs its archive operations, a notice appears onscreen to alert you that Outlook is ready to begin archiving. You can choose to accept or decline. If you decline, the notice appears each time you open Outlook until you accept the operation or until you reset the AutoArchive schedule in the AutoArchive dialog box.

Archiving Manually

If you prefer to archive your Outlook database manually, you can do so by choosing File, Archive. The Archive dialog box enables you to archive according to the AutoArchive settings—which can differ from folder to folder, depending on how you set the properties. Otherwise, you can choose to archive entire folders by the same standard, such as archiving all items older than October 19, 1997.

To Do: Manually Archiving a Folder

1. Choose File, Archive.

2. In the Archive dialog box, highlight the Journal folder. As shown in Figure 17.4, you can specify the age the messages must be in order to be included in the archive. In the Archive Items Older Than text box, either type a specific date or click the down arrow to drop down the calendar and choose a date.

3. If you would like to differentiate this archive file from your usual AutoArchive files, choose a new filename by clicking the Browse button and typing a new filename.

▼   4. When you are ready to archive your files, click OK.

FIGURE 17.4.

Specify how old Journal items should be in order to be archived.

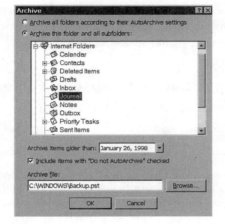

▲

17

Removing a Folder After Archiving

If you archive all the items in a folder, the empty folder remains in the Personal Folders File. If you no longer have any use for the folder and would like to remove it, right-click the folder and choose Delete.

Deleting a folder must be done from the Folder list. You cannot delete the primary folders (the ones automatically created by Outlook), only the sub-folders that you have created.

Restoring from an Archive

You can restore a file from an archive by one of two methods: Either open the archive as a separate Personal Folders file by choosing File, Open, Personal Folders File, or importing from the archive (discussed further in the next topic).

Opening an Archive as a Separate Personal Folders File

When yo open your archive as a Personal Folder, it will show up in Outlook as an additional Personal Folder in the Folder list. When it's open, you can copy items, open messages, and do all the things with the items that you need to do. You can even open multiple Personal Folders withing Outlook at the same time.

Before beginning the following exercise, you should know the location of the archive file you want to restore. If you don't already know the location of the file, open Windows Explorer and choose Tools, Find, Files or Folders and search for all files ending in .pst. The default name for archive folders is archive.pst. If, however, you have named your archive folder something else, it should appear on the list of found .pst files. Make a note of the folder location of this file.

To Do: Restoring an Archive as a Personal Folder

1. Click Tools, Services to open the Services dialog box.

2. From the Services tab, click Add.

> If you don't have Services as an available option, it's because you don't have Microsoft Exchange installed if you have revision A of Windows 95, or haven't installed the Windows Messaging System if you have revision B of Windows 95. These can be installed from the Windows Setup tab of the Add/Remove Programs folder in the Control Panel.

3. From the Add Service to Profile dialog box, as shown in Figure 17.5, select Personal Folders.

FIGURE 17.5.

The Add Service to Profile dialog box is used to add a folder to your profile.

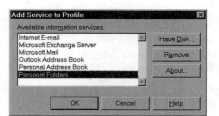

4. Click OK. The Create/Open Personal Folders File dialog box, as shown in Figure 17.6, is displayed. Notice that at this time, there are three Outlook files showing, all with a .pst extension: Backup, Outlook, and TYOL98.

5. Choose the archived file that you want to restore, and click Open.

> You may need to double-click the desired folder to locate the file.

6. You can specify a new name for your folder when it is restored from Archive. I named mine Un-Archived Folder. Type a name for your restored folder, and click OK.

▼ **FIGURE 17.6.**

Add the archived folder under the Add Services dialog box.

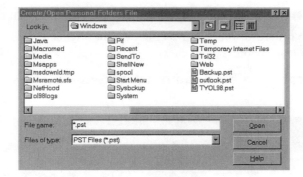

 I mentioned that the folder was restored, and it may have confused things. The Archive folder is a standard folder, and is never deleted or unavailable. What I did here was essentially make a copy of it and give it another name.

17

7. Outlook has now added your restored file to your profile. Click OK.

8. In your Inbox, click the Folder Banner, click the plus sign to open the archive folder, and highlight your new, restored folder (see Figure 17.7). Your archived files should now be available for use.

FIGURE 17.7.

Select your folder from the Folder Banner.

Folder Banner

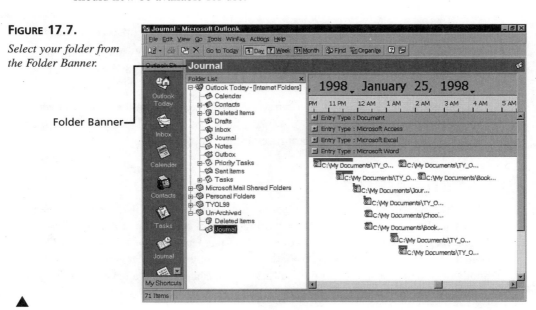

▲

Importing an Archive into Your Personal Folder File

You can also restore all your archived files to your original Personal Folders file. This puts your archived items back in the appropriate folders.

To Do: Restoring an Archive to Its Original Personal Folder

1. Select your Inbox.
2. Click File, Import and Export to start the Import and Export Wizard.
3. As shown in Figure 17.8, select Import from Another Program or File. Click Next.

FIGURE 17.8.

Choose to Import from another program or file.

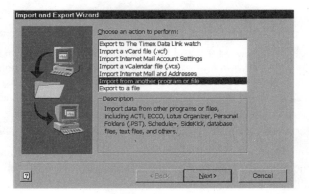

4. In the Import a File dialog box, select Personal Folder File (.pst) and click Next.
5. Enter the location of your archived file. Select whether you want Outlook to replace duplicates, allow duplicates, or import duplicates, and click Next. (This helps you avoid having several copies of the same data.)
6. As shown in Figure 17.9, you can select the folders or subfolders that you would like restored from your archive. Make your selection and click Finish. Your files are now restored to their appropriate destinations.

Exporting Items

The difference between exporting and archiving items is that archiving removes them from your Personal Folders file and exporting makes a *copy* of them in a new file. Exporting also gives you the option of exporting the data either as a Personal Folders file (which can be read by Outlook), a Windows Messaging file (readable in Exchange), or as another file type, such as a text file, an Excel spreadsheet file, or a database file.

FIGURE 17.9.

Select the folders and subfolders you want to restore.

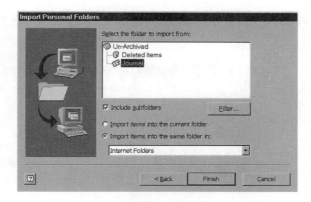

Exporting to a Personal Folders File

Exporting is a good way to share Outlook items with other Outlook users or between computers. For instance, if you work with Outlook at work and home, you can export items, such as your Contacts list or email messages, to a file and then import them into your Outlook folders at home.

To Do: Exporting Email to a Personal Folders File

1. Select your Inbox.
2. Click File, Import and Export.
3. In the Import and Export Wizard, choose Export to a file. Click Next.
4. In the Export to a File dialog box, as shown in Figure 17.10, select Personal Folder File (.pst). Click Next.

FIGURE 17.10.

Outlook enables you to export to a variety of file formats.

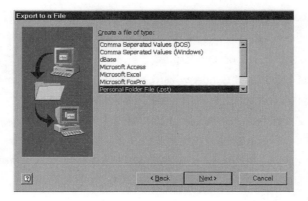

▼   5. In the Export Personal Folders dialog box, as shown in Figure 17.11, choose the
          folder that you would like to export *from,* and click Next.

FIGURE 17.11.

*Choose the folder
where your data exists.*

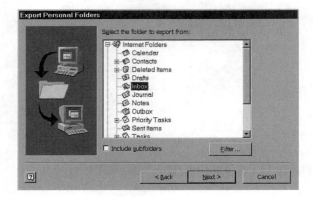

       6. Specify a directory and a name for the file you are creating. Click Finish. The
          Create Personal Folders dialog box is displayed. Click OK to continue.

          Your file is now ready to be saved onto a disk and transported to another computer
▲   for importing.

Exporting to Other File Formats

At times you may want to transfer your Outlook data to another file format. For instance,
suppose you want to give your Contacts file to a friend, but he or she does not have
Outlook. To accomplish this task, you can export your Contacts list as an Excel spreadsheet, which can be opened just like any other Excel file.

To Do: Exporting Data as an Excel Spreadsheet

▼ To Do

       1. Click the Contacts icon on the Outlook Bar.

       2. Choose File, Import and Export.

       3. In the Import and Export Wizard, choose Export to a File and click Next.

       4. In the Export to a File dialog box, choose Microsoft Excel and click Next.

       5. The Contacts folder should already be highlighted. Click Next.

       6. Select the location and filename for the newly exported data. Click Next.

       7. Outlook specifies the actions that will be taken in the exporting process. As shown
          in Figure 17.12, Outlook will export the Contacts file from the Contacts folder.
▼   Click Finish.

▼ **FIGURE 17.12.**

Outlook specifies the tasks to be done.

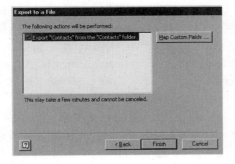

8. Outlook indicates the progress of the file transfer. When finished, your file is ready to be given to your friend.

9. Open the new file using Excel, if you have it on your computer. It should be similar to Figure 17.13.

FIGURE 17.13.

The file appears as a worksheet in Excel.

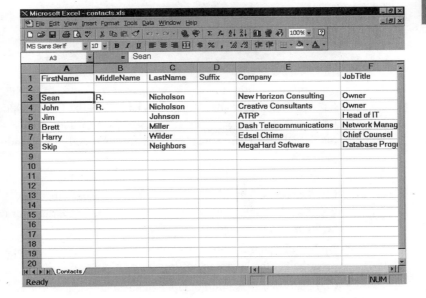

17

Tips on Making Your Outlook Files as Small as Possible

There are a few things you can do periodically to save hard drive space on your computer while you use Outlook. The following are some suggestions:

- Frequently empty the Deleted Items folder by selecting it and choosing Tools, Empty "Deleted Items" Folder. You can also right-click the Deleted Items Folder and choose Empty "Deleted Items" folder.

- If you want the Deleted Items folder to automatically empty each time you exit Outlook, choose Tools, Options and select the Other tab. Select the Empty Deleted Items Folder Upon Exiting check box.

- If you request receipts when you send email messages, choose Tools, Options, and select the Preferences tab. Click the E-mail Options button, and click the Tracking Options button in the E-mail Options dialog box. As shown in Figure 17.14, select the Delete Receipts and Blank Responses After Processing check box. (It should already be selected, but make sure.)

FIGURE 17.14.

Manage your receipts in the Tracking Options dialog box.

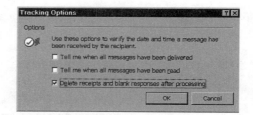

- Turn off the option to save messages that you send. To do this, select Tools, Options and choose the Preferences tab. Click the E-mail Options button and uncheck the option to save messages in the Sent Items Folder (again, this should be the default, but make sure). You can always specify on an individual basis when you want to save a message that you are sending.

- Be conservative in choosing options to be tracked as automatic Journal entries. Choose Tools, Options and select the Preferences tab. Click the Journal Options button and de-select any unnecessary Automatic Journal entries. By default, they begin as all unselected.

- Archive frequently either by choosing AutoArchive or archive manually, as described at the beginning of this hour.

- Compact your Personal Folders by choosing Tools, Services. Select Personal Folders and click the Properties button. Choose Compact Now.

Summary

Managing your data effectively can save you both time and space on your hard drive. Outlook's archiving feature, along with the import and export tools, should enable you to reduce the amount of space your Personal Folders occupy, while giving you the ability to transport files between users and computers.

Q&A

Q I am interested in exporting my files to a Microsoft Office program other than Excel. Can I do that?

A Sure. Hour 18, "Integrating the Office Neighborhood," covers Outlook's compatibility and integration with the other Microsoft Office products.

Q When I export a file, do I have to save it to my hard drive and then copy it to a floppy?

A No. You can export a file directly to a floppy by simply specifying your floppy drive as the target for the file when you name the file and its destination.

> You may want to check the file size. Outlook files can quickly grow past the 1.44 Mb floppy disk limit. You could run WinZip to compress the file before copying it to the disk.

Q Which is better: AutoArchive or manual archives?

A This depends on your needs. AutoArchive is handy for those who don't want to go to the trouble of periodically freeing up hard drive space. manual archives, however, let you keep tabs on the amount of space your files are taking at all times. Pick whichever is best for you.

Q Can I specify the time of day that Outlook archives files?

A No. At this point, you can specify the Outlook period only on a daily basis or greater (such as, weekly or monthly).

17

HOUR 18

Integrating the Office Neighborhood

If you think Microsoft has the patent on office tool integration, think again. It has been done before. The most commonly used integrated office tool appeared in offices, schools, and homes as early as the mid-nineteenth century.

The first part of the device has been in existence in primitive form since the Aztec civilization. A more modern form was developed in Germany in the sixteenth century, and until 1812, that device dominated the world market.

It was then that William Monroe opened an American manufacturing plant, and soon broke the German hold on the market, giving America independence from one more European monopoly.

The second part of the device was added in 1858 by Philadelphia inventor Hyman Lipman, thus creating a multipurpose integrated tool. A *wooden pencil*, with its rubber eraser, is certainly a greater tool than any of its individual parts: wood, graphite, and rubber.

Office 97 integrates its components as much as possible so that the uses are far greater than for each module when used individually. Some of the integrative methods are fairly obvious, thanks to document Object Linking and Embedding (OLE). Other aspects of the integration are more subtle, so you are scarcely aware of them.

Such is the integration between Outlook 98 and the Office 97 programs. Some of the possibilities are obvious, such as WordMail, and some subtle; for example, you can schedule a meeting from the middle of a PowerPoint slide show.

This hour covers different ways that Outlook interacts with its Office buddies and how this can make your work go quite a bit smoother.

Outlook and Word

If you think of Office as a family, Outlook is sort of like John Boy and Word is like Grandpa Walton. Both are valued members of the family, but it is quite clear who has the experience and power in the family and who is the new kid on the block.

This is not so strange if you think about it. Since its inception, a document-focused application has been promoted by Office. Microsoft asserts that all Office files are documents of one form or another, so what better place to put most of the document controls but in Word? That argument still holds true today in Office 97, even though Outlook items are not really documents, but rather database entries.

 Actually, Outlook items, when saved as separate files, are Mail Message files. You can see this every time you drag and drop a task or other Outlook item onto the desktop, which is essentially saving the item to a separate file.

Appropriately, Word and Outlook have the most levels of interaction. Using both programs, you can send email messages, create mail merge documents, and generate tasks.

WordMail

When you send email messages from Outlook's Inbox, there are some pretty good tools to format your message. You can apply bold, underline, or italic formatting, change the text's font and size, and create bulleted lists. These basic formatting options are often all you will need for your email.

However, sometimes you need more comprehensive word processing tools. No offense, but Outlook's message tool is simply not a word processor. Therefore, Outlook gives you the option of using Word as its email editor.

> As covered in Hour 8, "Setting Up the Mail Services," using a full-blown word processor as your email editor makes creating a message a bit slower. In fact, Microsoft recommends that your computer have at least 16MB of RAM before even using WordMail.
>
> The biggest advantage of using WordMail is that you can send nicely formatted documents to other people. But if the recipient does not use WordMail, most of your formatting is for naught: The message will only be read as plain text. In that case, it is better if you continue to use Outlook's Inbox editor.

If you decide to use WordMail, you need to inform Outlook. Choose Tools, Options. In the Options dialog box, choose the Mail Format tab, as shown in Figure 18.1. Select Microsoft Word from the Message Format drop-down box and click OK.

FIGURE 18.1.

Choosing Word as your email editor provides a wide variety of formatting options.

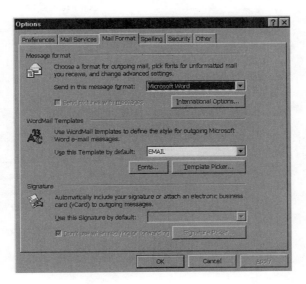

The next time you create a new mail message, you will see a little message box that says "Starting Word as your e-mail editor," followed by the appearance of a brand-new message tool that looks similar to Outlook's message tool (see Figure 18.2).

FIGURE 18.2.

The super deluxe WordMail Message tool.

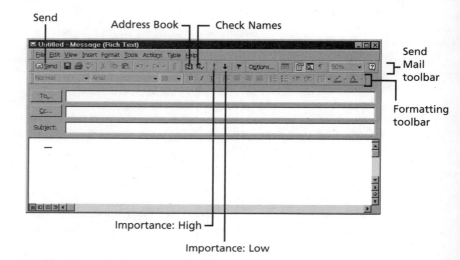

Look at those toolbars again. There are a lot more tools on them than on the Outlook toolbars. To see the difference, compare Figure 18.2 with Figure 18.3, which shows a standard Outlook message tool.

FIGURE 18.3.

The mild-mannered Outlook Message tool.

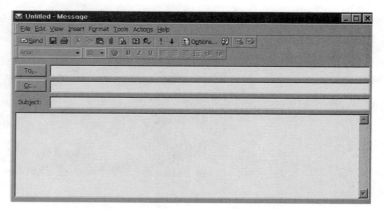

Tools of the Trade

You can see that the toolbars and menus of the WordMail Message tool have more in common with Word 97 than Outlook. The Formatting toolbar has expanded to match the one in Word, and the Standard toolbar has been replaced with the Send Mail toolbar.

> In case you are wondering, the WordMail function does not go both ways. You can't send a Word-formatted email message directly from Word, even when the WordMail option is on. However, you can send an email message with the most recent version of the open Word document attached. Just click File, Send To, Mail Recipient.

Different Strokes for Different Buttons

By using Word as your email editor, you gain several functions not available in the standard Outlook message editor. You can

- Check the spelling in your message
- Undo and redo your last 100 actions
- Use the table features
- View the Document Map (which enables you to quickly navigate a long document containing heading styles)
- Show/Hide hidden marks (such as spaces and paragraph marks)
- Adjust the zoom of the message (make the contents appear larger or smaller without changing the size of window)
- Use character and paragraph formatting styles
- Create numbered and bulleted lists
- Add borders to paragraphs
- Add highlighting to words or phrases

As you can see, there are many advantages to using Word as your email editor. You can also click the Options button to open the Message Options dialog box, as shown in Figure 18.4, to set several features of your email message.

18

FIGURE 18.4.

The Message Options dialog box enables you to customize your message.

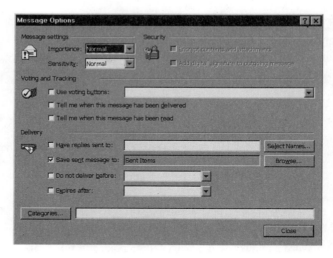

As for the rest of the buttons and fields, you will find that they function like Word 97's Standard and Formatting toolbars. In addition, the To, Cc, and Subject fields work exactly like Outlook's Message tool.

It's Got the Look

There is, however, one more thing WordMail can do to make your messages sparkle. Using templates, you can create an entirely new look for an email message.

To Do: Attaching a New Template to a Message

1. Open Outlook if it isn't already running.

2. Choose Tools, Options and click the Mail Format tab.

3. Click the Template Picker button. It shows a folder view and enables you to navigate through the system to select a template in a file (see Figure 18.5).

4. In the WordMail Template dialog box, choose the template of your choice and click OK.

> Although nothing appears to have changed, the next time a new message is created, that template will be used. This template will continue to be used for future messages until it is changed again.

FIGURE 18.5.

Use the WordMail Template dialog box to locate the WordMail templates.

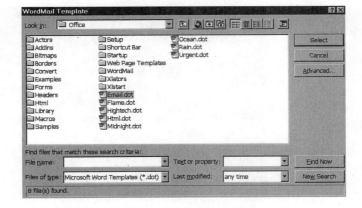

Figures 18.6 and 18.7 show examples of the same message, using the Hightech and Ocean templates, respectively.

FIGURE 18.6.

A WordMail message using the Hightech template.

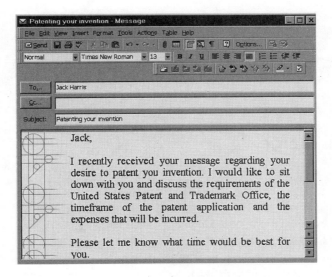

18

FIGURE **18.7.**

The same message using the Ocean template produces a slightly different effect.

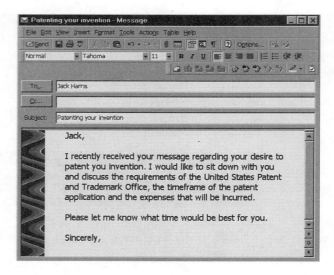

If you are really impressed by one of these templates, you can make it the default template for every email message you create with WordMail. Just choose Tools, Options and click the Mail Format tab. In the WordMail Templates section, select your default template from the drop-down list, and click OK.

Mail Merge

I have a confession to make: Mail merges give me the willies. I know I'm not alone. However, Word 97 and Outlook 98 have made them a lot easier. Really!

Now that I've made you nervous, let me first explain what a mail merge is for those who have never had to run one. Simply put, mail merging is the process used by Word to create a form letter, envelope labels, or any other document that needs multiple copies generated for many people. Instead of creating a separate copy for each person, you create one master document with a data list of the different names and addresses. Word then places the personal data in the master document in the correct order.

The data can come from a variety of sources: an Excel spreadsheet, an Access database, and now Outlook's Address Book.

Before we rush into the procedure of creating a mail merge document, some questions must be asked. Table 18.1 shows the Outlook fields that can be directly merged into Word 97. After looking at this table, ask yourself the following:

- Will my master document need any fields listed in this table?
- Will my master document need an Outlook field that's not listed in this table?
- Will my master document need a completely new custom field?

TABLE 18.1. MERGE-CAPABLE FIELDS.

Contact Field Name	Word Field Name
Assistant's Name	Assistant_Name
Assistant's Phone	Assistant_Phone
Business Fax	Business_Fax
Business Phone 2	Business_Phone_2
Business Phone	Business_Phone
City	City
Company	Company
Country	Country
Department	Department
E-Mail	Email_Address
First Name	First_Name
Home Address City	Home_City
Home Address Country	Home_Country
Home Address Postal Code	Home_Postal_Code
Home Address State	Home_State_or_Province
Home Address Street	Home_Street_Address
Home Fax	Home_Fax
Home Phone 2	Home_Phone_2
Home Phone	Home_Phone
Job Title	Title
Last Name	Last_Name
Mailing Address	Street_Address
Mobile Phone	Mobile_Phone
Office Location	Office_Location
Other Address City	Other_City

continues

18

TABLE 18.1. CONTINUED

Contact Field Name	Word Field Name
Other Address Country	Other_Country
Other Address Postal Code	Other_Postal_Code
Other Address State	Other_State_or_Province
Other Address Street	Other_Street_Address
Other Fax	Primary_Fax
Other Phone	Other_Phone
Pager	Pager_Phone
Spouse	Spouse
State	State_or_Province
Street Address	Street_Address
Suffix	Generation
Title	Courtesy_Title
ZIP/Postal Code	Postal_Code

Your answers to these questions will determine the method you use to transfer the merge data into Word. We'll examine all three methods.

Before you begin any of these methods, it is a good idea to create a new Contacts folder and *copy* the appropriate people into it. That way, you can be sure you will have the correct people for your mail merge document.

My Document Uses Only the Standard Merge Fields

You are the type of conformist that makes books like this easy to write. Take pride in your conformity. Now, let's merge!

To Do: Merging a Document Using the Standard Fields

1. Start Word 97.
2. Open an existing document to mail merge, if you have one. If not, create a new document and type a simple personal letter.
3. Choose Tools, Mail Merge. The Mail Merge Helper dialog box is displayed.
4. In Section 1, click the Create button. You can either create form letters, mailing labels, envelopes, or catalogs (see Figure 18.8). Click Form Letters.

FIGURE 18.8.

Choose your Mail Merge type.

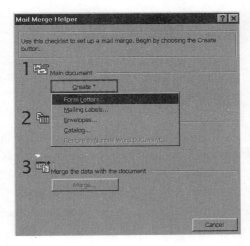

5. When you choose the document type, a query pops up, as shown in Figure 18.9, asking if you want to use the currently open document or create a new document. Choose <u>A</u>ctive Window.

FIGURE 18.9.

Choose the active document as your master document.

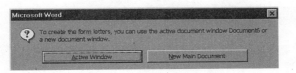

6. In Section 2, click the Get Data button.

> If you perform a mail merge without this trusty book by your side (shame on you), keep an eye on the very top section of the Mail Merge Helper dialog box. It tells you what you are to do at each step.

7. Click the Use Address Book command. Word opens the Use Address Book dialog box, as shown in Figure 18.10.

18

▼ **FIGURE 18.10.**

Select your Address Book.

8. Select the Outlook Address Book option and click OK. Unless you are using an old master document that already has merge fields, you will get a message box asking you to insert merge fields. Click Edit Main Document to begin this process.

9. Move the insertion point to the position where you want to place the first field.

10. Click the Insert Merge Field button on the toolbar, as shown in Figure 18.11, and select the appropriate fields to be placed in your document.

FIGURE 18.11.

Select the fields to be merged.

Insert Merge Field button

When adding your fields, create your document using each field as though it were an actual word, using the correct punctuation and spacing.

▼

▼ 11. When you finish adding fields, click the Mail Merge Helper button.

12. In Section 3, click the Merge button.

13. In the Merge dialog box, select the desired options and then click the Merge button, as shown in Figure 18.12.

FIGURE 18.12.

Finalize your merge options.

▲ 14. After some processing from the computer, your document will soon be merged with the Outlook data. Close the file, either saving it or discarding the changes.

My Document Uses Outlook Fields, But Not All Are Standard

If you want to use fields that are not on the standard merge list, you will need to prepare the data in Outlook before Word can use it.

To Do: Merging a Document Using Outlook Fields

1. In Outlook, click File, Import and Export to start the Import and Export Wizard.

2. In the Import and Export Wizard, as shown in Figure 18.13, select Export to a File and click Next.

3. Because you are merging your data into a document in Word 97, choose Tab Separated Values (Windows), as shown in Figure 18.14, and click Next.

FIGURE 18.13.

Export your data to a file.

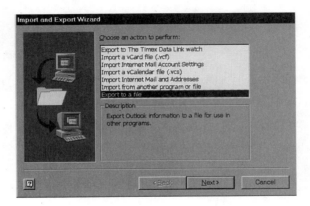

18

▼

FIGURE 18.14.

Choose a Word-compatible file format.

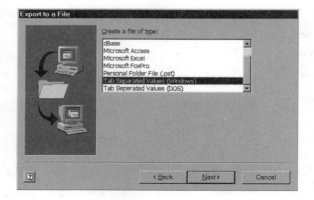

4. Select the folder where the desired Outlook data is located. Click Next.

5. Select the Contacts folder as the source of the data you want to export. Click Next.

6. Type `mailmerge` as the name for the soon-to-be-exported data file. You can name this file anything you want, but for the purposes of the exercise, use `mailmerge`. Click Next.

7. As shown in Figure 18.15, Outlook shows you what actions will be taken when you choose Finish. Because you want to merge nonstandard merge fields, click the Map Custom Fields button.

FIGURE 18.15.

Outlook shows you what it is going to do.

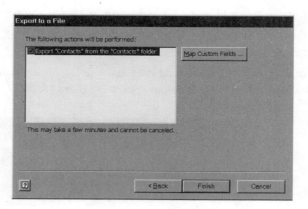

8. In the Map Custom Fields dialog box, as shown in Figure 18.16, you can assign the fields from your Contacts folder that correspond to Word's merge fields.

▼ FIGURE 18.16.

Assign your fields to match Word's.

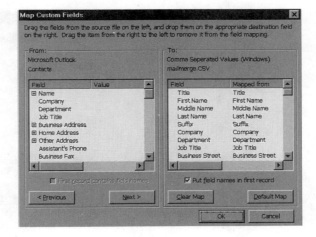

If you can't find a field among the Word fields that is similar to your unmatched Contact field, go ahead and choose a Word field (one that you do not normally use). The field's name won't matter when you create your master document.

18

9. When your nonstandard fields are assigned to Word fields, click OK and then click Finish in the Wizard. Outlook then exports the assigned data to the file you named earlier in the wizard.

10. Now start Word 97 and follow Steps 1 through 6 of the mail merge setup process, shown in the "My Document Uses Only the Standard Merge Fields" section earlier in this hour.

11. When you reach Step 7, click the Open Data Source command.

12. As shown in Figure 18.17, select the mailmerge file and click Open.

13. Proceed with steps 10–12 of the "My Document Uses Only the Standard Merge Fields" section to complete the merge.

My Document Uses Custom Fields

If your Outlook file is using a completely customized field, the mail merge procedure is exactly the same as that outlined in the preceding section: Prepare the contact data and then open a data source file, as opposed to using the Outlook Address Book directly. However, instead of exporting the Contacts, you will manually create the data source file.

FIGURE 18.17.

*Select the file to
which you exported
your data.*

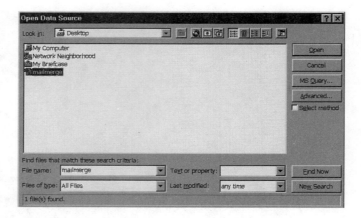

To Do: Manually Creating a Data Source File

1. In the Contacts view, create a new table view containing the fields you need by selecting View, Current View, Edit Current View and clicking the Fields button. Select the fields you want in your mail merge and click OK. Click OK in the View Summary box.

2. In your new view, select all the contacts you need for the merge.

3. With the contacts selected, copy them to the Clipboard by pressing Ctrl+C, or by choosing Edit, Copy from the menu bar.

4. Open a new document in Word 97.

5. Press Ctrl+V, or choose Edit, Paste to paste the selected contacts.

6. Save the document. Remember the name because this will be your data source file.

7. Open the Word document you want to use as the master mail merge document, and begin the mail merge process.

8. When asked for the source file, select the document you just saved.

Creating Tasks

In addition to using both Word and Outlook to create your email, you can perform other Outlook options from Office 97 modules. Back when you were learning how to create tasks in Hour 13, "Getting Things Done," you may have thought, "Sure, tasks are cool, but to stop what I'm working on, switch to Outlook, and make the task doesn't seem very productive."

Unfortunately, this is true. No one likes his or her train of thought interrupted. So why do it? Fortunately, with Word 97, you can create a task from any Microsoft Office document in which you are working. The new task will even have the open document linked to it for more convenience.

> If you display the Microsoft Office Shortcut Bar, you can always click the New Task button whenever you want to create a task.

To Do: Creating a Task from Within Word

1. Right-click any toolbar in Word.
2. Select the Reviewing toolbar from the menu.
3. On the Reviewing toolbar, as shown in Figure 18.18, click the Create Microsoft Outlook Task button.

FIGURE 18.18.

Creating a task in Word is as simple as pointing and clicking.

Reviewing toolbar

Create Microsoft
Outlook Task button

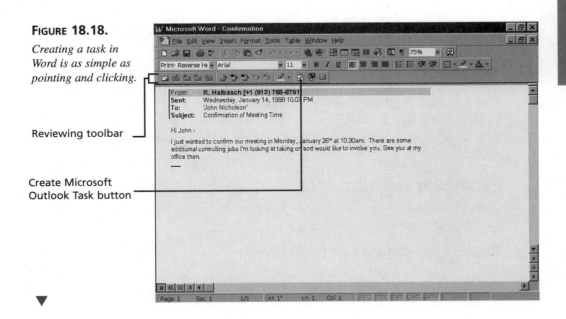

18

▼   4. A Task tool appears with the open filename in the subject field, a shortcut to the document, and the first line of the document in the note box. Finish filling in the rest of the task information, and click Save and Close.

> If you create a lot of these document-related tasks, you can move the Task button (located on the Reviewing toolbar) into either the Standard or Formatting toolbars. Then you'll have the tool present all the time. To move the button, you must have the Reviewing toolbar displayed, as well as the destination toolbar.
>
> 1. Right-click any of the toolbars.
> 2. Click the Customize command in the pop-up menu that appears.
> 3. Ignore the Customize dialog box when it appears. Drag the dialog box down until all the toolbars are uncovered.
> 4. Drag the Task button from the Reviewing toolbar to the place you want it on the destination toolbar.
> 5. When you close Word 97, you will be asked to save changes to the current template. If you say Yes, this toolbar change remains in place until you change it.

▲

Outlook and Access

As you may have guessed, because Outlook is essentially a database and Access is a database creation tool, they are fairly compatible. However, the transition is not exact in all cases. Outlook, a descendant of Exchange, uses a database format slightly different from that of Access. Fortunately, it is not too hard to share information between the programs.

Exporting Data to Access

If you need to have Access use the data contained within Outlook, you must first export the data to an Access 97 database file.

To Do: Exporting a File to Access

1. In Outlook, choose File, Import and Export.
2. In the Import and Export Wizard, select the Export to a File option, and click Next.

▼

3. Select the file type as Microsoft Access file. Click Next.

4. From the next dialog box, select the folder where your Outlook data is contained. Click Next.

5. Enter a name for the exported Access file. Do not use a period or extension. Click Next.

6. Finally, Outlook specifies what actions will be taken. Click Finish. Outlook exports the data to a file that can now be opened from Access.

▲

Importing Data from Access

So far, all the interactions with Office programs have been one way: The other office family members use the data stored in Outlook. With Access, however, Outlook can import data that you can store in any of your personal folders.

The steps for importing data are identical to those used in exporting data, and the Import Wizard screens all have the same functionality as the Export Wizard. In fact, only the last screen has a difference, and it's minor: a Change Destination button that gives you one more chance to choose the destination folder of the new data.

You can only import data to the predefined fields. You can't import to any user-defined fields.

18

Outlook and Excel

After all the great interactive possibilities you learned about Word or Access and Outlook, you're in for a letdown when it comes to Excel. Excel 97 and Outlook can do only two things together: create a workbook-related task and share data.

To Do: Creating an Outlook Task in Excel

1. Open Microsoft Excel 97.

2. Right-click any toolbar.

3. Select the Reviewing toolbar from the menu.

4. On the Reviewing toolbar, click the Create Microsoft Outlook Task button.

5. As with Word, a Task tool appears, and you can fill in the necessary information. Click Save and Close to complete the task.

To Do

▼

▲

If you anticipate creating a lot of workbook-related tasks, use the tip procedure suggested in the previous section and move the Task button to another toolbar.

If you need to share data between the Excel and Outlook, use Outlook's Import and Export Wizard, as described in the "Outlook and Access" section earlier this hour.

Outlook and PowerPoint

When you look at these two applications of Office 97, no two could seem more different. One's a personal information manager and one's a slide show maker, so how can there be any commonality between them?

The key is to remember that PowerPoint is not just a "slide show maker." It's a business presentation tool, and that one word—*business*—is the common connection with Outlook. However, as you were warned earlier in the hour, some interactivity is not easy to see.

After you have created a presentation in PowerPoint, one of your options is to use a computer monitor to project the presentation. While the presentation is made, PowerPoint's Meeting Minder can take notes, schedule a meeting, or create a task. It's those last two capabilities that relate directly to Outlook.

Scheduling a Meeting

Scheduling a meeting with PowerPoint's Meeting Minder is simple. Choose Tools, Meeting Minder, and PowerPoint opens the Meeting Minder dialog box, as shown in Figure 18.19.

FIGURE 18.19.

Creating a meeting in PowerPoint is simple.

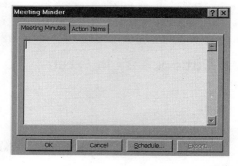

When you click the Schedule button, a Meeting tool appears. Using this, you can quickly schedule a meeting without starting Outlook.

Creating Tasks

As with Word and Excel, you can create an Outlook task in PowerPoint by viewing the Reviewing toolbar and clicking the Create Microsoft Outlook Task button. As with the other modules, fill in the necessary information and click Save and Close when you are finished.

You can also use the Meeting Minder to create some tasks. If you click the Action Items tab, you can enter the task's subject into the Description field and the due date and assignee into their respective fields. When this information is entered, click the Add button.

You can add as many action items as you desire. When you are finished, don't click the OK button. Click the Export button instead. This will activate the Meeting Minder Export dialog box, as shown in Figure 18.20.

This dialog box offers two choices: You can export meeting minutes and action items to a Word 97 document, or export just the action items to Outlook. If you check the latter option and click Export Now, the action items will be placed directly into Outlook's tasks.

18

FIGURE 18.20.

You can export Meeting Minder Action items from PowerPoint into a Word document or directly into Outlook.

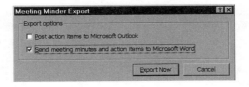

Summary

This hour focuses on Outlook's capability to interact and share data with the other Microsoft Office modules. With the capability to share data and email tools and create tasks from most of the Office programs, Outlook is truly an integral part of the Office 97 family.

Building on the concept of sharing data, Hour 19, "Share, Show, and Tell: Working with a Group," focuses on sharing data between the members of a workgroup.

Q&A

Q Can Outlook 98 share data with programs other than Microsoft Office applications?

A Yes, but its data-sharing capabilities are limited to FoxPro, dBASE and Schedule+.

Q Can I use another word processor as my email editor?

A Nope. Outlook can only use Word as an external email editor.

Q Where can I turn to get more information about mail merges?

A It depends on your needs. Microsoft Word has quite a bit of information on how to perform and troubleshoot mail merges in its Help files. If this doesn't help you, check your local bookstore for a book that focuses on the advanced features of Word.

HOUR 19

Share, Show, and Tell: Working with a Group

Since kindergarten, we've been taught that sharing is important. Whether it was snacks, toys, or crayons, we were taught that sharing is polite and courteous. What our kindergarten teachers didn't tell us is that sharing can save time and effort by reducing the workload of a single person and spreading the tasks of a project over the entire workgroup. Consider this: Through the use of networked computers we can share information by sending email messages, transferring information stored in files, and even navigating the Internet for pertinent Web sites.

Outlook 98 has embraced the idea of sharing by providing various features that can save you time and effort in your day-to-day tasks.

Sharing Your Personal Calendar

In Hour 12, "Power Calendaring," you learned how to set meetings using Outlook 98. We briefly covered the way that Outlook enables you to permit other users on your Exchange Server or on your Postoffice to view your schedule. This feature has such time-saving potential, I think it's important to mention it one last time.

By sharing your calendar, you allow others to see when you are busy and when you are available for a meeting, lunch, or even a tee time. Although the other users can see *when* you are busy, they can't see *why* you are busy. In other words, your boss may see that you are busy from 9 a.m. until noon, but he doesn't know that you are meeting a client on the golf course. Therefore, sharing your personal calendar doesn't reduce the amount of privacy you have on your network; it merely gives others the ability to schedule around your calendar without having to call you and confirm each meeting.

To Do: Sharing Your Personal Calendar

1. Open Outlook if it is not already open.
2. Choose Tools, Options. In the Preferences tab, click the Calendar options button.
3. In the Calendar Options dialog box, click the Free/Busy Options button, which opens the Free/Busy Options dialog box (see Figure 19.1).

FIGURE 19.1.

The Free/Busy Options dialog box enables you to grant or deny network access to your calendar.

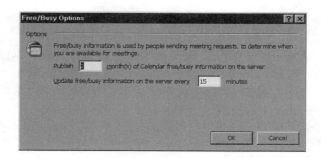

4. In the Free/Busy Options box, set the number of Calendar months that you want to make available to others on your Exchange Server or Post Office. If you don't want your calendar accessible at all, choose 0. Click OK.
5. In the Calendar Options box, click OK.
6. In the Options box, click OK.

Assigning and Reassigning Tasks

One of the greatest things about sharing is the ability to delegate to others. Just think: Isn't delegation just a sharing of the workload? Outlook's delegation tools come in the form of tasks. You learned how to create a new task in Hour 13, "Getting Things Done;" you learn how to assign tasks to other users on your network during this hour.

Essentially, Outlook has a two procedures for assigning tasks to others: You can either create a new task request, which the other person will either accept or decline, or you can assign one of your current tasks to another person.

Creating a New Task Request

Let's do a quick refresher on how to create a task: You can then request that the task be assigned to a coworker.

To Do: Creating a New Task Request

1. Select the Task folder and choose Actions, New Task Request. As you can see in Figure 19.2, the New Task Request screen is similar to the Task screen that you used in Hour 13. The differences, however, are the addition of the following:

   - **To field.** This field functions exactly like the field of the same name in the Inbox. If you click the To button, the Select Task Recipient dialog box is displayed (see Figure 19.3). This is identical to the Select Names dialog box seen when clicking the To button in a new message.

   - **Keep an Updated Copy of This Task on My Task List check box.** This check box, when enabled, keeps a current version of the task on your task list even after you have assigned it. This does not mean you still own the task. However, if you decide that you need to assign the task to somebody else, you'll need to re-create an unassigned task. If you keep this updated copy now, you won't have to re-create an entirely new task later.

> When the person you assign the task to checks it as complete on his task list, it is (almost immediately) checked as completed on your task list as well.

   - **Send Me a Status Report When This Task Is Complete check box.** When enabled, this check box attaches the request for a status report to the task request. When the recipient gets it, and if he accepts the task, every time he wants to give the task's original owner an update on how things are going, all he needs to do is click the Status Report button to begin creating a status report that is already addressed to the original task owner.

19

▼ **FIGURE 19.2.**

The New Task Request screen offers some enhanced options over the standard Task screen.

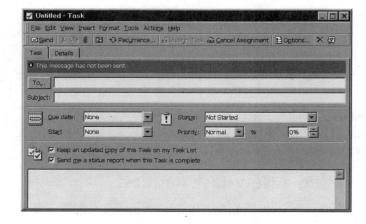

The recipient can send a status report at any time just by clicking the Send Status Report button on the toolbar of the task. This box is not a prerequisite for that feature. Checking this box causes a status report to be automatically generated when the other user checks the task as completed.

2. In the Task dialog box, click the To button. As shown in Figure 19.3, Outlook opens your Personal Address book, just as though you were sending an email message.

FIGURE 19.3.

Outlook uses your Personal Address Book to address your tasks.

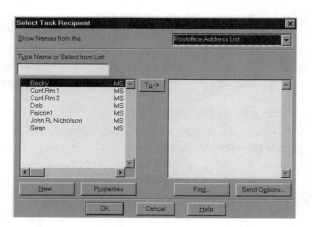

▼   3. Select a recipient for your task request and click To. Click OK.

4. In the Subject field, type Network Install.

5. In the <u>D</u>ue Date drop-down box, select a due date for the task.

6. In the Sta<u>r</u>t drop-down box, select the start date for the task.

7. If the task is already in progress, select Started in the Stat<u>u</u>s drop-down box. Otherwise, choose Not Started.

> Not Started is the default value.

8. Select both check boxes at the bottom of the screen to keep an updated copy of the task and to receive a status report when the task is completed. Your dialog box should look similar to the one shown in Figure 19.4.

FIGURE 19.4.

Your task request is ready to send.

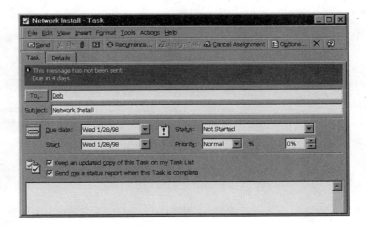

9. Click the <u>S</u>end button.

Creator or Owner? Which Am I? Or Am I Both?

This is how Outlook has defined ownership of tasks, assigned or unassigned. Every time you create a task, you are that task's creator. You are also, however, the task's owner. You remain the owner of the task for as long as it remains assigned to you. When you assign the task to someone else who accepts it, then that person becomes the new owner, while you are merely the recipient of a status report.

So remember, a task owner is not necessarily the one who initially creates the task, but the one who is responsible for completing the task.

19

Assigning One of Your Current Tasks

If you're like me, biting off more than you can chew is a daily occurrence. Fortunately, Outlook has planned for this contingency by enabling you to reassign your tasks to other workers. This feature is handy when you realize that a coworker may have superior knowledge or skill in finishing the task, or when an emergency arises and you need someone else to complete the task.

To Do: Reassigning a Task

1. After you have created the task or received it from someone else, open the task by double-clicking it in the task list.

2. When the Task tool opens, click the Assign Task button in the toolbar, or choose Actions, Assign Task.

3. As you can see in Figure 19.5, Outlook opens the Task Request tool, which enables you to select a recipient just as you did in the preceding exercise.

FIGURE 19.5.

Reassigning the task is as easy as opening the task and requesting that someone else take it over.

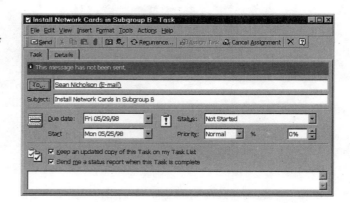

4. Fill in the To field and click Send. As shown in Figure 19.6, Outlook informs you that your task reminder has been turned off because you no longer own the task.

FIGURE 19.6.

Because you no longer own the task, your reminder is turned off.

5. Click OK.

6. When the recipient accepts the task, you receive a notice in your Inbox similar to the one shown in Figure 19.7.

▼ **FIGURE 19.7.**

The recipient has accepted the task.

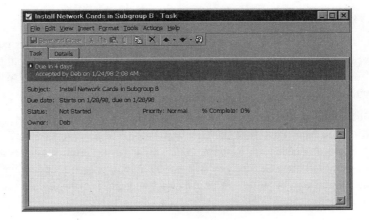

7. If, however, the task is declined, the returned message states that the task was declined by the recipient, as shown in Figure 19.8. You must then either complete the task yourself, or assign it to another user.

You can often deter others from handing their tasks off to you by keeping the following sign prominently posted in your office:

"Lack of preparation on your part does not constitute an emergency on my part."

19

FIGURE 19.8.

The task was declined.

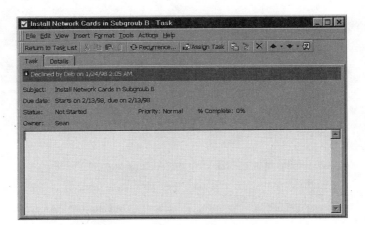

▲

Responding to Requested Tasks

Unless you are the supreme ruler of your company, sooner or later you will be on the receiving end of a task request. The important thing is to remain calm and make no sudden moves. By acting in a rational fashion, you may even be able to deal with the request without overloading your schedule.

Task requests first appear in your Inbox. If you are using Microsoft Exchange Server or a Microsoft Mail Postoffice, task requests appear as a request message, with a Task Request icon next to it. Remember: If you are using a messaging system other than MS Mail or Exchange Server, you will not be able to respond, update, or send status reports through tasks; you will have to use email and other forms of communication to pass this information around.

If, however, you do have a Microsoft messaging system running, you are in luck. As you can see in Figure 19.9, task requests have their own special tools to help you quickly respond to them.

FIGURE 19.9.

You've been asked to take over a task.

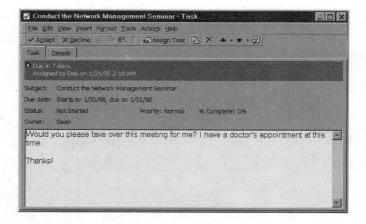

As you can see, there are basically three options you can take when you receive a task request:

- Accept the task by clicking the Accept button.
- Decline the task by clicking the Decline button.
- Reassign the task to someone else by clicking the Assign Task button.

After examining your own task list and your calendar, suppose you decide to take on the task. When you click Accept, a warning appears, as shown in Figure 19.10.

FIGURE 19.10.

If necessary, you can make changes to the response before sending it.

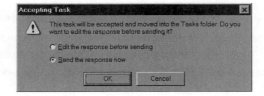

When you accept or decline the task, you can add your personal comments to the accept or decline message. If you choose not to add any comments or stipulations to the acceptance of the task, just click the Send the Response Now option button. If, however, you have something to say to the sender, click Edit the Response Before Sending. A Task Request tool appears. In the note box at the bottom of the tool, insert any reply you want. When finished, click the Send button.

Checking Task Status

After you have assigned a task to someone else, you can monitor the progress of the task through progress reports if you checked the option that kept a copy of the item in your task list. When the person who accepted the task makes progress and reflects that in his task list, your copy of the task is automatically updated, and the changes are reflected in your task list.

In addition, if you checked the box stating that you would like an update when the task is complete, you will automatically receive a message similar to the one shown in Figure 19.11 in your Inbox when the person responsible for the task marks it complete.

19

FIGURE 19.11.

This task has been completed.

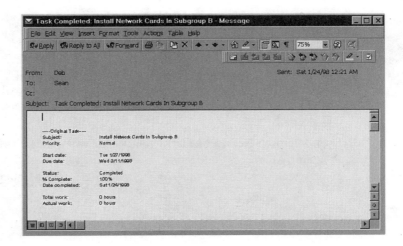

Creating and Conducting an Online Meeting

The final way Outlook can help you share your thoughts, ideas, and even files is through online meetings. By using Microsoft NetMeeting (which comes with Outlook 98), you can schedule and conduct a meeting on the Internet. This enables people from around the world to conduct a meeting without ever having to leave their desks. In fact, during an online meeting, the attendees have the capability to chat with one another by typing, or—if they have full-duplex modems, sound cards, and microphones—speak with each other using the speakers and microphones attached to their computers.

You can also transfer files and conduct a number of other activities online. Imagine: no more red-eye flights across the country and no more sleeping in lumpy hotel beds. Just connect to the Internet, and you can speak with all the members of your project team whether they are in the next cubicle or in Rangoon.

Before you can create and conduct an online meeting, you must first set up Microsoft NetMeeting. When you open NetMeeting for the first time, a wizard will guide you through the process. You will need to have your microphone and speakers attached to your computer *before* you set up NetMeeting if you want to take advantage of the full-duplex capabilities that NetMeeting supports.

What is *full duplex,* you ask? It is the capability to send and receive simultaneously so that if you speak when the person on the other end speaks, you can still hear each other—like a regular telephone call.

To Do: Installing Microsoft NetMeeting

1. Make sure you have the most recent version of NetMeeting. Establish an Internet connection with your Internet service provider and go to www.microsoft.com/ie/download/. Choose the most recent version of NetMeeting. Make sure you note the directory where you are downloading the file. You can then install NetMeeting by choosing Start, Run, and selecting the file you downloaded.

2. Open Microsoft NetMeeting from your Windows 95 Start Menu by choosing Start, Programs, Microsoft NetMeeting. As shown in Figure 19.12, NetMeeting's welcome screen provides information about the uses of NetMeeting.

FIGURE 19.12.

The welcome screen of NetMeeting whets your appetite with a list of savory features.

3. The first screen simply informs you that NetMeeting will be set up on your computer. Click the Next button.

4. NetMeeting has a variety of servers available at its Internet site so that it can accommodate a large number of users at the same time. In the directory server box, make sure the box specifying that you be listed in a directory is checked, and drop-down the server list to choose ils.business.four11.com (see Figure 19.13). This server has worked well for me in the past and is rarely too busy. If, however, this server doesn't work for you, you can change this setting later.

FIGURE 19.13.

Choose a directory server.

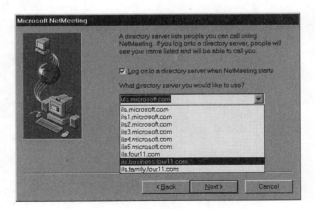

19

5. Enter your personal information in the text boxes, as shown in Figure 19.14. Note that First Name, Last Name, and Email Address are required fields, but the rest are optional. When you are finished, click Next.

▼ **FIGURE 19.14.**

Enter your personal
information so that
others can find you.

6. Select a category that suits your NetMeeting needs. People use NetMeeting for a variety of purposes: some for business, some to talk to their families, and some to meet other people. Select the category you want to use, and click <u>N</u>ext.

7. In this dialog box, select the speed of your modem or type of connection and click <u>N</u>ext.

8. To proceed to the Audio Wizard, click <u>N</u>ext.

9. As shown in Figure 19.15, NetMeeting's Audio Tuning Wizard tests your sound volume levels. Click the <u>T</u>est button (which changes to a Stop button), and adjust your volume to a comfortable level. When you are done, click Stop and then click <u>N</u>ext.

FIGURE 19.15.

Test your speakers and
adjust the volume as
needed.

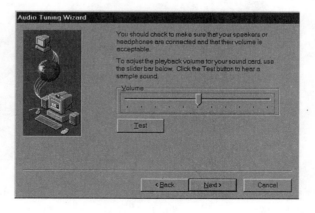

▼   10. NetMeeting tests your microphone volume levels, as shown in Figure 19.16. Read
         the statement on the screen into your microphone at a normal speaking level and
         then click Next.

FIGURE 19.16.

*Check your micro-
phone volume.*

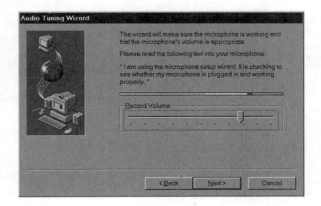

11. When your audio and microphone levels are tested, you are ready to use
    NetMeeting. Click Finish.

▲

When you've finished setting up NetMeeting, you are ready to conduct your online meeting. The next section gives you a brief overview on how to organize and conduct an
online meeting.

To Do: Conducting an Online Meeting

1. To conduct an online meeting, open Microsoft NetMeeting. Depending on how
   your Internet connection is set up, NetMeeting may connect for you or wait for you
   to establish a connection with your Internet service provider.

When logging on to your NetMeeting server, you may get a message telling
you that you are not able to log on to the server because it is busy. In this
case, try choosing a different server by clicking Call, Change My Information,
and select the Calling tab. In the Server Name drop-down box, choose any
of the other servers. In the past, ils.business.four11.com has worked well and
is usually not busy. When you have chosen the new server, click OK.

▼

19

▼   2. A notice in the lower-right corner of your NetMeeting screen, as shown in Figure 19.17, shows your connection status (either `connected` or `not logged on`).

FIGURE **19.17.**

Are you logged on? Find out by looking at the lower-right corner of the NetMeeting screen.

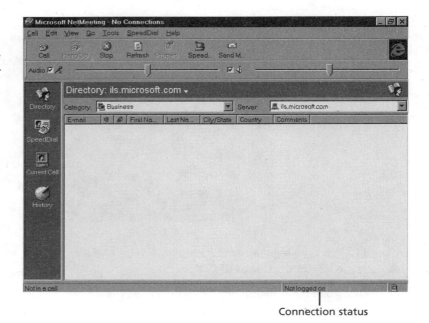

Connection status

3. To conduct your online meeting, you must call the other attendees. To do this, you can select an attendee from the server directory, as shown in Figure 19.18, or you can click the Call button on your toolbar. NetMeeting asks you the email address of the person you would like to call. Enter the address and NetMeeting will attempt to contact that person.

If the person is logged on to the server, he will receive an invitation to join a meeting with you. If he is not logged on, you will receive a notice that the person could not be contacted.

Each person must be logged on to the *same* NetMeeting server, such as `ils.business.four11.com`. If an attendee is logged on to another server, he or she will not be able to receive invitations from you. Therefore, when setting up an online meeting, make sure you specify a backup server where everyone can log on just in case your primary server is busy.

▼

FIGURE 19.18.

Find the attendees of your meeting.

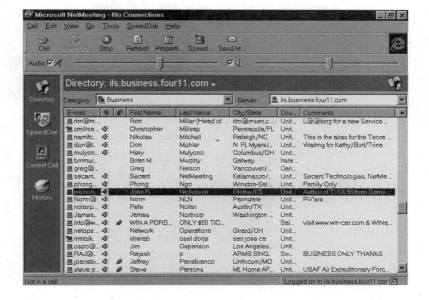

4. If you have set up your sound card and microphone, you can speak directly to the other attendees (depending, of course, on their equipment). You should note, however, that if you do not have a full-duplex sound card, you will have to wait for the other person to stop speaking before you can speak.

5. After you have contacted all the other attendees, you should see a screen similar to the one shown in Figure 19.19. On the right side of the screen is a video box that allows videoconferencing if your computer is configured for it. The center box lists the attendees, and the toolbar enables you to select from a variety of options.

6. On the toolbar, click the Chat button. NetMeeting enables you to type messages back and forth between the different attendees. The Chat box, as shown in Figure 19.20, is useful when one or more of the attendees doesn't have a sound card or a microphone. Close the Chat box.

7. On the toolbar, click the whiteboard button. NetMeeting opens a whiteboard, as shown in Figure 19.21. NetMeeting enables every member of the meeting to see the images and changes on this whiteboard, just as if it were in a conference room in front of everyone. The whiteboard tools on the left of the whiteboard are simple to use and can perform a variety of tasks. Close the whiteboard.

19

▼ **FIGURE 19.19.**

Your online meeting screen is ready to go.

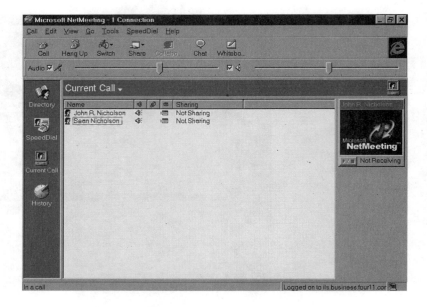

FIGURE 19.20.

The Chat box in NetMeeting enables real-time communication among meeting attendees.

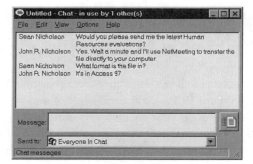

8. You will also notice that by choosing Tools, File Transfer, you can send files to the different members of your meeting.

9. Close NetMeeting.

This has been a *brief* introduction to Microsoft NetMeeting and a basic lesson on how to set up an online meeting. If you are interested in using NetMeeting on a regular basis, you should consider consulting books that specifically address the features and capabilities of NetMeeting.

▼

▼ **FIGURE 19.21.**

The whiteboard enables you to add a visual aspect to your meeting.

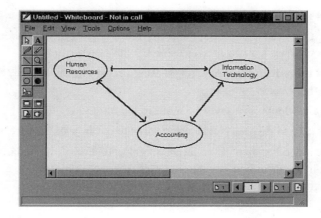

▲

Summary

Sharing is an important part of today's business. By accessing coworkers' calendars, files, or ideas, Outlook—in combination with Microsoft's NetMeeting—can help you schedule and conduct online meetings with a few keystrokes and clicks.

Q&A

Q Where do I find out more information about Microsoft NetMeeting?

A Check out the Microsoft Web site at: http://www.microsoft.com.

Q I have Windows 95, revision B and NetMeeting was already installed on my computer. Can I use it?

A Yes, but it is version 1.0. If you download the newest version of NetMeeting, you will be able to take advantage of numerous features that were not included in version 1.0.

Q Can I restrict access to my personal calendar to just a single person?

A At this time, when you publish your calendar on your Exchange Server or MS Mail Postoffice, you must make it available to everyone.

Q When I use the Voice feature, the sound sometimes breaks up. What can I do?

A Try adjusting your speaker and microphone volumes, speaking more slowly, getting a faster Internet connection, or use the telephone. Unfortunately, Internet voice capabilities have been beaten by two cans attached to a string. The technology is getting better all the time, but it's still not very good.

19

Q **Can I keep others from changing the whiteboard during a meeting?**

A Yes. Click the lock tool in the lower-left corner of the whiteboard toolbar. You can also save whiteboard images using the _S_ave command.

Q **Will there be additional NetMeeting servers in the future? The few that are out there seem to be busy.**

A Have no doubt, there will be more in the future.

Q **Is it safe to display NetMeeting topic areas in a public presentation?**

A Like any other area of the Internet, appropriateness of language is not always a requirement for being on the Internet. There are rude, crude, and abusive users who delight in shocking others. Just be careful anytime you are doing a live presentation on the Internet.

PART VII
Is That All There Is?

Hour

HOUR 20

It Takes a Licking...

> "Far out in the uncharted backwaters of the unfashionable end of the Western Spiral arm of the Galaxy lies a small unregarded yellow sun. Orbiting this at a distance of roughly ninety-eight million miles is an utterly insignificant little blue-green planet whose ape-descended life forms are so amazingly primitive that they still think digital watches are a pretty neat idea."
>
> —Douglas Adams, *Hitchhiker's Guide to the Galaxy*

Many of us (particularly the older generation) still think digital watches are a pretty neat idea. (At least, better than a sundial in most cases.)

And when we were kids, how many times did we look at Dick Tracy's watch communicator and exclaim, "Ooooo?" Or did you drool with envy over Mr. Spock's tricorder? Fancy stuff, from fanciful shows.

Today, reality has begun to overtake fiction. Portable TVs are as small as watches, and cellular phones are nearly identical to the Star Trek communicators (the old flip-open ones, not the chest pins). Digital personal assistants, once the size of an old calculator, can now be worn on your wrist. In fact, I wear one on mine: It's called the Timex Data Link™. It can store up to 150 pieces of information with up to 31 characters each. Where does it get this data? One good source is from your Outlook 98 program.

Introducing the Timex Data Link Watch

The Timex Data Link Watch is a wrist-sized personal information manager (PIM). In addition to being a watch with many standard features, it can also be used to download data from your computer and enables you to retrieve it on command. You can store phone numbers, lists, and appointments. It is available with either a leather or stainless steel band. You can buy one at most office or computer supply stores, as well as directly from Timex (1-800-367-8463).

Required Hardware

The first thing you need is a Data Link Watch (see Figure 20.1). At the time of this writing, the Data Link 150 was selling for under $100—not much more than other medium-priced watches. The system monitor for your computer must be VGA or higher to interact with the watch. It won't work with a Macintosh or any other Apple computer.

FIGURE 20.1.

The new Timex Data Link 150 watch enables you to wirelessly download up to 150 entries from your personal computer.

You also need to have a 386 or higher processor in your computer, 2.5MB of hard drive space, and a mouse. (If your computer didn't meet these requirements, you wouldn't be able to run Outlook 98, so you should be okay.)

Adapting to a Laptop

You can't directly download information from a laptop or notebook computer unless you purchase a special adapter that is temporarily attached to the serial port, as shown in Figure 20.2. The adapter is so small that you can easily stick it in one of the pockets of your laptop case. It is required because the data from your computer is read visually by your watch. The circle above the watch display is a lens. When the watch is set to receive, the lens reads a series of bar codes that flash across your screen, or reads the flashing LED on the optional notebook adapter.

If you have an external VGA or higher monitor attached to your laptop either directly or through a docking station or bar, you don't need to use the notebook adapter. The adapter is required only if you have no screen other than your laptop display.

At the time of this writing, the adapter was priced at about $30. Most stores that carry the watch should carry the adapter. Remember: You need it only if you will be setting your watch using your notebook.

FIGURE 20.2.

Using the new notebook adapter, the Data Link can communicate with notebook and laptop computers.

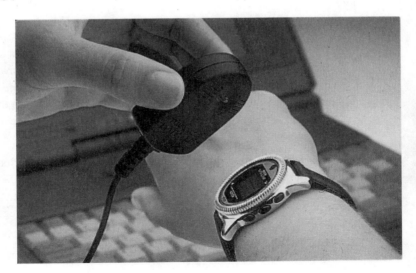

20

Required Software

You must have software to transfer data from your computer to the Data Link. Each watch comes with software, and you will probably want to install it because there are many additional things you can do with the Timex software that can't be done from within Outlook.

You can also download information directly from Outlook 98, but you'll need to make some minor adjustments to the program before it will work.

> Often computer users set the time on their computers, and then assume that it will keep time like a watch or alarm clock. Unless you have special software, this generally isn't the case. Before you begin installing the Timex software, make sure that your clock is set accurately. To set it, double-click the time in the bottom-right corner of the task bar. In the Date/Time properties dialog box, make sure the time and date are correct. Click OK when you are finished.

Getting the Time of Day from the Internet

If you're going to go to all the trouble to get a nifty watch like the Data Link, you need to set it correctly. Before you begin setting the watch, you need to set your computer's time accurately. You can get the current time by going to the Boulder Atomic Time Clock at

```
http://www.bldrdoc.gov/doc-tour/atomic_clock.html
```

However, because you probably like toys, you might want to get a software program to automatically set your computer time for you. If you are compulsive about the accuracy of your watch, go to www.hotfiles.com and search for *atomic time*. I recommend two programs. Atomic Clock is a freeware, no-frills program that uses the Internet to get the time from the National Institute of Standards and Technology (the atomic time clock in Boulder, Colorado).

AccuSet, a different program, uses your modem to call the time clock (probably a long distance call, but it takes less than a minute to set the time). AccuSet is a shareware program and costs $10 to register. You can try it free for 21 days. It can track the required adjustments to your clock, and can add or subtract seconds on a regular basis to keep your clock accurate. Definitely worth the price!

You can also get the current time from Timex at:

`http://www.timex.com`

Installing the Timex Data Link Software

The screen captures used in this section are from version 2.0 of the Timex Data Link software. If you are using a later version of the software, your screens might look slightly different.

Software installation is simple and quick. Remember: Just because you are using Outlook 98, don't discount the Timex software; it gives you some capabilities not available from within Outlook. In the following exercise you learn to install the Data Link software.

To Do: Installing the Timex Data Link Software

1. Insert the Data Link floppy disk into your computer. Click Start, Run; type `A:\Setup` in the Run dialog box; and press Enter. (If your floppy drive is designated other than as A, replace the first letter with the appropriate drive designation.) The Welcome dialog box is displayed. Read it and click Continue.

2. In the Timex Data Link Setup dialog box, you are reminded to close any open programs. Follow the directions on the screen if you have programs open. Click Continue.

3. In the Setup dialog box, leave the location as listed, unless you need to put the software on another drive. Click OK to continue the installation.

Although you are using Windows 95 or later, the Timex software *doesn't* support long directory names. Any new directory name must be eight characters or fewer.

20

4. Sit tight for a few minutes. When the software is finished installing the files, you are prompted to reboot Windows. Do so now, or the software might not function as expected.

Working with the Timex Data Link Software

Before you begin using Outlook to control your new watch, you need to learn the capabilities of the Timex software. It is so easy to use that it is nearly intuitive. Table 20.1 shows the categories used by the Timex software.

TABLE 20.1. TIMEX SOFTWARE CATEGORIES.

Data Category	Description
Appointments	Appointments and meetings (even recurring) can be transferred.
Anniversaries	Recurring events can be transferred. A special icon in the watch informs the wearer one week before an anniversary or event, and flashes on the day of the event as a final reminder.
Phone Numbers	Contact names and phone numbers can be transferred.
Make a List	Tasks can be transferred.
Time Settings	Time and date for two time zones can be entered.
Alarms	Up to five daily alarms can be transferred.
WristApps™	Specialized watch functions can be loaded one at a time. The watch comes with a chronometer.
Watch Sounds	Sound schemes are provided for the watch.

As you can see from Table 20.1, Data Link software still has a lot of functionality of its own, despite the overlap with Outlook, so don't abandon it. The WristApps applets alone make it worth saving.

 Downloading any information from the computer into the watch erases *all* data already contained in the watch (with the exception of the current Wrist App).

In the next exercise, you'll begin working with the software supplied with your watch.

To Do: Readying the Timex Software

1. Close the Timex folder if it is open. To begin running the program, click Start, Programs, Timex Data Link, Timex Data Link. (You have to click Timex Data Link in two locations.)

2. The screen will go black for a few seconds, and you will see an auto-calibration message for your monitor. When the calibration is completed, click OK. After that, a short tutorial is run.

3. When it's complete, press Enter to continue. The main Timex Data Link screen, as shown in Figure 20.3, is displayed.

> If there was a problem with the download, click the Retry button. If it still doesn't work, see the online help area for troubleshooting tips.

FIGURE 20.3.

The main Timex Data Link screen offers several options for entering data.

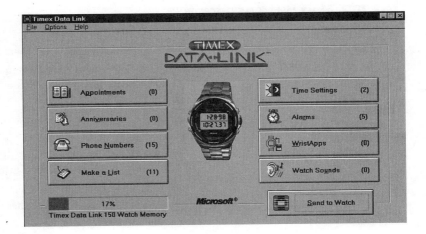

> If you travel often, download all the pertinent data you need or even think you'll need before you leave. However, keep a current version of your Outlook folders on your laptop, just in case.

Timex Tips

The following are a few important issues to understand about the watch and software:

- If you don't send a particular database (such as Notes) when you download information, that category won't appear as you cycle through the various modes.

- To scan quickly through a series of data on the watch, press and hold the Next or Previous button.

20

- Appointments have a variable pre-alarm (early warning) time. This is set in the Appointments control in the Timex (not Outlook) software. You can vary the warning time from 0–30 minutes.
- If your company is on a tight budget (the boss is too cheap to buy more than one watch), you can install the software in a separate folder for each person.

A Few Words About WristApps

WristApps are miniature software programs. Those listed in Table 20.2 are included with the Data Link watch.

TABLE 20.2. TIMEX WRISTAPPS DESCRIPTIONS.

WristApp	Description
Stopwatch	Event timer. Starts at zero and counts up.
Week of the Year (U.S.)	Displays current week number, current day number, and number of days left in the year. Uses Sunday as the first day of the week.
Week of the Year (International)	Same as U.S. version, except uses Monday as first day of the week.
Countdown Timer (Adjustable)	Allows setting from one minute to 100 hours in one-minute increments. Counts down from the set time to zero.
Countdown Timer (Preset)	Same as Adjustable version, but only allows preset times of 5, 10, 15, 20, 30, 45, or 60 minutes.
Note	Displays note of up to 255 characters (30–40 words). Use for directions or other, more complex, instructions.
Melody Tester	Used to test watch tones, rather than waiting for them to sound.

Only one WristApp can be downloaded to the watch at a time. You must download them using the Timex software. Outlook cannot handle WristApps.

You can order an additional set of WristApps directly from Timex (1-800-448-4639). They include a golf scorekeeper, CopyMe! game (match musical tones), Pulse Calculator, Value Converter, and Word Time modules. The price is around $20 for all five. They add to your current WristApps, and do not replace the others (so you have ten to choose from). You can still have only one loaded into the watch at a time.

Setting the Time Using the Data Link Program

Before you learn how to use Outlook and the Data Link watch, learn to download information from the Data Link program so that you can see the differences when you later work with Outlook.

To Do: Downloading the Time and Date

1. Open the Data Link software.
2. Click the Time Settings button.
3. In the Time Settings dialog box (see Figure 20.4), you can set your computer's current time and the time and date for two time zones. Configure the settings as required.

FIGURE 20.4.

The Time Settings dialog box is used to set the current time zone as well as an additional one, if desired.

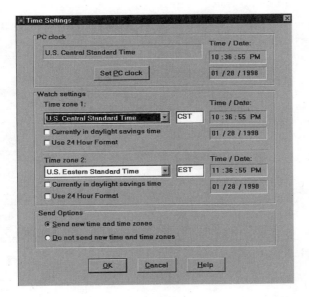

 If you do not want to set your watch for more than one time zone, just make sure the information in both time zone sections is identical.

4. In the Send Options panel, click the Send New Time and Time Zones option button.
5. Click OK.
6. In the main screen, you will see that a 2 appears next to the Time Settings label. This is because you are ready to download information for two time zones.

20

Also in the lower-left corner of the main screen is a percentage bar that indicates the percentage of the watch's memory that is used when the download occurs. Keep an eye on this because you will not be allowed to overflow the watch.

The WristApps features can be downloaded only one at a time. The memory requirements for them are already built into the watch; therefore, downloading a WristApps feature does not affect the watch's storage capacity.

7. Click the Send to Watch button.

8. Prepare your watch as the Data Link software tutorial showed you. The Get Ready dialog box appears to remind you of this (see Figure 20.5).

FIGURE 20.5.

The Get Ready dialog box indicates that the program is ready to send data to the watch.

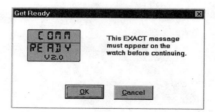

9. When your watch is ready and in position, click the OK button in the Get Ready dialog box.

10. While the data is downloading, your watch produces short beeps. When completed, a single long tone sounds.

If no tones sound, you probably forgot to put the watch in the Communication mode before starting the download.

11. When the download transmission is complete, a Timex Data Link dialog box appears to confirm that you heard no warning alarms from your watch, which would have indicated faulty transmission (see Figure 20.6). If you did hear an alarm, click Retry; otherwise, click OK.

▼ **FIGURE 20.6.**

The Timex Data Link dialog box asks you to confirm that the information was successfully downloaded to the

▲ *watch.*

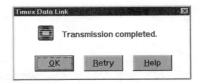

Outlook and Data Link

Now that you've seen how the Timex Data Link software works, it's time to see how Outlook can be used to transmit data to the watch.

Only three folders of data can be transferred from Outlook to the watch: Calendar, Tasks, and Contacts. This may seem limited, but these are very useful folders, and you can't email with your watch (yet), anyway.

To prepare Outlook to download its data, you must first install the Data Link system add-on. This add-on is an executable wizard located on your Outlook 98 CD-ROM. If you aren't sure if the Outlook Export filter has been installed yet, click File, Import and Export. The Export to the Timex Data Link Watch option should be chosen. When you click Next, you get an error message if the filter hasn't been installed yet. Close Outlook and follow the instruction shown in the Description panel. In the following exercise, you use Outlook to download data to your watch.

To Do: Using the Basic Timex Commands in Outlook 98

1. Click File, Import and Export.
2. In the first screen of the Import and Export Wizard, select The Export to The Timex Data Link Watch option (see Figure 20.7), then click Next.

FIGURE 20.7.

Start the exporting process.

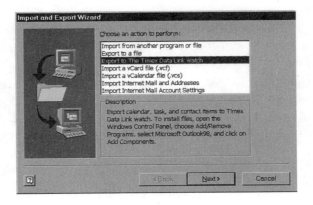

20

▼ 3. In the second screen of the wizard, as shown in Figure 20.8, you select which types of data from Outlook you want to download into the watch. Check and uncheck the options as desired. When you are finished, click Next.

FIGURE 20.8.

Choose the data to send to the watch.

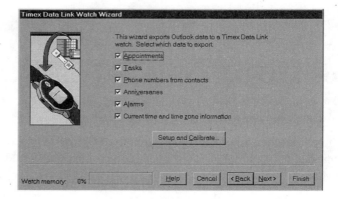

The remaining screens in the wizard are displayed if the associated data category was checked in the second screen. In other words, the Tasks screen of the wizard will not appear if the Tasks option was unchecked.

The remainder of these steps assume that all options were checked. If at any time, you want to stop configuring the downloading procedure, click the Finish button.

4. The third screen enables you specify how much appointment data you want to transmit (see Figure 20.9). Keep an eye on the watch memory bar at the bottom of the wizard—the more data you download, the more memory will be used. Click Next when finished.

5. The fourth screen is for configuring the tasks that you want to download into the watch (see Figure 20.10). Notice that task priority is a factor, not just the chronology of the task. Click Next when finished.

6. The fifth screen, as shown in Figure 20.11, enables you to select the phone numbers that will be downloaded to the watch. Select the rows (contacts) to be downloaded by clicking each one. Remember, keep an eye on the watch's memory box
▼   so that you don't overload the watch. Click Next when finished.

FIGURE 20.9.

With the appointment configuration screen, determine the number of days to download into your watch.

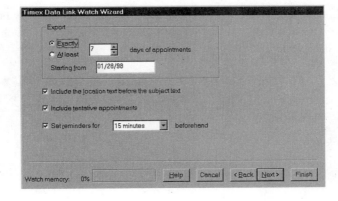

FIGURE 20.10.

With the tasks configuration screen, determine the number of to-do items to download into your watch.

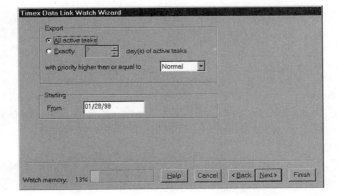

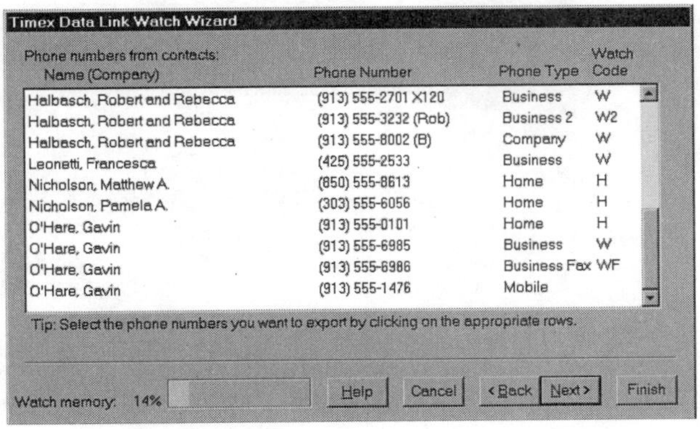

FIGURE 20.11.

With the phone number configuration screen, determine which phone numbers from your contact list to download into your watch.

20

▼   7. In the sixth screen, select the anniversaries, birthdays, or any other annual events
       you have in Calendar that you want downloaded into the watch (see Figure 20.12).
       Click Next when finished.

FIGURE 20.12.

*With the annual events
configuration screen,
determine which
events to download
into your watch.*

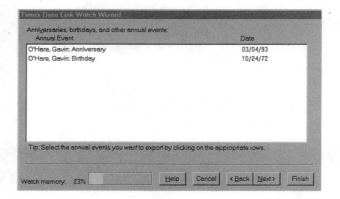

8. The Data Link watch can have up to five alarms set for it on a daily, weekly,
   monthly, or yearly basis. The seventh screen (see Figure 20.13) sets these alarms.
   If an alarm is set with one of the latter three intervals, a Date field appears in that
   alarm row. Click Next when finished.

FIGURE 20.13.

*With the alarms con-
figuration screen, you
can set up to five
alarms.*

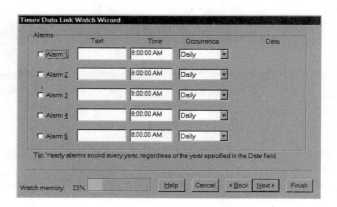

9. The eighth screen sets the time zone information for the watch. Compare Figure
   20.14 to the Timex Data Link Watch Time Settings dialog box shown in Figure
   20.4. They use the same information, but are arranged differently. (The choice of
▼   which to use is up to you.) Click Next when finished.

FIGURE 20.14.

You can use the time zone configuration screen in lieu of the Time Settings dialog box (refer to Figure 20.4).

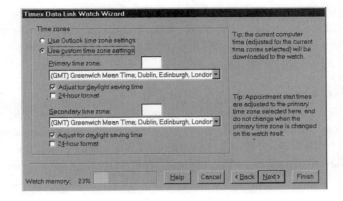

10. In the ninth screen you will briefly see a display similar to the main screen of the Data Link software, which will quickly be covered by the Export to Watch dialog box (see Figure 20.15). When your watch is ready, as the dialog box specifies, click OK.

FIGURE 20.15.

The Export To Watch dialog box indicates that your watch is ready to receive the data that you've configured.

11. When the download transmission is complete, a message dialog box appears to confirm that you heard no warning alarms from your watch, which would have indicated faulty transmission (see Figure 20.16).

    If you *did* hear an alarm, click No so that the wizard will recycle the transmission sequence. If you *did not* hear a warning alarm, click Yes.

FIGURE 20.16.

The Timex Data Link Watch Wizard asks you to confirm the transmission.

20

Congratulations, you have entered the world of the truly connected. Some would say the world of the geek, but pay them no mind. You have the world at your fingertips—or at your wrist.

Summary

Now that you have learned how to use the Timex Data Link watch, you will be able to take your Outlook information anywhere. It's even water-resistant, in case you want to take it to the beach. Like all high-tech tools, you need to take care of it. Don't bang it on the sidewalk because you don't hear it ticking. (It really doesn't tick at all.)

 If you really insist on licking the watch, clean it off before downloading data. Smudges tend to goof up the transmission.

In Hour 21, "Keeping Up with the Gateses," you learn to keep your copy of Outlook up-to-date, as well as suggestions for getting a lot of information from the Microsoft Web site and other sources.

Q&A

Q I can't get the watch to download properly. Is there some trick?

A This is why you should go through the Timex Data Link watch tutorial. It will help you get the angle and position right. Basically, if the watch is reading correctly, it will emit a steady stream of beeps. Run through the calibration sequences available in the Data Link software or on the second page of the Import and Export Wizard until you find the right place.

Make sure your room is well lit and that the screen is fairly bright. Also, try taking the watch off and holding it in your hand. That might make it more steady. Make sure that your monitor and the lens of your watch are clean.

Q I have been using an older model of the Timex Data Link watch. Can I use it with Outlook?

A Not very well. The wizard is geared for the Model 150 watch and cannot adjust for the lack of functionality of the earlier model. You can use the Data Link software, however. It can be adjusted by clicking the File, Advanced menu command.

Q Can I change the time or set alarms without using the software?

A Yes. The instructions for doing so are included in the box with the watch. It's basically the same as any other digital watch.

Q When the battery wears out, can I change it myself?

A No. Take it to an authorized Timex repair shop. Otherwise, your watch will probably not be water-resistant anymore.

Q The box says the watch is water-resistant up to 30 meters. If I do wear it in water, are any special precautions necessary?

A Just make sure you don't press any of the buttons while you are in the water; or water might leak into your watch.

20

Hour 21

Keeping Up with the Gateses

If you have kept track of everything Microsoft has released and know exactly what each component does, you should probably work for Mr. Microsoft (Bill Gates) himself. However, considering you are working through a book to learn about Microsoft Outlook 98, I assume you are not one of the designers of the program and therefore don't know all the little intricacies that have been added or deleted each time a new software version is released.

Every software application is tested and retested by beta testers months before it is released to the public. A beta tester is someone gullible enough to install bug-ridden software on his or her computer, causing it to crash on a regular basis. There is no financial compensation for doing this, so it doesn't sound too smart, does it? Actually, it's a lot of fun, although often frustrating. But you have a real sense of accomplishment when you detect a flaw and report it to Microsoft.

Because of Microsoft's extensive beta testing of its software, applications released to the public are relatively stable and bug free. (Remember, though, applications can consist of millions of lines of computer code. When I consider all the hardware and software variations and interactions throughout the world, I'm amazed they run at all!)

A lot of people think, okay, I just bought this software. I have the latest version. I don't have to worry about anything else until they release another version. However, that is seldom the case. Sometimes the developers find things that need to be fixed or updated that don't necessarily warrant a new version of the software. These are called *service updates*, *service releases*, or *patches*. They are small- to medium-size programs you either can download from the Internet or order directly from the manufacturer to enhance the software you already own. There has been a lot of speculation in the press recently that this model of software distribution—lots of little upgrades instead of big releases—may soon become the norm from Microsoft and the rest of the developers.

In addition, many companies offer helpful hints on their Web sites on how to work with specific software, including Outlook. Hints that you might not find in instruction manuals or how-to books can often be found on the Web. Books and manuals are usually released at the same time the software becomes available, and thus don't always contain all the tips and tricks that are discovered by the everyday user. In fact, if the manufacturer says a piece of software *can't* do something, the chances are excellent that another user of the program can tell you how to do it.

During this hour, you will find references to Office 97 information, rather than information specific to Outlook 98. In most cases, each reference includes some way to access additional information about Outlook because it is part of the Office 97 suite.

This hour offers many activities, but we are making some assumptions that may not be true for you. To do most of the exercises in this hour, you'll need an Internet connection and a newsgroup server. The Internet is always changing, so the figures in this hour may not be the same as those on your monitor. Some newsgroups referred to might no longer be in existence, and new ones may have appeared to take their places. We will cover some of the most popular Web sites where you can locate more information about Outlook 98. The search skills that you learn can also be used for other software and, actually, any other topic you can think of. There is a lot of information out there; you just need to know how to get to it.

Words of Wisdom and Warning

Although this book discusses the Internet, it isn't about the Internet. Most people can figure out how to use a basic browser to access the Internet, but they may have difficulties in understanding the complexities of such features as discussion groups (newsgroups) and list servers. This hour has a lot of Internet information in it. If you are not yet fully comfortable with the Internet, you may want to get a copy of *Sams' Teach Yourself the Internet in 24 Hours* (Sams Publishing) by Noel Estabrook. If you want to "check out" Macmillan's latest books (and even temporarily check out up to five books from its library), take a look at Macmillan's Web site:

www.mcp.com

What, Exactly, Do We Have Here?

Before beginning your Web exploration for Outlook information, it's helpful to know exactly what version of Outlook you have. You can find this by choosing Help, About Microsoft Outlook. The About Microsoft Outlook dialog box, similar to the one shown in Figure 21.1, is displayed. Your version will be different from the one shown in the figure.

FIGURE 21.1.

The About Microsoft Outlook dialog box displays the version you currently have installed. You may need to upgrade it at the Outlook Internet site.

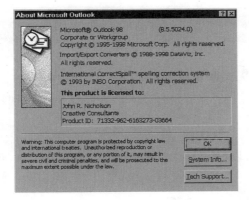

Write down the version of Outlook you are using. Some of the extra software that you will read about in Hour 23, "Adding Extras to Outlook 98," will work only with specific versions of Outlook. You learn more about upgrading later in this hour.

Going to the Source

A Microsoft home page is shown in Figure 21.2. The one you see when you access the Web site will be different—perhaps totally different. Microsoft updates its Web site often, making it easier to navigate, and adding new information to the pages.

Your screen may also look different depending on your browser (probably Microsoft Internet Explorer (IE) or Netscape Navigator or Communicator). All the figures in this book use Internet Explorer.

21

FIGURE 21.2.

Microsoft's home page on the Internet is a good place to begin your search for Outlook help.

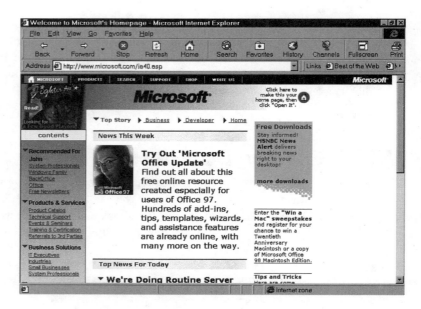

To get to the Microsoft home page that you saw in Figure 21.2, use the following Internet address:

www.microsoft.com

This site will quickly update you concerning major changes on the Microsoft Web site, as well as any major additions and changes to Microsoft software. If you are interested only in Office, read on.

Checking In at the Office

When you access the Internet and go to the following address, you will find a wealth of information about Microsoft Office 97, and even Outlook 97 and 98 specifically. This site should serve as your first source of information for specific Office product information. You can go directly to the Office home page, bypassing the Microsoft home page, by setting your browser to:

www.microsoft.com/office

At this Web site, you can discover a lot of interesting information regarding all the components of the Microsoft Office Suite. Because Outlook is part of the Office suite, this is obviously a very good place to start. Figure 21.3 shows an example of the Office 97 home page.

FIGURE 21.3.

The Microsoft Office home page keeps you informed about changes in the Office suite.

Visit the Office home page frequently and explore it carefully. You need to learn to use the references on this page to the fullest.

In February 1998, Microsoft released a new service on its Web site for registered Office 97 users called Microsoft Office Update: When you are registered online, your version of Office is automatically checked each time you access the site to ensure that it contains all the latest update files. If it does not, your copy of Office is automatically updated to the most recent version.

If you need to reinstall Microsoft Office 97 or any of its components, you will immediately want to return to the update site to have the most recent upgrades applied to Office.

Finding the Outlook Internet Site

If you want information that is specific to Outlook, you may want to go directly to the Microsoft Outlook Web site:

www.microsoft.com/office/outlook

21

An example of the Outlook home page is shown in Figure 21.4. Because this page is frequently updated, yours will look different, but the figure will give you an idea of what you can expect.

FIGURE 21.4.

The Outlook home page can be directly accessed to get updated Outlook information.

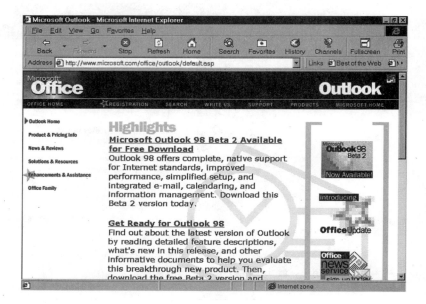

Before you move on, there's one Web site that you *can't* miss. It's probably the best site for Outlook information. You can find it at:

www.slipstick.com

Now that we've described a few of the Web sites you need to access to keep your Outlook 98 (and Office 97) up-to-date, let's do a little hands-on exploring.

To Do: Exploring the Microsoft Web Site

1. Open your favorite Internet browser and, if required, connect to the Internet. (If you are connected to a network, you may be immediately on the Internet as soon as you open your browser. If you are working from home, you might have to use a dial-up connection.)

2. In the Address box, type www.microsoft.com. Press Enter.

Most browsers do not require http:// to be typed to access the address. Additionally, if you just type *microsoft*, most browsers assume the beginning *www* and the ending *com*.

In version 4 and later of both Microsoft Internet Explorer and Netscape Communicator, as you begin typing the address, the browser automatically tries to fill in the rest of the address. If the displayed address is correct, just press Enter. If not, keep typing until the entire address is displayed and then press Enter.

3. Use the scroll arrows to explore the entire page so that you get some idea of what is available. Keep in mind that this page may change daily, although the basic controls will remain the same. At the top of the page are several options you may need later; the most important is Support. Locate it, but don't click it just yet.

4. In the Address box, type www.microsoft.com/office and press Enter. (If, as soon as you begin typing, the first part of the address appears, press Tab to move the insertion point to the end of the address, and type the rest of it.)

5. Explore the Office home page. Again, this changes on a regular basis, so it may be different each time you return. Visit it frequently.

6. Now take a look at www.microsoft.com/office/outlook. From here, you can download various software programs that work with Outlook, as well as get the latest tips for working with Outlook.

7. Close your browser, but leave the Internet connection open.

A Brief Guide to Newsgroups and List Servers

Two additional sources for Outlook information on the Internet are newsgroups and list servers. Each has advantages and disadvantages. You may find that they are difficult to use (in some cases, too much or inappropriate information overshadows the useful tips). In this hour, we assume that you know how to access newsgroups and list servers. If you are using Outlook and are unfamiliar with these, you might want to skip ahead to Hour 24, "Taking the Outlook Express," and then return to this hour. Outlook Express is used as an email tool, as well as offering access to newsgroups.

The version of Outlook Express that ships with Outlook 98 provides only news services. If you want the email version, download it from the Microsoft Office Web site. If you download a complete version of Internet Explorer, Outlook Express is automatically placed on your desktop.

21

More About Newsgroups

Newsgroups, also called *discussion groups*, are a part of the Internet that functions as a gigantic community bulletin board. There are tens of thousands of newsgroups on the Internet, each dedicated to a specific topic. As you can imagine, *any* topic is available in newsgroups. Most are public, but some are private, and you can only discover their existence when you are given the address by someone. You may even need a password to access private groups.

Newsgroups are active: To read the information, you must access the material using the appropriate software. Think of newsgroups as bulletin boards. You must first choose from a list of available ones, and then you must read each posting, or at least scan the headings.

To read a newsgroup, you must first have a newsgroup server (see Hour 24 for additional information). When you have identified the server, open Outlook Express. If you are not subscribed to any newsgroups, you will see the message shown in Figure 21.5.

FIGURE 21.5.

A warning message is displayed stating that you are not subscribed to any newsgroups.

Clicking <u>Y</u>es displays the dialog box shown in Figure 21.6. (The newsgroups you see will probably be different from those shown in the figure.) It may take a few minutes to load a list of the available newsgroups because there are so many.

To see all the newsgroups that contain the word *Outlook*, type `Outlook` in the Display Newsgroups Which Contain text box. After a few seconds, you will see a list of all public newsgroups carried on the selected server that contain the word *Outlook*, as shown in Figure 21.6.

> Not all newsgroups that contain the word *Outlook* pertain to the Microsoft product. For instance, the site may cover economic news, reporting the outlook of the stock market for the next year.

To subscribe to a newsgroup, select it and click the <u>S</u>ubscribe button on the right side of the dialog box. After you have subscribed, you can click the <u>G</u>o To button to open the newsgroup, or OK to close the dialog box. Figure 21.7 shows postings to the `microsoft.public.outlook97` newsgroup. Topics and sender information are shown in the top-right window with the selected message displayed beneath it. (You may need to use the scrollbars to see all the message.)

FIGURE 21.6.

*The search returned a list of all the newsgroups that contain the word **Outlook**.*

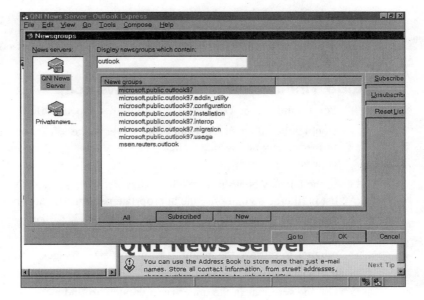

FIGURE 21.7.

A variety of topics relevant to Outlook are posted to the microsoft.public. outlook97 *newsgroup.*

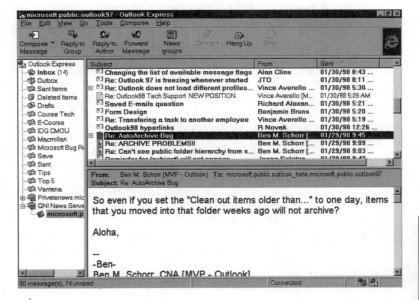

21

The basic function of a newsgroup is to act as a forum where you can leave a question that another user may have the answer to. You can also read questions from others that you might be able to answer. In other words, it's a place for questions, answers, and/or comments. Some of the information is relevant; some isn't. You need to sort the wheat from the chaff. In the next exercise, you'll have an opportunity to view a newsgroup. The exercise assumes you have already subscribed to a news server. If not, skip ahead to Hour 24.

To Do: Finding and Viewing a Newsgroup

1. You should still be connected to the Internet. Open Outlook Express.

2. Double-click the name of your news server in the left frame. If you aren't subscribed to any newsgroups, click Yes to see a list of all newsgroups available on your news server.

3. In the Display Newsgroups Which Contain text box, type Outlook. Wait until the list is filtered so that only the appropriate newsgroups are shown.

4. Select a group that looks interesting. Click Subscribe. Click Go To. Depending on the number of postings in the group, it may take from several seconds to several minutes to retrieve the headings from current messages. Soon, though, the current postings are displayed on the screen.

5. Use the scrollbar in the upper-right window to find a message that may be of interest to you. Click it once to select it. After a few seconds, the full text appears in the lower-right window.

6. Use the scroll arrows in the lower-right window to scroll through the individual message.

7. To unsubscribe to a newsgroup, highlight it in the left window, right-click, and select Unsubscribe From This Newsgroup. Confirm that you want to unsubscribe.

> As long as you subscribe to at least one newsgroup, you won't see the message that you are not subscribed to a newsgroup. If you want to see the list of available newsgroups on your server, right-click the name of the news server (*not* a newsgroup), and choose Newsgroups to display the Newsgroups dialog box. The All tab shows all newsgroups that were carried on the server the last time you checked. The Subscribed tab shows the groups to which you are currently subscribed. The New tab lists new newsgroups (which are constantly being created) that were not in the original All listing.

 8. Close Outlook Express but keep the Internet connection open.

The Magic of List Servers

List servers are similar to newsgroups, but their information comes directly to you; that is, postings show up in your Inbox as email. Active list servers may send dozens of messages every day, so choose your groups wisely. Some groups are moderated, which means that you send email to a specific person, and if the moderator thinks the information is worth sending, he or she distributes it to the group. This means that you are more likely to get meaningful, relevant information.

To subscribe to a list server, you generally send an email message to a specific address with the word *Subscribe* in the subject. However, each group operates slightly differently, so you need to find out the exact procedure for the group you are interested in. Usually, you get list server names from others with similar interests.

A good place to begin finding a list of list servers is at CataList. As of January 31, 1998, they had a searchable index of 16,132 of the 77,326 list servers on the Internet. They are on the Web at:

www.lsoft.com

If 16,132 sites aren't enough, use your browser to go to the Excite search engine and search for List of Lists. We discuss search engines and how to use them in the next section. Meanwhile, Excite can be found at:

www.excite.com

Defining Subscriptions

We have talked about subscribing to list servers, but you should realize that there are two types of subscriptions: unpaid and paid. Nearly all list servers offer free subscriptions. In some cases, commercial list servers carry paid advertising. In other cases, the list owner (or moderator) may charge a small fee for a subscription. Paying for a subscription is unusual, so make sure that you preview a commercial list serve before you pay for one.

Commercial (But Free) Help Sources Delivered to You

If you would like a daily tip delivered to you via email, one place to begin is at:

www.tipworld.com

From there, you can choose from dozens of subjects. The Microsoft Office Tips is particularly helpful, and often has tips on Outlook.

21

Be careful how many you choose to subscribe to. If you aren't careful, you'll be subject to a glut of information, and be unable to process most of it. At any time, you can return to the site and unsubscribe.

A weekly newsletter that you won't want to miss is WOW (Woody's Office Watch). To subscribe, and to see an amazing Web site, be sure to visit

www.wopr.com

Make sure you check out the Annoyances books. He has one on Office 97, but not one specifically on Outlook yet.

The Little Search Engines That Could

There are hundreds of search engines that can search the Internet for items about your choice of subjects, including Microsoft Outlook. Table 21.1 shows some sample searches that I conducted using Microsoft Outlook 98 as the search term. Hits are the number of items found. *More is not always better.* If you get too many hits, refine your search: Make it more restrictive by adding words to the search terms.

TABLE 21.1. SAMPLE SEARCHES OF WORLD WIDE WEB SEARCH ENGINES.

Name	Address	Hits or Comments
AltaVista	www.altavista.com	1,330 using advanced search.
Excite	www.excite.com	Top 50 matches.
Hotbot	www.hotbot.com	17,701 hits.
Mamma	www.mamma.com	59 hits.
Web Crawler	www.webcrawler.com	1,238 hits.
Woody's Parallel Search (Inference Find)	www.wopr.com	29 hits.
Woody's Super Search	www.wopr.com	Choose 8 of 14 search engines to search at one time.
Yahoo!	www.yahoo.com	None, but link to AltaVista offered with 96,945 matches.

All search engines don't access all Web pages. Each has a different set, although they often overlap. Therefore, if you don't find what you need with one search engine, try a different one.

If you want to get a large listing of search engines with links to them, try:

`www.1sf.com/ws/searchengines.htm`

Another good method is to go to the Yahoo! Web site and use *search engines* as the search term. You will find more references to search engines than you could ever use.

All Cobb—No Corn

The Cobb Group is a publishing division of Ziff-Davis. It publishes magazines on many subjects. You can get a free copy of one of its magazines by going to:

`www.cobb.com`

These magazines contain no advertising, and are filled with tips and solutions that work in the real world. Unlike other items I have mentioned in this hour, these are paper magazines, and have a varying subscription rate. However, I personally subscribe to several of them, and find them well worth the price.

The Ziff-Davis World of Information

If you want to keep up-to-date on what's going on in the world of technology, be sure to check out the Ziff-Davis home page at:

`www.zdnet.com`

One of the best updates to arrive in my Inbox is Jesse Berst's AnchorDesk letter. It summarizes everything that's going on in the industry. This should be a must for everyone working with technology. There is no charge for the subscription. To apply, go to the Ziff-Davis home page and click AnchorDesk in the left window. At the bottom of the AnchorDesk page, click Subscribe. You'll be glad you did.

Summary

As you have seen during this hour, there are many ways to keep informed as to the new programs Microsoft releases. In addition, there are quite a few companies out there showing you neat ways to do things more quickly. Using the methods discussed, you now have the power to go out and explore. Find what you didn't know you could find. Learn everything you can to keep up with the Gateses.

21

Q&A

Q As I was surfing the Net, I saw several advertisements for free email accounts. Should I consider one of these?

A Probably not. They usually provide only email access free, and charge for other services. If you already have a provider and need another email account, check with them. In many cases, you can get an additional account inexpensively.

Q Do I really need to keep up on the enhancements to Outlook? Won't it work just fine without them?

A Although you may not have any problems running Outlook 98 out of the box, there will often be tiny bugs that might cause problems you seldom notice (such as when you are running another piece of software). Your best bet is to keep up with the updates, service releases, and patches. Then you won't need to worry.

Q I've heard that sometimes the patches or updates cause more problems than they resolve. Is that true?

A In the past, there have been updates that caused problems. These problems are usually pointed out by users within the first few days of release. You might want to wait a couple of weeks before getting an enhancement, just to make sure that there aren't any problems being reported.

Q Wading through information provided by search engines seems to take a lot of time, and doesn't always prove helpful. Are they really worth using?

A There is so much information on the Internet that it can be very difficult to find exactly what you need, even using a search engine. If you keep up with the Outlook Web site, subscribe to a couple of Outlook discussion groups, and generally keep your ears open, you should be fine without a lot of search engine use.

HOUR 22

New and Fun Outlook Features

Many years ago, when my wife gave me flying lessons as a Christmas present, the first thing I got to do was take a ride in a plane. The instructor took me up for a test flight just so I could see what it was like. He didn't explain all the instruments, the tower chatter, or the exact procedures for takeoff and landing. I just got the chance to experience the wonder and joy of flight. I didn't need to know the specifics to make a decision that I wanted to continue to learn to fly.

Learning Outlook is a lot like my first flight. You need to experience it first (as you did in Hour 1, "The View from the Outlook") and then learn a few features at a time, absorbing each new skill and integrating it into your work environment. This is a book for beginners. Why should you read about features that you might not need? There are two reasons that this hour is included in this book:

- It will give you an introduction into some of the things that Outlook is capable of doing, but that we haven't discussed yet.

- It will give you some direction in choosing new features that you might want to learn more about.

This hour is quite different from previous ones. There are fewer exercises. Although you probably learn best in a hands-on environment (which is why all the previous hours contain a multitude of exercises), some of these topics require a lot of explanation before you can actually do anything with them. However, if you know the features exist, you can learn to use the ones most helpful to you. You can use the online help feature to get additional information, or you can buy a more advanced book on Outlook to learn exactly how to use the additional features.

Taking an Advanced Shortcut

I tell my students that the purpose of having a computer in the office is to increase productivity. However, I don't always begin by teaching them all the shortcuts. I teach them the standard way to accomplish tasks and then show them shortcuts. If students understand how something works, it's easier for them to understand when a specific shortcut will or won't work.

Similarly, throughout the previous hours, you haven't been shown all the available shortcuts. Now, though, you're going to see one that's pretty nifty.

To Do: Displaying and Using the Advanced Toolbar

1. Open Outlook. Click the Outlook Today folder in the Outlook Bar.
2. Choose View, Toolbars, Advanced. The Advanced toolbar, as shown in Figure 22.1, is added beneath the Standard toolbar. When it is turned on, the Advanced toolbar is added to all folders. You'll view the others shortly.
3. Point to each of the buttons on the Advanced toolbar. From the left, they are Outlook Today, Back, Forward, Up One Level, Folder List, and Undo. Some are currently grayed, and will become available later.
4. Click the Inbox folder. The Advanced toolbar remains in the same place, but the buttons changed somewhat. The first five buttons are the same as in Outlook Today. The new buttons, beginning to the right of the Folder List button, are Print Preview, Undo, Rules Wizard, Current View, Group By Box, Field Chooser, and AutoPreview. With the exception of the Rules Wizard, all the features have been discussed in earlier hours. You accessed them with the menu commands, rather than simply clicking a single button.
5. Click the Calendar folder. The Plan a Meeting and Current View buttons are added to the right side of the toolbar. Again, there is nothing here that you haven't used before.

▼ **FIGURE 22.1.**

The Advanced toolbar offers shortcuts for performing various tasks.

Advanced toolbar ⎯

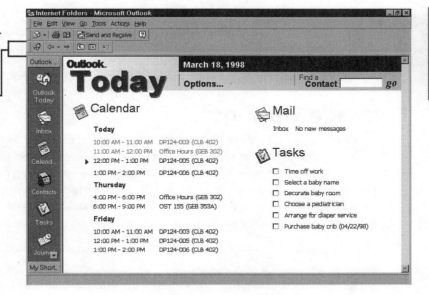

6. Click the Contacts folder. The first button to the right of the Undo button is New Meeting with Contact followed by New Task for Contact, Call Using NetMeeting, and Explore Web Page. The final button, as in the previous step, is the Current View button. The only new button here is the Explore Web Page. If a contact is selected and has a Web page listed, clicking the Explore Web Page button opens your Internet default browser (even if it's Netscape), and connects to the contact's Web page.

If you don't have a connection to the Internet already established when you click the Explore Web Page button, you won't be able to connect to the Web page.

7. Click the Tasks folder. You have seen all these buttons before. They were arranged differently in earlier screens.

8. Click the Journal folder. All the buttons should be familiar.

9. Click the Notes folder. Buttons are the same as in previous folders.

▲ 10. Click the Deleted Items folder. The toolbar is the same as the Inbox folder.

Turn the Advanced toolbar on and leave it on. It will still be there after exiting and returning to Outlook. Learn to use the shortcut buttons: They save time and mouse clicks.

Message Options

When you create a message, you can set several message options, as shown in Figure 22.2. The importance and sensitivity (privacy requirements) can be set. You can choose to add one of three voting button sets to the email (discussed in the "Voting" section later this hour). You can have the mail server tell you when the message has been delivered to the recipient, and when it has been read. This is a great way of ensuring that people don't ignore your email. (After all, you would never send junk mail, right?)

Not all servers support these types of features. You won't know until you ask your system administrator, the recipient, or at least give it the "old college try."

FIGURE 22.2.

The Message Options dialog box enables you to set various criteria for message sending and delivery.

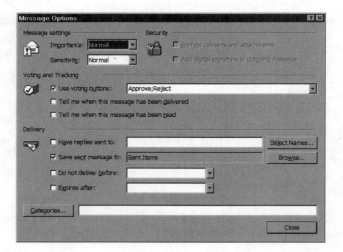

Using the Delivery options, you can choose to have replies sent to a different address. You can specify where to save copies of sent messages. You can postpone delivery until a specified date, and you can put an expiration date on the message, meaning that it can't be read after the listed date. The Message Options dialog box also provides two methods for security.

22

Taking Back What You Said

My mother always taught me that after I write someone a harsh letter, I should leave it under my pillow for 24 hours. If I still feel the same way the next day, then I can mail it.

In this age of instant communication, sometimes we send notes saying things that we later realize might not have been as tactful (or smart) as we thought at the time. This is a particular problem with email, where sarcasm is generally lost. Because a lot of our communication is nonverbal, email is at the low end of the communication efficiency ladder.

Microsoft has added an improved feature called *message recall* to Outlook 98. If you have sent an email message to another Outlook user, either through the Internet or using Microsoft Exchange Server, you can recover the message, as long as the recipient hasn't either read it or moved it to a new location. Additionally, you can replace a sent message that meets the preceding conditions with a new message of your choosing. Although this sounds like a nice feature, don't depend on getting your mail back. People often read their mail as soon as it arrives. As with all the specialized mail features, the receiving server may or may not support message recall.

Setting the Rules

If you haven't heard of spam yet, you will. No, it's not the meat product, but unsolicited email—sometimes referred to as junk mail. Just as snail mail (the United States Post Office) delivers 4th class bulk mail, the Internet has tools to send junk mail to any number of unsuspecting people. Although it may not directly cost you anything (unless you are paying an hourly fee), time wasted in looking at junk mail with clever headings (such as Hi from an old friend) costs you time and productivity. Luckily, Outlook 98 includes an improved feature called the Rules Wizard. (A Rules Wizard is available for Outlook 97, but you must download it from Microsoft.)

A *rule* is a set of conditions and actions (at least one of each is required) that instructs Outlook how to handle various items, including messages, task requests, and meeting requests. To specify a rule, you must be in the Inbox folder. Choose Tools, Rules Wizard. The Rules Wizard dialog box, as shown in Figure 22.3, is displayed.

The Rules Wizard can also be accessed from any folder containing mail items (although it works only on items received in the primary delivery folder). Oddly enough, you can also access the Rules Wizard from the Deleted Items folder.

FIGURE 22.3.

The Rules Wizard dialog box is used to control existing rules or to create new rules.

Rules can do quite a few things (as you will see shortly). For example, you could have Outlook play a special sound when a high priority message arrives. You can have Outlook forward mail from a particular person to someone else. Or, if you receive junk mail, you can instruct Outlook to automatically send future messages from that address directly to the trash.

In the following exercise, you'll get a first taste of applying rules. For additional information about rules, see the online help guide.

To Do: Setting Up the Rules Wizard

1. Outlook should already be open. Click the Inbox in the Outlook Bar.
2. Choose Tools, Rules Wizard. The Rules Wizard dialog box, as shown in Figure 22.3, is displayed. The first time you open this dialog box, it is empty (you haven't created any rules yet).
3. Click New to display the first step in the wizard, as shown in Figure 22.4.
4. Read each of the rule types in the upper panel. You will probably need to use the scroll arrows to be able to see all the rules.
5. Highlight Notify Me When Important Messages Arrive. Read the description in the lower panel.
6. Click Next. In the dialog box shown in Figure 22.5, you choose the condition or conditions under which you want the rule applied. Again, use the scroll arrows to view each of the conditions and its description. Make sure there are check marks in the first two options.

22

▼ **FIGURE 22.4.**

In the first step of the Rules Wizard, you choose the type of rule you want to create. The Rule Description panel shows what the rule will do when applied.

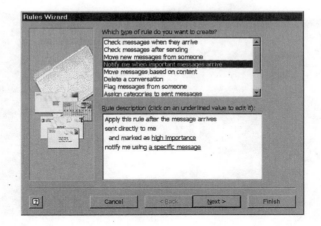

FIGURE 22.5.

This dialog box enables you to specify the conditions under which you want the rule applied.

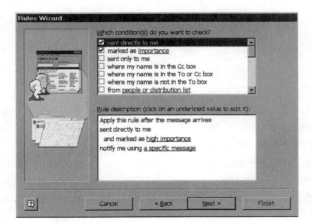

7. Click <u>N</u>ext. (Notice that each time you make a selection from the Rules Wizard, a sentence is added to the description of the rule.) The dialog box shown in Figure 22.6 is displayed. Here, you tell Outlook what to do with messages that fit the criteria specified in the previous dialog box. Leave the check mark in the first option.

8. Look in the lower panel. There are two underlined phrases, High Importance and A Specific Message. At first, underlined phrases are in blue. This means there is a value that must be completed before the wizard is finished. You can set each value as it appears, or wait until the wizard says you must complete all values. Click High Importance. The Importance dialog box, as shown in Figure 22.7, is displayed. High should already be selected. Click OK. Notice that the underlined phrase now appears in dark green (it may even look black).

▼

▼ **FIGURE 22.6.**

Here you tell Outlook what you want done with items meeting the specified criteria.

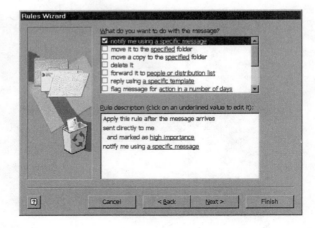

FIGURE 22.7.

A dialog box appears telling you to select the appropriate importance value.

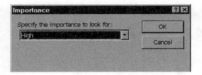

9. Click A Specific Message. The Notification dialog box is displayed, asking for the message you want displayed. Type A high importance message has just been delivered to your inbox. Click OK.

10. Click Next. The dialog box shown in Figure 22.8 asks you to place a check mark next to any exceptions. Use the scrollbar to view the exceptions. Don't place a check mark in any of the boxes because you don't want any exceptions to this rule.

FIGURE 22.8.

This dialog box enables you to specify exceptions to the rule you are creating.

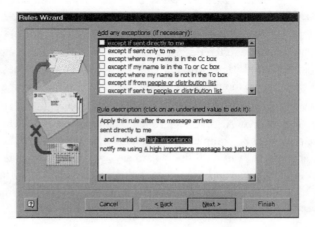

22

▼ 11. Click <u>N</u>ext. In the final dialog box, as shown in Figure 22.9, you have several options. You can name the rule, turn it on (which it is by default) or off, and have a final opportunity to change the values in the lower panel. In the Please Specify a <u>N</u>ame for This Rule text box, type `High Priority Message`.

FIGURE 22.9.

The last dialog box in the Rules Wizard enables you to name the rule and turn the rule on, and offers a final chance to edit any of the values in the lower panel.

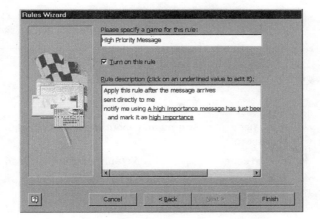

12. Click Finish to complete the wizard. The Rules Wizard dialog box now shows the rule you created (see Figure 22.10). You can copy it (if it is a complex rule to which you are going to make a few modifications), modify it, rename it, or delete it.

FIGURE 22.10.

Back at the beginning of the Rules Wizard, the dialog box shows the names of any rules you have created and a description of the selected rule.

▼

▼   13. If you have multiple rules, you can use this dialog box to change their position in
        the hierarchy, using the Move <u>U</u>p and Move Do<u>w</u>n buttons. The rule at the top is
        processed first, then the others are processed in order.

> Give careful consideration to the order in which the rules are placed,
> making sure that a later rule doesn't contradict an earlier one.

▲   14. Click OK to close the dialog box and turn on the rule.

> If you need more information about the Rules Wizard, point your
> browser to:
>
> www.microsoft.com/outlook/enhancements/rwfaq.asp
>
> This is a listing of Frequently Asked Questions (FAQs) about the Rules
> Wizard.

Miscellaneous New Features

There are many new features in Outlook 98 that we haven't had a chance to discuss.
Here is a brief overview of a few of those features so that you at least know they exist.
Use the online help manual to get more information, or visit:

www.microsoft.com/outlook

Encrypted Sealing and Electronic (Digital) Signatures

Using the Message Options box, you can add a password to a message, ensuring that
only the recipient can read the message. As with all things electronic, codes can be broken (some more easily than others). As a rule, don't put anything in an electronic communication that you don't want to see posted on the entire Internet at a later time.
Passwords keep honest people honest, rather like a lock on a diary.

For more information about setting a password or obtaining a digital signature (so the
receiver knows the mail is really from you), see the online help feature.

Signing Your Message Automatically

You can instruct Outlook to automatically add a signature line or lines to the bottom of
every message you send. This feature is called AutoSignature. Often, senders attach their

22

names, addresses, phone numbers, or witty sayings to their messages. I like Will Rogers's saying, "Half our life is spent trying to find something to do with the time we have rushed through life trying to save."

If you use a quote at the bottom of your email, make sure to change it on a regular basis. That keeps the readers alert to changes in your message. In fact, a new quote every day would be a good way of getting people to read your messages. Keep the signature to four lines or fewer. A 10-line signature under a two-line message is annoying.

To create an AutoSignature, create a new mail message, type the AutoSignature you want to use, format it, and then choose Tools, AutoSignature. You will see the AutoSignature dialog box shown in Figure 22.11. By default, Outlook leaves a blank line between the ending of your message and the beginning of your AutoSignature. Remove the check mark if you don't want the blank line.

FIGURE 22.11.

The AutoSignature dialog box is used to create an automatic signature line at the end of each message you create.

Junk Email

In the section "Setting the Rules" earlier this hour, you learned about the Rules Wizard. You can also use the wizard to eliminate junk email. From the Inbox folder, choose Tools, Rules Wizard. Click the New button. In the first dialog box, leave the rule at Check Messages When They Arrive. Click Next. Use the scroll arrow until you see the option to Suspected to Be Junk E-Mail or from Junk Senders. Click Next. At this point, you can delete it or move it to a special folder. Finish the wizard.

Outlook 98 has a built-in wizard to shortcut this particular feature. With Inbox open, click Organize and Junk E-Mail. It enables you to easily create custom actions for junk email. Click the Close button in the Organize box to close it.

If you are reading a message and realize that it is junk mail, choose Acti<u>o</u>ns, <u>J</u>unk E-mail, Add to <u>J</u>unk Senders List. From then on, messages from that source will automatically be deleted.

Virtual Cards and Calendars

vCard and vCalendar are developments of the Internet Mail Consortium (IMC). They are a standard that is used by Outlook 98 in conjunction with the Internet. More information on these are available from the IMC Internet site at:

www.imc.org

A vCard is similar to a business card. It contains the personal and corporate information of an individual. It can be sent to you as an attachment to email, or you can download it from the individual's Internet site. Outlook directly reads the information into your Contacts folder. No more having to enter information by hand (at least when you are contacting those who use vCards). In addition to standard information, vCards can also contain photographs, company logos, and audio clips.

The vCalendar enables users to schedule meetings and check one another calendars. The major difference between vCalendar and the Outlook calendar features is that vCalendar is platform independent. That is, it works as well on an Apple Macintosh as it does on a Windows-based system.

Change-Only Offline Address Book

Previously, when you downloaded the public address book from the server to your computer, the entire file was downloaded. In large companies, this could take a lot of time. Outlook 98 downloads only the changes to your computer, potentially saving time.

Network Deleted Item Recovery

You'll need to check with your system administrator for the details on this feature. Basically, if you keep messages in a public folder on the server, and you empty the Deleted Items folder, the system administrator can set up a folder that keeps deleted items. Even if you have the feature enabled, any items deleted from a folder on your hard drive are forever lost.

Voting

One of the enhanced Outlook 98 features is the capability to conduct polls and tally votes. Voting buttons are placed in the header of a message.

To Do: Setting Up a Voting Message

1. Click the Inbox folder in the Outlook Bar.

2. Click the New Message button on the Standard toolbar.

3. Click the Options button on the Standard toolbar. The Message Options dialog box is displayed, as shown in Figure 22.12.

FIGURE 22.12.

The Message Options dialog box enables you to set up voting for those who receive your email.

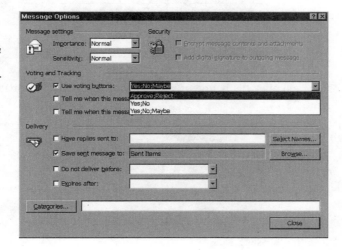

4. You can choose from one of three default button sets from the Use Voting Buttons drop-down list:

   Approve;Reject

   Yes;No

   Yes;No;Maybe

>
> You can create your own voting buttons. Type the choices in the Voting Buttons field, separating each by a semicolon. For example, you could type $10;$100;$500;One Year Salary.

5. Click Close to close the dialog box. When you return to the message, nothing is different. If your email is connected, send a copy of it to yourself. When the message is received and you are in the Inbox view, you will not see any buttons. To see the buttons and cast a vote, double-click the message to edit it. A sample message is shown in Figure 22.13.

▼ **FIGURE 22.13.**

This sample message displays the voting buttons.

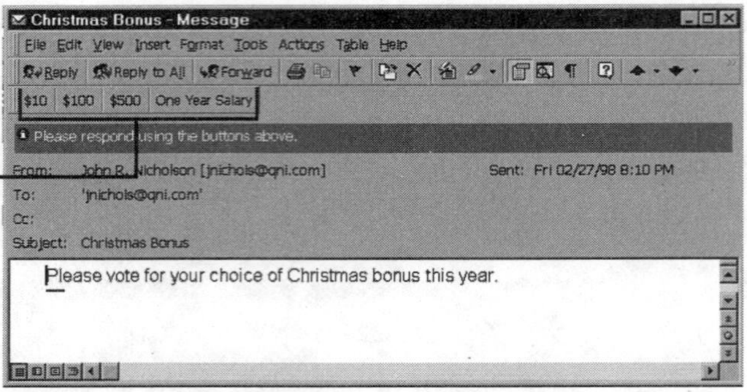

Voting buttons ——

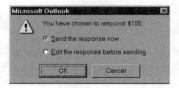

6. When you click the button of your choice, you see a confirmation, as shown in Figure 22.14.

FIGURE 22.14.

The verification box is displayed before sending your vote.

7. Close the message.

To view the vote responses, open the original message with the vote in it. It is usually located in the Sent Items folder. Click the Tracking tab. For additional information, see the View Vote Responses to a Message online help topic.

▲

Automatic Mapping of Contact Information

The last thing we'll look at is Outlook's new capability to build a map based on the contact's address. To use this feature, you must be connected to the Internet. When you are viewing a contact card that has an address, choose Actions, Display Map of Address. In Figure 22.15, I have typed in the address of the college where I work.

The map opens in your default browser. Even if you have Internet Explorer open and connected to the Internet, if Netscape Communicator is your default browser, the map is opened in Netscape.

FIGURE 22.15.

A map of the contact's address is displayed.

22

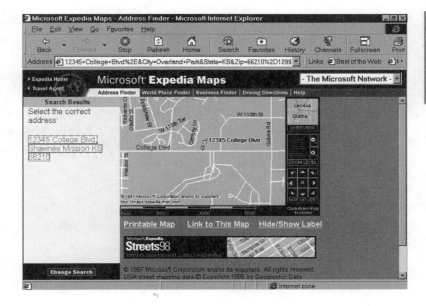

Summary

Although we covered a lot of new features in this hour, remember that they are only a fraction of what Outlook 98 is capable of doing. In Hour 23, "Adding Extras to Outlook 98," you'll see some of the capabilities of Outlook for which it was not originally designed. This is accomplished by using add-ons: extra programs developed either by Microsoft or third-party vendors.

Q&A

Q **The voting buttons allow only one button to be pushed. Does each button have to be exclusive, or can I configure it so the user can make more than one selection?**

A The user can make only one selection using the voting features of Outlook 98.

Q **If someone has already read a message I sent, is there any way of getting it back?**

A Unfortunately, the only way to get a message back after it's sent is to request the recipient send you a copy. When it is read, it's too late to take back what you said.

Q **When I set up several rules using the Rules Wizard, do they all have to stay active?**

A No. You can turn off a rule by opening the Rules Wizard and removing the check mark to the right of the rule. You don't have to have any rules turned on, or you can turn on several rules.

Q **You mentioned that if I emptied the Deleted Items folder contained on a network, I can recover the deleted items. Is that feature set automatically?**

A No. Your system administrator must set the options on the server.

PART VIII

Outlook Extras

Hour

Hour 23

Adding Extras to Outlook 98

At the time you purchase a car, you need to decide exactly which options you want. When you have taken possession of the vehicle, there are few options that you can add without considerable time and expense. Outlook 98, however, enables you to continue to add options as needed, increasing your productivity and better meeting your needs.

There are several types of add-ons. The most obvious ones are available from the Microsoft Web site. However, there are other ways of getting software to enhance Outlook. *Shareware* is software that you are allowed to try for a specific time period (generally 30 days) and then either submit a small payment for continued use or erase it from your computer.

There also some additions that are free. In this hour, we'll take a look at all three kinds of software, and review ensuring that you are updated whenever new add-ons are released.

Rather than having a lot of exercises in this hour, we'll spend most of the time on the Internet, pinpointing some sites that you may want to look at on your own.

After 22 hours of working with this book, I hesitate to remind you of this, but I will anyway: Because this is the Internet and it changes daily, the screens you see will probably be different than those shown in the figures. They are shown only to give you some idea of what was available for Outlook at the time of this writing. Checking things out for yourself will probably reveal a lot more goodies than are shown here. Good luck, and good hunting.

Microsoft Free Stuff

The first place to begin looking for extra Outlook software is on the Microsoft Web site at:

```
www.microsoft.com/office/outlook
```

The Outlook home page, shown in Figure 23.1, will probably look considerably different by the time you visit it. Regardless, it's a great place to begin looking at what's new for Outlook.

FIGURE 23.1.

The Outlook home page on Microsoft's Web site is a good place to begin looking for Outlook extras.

Clicking the Enhancements & Assistance option takes you to the site shown in Figure 23.2. From here, you can choose to look at the enhancements (also called add-ons), display the assistance page to get help using Outlook, or sign up for the automatic Outlook (and Office 97) updates.

FIGURE 23.2.

The Enhancements & Assistance page leads you further on your quest for Outlook excellence.

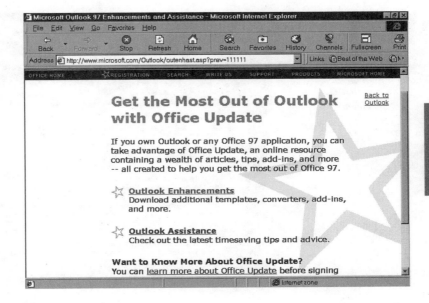

23

The first choice is a calendar template that enables you to import your month-by-month calendar directly into Microsoft Word. With Word's capability to create Web pages in a matter of minutes, you can easily place your Outlook calendar on the Internet for everyone to view, even if they don't have the Outlook program.

Next is a Help file that integrates into your current Outlook Help file. It gives you direct links to help topics, knowledge base articles concerning Outlook, and other Web sites that concentrate on Outlook.

There is an updated Rules Wizard for users of Outlook 97 to give it some of the functionality found in Outlook 98. Skipping to the bottom of the page, you'll find a link to Other Outlook Enhancements, which takes you to the page shown in Figure 23.3.

Notice that some items (marked with a star) are available only to registered owners of Office. So make sure that you register your program. Besides making you eligible for technical support on the Office products, you'll also receive regular updates concerning changes to Outlook. Figure 23.4 shows only a partial list of the enhancements available to registered users.

If you're getting tired of the available actors for the Outlook Office Assistant, download Rocky (see Figure 23.5), a well-trained dog to help you out that is sure to make you the envy of your colleagues. (Be careful, though. Rocky's sound and animation takes up over 2 MB of memory.)

FIGURE 23.3.

The Outlook Enhancements page describes current updates and offers links to other Outlook enhancements.

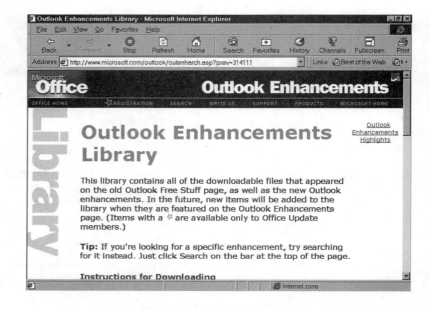

FIGURE 23.4.

A sample list of down-loads available to enhance Outlook.

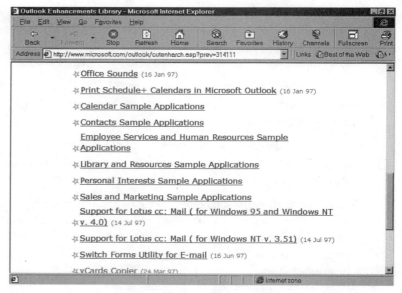

FIGURE 23.5.

You can download new actors for the Outlook Office Assistant from Microsoft's Web site.

Now you have an idea of some of the Outlook enhancements that are available free from the Microsoft site. In the next section, we'll examine some other programs that work with Outlook.

Sampling Third-Party Add-Ons

Many of the third-party software applications designed for Outlook 97 have been directly incorporated into Outlook 98, so there is no need to load them separately. In the following sections, we'll take a look at a few of the applications that can add functionality to Outlook. This is by no means an exhaustive list. For additional information, go to the Microsoft home page and search for *Outlook add-ons*. You'll be amazed at some of the enhancements that are available to you.

Not all of the following applications integrate with Outlook, but they all work in conjunction with Outlook data to offer you a more complete communications package.

Active Voice

www.activevoice.com

Active Voice is the maker of several communications software accessories. Using PhoneMax, you can manage telephone calls onscreen. View Mail enables you to manage voice and fax messages.

Algo Communications Corporation

www.algocommunications.com

Pop! increases the power and usefulness of Outlook by opening it to the record of the calling party before you answer your telephone. This is a macro, and can be downloaded from Algo's site.

Algo also produces NetPop! When a call is received, users can click a *pop* button to automatically launch the Outlook contact form that contains additional information about the caller. NetPop! requires the user to have caller ID (available from most local telephone companies).

Algo suggests several ways that NetPop! can be used. Sales representatives can automatically launch Outlook with the caller's personal information every time a call is received. Customer support organizations use NetPop! to automatically display customer history, product, or warranty information whenever calls are received from registered users. Attorneys can use NetPop! to automatically launch and display client information when calls are received from important clients.

Putting Scrambled Data Back in Order

www.dataviz.com

DataViz created several of the niftiest programs I saw while searching for Outlook enhancements. The first is called E-ttachment Opener. E-ttachment can solve many problems, including the following:

- You open the mail message, there is garbage text at the end of the message, and you don't receive the files.
- You are able to save the attached files, but Windows is unable to open them.
- You are actually able to retrieve the attachment, but when you double-click the file, Windows cannot open it.

DataViz also produces Desktop to Go (for Palm Pilot). If you use a Palm Pilot and different personal information managers in your company, take a look at this. It synchronizes Outlook 97, 98, & Schedule+ files.

This Web site carries multiple products that work in conjunction with Outlook. You should definitely take a close look at it if you receive files in multiple formats from other users.

Faxing Made Easy

www.symantec.com

If you have used Microsoft Fax, you realize what a limited program it really is. (What do you expect from a free program?) Outlook 98 comes with a starter edition for Symantec's WinFax (if you install in Internet-Only mode; Corporate mode still uses Microsoft Fax). The full version of the software, WinFax Pro, integrates directly with Outlook 98 to offer one of the easiest-to-use interfaces for sending faxes.

Getting Email with Your Pager

www.ikon.net

Ikon Office Solutions offers a program that integrates directly into Outlook: MobileCHOICE Messenger for Microsoft Outlook. It offers one-way and two-way wireless messaging, which enables you to forward important messages or send Outlook's reminders to your pager. MobileCHOICE Messengers offers four major features:

- Send email to any paging device
- Send Outlook reminders directly to your pager
- Forward important email to your paging device
- Add pager information directly to your Outlook Contacts

If you travel and use a pager, this is a program that you might want to check closely. The added features can be a tremendous advantage to today's "road warriors," particularly if you aren't working with a large support staff to forward information to you.

Listen to Email and Faxes

www.msw.com

If you travel a lot, but don't take your computer with you, you can purchase a program from Millennia Software that enables you to have your email and faxes read to you over a regular telephone line. EmailReader Plus enables you to dial your computer using a touch-tone telephone to browse and retrieve email and faxes, as well as record and send a reply to the sender. It can send a preprogrammed reply to acknowledge receipt of specific messages. You can even listen to Microsoft Word documents.

Viewing Attachments from Within Outlook

www.inso.com

QuickView Plus from Inso Corporation is a handy utility. You can find, access, view, and print virtually any document from within Outlook, even if you don't have the native application on your desktop. You can instantly access fully formatted views of all files and attachments.

Automated Invoicing

www.studio848.com

Bill Power from Studio 848, Inc., is an Outlook attachment for automatic billing based on Outlook entries. It creates invoices directly from Outlook entries. Billings can be based on hourly rates, fixed fees, costs, payments, accounts, and tax rates. A complete set of invoice formatting options is included. Invoices can be stored as files for record keeping. In December, 1997, ZDNet made Bill Power a four-star Editor's Pick! If you use Outlook and write invoices, you should definitely check this one out. You can even download a free 30-day trial from Studio 848's Web site.

Final Words on Outlook Add-Ons

There are too many extras to cover each individually. The examples I have offered looked interesting to me given tasks that I routinely perform. I mentioned about 10 percent of the programs listed on the Microsoft site. At the time of this writing, the enhancements were listed at:

www.microsoft.com/Outlook/documents/thirdparty-addons.htm

Many of the third-party add-ons listed on the Microsoft site are no longer required, having been built into Outlook 98. Before buying an add-on, make sure that the features have not already been incorporated into your version of Outlook.

All the programs mentioned in this hour are copyrighted and trademarked by their respective developers. For additional copyright and trademark information on individual products, visit the listed Internet site.

Outlook Enhancements Provided with the Program

When you first install Outlook 98, it doesn't automatically install all available components. (Why waste the hard drive space and memory?) Outlook can automatically check for installed components, and update your version so that it fits your needs. The update is done from the Control Panel and through the Internet. In the following exercise, you'll get an opportunity to see which components are currently installed and which are available to you.

To Do: Checking for Outlook Optional Programs

1. Close any open programs, including Outlook.

2. Choose Start, Settings, Control Panel. Double-click the Add/Remove Programs icon. The Add/Remove Programs Properties dialog box is displayed (see Figure 23.6). The Install/Uninstall tab should be selected.

Make sure that you have an active Internet connection before continuing this procedure.

3. Scroll down and click Microsoft Outlook 98. Click Add/Remove. The Outlook 98 Active Setup dialog box (the first step of the Maintenance Wizard) is displayed, as shown in Figure 23.7.

4. Click Add New Components. Internet Explorer is automatically opened and connected to the Internet upgrade site.

▼

▼ **Figure 23.6.**

*The Install/ Uninstall
tab of the Add/Remove
Programs Properties
dialog box is used to
begin the Outlook
update procedure.*

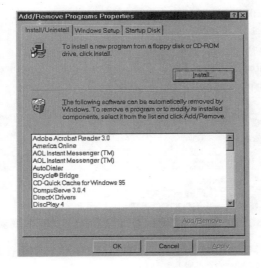

Figure 23.7.

*The first step of the
Maintenance Wizard
enables you to add new
components.*

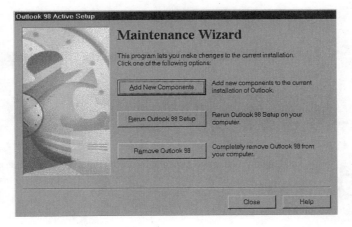

If Internet Explorer isn't your default browser, it may appear to open for a
second and then disappear. You may need to move or minimize any open
windows to see the message about making Internet Explorer your default
browser. Click <u>N</u>o to continue.

5. The Outlook 98 Component Install screen is displayed. Notice the right-pointing
   arrows to the right of each option. Click one to see the instructions for that particular item. Click it again to hide the instruction.

▼ 6. Outlook will take a few minutes to initialize. When the initialization is completed, you see the Active Setup dialog box, asking permission to examine your system for installed Outlook Components. Click Yes to continue.

7. After a few more minutes, Outlook shows you a list of items that are installed, not installed, or require upgrading, as shown in Figure 23.8.

FIGURE 23.8.

The Outlook 98 Component Install site evaluates the components already installed in your system.

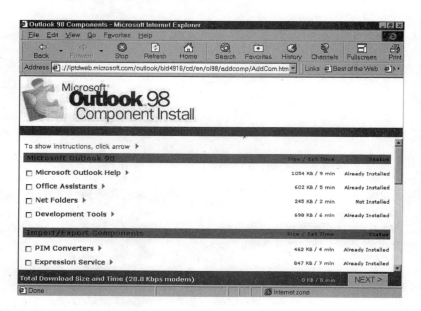

 These screens and procedures can (and will) change. What you see and do may be different from the instructions in this exercise. But remember: Being flexible is what technology is all about.

8. Scroll through the list to see the different options. Table 23.1 shows each of the groupings and the items contained within each one. Place a check mark in each item you want to download or upgrade. When all items have been selected, the total download time is displayed at the bottom of the list. Click Next to continue.

TABLE 23.1. OUTLOOK 98 COMPONENTS AVAILABLE FOR INSTALLATION.

Grouping	Component
Microsoft Outlook 98	Microsoft Outlook Help, Office Assistants, Net Folders, Development Tools
Import/Export Components	PIM Converters, Expression Service, Lotus Organizer Converters, Export Wizard for Timex DataLink Watch

▼

Grouping	Component
System Tools	MS Info, Integrated File Management
Extra Components	Office Sounds and Animated Cursors, Microsoft Outlook Newsreader
Mail Components	Schedule+ Support, Internet Only E-mail Service, Corporate or Workgroup E-mail Service, Microsoft Mail 3.X Support, Fax Update for Corporate or Workgroup E-mail Service
Proofing Tools	Microsoft Shared Proofing Tools—English: US, Microsoft Shared Proofing Tools—English: Australian, Microsoft Shared Proofing Tools—English: Great Britain

23

9. The Component Confirmation and Installation screen is displayed for you to check the selected options. If they are okay, click Install Now, as shown in Figure 23.9.

FIGURE 23.9.

The Component Installation and Confirmation screen is used to select the site from which the upgrade is to be downloaded.

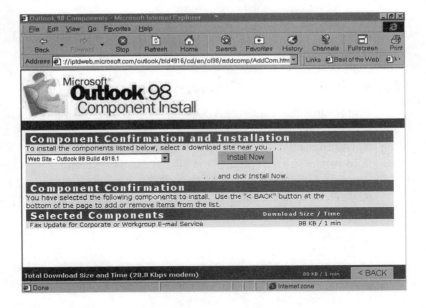

 Generally, the fastest download time is from the Web site geographically nearest to you. However, if you try to download at a busy time, you may get a faster download from across the world where the server has fewer users at that time.

▼ 10. As the download progresses, you will see the Outlook 98 Active Setup dialog box displaying the amount of the download that is completed, as shown in Figure 23.10, and the approximate time left to complete the download.

FIGURE 23.10.

The information box displays the amount downloaded and the approximate time left to finish the download.

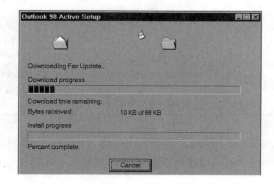

▲ 11. When you get a confirmation message saying that everything has been installed correctly, close all the open windows.

The Future of Enhancements

Rest assured that Outlook 98 does not yet live up to its full potential (and who among us does?). There will continue to be free Outlook enhancements from Microsoft (for registered users). Given the number of entrepreneurs in the world, we'll continue to see third-party software designed to make us more productive using Outlook. Designers are amazing: Every time you think they can't add anything else worthwhile to a software package, an announcement is made that proves you wrong.

Summary

There are many enhancements to improve the functionality of Outlook 98. Many of the add-ons that were required for Outlook 97 are built into Outlook 98, so they are no longer required as add-ons. Microsoft's automatic upgrade Web site ensures that your copy of Outlook 98 can always be up-to-date.

Hang in there: You're almost finished. In Hour 24, "Taking the Outlook Express," you learn about Outlook Express, a Windows 95 utility that functions as a mail reader and discussion group tool. You need to understand the differences between the Outlook and Outlook Express.

Q&A

Q If I bought Outlook 98, why do I have to keep upgrading it?

A Actually, you don't *have* to upgrade, but small fixes to problems discovered after the software was released can save you a lot of troubleshooting time if you do run into a problem.

Q Are there other enhancements to Outlook 98 that you haven't covered?

A Use the search engines to find Outlook 98 enhancements. In many cases, you will be able to try them free for 30 days before purchasing them. That way, if you really don't use the features, you don't have to pay for them. In many cases, they are even available at no charge!

Q What if Office 97 was already installed on my computer when I purchased it, but I didn't get any disks for it?

A In reality, this probably means you have a pirated copy of Office 97. Some unscrupulous individuals who sell computers install Windows and Office on the computer, but don't give you the disks. The first time you try to make a change to Office or Windows, you are asked to put the disk in the CD-ROM drive. You are probably not a registered owner of either Windows or Office 97 if you don't have the original disks, and will be unable to get support or upgrades for your product.

Another possibility is that it was installed from a network directory. If that's the case, you'll need to contact the network administrator to get things upgraded or installed.

23

HOUR 24

Taking the Outlook Express

At some point in the future—if it hasn't happened already—a shortcut to Outlook Express will pop up (probably unbidden) on your desktop. As I did, you may wonder how it got there and just what it is. Because it's called Outlook Express, it seems to be connected to Outlook in some way. When you open it, though, you can see that it appears to be an email program and newsreader (even though it has a few extras).

It seems that Microsoft has given you another gift. Is it worth the space it takes up on your hard drive? Do you need it if you already have a program, such as Outlook 98, to read your mail and news? These and other questions are answered during this hour, so read on to become an expert on Outlook Express. Then, when your colleagues ask you just what that new icon is on their desktops, you can jump right in and explain it, impressing them with the depth of your knowledge.

What Is Outlook Express?

When you first open Outlook Express, you see a screen similar to the one shown in Figure 24.1. It looks pretty simple. In fact, that is the purpose of Outlook Express. It is capable of acting as your primary email service and newsreader.

FIGURE 24.1.

The opening screen in Outlook Express indicates that it is basically an email program and newsreader.

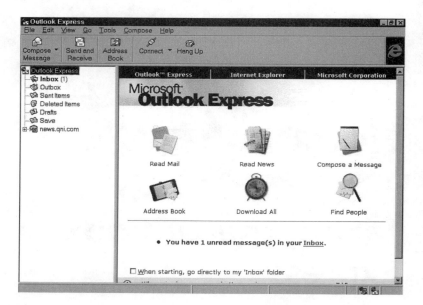

If you have Netscape Communicator, Outlook 98, Microsoft Internet Explorer, Eudora Pro, Microsoft Exchange, or other program designated as your email service, you can easily make the transition to Outlook Express. Running the Configuration Wizard is all it takes.

When the Outlook Express icon appeared on my desktop, my first question was, "Where did that come from?" My next was, "How is Outlook Express different from Outlook 98?" In the next few minutes, you'll know the answer to both of these questions.

Outlook Express is automatically installed when you install version 4 or later of Internet Explorer. It is actually the mail and newsreader portion of Internet Explorer. If you are familiar with Netscape Communicator, with which you can access email and newsgroups from within the program, it may seem that separating the Internet browser features from the email and news features is a little strange.

Microsoft's purpose in separating the programs is to make each one easier to use. Outlook Express has an extremely simple user interface. It's easy to use and understand.

That's what Microsoft was aiming for, and that's what it achieved. In comparison tests by leading computer magazines, Outlook Express often excels in the email category, beating even such powerful programs as Eudora. The reviews are consistently positive: Outlook Express is indeed simple to use and easy to learn.

How Is Outlook Express Different from Outlook 98?

Outlook Express is a slimmed-down version of Outlook 98. You don't need to worry about all the features in Outlook 98 just to access email and read newsgroups. Do you need both? Maybe. Do you want both? For me, the answer is yes. I love the simple interface of Outlook Express. It makes my life simpler, and that's what I want from my computer and software.

Although Outlook Express provides two of the functions available in Outlook 98, I think you'll want to have both programs, as you'll see when you've finished this hour. Outlook Express is a simple, addictive program, well worth its price (free).

24

Configuring Outlook Express for Email

Configuring Outlook Express couldn't be easier. Before beginning, you need to know how to access your mail and news from the server. You need this information before proceeding with the next exercise.

> Before beginning the next exercise, skim through it to make certain you have all the information you need to complete it.

To Do: Configuring Outlook Express to Handle Email

1. Open Outlook Express.
2. To run the Internet Setup Wizard, choose <u>T</u>ools, <u>A</u>ccounts. The Internet Accounts dialog box is displayed, as shown in Figure 24.2. (Your accounts will be different from those shown in the figure.)
3. Click the Mail tab. If you already have a default account established, you can skip the rest of this exercise. If you don't have an account or want to add another account, click <u>A</u>dd, <u>M</u>ail. The first step of the Internet Connection Wizard is displayed (see Figure 24.3).

▼ **FIGURE 24.2.**

Setting up an email or newsgroup account begins in the Internet Accounts dialog box.

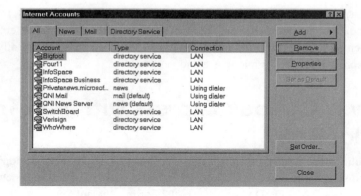

FIGURE 24.3.

The first step of the Internet Connection Wizard begins the actual identification of an existing mail account.

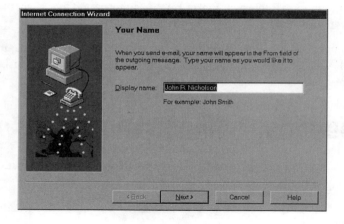

4. Fill in your name as you want it displayed on the email messages you write. This can be your real name or a nickname. Click Next to advance to the next step of the wizard.

5. In the second step of the Internet Connection Wizard, as shown in Figure 24.4, enter your email address. After entering your address, click Next.

6. In the third step (see Figure 24.5), you need to know the type of account you want to set up (usually POP3). You can get this information from your email provider (assuming you have one), using either email or the telephone.

7. After entering the information, click Next. The next step is used to enter your account name and password, as shown in Figure 24.6. Your password will appear

▼ as asterisks onscreen so that anyone watching won't be able to see it.

FIGURE 24.4.

The second step of the Internet Connection Wizard is used to input your email address.

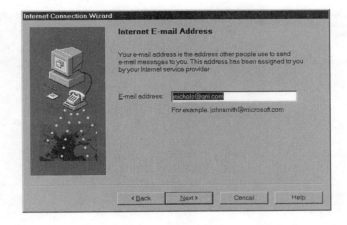

FIGURE 24.5.

The third step is used to establish the type of mail account you are setting up, and the incoming and outgoing mail addresses.

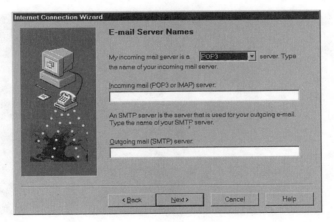

As with all passwords, you need to choose one that you are unlikely to forget.

8. Click <u>N</u>ext. In the Friendly Name screen, type in a name to identify the account, as shown in Figure 24.7.

9. Click <u>N</u>ext to move to the Connection Type screen, as shown in Figure 24.8. Here, you establish the means by which you will begin Internet access.

10. If you choose Connect Using My <u>P</u>hone Line, the screen shown in Figure 24.9 is displayed. Here, you can choose an existing dial-up account or create a new one. Choose the option you want and then click <u>N</u>ext to continue.

▼ **FIGURE 24.6.**

The fourth step is to identify your account name and password.

▼ **FIGURE 24.7.**

The next step is to assign the account a name that is easy to remember.

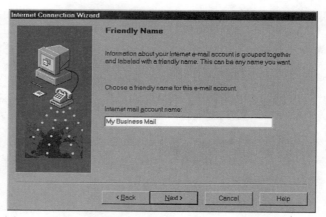

FIGURE 24.8.

This step enables you to specify how you connect to the Internet.

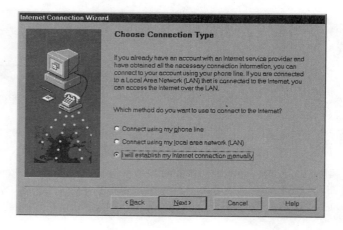

▼

▼ **FIGURE 24.9.**

The Dial-Up Connection screen enables you to choose from an existing dial-up connection or create a new one.

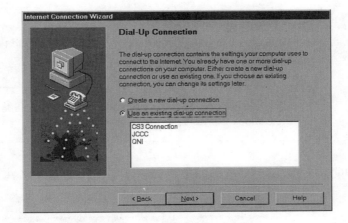

11. At the Congratulations screen shown in Figure 24.10, click Finish to complete the wizard. You will see the account name in the Internet Connection Wizard dialog box. If this is your only mail account, it is marked as the default. If you have more than one account, select the one to be used as the default account, and click Set as Default. You are not asked for confirmation. You can change the default account at any time by choosing Tools, Account and clicking the Mail tab to return you to this dialog box.

FIGURE 24.10.

The Congratulations screen is the final step of the Internet Connection Wizard.

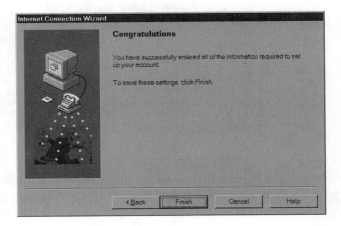

▲ 12. Click Close to close the dialog box and finish the process.

24

Using the Mail Features

From the Outlook Express opening screen, click Read Mail to read the mail in your Inbox.

 Instead of clicking the Read Mail button, you can click the Inbox folder on the Outlook Express Bar.

The Inbox shown in Figure 24.11 is displayed. If the toolbar isn't visible, choose View, Toolbar.

FIGURE 24.11.

The Inbox is similar to the one you used for sending mail in Outlook 98.

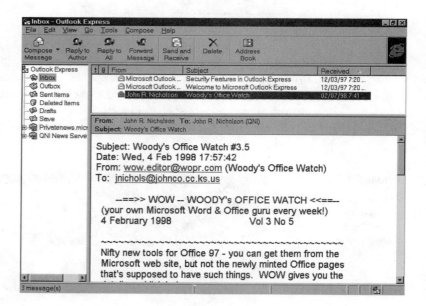

When you create a new mail account, you will find two messages in it: the first welcoming you to Outlook Express and the second discussing the security measures. After you read these, you can delete them, if desired, by selecting each one and clicking the Delete button on the toolbar.

Filing Messages

You can easily organize your messages using Outlook Express. For example, if you want to add a folder for memos, select the folder where you want to create the new folder (for example, either the main Outlook Express folder or the Inbox folder). Choose File,

Folder, New Folder. In the Create Folder dialog box shown in Figure 24.12, make sure the correct folder is selected, type the name for the new folder, and click OK.

FIGURE 24.12.

The Create Folder dialog box is used to create a new folder used for organizing your messages.

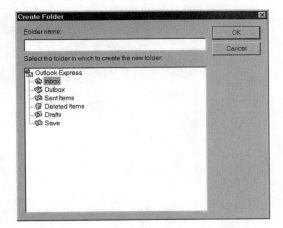

When you have created the necessary folder or folders, you can drag the message from the upper-right pane into the folder in the Outlook Express Bar.

You aren't *required* to create additional folders. However, sorting your email into subject-specific folders enables you to easily find it later.

Using Special-Occasion Stationery

One of the clever Outlook Express features is the stationery feature. It enables you to add a background image, insert a picture, add a signature, or attach your business card (in vCard format, taken from your address book) to your email. In the next exercise, you'll create a new message and send it to me.

To Do: Creating Specialized Messages

1. If the Inbox folder isn't selected, click it now. (You don't have to start from the Inbox, but this way we're "on the same page.")

2. Choose Compose, New Message Using. A fly-out menu (one that appears when you select a menu option) is displayed (see Figure 24.13).

3. Explore several of the options. After you have seen them, close the message without saving it, and compose another message using different stationery.

▼ **FIGURE 24.13.**

The New Message Using command on the Compose menu displays several options.

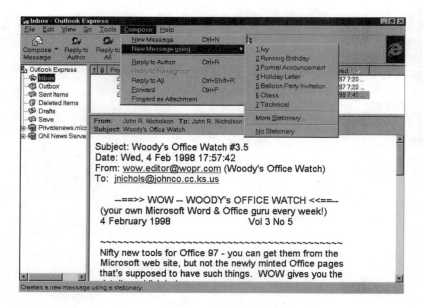

4. If you don't like the available options, choose Compose, New Message Using, More Stationery. Outlook Express comes with two dozen stationery backgrounds, as shown in Figure 24.14.

FIGURE 24.14.

The Open dialog box displays available stationery.

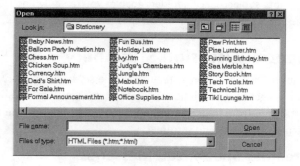

5. Choose a background that you like. Click Open. For Figure 24.15, I chose the Paw Print.htm stationery as the background.

6. The insertion point should already be in the To box. Type jnichols@johnco.cc.ks.us (do not put a period at the end of the address). Click the Subject line. Type TYOL98 Comments. Click in the message area and write me a note. Comments on the book are welcome. Format it as you please.

▼

FIGURE 24.15.

*Composing a message
using Paw Print.htm as
the background.*

24

A winner will be drawn from a list of all submissions. That person will win a
one week, *no expenses paid*, vacation in Kansas. Losers will receive two
weeks of the same. (OK, so it's an old joke. Those of us who live in Kansas
still think it's funny!)

7. To send the message, click the Send button in the upper-left corner of the toolbar.

You can use any HTML page as the background for your messages.

Replying Smartly

By default, Outlook Express sends messages in HTML format. However, if you are
replying to a message, Outlook Express returns the reply in the same format as it was
originally sent. This ensures that any replies you make will be readable by the recipient.

Using Rules to Protect Against Spam

Outlook Express has built-in rules for email, just like Outlook 98. However, they aren't
nearly as powerful as Outlook's. If used correctly, though, they can eliminate most junk
mail. When you get a piece of junk mail, open it and highlight the sender's name. Press
Ctrl+C to copy the name. Choose Tools, Inbox Assistant to display the Inbox Assistant
dialog box. Click the Add button to display the Properties dialog box, as shown in
Figure 24.16.

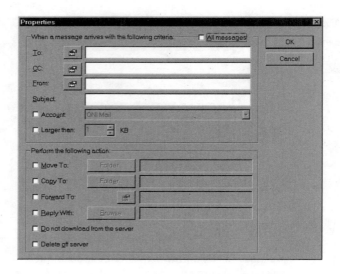

Place the insertion point in the From box and press Ctrl+V to paste the name into the text box. At the bottom of the dialog box, select the Delete Off Server option. Click OK to return to the Office Assistant, and click OK again to close the dialog box. From now on, any time mail arrives from that address, it is automatically deleted without your having to bother with it.

Discussing Newsgroups

Newsgroups (also called *discussion groups*) are similar to a community bulletin board. You can use Outlook Express as a newsreader: You can read postings either while you are online, or you can download messages and then read them offline. This is particularly helpful if you subscribe to newsgroups generating a lot of discussion, and your Internet service provider charges by the hour.

Adding a Newsgroup Server

To read newsgroups, you must have a server that provides access to the newsgroups. Different servers carry various newsgroups. Normally, though, you use your Internet service provider (ISP) to subscribe to newsgroups. Check with your ISP to find the correct name of the news server.

To specify a news server, follow the instructions given in the first exercise. Instead of adding a mail account, add a news account. After you have successfully added a news server, it appears in the Outlook Express Bar.

Reviewing Available Newsgroups

When you have specified the news server, then it's time to see what newsgroups are available to you. Click the news server entry in the Outlook Express Bar. If you get a message telling you that Outlook Express is not your default newsgroup reader, change it to the default by clicking Yes, or click No to continue.

At first, there won't be any newsgroups available for you to view. Because you are not subscribed to any newsgroups yet, you are prompted to see a list of the newsgroups when you click it. A sample listing is shown in Figure 24.17.

FIGURE 24.17.

The Newsgroups dialog box is used to subscribe to various newsgroups.

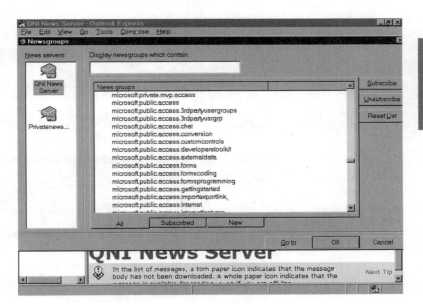

24

Filtering Newsgroups

Choosing from thousands of newsgroups can be a time-consuming process. Normally, you want to choose specific newsgroups based on their topics. For example, if you are interested in scuba diving, type scuba in the Display Newsgroups Which Contain text box. The result (at least on my server) is shown in Figure 24.18.

To subscribe to a group, double-click it, or select it and click the Subscribe button on the right side of the dialog box. You can also view a group without subscribing to it by selecting it and clicking Go To at the bottom of the page. In the Outlook Express Bar, it will look like you're subscribed until you quit the newsreader. When you reopen the newsreader, you will not be subscribed to the groups you only viewed. In Figure 24.19, you can see a sample message from the rec.scuba forum.

FIGURE 24.18.

The newsgroups have been narrowed to only those containing the word scuba.

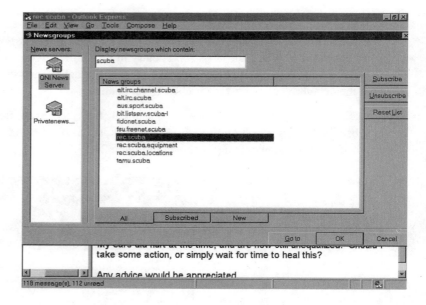

FIGURE 24.19.

A subscriber to the rec.scuba newsgroup is asking for advice. Other subscribers can respond with suggestions.

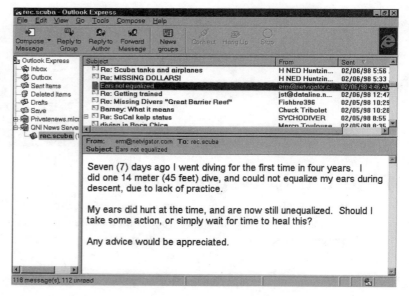

There is something on the Internet (and particularly in the newsgroups) to offend everyone. If you don't like what you see, move on to the next item. Don't bother to lecture those with beliefs different from yours. If you do, you will be bombarded with hate mail. Keep your comments constructive.

Answering a Newsgroup Message

So far, you've only learned to read newsgroup mail. Now it's time to jump into the action. In Figure 24.19, you can see the control buttons. If you want to begin your own topic, click Compose Message. The New Message window, as shown in Figure 24.20, is similar to an email message window. The Newsgroup name is already inserted. (By the way, this is the same as if you click the Reply to Group button.) Type your message and click the Post button.

FIGURE 24.20.

The New Message dialog box is used to post a message to a newsgroup.

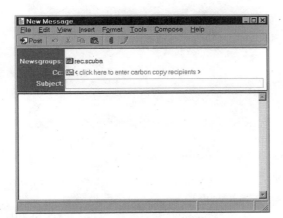

Clicking Reply to Author, instead of Compose Message or Reply to Group, sends an email message only to the author of the message, and does not post it so others can see. It is a private message, completely independent of the newsgroup.

Reading Discussions Offline

If you are charged by the hour for Internet access, you may want to download messages and then view them when you are not connected to the Internet. To read a newsgroup offline, you must first subscribe to it. The following exercise shows you how to read newsgroups offline.

To Do: Reading Newsgroups Offline

1. In the Outlook Express Bar, click the newsgroup you want to read offline.

2. Choose File, Properties. Click the Download tab. On the Download tab, select the When Downloading This Newsgroup, Retrieve check box (see Figure 24.21). Selecting that option makes the other options available.

FIGURE 24.21.

Select the downloading options for offline newsgroup reading.

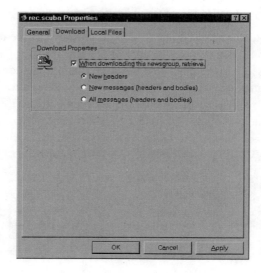

3. Choose one of the following options:

    - *New Headers*. Downloads only the headers (just the titles, not the messages or any attachments).

    - *New Messages*. Downloads only new messages (the headers plus the messages and attachments).

    - *All Messages*. Downloads all messages.

    The second choice is the one most often used. (Downloading only the headers isn't useful for offline reading.)

 4. Click OK.

Summary

This hour focuses on Outlook Express, a mail and newsgroup reader provided free by Microsoft. It is a simple program to use, and that is its strength.

During the last 24 hours, you have gotten a good, general overview of Outlook 98. You learned to use it to send email, to keep track of appointments, and to track information about people you deal with on a regular or occasional basis. You learned about using Outlook 98 to track the things you need to do, to track contacts and the use of multiple Office 97 programs, and even to create "sticky notes" so you don't forget ideas that occur to you as you are working.

Remember: This book has only touched on the many features of Outlook, almost like flying over the Grand Canyon. You get a good overview of the area, but you can't tell much about the details.

The rest of this book contains three appendixes that you might find useful. Appendix A, "Getting, Installing, and Upgrading Outlook 98," concerns acquiring and installing Outlook 98 (although by the time you reach the end of this hour, you have already performed these tasks). You can see a partial listing of the new features of Outlook 98 in Appendix B, "What's New in Outlook 98." Appendix C, "Using the Microsoft IntelliPoint Products," covers the use of the Microsoft IntelliPoint devices, including the mouse and trackball.

Continuing your studies by consulting more advanced books as well as the online help system can assist you in using Outlook 98 and Outlook Express and broaden you skills. Use it regularly, and you will find it an important part of your life.

Q&A

Q Do I need to close Outlook 98 to open Outlook Express?

A You don't need to close Outlook to use Outlook Express. If you only want to read newsgroups, you can choose G̲o, New̲s. If you open Outlook Express in this mode, mail services aren't available. To get the mail services, you must open Outlook Express separately from Outlook 98.

Q How can I find more about available newsgroups?

A The best place is to buy Internet magazines. For beginners, *Yahoo! Internet Life* is an excellent choice. It covers hundreds of new Web sites and newsgroups each month. You're sure to find something that you like. Generally, books are not a good source of new newsgroups; in fact, by the time a book is published, it may be out of date.

Q I read a posting on a newsgroup, and the information given was absolutely wrong. What should I do?

A There are several answers, depending on your level of knowledge, your degree of tact, and the thickness of your skin. One approach is to just ignore it. The first thing you will notice about newsgroups is that ignorance is rampant. Everyone has an opinion about something. Lecturing the author of the message is not a good idea. It is better to write a light note, and try not to call the author's intelligence and intentions into question.

Whenever possible, use emoticons to add a flavor of non-verbal communication. A :-) is a smiley face turned on its side. <G> means grin, which makes it seem like you're making a joke. There are dozens of other emoticons. Go to Yahoo! and search for *emoticons* for additional information.

Q I have America Online. Can I use Outlook Express with it?

A As of this writing, the answer is no. If you use the Windows 95 version of the AOL software, you can use Internet Explorer or Netscape Navigator to surf the Web, but not to check your mail or subscribe to newsgroups.

Q Many of the newsgroup names I see begin with *alt*. What does this mean?

A When newsgroups first began, they needed to be approved by an agency who assigned specific group names. Newsgroups that begin with *alt* are not sanctioned by the agency. It just means that an individual wanted to begin a discussion on a topic not currently addressed.

Q Is there someplace I can look to see a list of newsgroup names and a summary of what each is about?

A The closest resource you'll find is at

```
http://www.liszt.com/news/
```

PART IX
Appendixes

APPENDIX A

Getting, Installing, and Upgrading Outlook 98

There are two ways to get the Outlook 98 upgrade. First, the easiest and least expensive way is to download the upgrade from the Internet. However, because the downloading probably will take more than 45 minutes, users of America Online should avoid this method, unless they are willing to monitor the download, pressing Enter when prompted. Otherwise, AOL will probably terminate the connection.

Another way is to order the upgrade on CD-ROM directly from Microsoft. This method has two distinct disadvantages: It takes time to receive the update, and Microsoft probably will charge you a small fee for mailing the disk. Check the Microsoft Office home page for additional upgrade information:

www.microsoft.com/Office

Installing Outlook 98 from the CD-ROM

Installation of the Outlook 98 CD-ROM is simple, but you may have outdated files even if you just received the CD-ROM. No problem: You'll learn how to check your version shortly. In the following exercise, you learn to install Outlook 98 from the CD-ROM.

To Do: Installing Outlook 98 from the CD-ROM

1. Place the CD-ROM in the computer's CD-ROM drive. The installation screen, as shown in Figure A.1, is automatically displayed.

FIGURE A.1.

The beginning installation screen is displayed when you insert the Outlook 98 CD-ROM into the drive.

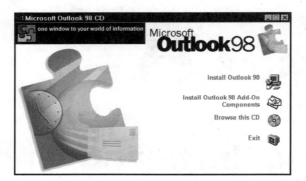

If for some reason you don't see the screen automatically displayed, click Start, Run. In the Open text box, type D:\SETUP.EXE (assuming that your CD-ROM is the D drive).

2. Click Install Outlook 98. The Outlook 98 Active Setup dialog box is displayed. You are warned that continuing replaces all previous versions of Outlook.

If you have already installed Outlook 98 (from a Beta version) and are doing an upgrade, you see the first step of the Maintenance Wizard, as shown in Figure A.2. Skip ahead to the "Upgrading Outlook 98" section of this appendix.

▼

▼ FIGURE A.2.

If you see the first step of the Maintenance Wizard, skip ahead to the "Upgrading Outlook 98" section of this appendix.

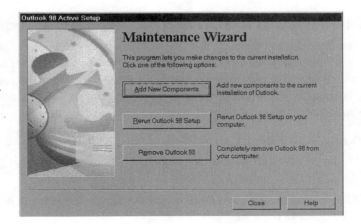

3. Click Next. The Registration screen is displayed. Enter your name and company if they aren't already listed.

4. Click Next. You can choose from four installation types: Minimal, Standard, Enhanced, and Full. Choose each of the four types from the drop-down list. A description of each installation is shown. Select the one that best suits your needs.

5. Click Next. Outlook 98 analyzes your present email capabilities and offers you the option of importing the messages into Outlook. This has no effect on existing email programs. (In other words, it doesn't delete the mail.)

6. Click Next. The E-mail Services Option screen offers three choices: Internet Only, Corporate or Workgroup, and No E-mail. Unless you have a compelling reason, choose the Corporate or Workgroup option. This makes sure that all the files you need will be installed.

7. Click Next. On the Schedule+ Support screen, choose to continue using Schedule+ as your group scheduling program, or choose Outlook. Unless you are on a network using Schedule+ for group scheduling, choose the Outlook option.

8. Click Next. Choose the default installation location, unless you have an overwhelming reason for changing it.

9. Click Next. At this point, you may have to wait for a few minutes. Outlook is preparing to install Outlook 98 and Microsoft Internet Explorer 4 on your hard drive. If any programs are open (including the Office shortcut bar), you are prompted to close them. Otherwise, installation will continue.

10. When the installation is complete, you will need to reboot your computer for the changes to take effect.

▲

Installing Outlook 98 from the Internet

Installing from an Internet connection is a slower way of upgrading than using the CD-ROM, even if you have a fast connection. Unless you have a T1 or faster Internet connection, it will take over an hour to download the appropriate components for the installation. If you decide to install from the Internet, follow the instructions in the next exercise.

To Do: Installing Outlook 98 from the Internet

1. Open your Internet browser, and go to

   www.microsoft.com/outlook

2. This installation takes place in two distinct steps. First, you download the Setup.exe file from the Web site.

3. After Setup is downloaded, you can run it, as in the previous example. Make the appropriate choices, and take a long lunch break when the installation begins.

4. When the installation is completed, restart your computer.

Upgrading Outlook 98

If you are upgrading from a previous version of Outlook 98 (*not* Outlook 97)—either from a disk or from the Internet—the Maintenance Wizard is displayed when you run Setup (refer to Figure A.2). On this screen, you can choose to perform one of the following procedures:

- Add new components (ones that were not previously installed)
- Run the Outlook Setup again
- Remove Outlook 98 from your computer

Using the last two options is self explanatory. In the next exercise, you learn to add Outlook 98 components to an existing installation.

To Do: Adding Outlook 98 Components

1. Close all programs, including the Office shortcut bar.

2. Place the CD-ROM in the computer's CD-ROM drive. The installation screen is automatically displayed (refer to Figure A.1).

3. Because Installing New Components requires the use of Internet Explorer, you need to have an active Internet connection already established.

▼ 4. Click Install Outlook 98. The Maintenance Wizard is displayed. Click A̲dd New
   Components. Internet Explorer starts, and you are taken to the Outlook upgrade
   page.

5. At this point, you might be asked for a registration code. If so, enter it.

6. After the program is initialized, you are asked for permission to check your hard
   drive to determine which versions of the components are currently installed, as
   shown in Figure A.3. You must click Y̲es to upgrade Outlook 98.

FIGURE A.3.

*The Upgrade Wizard
politely asks to check
your hard drive.*

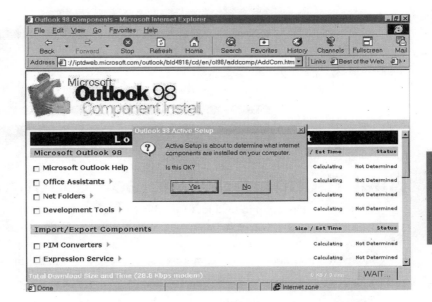

7. After a few seconds (or minutes) of checking, you see a screen similar to the one
   shown in Figure A.4. You can scroll through it to see the components that are
   already installed, not yet installed, and need to be upgraded.

8. Click the check box to the left of each option that you want installed or upgraded.
   Click Next to continue.

▼ 9. When the update is complete, shut down the programs and reboot your computer.

▼ FIGURE A.4.

Outlook Setup has determined which components are already installed and which need to be upgraded.

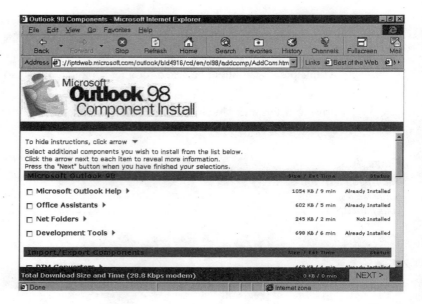

▲

Final Thoughts on Upgrading Outlook 98

Although it may seem to be a lot of trouble to upgrade Outlook 98, there are some distinct advantages. Because the upgrade program checks your versions of Outlook components, for example, you can always be sure of having the latest versions. You can get them over the Internet to avoid waiting for a disk to arrive in the mail.

Microsoft Office 97 has recently implemented upgrade services of a similar nature. Can Windows and other Microsoft programs be far behind? Although you may have misgivings about giving Microsoft access to your hard drive, your only choice is to do so, or wait for a mail upgrade (and possibly be charged for it). Although this may not be the best solution, it is the best available for the time being. Maybe in the future, Microsoft will figure out some way of "beaming" upgrades directly to us. Only time (and Microsoft) will tell.

APPENDIX B

What's New in Outlook 98

Nearly every area of Outlook has been improved. This appendix is a summary of some of the more important features that can increase your efficiency as you work with Outlook 98.

Managing and Prioritizing Information

The Outlook Today screen is an addition to the major views available to you. This screen displays appointments for the next three days, tells you how many new mail messages are in your Inbox, and lists the tasks you need to complete. You can also search for a contact by entering a name in the Find a Contact text box.

The Find dialog box, accessed by clicking the Find button on the toolbar, enables you to search for information in a variety of ways. It acts as a search engine for all the items in the various Outlook folders. The Find dialog box is not available from the Outlook Today screen.

In the original version of Outlook, you were able to flag messages for follow-up. You can now also flag contacts for follow-up. If you need to phone a contact with more information, for example, you can set a follow-up flag as a reminder to finish the job.

Organizing Your Inbox

A limited Rules Wizard was available as an add-on to the original version of Outlook. Outlook 98 has an enhanced Rules Wizard built into it, easing the operation of organizing your Inbox. For example, you can specify that messages from a certain person (maybe your boss) be displayed in a specific color. You can also select messages meeting specific criteria, sending them to separate folders. You can automatically flag junk email, and either send it to a specific folder or directly delete it from the server.

> You can delete mail directly from the server only if you're using Outlook Express as your mail reader. Otherwise, Outlook 98 will download it to the folders before the Rules Wizard acts upon it.

More views are available for organizing your Inbox. You can choose from several pre-defined views, or create custom views that best fit your needs. Switching between views requires only a few mouse clicks.

A Draft folder is automatically created. When you create a message, but don't finish it during a session, Outlook stores it in the Draft folder on the Outlook Bar. This enables easy access to unsent messages. In Outlook 97, unsent messages were stored in the Inbox, which made them easy to miss.

Sending and Reading Messages

If you use HTML for email, you can add various backgrounds (called stationery) to your messages, as well as customize the font, add pictures, and sign each message with an electronic and/or digital signature. You can create multiple electronic signatures—assigning one as the default, but easily modifying the signature attached to a specific message.

By using HTML mail, you can add anything to your message that could be contained on a Web page. Add pictures, movies, sounds, or other multimedia content to spice up your messages.

When you reply to a message, Outlook automatically recognizes the format of the original message and creates an answer in the same format, ensuring that the recipient will be able to read the mail.

The addition of the Preview Pane enables you to view the entire contents of a message in a separate window without opening a window for viewing each message. You can move the bar at the top of the Preview Pane up or down to display more or less of the message on your screen.

Exchanging Information over the Internet

Outlook 98 supports all major Internet mail protocols, ensuring that you can create messages in various formats that will best fit your needs. You can also use vCards and vCalendars to exchange information over the Internet, even with people who are not using Outlook.

Working with Other Programs

Outlook 98 is directly integrated with Internet Explorer 4.0. You can use Outlook Express from within Outlook to either send email messages or read newsgroups. If you are using HTML formatted email, you can move information from any Web site into a message that you create.

 If you open the Outlook Express news reader from within Outlook, you are only able to use it as a news reader. If you want to send email and read news, open Outlook Express directly.

B

NetMeeting is also an integrated part of Outlook 98. Using it, you can conduct an online conference using chat, voice, whiteboard, and other methods of exchanging information in a real-time meeting.

Hand-held devices that use Pocket Outlook with Windows CE can now be synchronized with the information on your main computer.

Using Basic Features with Greater Ease

Menus and dialog boxes have been simplified for easier use. The Actions option has been added to the Outlook 98 menu, organizing common actions that can be accessed from a single menu choice.

You can customize toolbars in Outlook 98, creating and modifying them to accommodate the way you work. You can remove a button from a menu by right-clicking it and choosing Delete.

The buttons are more clearly marked in the new version of Outlook. ToolTips have been enhanced to make the purpose of various buttons clearer to the user.

Using the Upgrade Wizard, you can now migrate from other mail programs to Outlook 98 automatically. Address books and connection and configuration information are automatically converted to Outlook format.

Discovering Improved Performance

Perhaps the biggest change you will notice is the increased speed of Outlook 98. You no longer have to wait ten seconds for Outlook to close. It also takes less time to complete most tasks than in earlier versions. Downloading email from the Internet is faster than in the original version of Outlook.

If you are sharing information between computers, synchronization is faster and easier. You can even specify which information gets downloaded, rather than having to update all of the files each time you synchronize your folders.

APPENDIX C

Using the Microsoft IntelliPoint Products

Microsoft has developed a new mouse and trackball, called the IntelliMouse and IntelliMouse Trackball, respectively, that makes it easier to navigate through applications. The mouse has a wheel located between the two buttons. On the trackball, the wheel is directly above the ball. The main purpose of the wheel is to replace the need to use the scrollbars in any window, but it has a few more bells and whistles. In the following instructions, we refer to the IntelliMouse. However, the IntelliPoint Trackball uses the same wheel movements.

There are four basic IntelliMouse moves that differentiate it from a standard two-button mouse:

- *Rotating the wheel.* This operation scrolls up and down through documents or windows without having to use the mouse to click the scrollbars on the edges of a window.

- *Holding the Shift key while rotating the wheel.* This combination can do a number of things, depending on where you are using it. Sometimes it toggles between views, and other times it expands and collapses folders.

- *Holding the Ctrl key while rotating the wheel.* This combination can be used to zoom in and out in a document window, such as a Word document.

- *Holding down the wheel while moving the mouse.* This operation can be performed to quickly scan through a document or a window. The mouse pointer appears as four arrows, and enables the user to scan sideways or up and down by moving the mouse.

> Get your mouse wheel to do special tricks. Open the Control Panel and double-click the Mouse icon. In the Mouse Properties dialog box, select the Wheel tab. From the Button Assignment drop-down box, choose what you want to happen when you click the wheel. You can set it to act as a double-click, display the Help screen (same as F1), start Windows Explorer, or open the Start menu.

How the IntelliMouse Works in Outlook 98

Because the IntelliMouse works differently with each program that recognizes it, this appendix focuses on the ways the mouse can be used in Outlook 98.

Using the IntelliMouse to Scroll

The most common way to use the mouse wheel is to scroll through documents (such as mail messages), or scroll up and down windows (such as the Inbox window). By rolling the wheel with your finger, you can scroll through a document or a list in a table view. Examples of table views are the Messages view in Inbox, the Events view in Calendar, and the Phone List view in Contacts.

In the Contacts folder, rotating the wheel in an Address Card view enables you to scroll through the list of contacts. By rotating the wheel, you can scroll sideways through the cards.

If you want to scroll through a *list* sideways, hold down the wheel while you move the mouse to the left or right. (If you do it correctly, the mouse pointer turns into a four-headed arrow.)

If you use Microsoft Word as your email editor, you can click the wheel button once in an open email message to have it AutoScroll through the message. Take your hand off the mouse and read; the document will slowly scroll down automatically.

Using the IntelliMouse to Change Views

Using the Shift key while you rotate the wheel enables you to switch views in some of the Outlook views, such as a Timeline view. For instance, if you change the Inbox view to Message Timeline, you can hold the Shift key down while you rotate the wheel to change the time being viewed. If you rotate the wheel, you can switch from viewing a few hours' worth of messages to viewing a day's worth of messages or even a few days' of messages.

In the Day, Week, and Month views in the Calendar folder, you can add the Shift key while you rotate the wheel to toggle between the Day view, Week view, and Month view.

Using the IntelliMouse to Expand and Collapse Groups or Folders

If you have folders and subfolders in Outlook, such as folders within your Inbox folder, you can expand and collapse them by placing the mouse pointer over the plus (+) or minus (–) sign and holding the Shift key while rotating the wheel up or down.

In some view formats in which fields group the items, you can place the mouse pointer over the plus (+) or minus (–) sign, hold the Shift key, and rotate the wheel up or down to expand and collapse the groups. A couple of examples of views with grouped items are the By Category view in the Inbox and the Events view in Calendar.

Using the IntelliMouse to Adjust the Width of Columns

Whenever you select a Card view in the Contacts folder, just hold down the Shift key and rotate the wheel to lengthen or shorten the columns.

Using IntelliMouse Features with Other Programs

By default, the wheel features can be used only in Office 97 and Office 98 products. Microsoft Internet Explorer also supports the wheel. If you want to use the wheel with *all* programs, you can purchase a shareware program called Flywheel. For more information, point your browser at

www.plannetarium.com

INDEX

beeper numbers for
contacts, 91
beepers (MobileCHOICE
Messengers software),
442-443
beta testers, 405
Bill Power software, 443
blind carbon copies
(email), 146
Bookmarks option (help
screen), 55
Boulder Atomic Time Clock
Web site, 390
bound/unbound controls
(forms), 117
bulletin boards, *see*
newsgroups
By Category view
Journal, 299-301
notes, 322
By Color view (notes),
322-323
By Contact view (Journal),
298-299
By Type view (Journal), 295

C

Calendar, 11-12
allowing access to,
245-246
appointments, 216-217
Appointment tool,
218-219
creating, 12, 217-223
date, changing,
225-226
date, entering, 220
deleting, 228
error messages, 218

hiding, 248
location, changing,
226-227
location, entering, 219
private, 234
rating importance
of, 248
reminders, 246-248
scheduling conflicts,
223-224
selecting, 224-225
subject, 219
subject, changing, 226
time, changing, 225
time, entering, 220-221
customizing, 216
events, 228-229
meetings, 235
acknowledging
requests, 244-245
canceling, 242
changing, 241
creating, 239-241
creating from appoint-
ments, 242
creating from
contacts, 242
creating with Exchange
Server or Microsoft
Mail, 236-239
recurring, 243-244
options, setting, 37-38
overview, 214-215
printing, 252, 254
recurring appointments,
228-230
changing, 232-233
creating, 231-232
deleting, 233
recurring events, 230-231
reminders, setting, 70

screen elements, 215-216
sharing data, 368
starting, 215
tasks, creating, 12
automatically, 266
time intervals,
changing, 249
time zones, changing,
249-250
views, 249
Daily, 249-250
Monthly, 252-253
Weekly, 252
Work Week, 251
Calendar Options dialog
box, 37-38
calendars, history of,
213-214
calling contacts, 110-111
troubleshooting, 112
canceling
appointments, 228
meetings, 242
captions
forms, editing, 129
Journal views, 296-297
CataList Web site, 415
categories
for contacts, 80-81, 97
assigning, 98-99
creating custom,
99-101
deleting, 100-102
email messages, 185, 187
Journal entries, viewing,
299-301
misspelled, 99
notes
changing, 316
creating, 328
viewing, 322
tasks, assigning, 15-16